INDIAN IN 1880

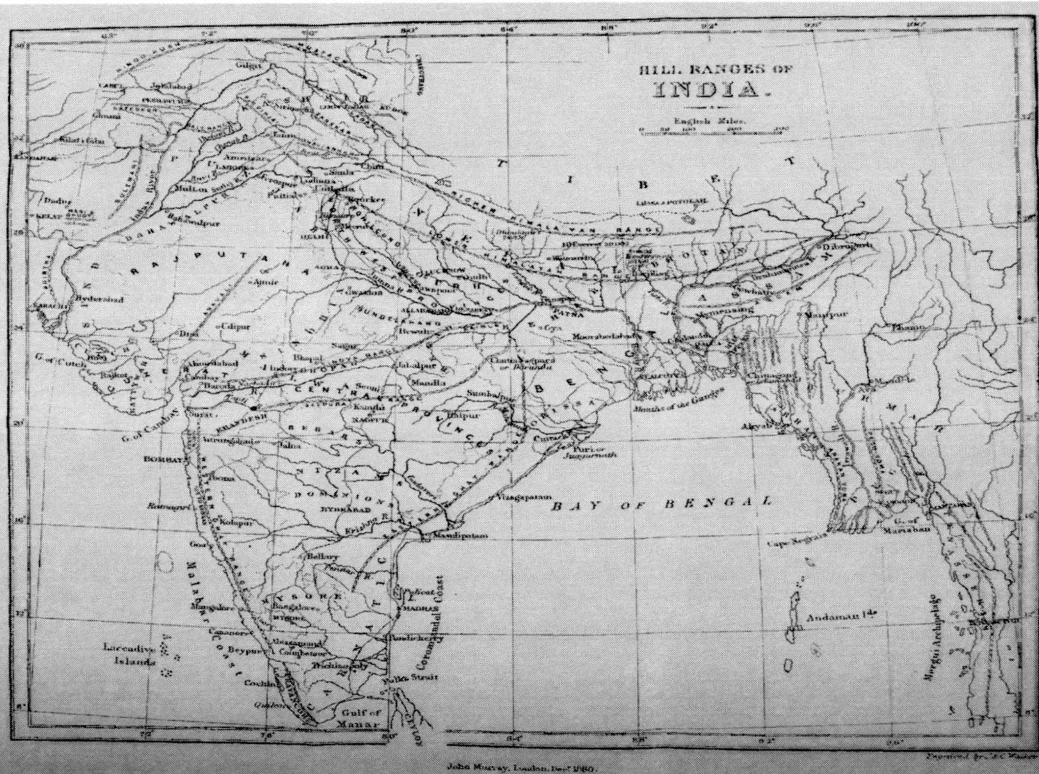
HILL RANGES OF
INDIA.
English Miles.
T I B E T
BAY OF BENGAL
RAJPUTANA
BENGAL
ASSAM
BURMAH
CENTRAL RANGE
MYSORE
DOMINIONS
HYDRABAD
BERARS
ORISSA
BUNDELKHAND
KHANDESH
Gilgit
Jelalabad
Kilat i Gilzi
Dadur
Multan
Lahore
Amritsar
Simla
Ludhiana
Patiala
Firozpur
Hyderabad
Karachi
G. of Cutch
G. of Cambay
Surat
Ajmir
Udipur
Disa
Ahmedabad
Baroda
Bhopal
Indore
Sagar
Jabalpur
Mandla
Kamthi
Nagpur
Jalna
Aurungabad
BOMBAY
Poona
Ratnagari
Kolapur
Goa
Bellary
Masulipatam
Vizagapatam
Kristna R.
Godavari
Sumbalpur
Cuttack
Puri or Jaggernath
Mouths of the Ganges
Patna
Gya
Moorshedabad
Chuta Nagpur or Dorunda
Mymensing
Dibrugarh
Manipur
Chittagong
Akyab
Cape Negrais
G. of Martaban
Andaman Is.
Mergui Archipelago
Malabar Coast
Mangalore
Cananore
Beypur
Calicut
Cochin
Quilon
Coimbatore
Bangalore
Mysore
Trichinopoly
Pondicherry
Pulicat
MADRAS
Coromandal Coast
Palks Strait
Gulf of Manar
CEYLON
Laccadive Islands
John Murray, London.

INDIAN IN 1880

By

SIR RICHARD TEMPLE, BART.,

GYAN

Published by

Gyan Publishing House
5, Ansari Road
Daryaganj, New Delhi-110002
Phone: 011-47034999, 9811692060
E-mail: books@gyanbooks.com

Distribution Network
gyanbooks.com
India, USA, Canada, UK, Australia, France

ISBN : 978-81-212-6613-0 (PB)
First Published, 1881

2nd Impression 2022

Printed at: Gyan Press, Delhi.

INDIAN IN 1880
Author: Sir Richard Temple, Bart.,

INDIA IN 1880.

BY

SIR RICHARD TEMPLE, BART.,

G.C.S.I., C.I.E., D.C.L.,

LATE GOVERNOR OF BOMBAY, LIEUTENANT-GOVERNOR OF BENGAL,
AND FINANCE MINISTER OF INDIA.

THIRD EDITION.

WITH TWO MAPS.

1881.

TO HIS ROYAL HIGHNESS

ALBERT EDWARD

Prince of Wales,

IN MEMORY OF HIS VISIT TO INDIA,
ON WHICH MOST AUSPICIOUS OCCASION
GREAT BENEFIT WAS CONFERRED
ON THE
PRINCES, NOBLES, AND PEOPLE
OF THAT EMPIRE
WITH A POTENT AND ENDURING EFFECT
ON THEIR HEARTS AND MINDS,

THIS BOOK IS,

WITH THE GRACIOUS PERMISSION OF HIS ROYAL HIGHNESS,

Dedicated,

BY HIS DUTIFUL AND LOYAL SERVANT,

THE AUTHOR.

PREFACE TO THE THIRD EDITION.

THE issue of a third edition seems to be a suitable opportunity for adverting in general terms to the notices which this book has received during the eighteen months that have elapsed since its first appearance. I am thankful to find that it has been favoured with some commendation from the Press, and that no material error whatever has been discovered. Still there has come from several organs of opinion some criticism which deserves attention, and may be considered as relating to, first, the want of definiteness in the expression of opinion regarding at least a few important points; secondly, the optimism alleged to characterize parts of the work.

The first heading of criticism, then, relates to the supposed want of definiteness in the expression of opinion regarding several important points. Now, as stated in the introduction, at page 3, the work was meant to be a dispassionate survey, and to supply the reader with the means of judging for himself regarding difficult and disputed questions rather than to establish any particular conclusions. I trust that this much is in some degree effected, and that the various sides, phases, or aspects of many doubtful matters are duly presented. Still in the course of the exposition, my own view was meant to be indicated, though it might not be dogmatically expressed. For instance in chapter IV. the political advantages accruing to the British Government from the existence of the Native States, the elements of security thereby afforded to the Indian empire, are positively set forth. By chapter VI. it was intended to imply distinctly that the

*

land can support the additional numbers which are yearly being added to its vast population, that the wealth of the people is increasing fast under British rule, and is fairly well diffused among all classes except the very humblest, that even these humblest are not so depressed as they were in former times, and feel poverty less than the corresponding classes among Northern and Western races. In chapters VII. and VIII. it is fully explained that the moral effect of British rule upon the various sections of the people is beneficial, with but few exceptions, that mental progress, though slow among the majority, is rapid among several important classes, that the character of the educated classes is greatly improved by the Western education, and that public instruction, though as yet defective and insufficient, is beginning to scatter blessings abroad. A large degree of success is claimed for the Christian missions in chapter IX., and a decisive influence for good is attributed to them. By chapter X. the legislation for India is declared to be excellent in all respects, and the charge of over-legislating is answered. In chapter XI. the repression of violent crime is affirmed, while the police and prisons are pronounced to have been really much improved, despite many defects still remaining. The settlement of the land revenue and of landed tenures is unreservedly commended in chapter XII., the recognition by the Government of a property in the land is declared to be a valuable concession to the people, and a perpetual boon, while the status of the proprietary classes, whether landlords or peasant proprietors, is held to be satisfactory. But while those tenants who have occupancy rights are protected against oppression, those who have not such rights are unprotected, and have a fair claim to better protection in future. Still the rank and file of the agriculturists are on the whole flourishing. In chapter XIII. the land revenue is declared to be well and carefully assessed, the salt-tax to be paid without real difficulty by the poor, and without sensibly affecting consumption, the opium is held to be a legitimate subject of taxation not truly open to the moral objections recently adduced against it. The entire abolition of the import duties on British piece goods is suggested. By chapters XIV., XV., and XVI. the canals of irrigation are shewn to be works of which any country might be proud, to be efficacious in times of famine, and financially profitable; the railways are proved to be successful whether under the guarantee system or under State management; the trunk roads are found to be finely engineered. Respecting natural and industrial products in chapter XVII. the need of forest conservancy is urged in the most emphatic manner, and the danger is indicated of stifling the art-genius of the Natives by the misapplication of European ideas. The allegations that India is drained yearly of much produce, receives an unequal amount in return, and is injured by the obligation to remit large sums annually to England in payment for value received or service rendered, are controverted in chapter XVIII. regarding commerce. The cause of sanitation is earnestly pleaded in chapter XIX., and the means of saving life in times of famine are clearly outlined in chapter XX. The requirements of agricultural instruction for the people are pressed strongly in chapter XXII. relating to physical science. By chapter XXV., regarding the army, the reduction of fighting strength is deprecated, and the need of maintaining the European and Native forces at full strength is set forth. The possible embarrassment to Indian interests from the Russian movements in the Turcoman country, and from the approach of Russia towards Afghanistan, are explained in chapter XXIV. Lastly, in chapter XXVII., regarding finance, endeavour is made to do justice to the objections which have been brought to bear upon the financial situation, but the soundness of that situation is vindicated.

Thus with the exception of those few chapters which are purely descriptive, the whole work abounds with opinions of mine definitely enuntiated. The reader may or may not accept these opinions; but he is always warned of any counter-opinions which may be known to exist, and he is apprised of the arguments on both sides in case he desires to form his own judgment. Thus, my opinions, though free, as I hope, from incisiveness or dogmatism, will not actually be found wanting in definiteness.

Doubtless the tenour of these opinions is very favourable to the Indian empire. Certainly I feel the pride which all Englishmen have felt on contemplating the wondrous achievements of our countrymen in the East. But if by optimism is meant the disposition to observe the bright parts only of the picture, and not its shadows, then I have no intention at all of being an optimist. Indeed, nothing in my judgment could be more dangerous than to encourage the British public in a belief that the Indian empire is free from disadvantages and perils, and may be left to take care of itself without incessant vigilance on the part of the governing race. My intention, therefore, was to point out every one of the troubles greater or lesser to which the empire is exposed; and I did this to the best of my recollection. A few references (following as nearly as possible the order of the pages) will convey some idea of the manner in which this part of my task has been fulfilled, for example:

the several kinds of discontent pent up in the British territories and needing a safety valve to be supplied by the Native States, p. 63;

the possible embarrassment from the military forces of the Native States being maintained at an excessive strength, and from their arsenals becoming efficient, p. 66;

the Arab element in the army of the Nizam in the Deccan, p. 68;

the national and perhaps hostile sentiment surviving among the Mahratta States and Mahratta mountaineers, p. 72;

the probability of the Gurkha nationality in Nepal asserting itself in event of any general commotion, p. 74;

the causes, climatic and other, producing more than ordinary sickness and mortality among the people, p. 81;

the impossibility of preventing the periodical recurrence of famine, pp. 87, 337;

the difficulty of sustaining the cattle at certain seasons, and the consequent murrains, pp. 99, 362;

the inadequate application of human labour and the extreme lowness of wages in some rural localities, p. 100;

the comparative poverty shewn by the smallness of the income tax proceeds, p. 102;

the inevitable unpopularity of British rule with certain classes of the people, pp. 107, 500;

the probability of the old spirit of plunder breaking out again if the bonds of order were loosened, p. 110;

the disaffection and fanaticism occasionally manifested among the Muhammadans, pp. 114, 120;

the uneasiness prevailing among the decayed Native aristocracy, p. 116;

the unconquerable pride of the Hindu priesthood, p. 118;

the inflammable character of Sikhism in the Punjab, p. 120;

the political ideas and aspirations of the educated Natives, pp. 125, 126;

the unfriendly tendencies sometimes evinced by the vernacular press, p. 132;

the discontent among highly qualified Natives who cannot find scope for their abilities, pp. 133, 134;

the paucity of children at school relatively to the vast population, despite all our educational efforts, p. 139;

the want of technical instruction, pp. 143, 144;

the backwardness of female education, p. 159;

the oppression practised by usurious creditors upon ignorant debtors, p. 187;

the political import of gang-robbery in Western India, p. 198;

the sudden outburst of rioting at various times, p. 199;

the faults remaining in the police even after the reorganization, p. 205;

the not infrequent occurrence of serious mortality in the prisons, p. 211;

the partial failure of the Permanent Settlement in Bengal to ensure the outlay of capital on the land, p. 115;

the indebtedness among some classes of the peasant proprietors, pp. 221, 222;

the want of elasticity in the revenues, pp. 244, 447;

the hesitation of the people in some provinces to use the water provided by canals of irrigation, p. 258;

the difficulty of framing projects for irrigation in a manner that shall ensure the State being repaid for the outlay, p. 262;

the extension of railways checked by expensiveness in construction, p. 277;

the mischief arising from wasteful cutting of the forests, p. 296;

the danger to the public health from impure drinking water, p. 323;

the bad ventilation of urban dwellings, p. 325;

the slow exhaustion of the soil and the absence of agricultural instruction, pp. 361, 362;

the insufficiency of naval force to fully protect British interests in Indian waters, p. 376;

the incompleteness of defensive works for the coasts and harbours, p. 377;

the destructive effects of cyclones, p. 380;

the limits of the fidelity of Native troops, p. 394;

the diminished attractiveness of British military service in Native estimation, p. 401;

the difficulties of military transport, p. 409;

the specific risk to India if Russian influence were to be established in Afghanistan, p. 434;

the menace to Herat from the Russian movements in the Turkoman districts, p. 431;

the drain upon the finances from the recurring expenditure for the prevention of famine, p. 459;

the loss by exchange on the remittances to England in silver to be measured by a gold standard, p. 459.

This may seem a long list of troubles for an empire which is in the main secure and flourishing. In fact the Indian empire teems with difficulties, and its security depends on the watchfulness of the ruling power. Still, if England is true to herself, the imperial interests are safe, and the difficulties will be encountered with more or less of success by English resources, while some of them may even be removed with English perseverance. But if the precautions heretofore so well maintained were to become relaxed, then the dangers, inherent in a foreign rule, would thicken fast, like clouds gathering to burst in a tempest.

Since the publication of this book in December 1880, the proceedings of Russia in the Turkoman country have been largely developed. The occupation of Merve has not been actually effected, only because a still more important line of operations has been adopted by Askabad and Serakhs, close along the north-eastern frontier of Persia. A railway has been made from the eastern shore of the Caspian to Kizl Arvat for the transport of Russian troops and material to the Turkoman territories, and will probably be soon extended along the Persian border in the direction of Afghanistan. The Turkomans appear to have been subdued with a completeness surpassing anticipation. Their almost unique resources in cavalry will be at the disposal of the conqueror. It may be foreseen that ere long the Russian forces will be within a comparatively short distance of Herat.

The favourable view taken in 1880 regarding the finances of India has been fully borne out by all that has since occurred. With the help of a contribution of five millions sterling from the English treasury, India has paid or will very shortly pay out of her own current revenues and cash balances the expenses of the late Afghan war, or twenty-one millions sterling, without making any addition to her public debt on that account.

This defrayal of the war charges by India is the more remarkable as she has paid from her current revenues fifteen millions sterling within the last few years for the relief of her people from starvation by famine. Even now, with considerable reduction of taxation both of the salt-duties and of the customs, her finance is in a condition of surplus. And notwithstanding the mortality from recent famines her population has increased by thirteen millions of souls during the last ten years.

R. T.

THE NASH, KEMPSEY, *near* WORCESTER.
April 22nd, 1882.

CONTENTS.

CHAPTER I.

CLAIMS OF INDIA ON THE CONTINUOUS ATTENTION OF ENGLAND.

CHAPTER II.

OBJECTS OF BEAUTY IN NATURE.

CHAPTER III.

OBJECTS OF BEAUTY IN ART.

CHAPTER VII.

MENTAL AND MORAL PROGRESS OF THE NATIVES.

CHAPTER VIII.

NATIONAL EDUCATION.

CHAPTER IX.

RELIGIOUS ESTABLISHMENTS AND MISSIONS.

CHAPTER X.

LAW AND LEGISLATION.

CHAPTER XI.

CRIME, POLICE AND PRISONS.

CHAPTER XII.

LAND-TAX AND LANDED TENURES.

CHAPTER XXII.

PHYSICAL SCIENCE.

CHAPTER XXIII.

WILD ANIMALS AND SPORTS.

CHAPTER XXIV.

NAVY AND MARINE.

CHAPTER XXV.

THE ARMY.

CHAPTER XXVI.

FOREIGN RELATIONS.

CHAPTER XXVII.

FINANCE.

CHAPTER XXVIII.

STATISTICAL SUMMARY.

CHAPTER XXIX.

CONCLUSION.

DIRECTIONS TO BINDER.

ERRATA.

Page **114, eighth line from top,** ***for*** **"Synd"** ***read*** **"Syud."**
Page **161, eighteenth line from top,** ***for*** **"natural"** ***read*** **"national."**

INDIA IN 1880.

CHAPTER I.

CLAIMS OF INDIA ON THE CONTINUOUS ATTENTION OF ENGLAND.

Need of steadfast attention to Indian affairs on the part of Englishmen—Changeful character of India under British rule—Necessity of observing current events—Therefore survey undertaken of India in 1880—Circumstances interesting to travellers and sportsmen—To those connected with art and science—To the friends of missions—To those concerned in public affairs—To economists and statesmen.

THE possession of India by England involves grave responsibilities, and comprises recondite problems. Consequently the attention of Englishmen is excited, and their conscience is stirred with emotions transcending the patriotic pride with which the Indian empire is regarded. But amidst the distractions of English life, such attention and such emotions are fitful and spasmodic, instead of being continuous. Nevertheless, continuity of thoughtfulness is essential, because, under British rule, India is changing with a rapidity of which eastern nations seldom afford an example. Immutability has heretofore been characteristic of India, and still is so in some respects. But in many other matters, mutation and mutability are rather to be attributed to the country and to its people. Some things indeed, such as the costumes and ornaments, the styles of domestic architecture, the festivals and ceremonies, the religious observances and structures, remain the same from epoch to epoch. Antique carvings, sculptures and frescoes are often found to represent in externals the same people whom we see to-day. But under the plastic touch of western civilization, the face of the land, the economic conditions of the country, are undergoing modification, and the religious ideas, the moral sentiments, the social habits, the political aspirations, of many classes of the people are changing fast. Whether these movements shall be for better or for worse, must depend on the conduct of England under the guidance of an all-wise Providence. Wonderful as India has been in her past, and is in her present, she will be equally wonderful in her immediate future.

This tendency to change produces some difficulties in the governance of India, which have been as yet imperfectly perceived. Men who have specially studied the country or travelled in it, or taken part in its administration, will naturally think that the knowledge acquired at the time and on the spot will be always valid, that the experience gained under certain conditions will be ever applicable. However valuable such knowledge and experience may be, as constituting a preparation for judgment, they must be supplemented constantly by fresh study and new observations. There is danger lest data, sound in themselves, should lead to unsound conclusions, by reason of the shifting character of the circumstances. Hard as may have been the labour of mastering the manifold conditions of the country at any given time, the further task must yet be undertaken of learning the variations which have subsequently occurred and are still occurring. Those who are conversant with the country must, by the study of current events, strive to march abreast of Indian progress, and to keep pace mentally with the advancing tide of change in the East. Otherwise they will be moved rather by the recollection of India as she was, than by the consideration of India as she actually is.

Therefore it behoves those who have fresh memories of the country, to record their recollections before the freshness begins to fade. By such a record they set up landmarks to denote the steps by which the age is advancing, and leave such vestiges on the sands of change as may help to guide the students and workers who are to follow. With this view I undertake to present a survey of the India of 1880, the year in which I left its shores. My work will be a survey as exact and comprehensive as can be contained in the limited space, and will be nothing more than a survey. It will comprise only such retrospect of the past as may be occasionally necessary to elucidate the present. It will not determine disputed matters, nor vindicate specially any set of opinions. It will often, however, present both sides of debatable questions, and indicate any dangers which seem to threaten the general weal. It will be a short account of the most interesting facts and circumstances, as developed at the time of writing. The exposition will not be technical, but will aim at being popular.

The statement must be as varied as the considerations are multiform, and the conditions many-sided. For India presents phases interesting to all sorts of men.

To the traveller she opens a field where the peculiarities of the eastern world and the results of ancient systems may be observed, in combination with the achievements of the Anglo-Saxon race and the effects of modern civilization.

To the painter she offers scenery, ranging by gradations from tropical to alpine conditions, and a variety of national features, figures and costumes, not to be seen in any other dominion under one Government.

To the architect and antiquary she presents either standing specimens, or ruins, or antique remains, of several styles of architecture, originating from different circumstances, and emanating from diverse states of the human mind.

To the hunter and sportsman she promises stirring adventures by flood and field, in burning heat, in frost and snow, wherein the wildness of nature may be enjoyed and the fierce courage of the brute creation admired.

To the geologist she displays, among countless other formations, the loftiest gneiss and granite peaks yet discovered, many coal-bearing strata, and one of the grandest masses of bedded trap to be found in the world.

To the botanist she yields, as the reward of plant-collecting toil, the specimens of vegetation varying from that which flourishes near the equator, to that which thrives near the line of everlasting snow.

To the entomologist she exhibits many of the finest and loveliest forms of insect life.

To the ornithologist she exemplifies in her woods and forests whole orders and genera of birds, together with many rare species and varieties.

To the meteorologist she manifests wondrous and mighty phenomena, which specially invite scientific cognizance, as they affect the rainfall and the contingencies of drought and famine.

To the ethnologist and philologist she shows several types of mankind, aboriginal or civilized, Caucasian or Mongolian, Scythian or Aryan; together with the roots or bases of several languages.

To the moralist she indicates the effects produced on human conduct by the three most wide-spread religions of the non-christian world, and by Christianity itself; also the influence exercised on the thoughts of men by several systems of philosophy.

To the missionary she holds out the hope of the largest field, yet seen in the world, for religious effort among the heathen, under the protection of a strong government, which ensures equal security to all religions.

To the journalist and publicist she originates discussions which may be conducted and controversies which may be waged, before an ever-widening circle of readers.

To the politician and administrator she furnishes a sphere for exercising the ability to arrange complex affairs on the greatest scale, divine the feelings and wishes of alien races, maintain diplomatic control over semi-independent States, and render foreign rule acceptable to an indigenous population.

To the jurist she demonstrates the manner in which foreign codes and systems of law may be considerately administered by a ruling nation, and the best principles of western jurisprudence applied to the governance of eastern races.

To the civil engineer she affords a scope for storing the bounteous resources of nature to be used by man, reducing the effect of distance in an enormous area, reclaiming the desert, and augmenting many fold the produce of cultivation.

To the soldier she propounds professional questions regarding the secure occupation of a vast country by scattered bodies of troops, the defence of mountainous frontiers, the concentration of forces for extreme efforts, and the organization of armies drawn from many nationalities.

To the merchant she develops large opportunities for barter between nations, raw produce being exchanged for manufactures, new products being introduced, and industries, with the aid of capital, being commenced, of which the growth may be indefinitely great.

To the mariner she discloses some few harbours of great extent, a rock-bound or sand-encumbered coast, and seas where the periodical phenomena demand nautical observation.

To the hygienist she proves the necessity of applying the principles of European sanitation to the conditions of tropical insalubrity.

To the economist and financier she suggests for solution many problems, relating to the balance of trade, the remittance of silver with value measured by a gold standard, the want of elasticity in the revenue, the returns on the capital outlay by the State, and the growth of the public debt.

To the statesman she proffers all these matters, as they collectively concern the maintenance of a widely-extended and progressive empire in peace, wealth, strength and safety.

CHAPTER II.

OBJECTS OF BEAUTY IN NATURE.

Objects of beauty in divers places—Improved facilities for travelling nowadays—Variety of climatic aspects—Phenomena of the rainy season—Different characteristics of the country on the north and on the south of hill ranges forming the backbone of the Indian continent—Pleasant mountain retreats during summer for European residents—Fine views from mountains looking towards the sea—Noble prospect from Himalayas looking towards the plains of India—River scenes—Marble rocks—Cascades—Mountains clothed with perpetual snow—Loftiest peaks yet discovered in the world—Lake region—Scenery of Cashmir valley—Features of the several Indian races—Picturesque effect of their costumes.

IF a series of sketches were to be made of the beautiful and interesting objects in every province throughout India, the spectator might imagine that the country is one vast book of beauty. But while some regions are continuously beautiful, many outlying districts have an ugly and ill-favoured appearance, to which no part of Europe, except, perhaps, Russia, can furnish a parallel. The objects of beauty and interest, which exist in India are, in their quality and variety, probably not surpassed in any country of the world, and exceed any description that can be given of them in words. But they are somewhat scattered; and though by no means few, they are far between. The intermediate spaces wear an aspect, often inattractive, and sometimes even repulsive. Visitors who, after becoming versed in the description of India, actually traverse expansive tracts of the country and find nothing to please the eye, may at first sight be disappointed. Such disappointment was more common in the past generation than it is in the present. Some thirty or forty years ago, it was impossible for a traveller to visit more than a few of the places worth seeing in the country. Men who spent the most active years of their lives in an empire containing many provinces, were acquainted with only one province. Hardly a person could be found who had seen most of the interesting views in the country. Indeed, to see them all would, in those days, have required the devotion of a lifetime to that single purpose. The search was tedious and protracted, while the gems of scenery or antiquity were rare. The pilgrimage was toilsome and troublous, while the spots, hallowed by beauty of aspect or by interest of association, were remote. Therefore the things seen were often disproportionate to the distances travelled, and to the time spent in travelling. This circumstance may have given to some the impression that the glories of India are overrated and overpraised.

But within the last twenty years the introduction of railways in the interior, and the employment of steamers along the coasts, have already caused many parts of the country to be easily and quickly approached, and will soon render almost every part accessible. The phrase of the grand tour of India represents a project which can be executed by an ordinary tourist. In the course of a few months a visitor may, without undue fatigue or imprudent exposure to the weather and climate, see most of the finest sights in India. By transit rapid and facile he is relieved from the tedium of slowly crossing the intermediate spaces devoid of interest; and proceeds straight to the point whither his thoughts and hopes are directed. Thus the knowledge of India has increased fast, and is increasing still faster, not only among the travelling classes of England, but also among those Englishmen whose lot is cast, and whose residence is fixed, in the Indian empire. Still, notwithstanding the augmented facilities for seeing and the ambition of so many to see everything, there lives not the man of whom it can be said that he has seen all India, so extensive is the country, so diversified is its configuration, and so dispersed are its wonders.

When the thoughts are fixed upon these wonders and glories,

it must at the same time be remembered that the greater part of the country is neither wonderful nor glorious, that much of it is commonplace, and that some portions of it are even hideous. Nothing for instance can be more wretchedly plain in appearance than the treeless, shrubless, shelterless plains in the northern province of the Madras Presidency, in the Bombay Deccan, or in the districts lying between Delhi and the Satlej. In western India and even in the southern slopes of the western Himalayas, there are low ranges of hills denuded of vegetation, which have all the bareness of the mountains in Arabian or African deserts. Indian villages are in some provinces, for instance in Bengal, in Behar, and on the western coast, eminently picturesque, but in many provinces are uncomely and unprepossessing. Still, even the plainest parts of the country often verge on the picturesque, and a chance collocation of objects produces an interesting scene. The sunlight brightens up rude objects, casting vivid lights against strong shadows, and fixing attention upon the play of light and shade. The dress and the implements of the peasant, though rough, are interesting. The costumes of most classes of the people are variegated in colour, and set off even the dullest landscape. Wherever the old ancestral tree in the midst of the village affords a spreading shade, the village folk cluster in very attractive groups.

As might be expected, the wonders and glories belong partly to nature and partly to art, and are all affected by climate.

By most Englishmen, who have not travelled in the East, the Indian climate is probably imagined to be damp, sultry, enervating, the prolonged stillness being broken occasionally by tempests, and to possess all the disagreeable characteristics of tropical latitudes. This is but too true of the Indian regions which first became known to Europeans, and from which traditional ideas have originated. But in the empire, now comprised under the territorial name of India, there are many varieties of climate. In some regions, for example the northern, the noteworthy characteristics are the constant agitation of the hot air for several weeks and even for some months consecutively; the sharp biting cold at certain seasons during the last hours of night and the first hours of morning; the generally prevailing dryness often verging upon drought; the moisture sufficient during the first months of summer and autumn, and deficient during the remaining months. Although, sometimes, unseasonable rains spoil the standing crops, and floods sweep away the reaped but ungarnered harvest, still it is the dread of drought which generally haunts the minds of the people. It is only in some lines of country that the rainfall can be described as unfailing, with variations often on the side of excess, but never on that of deficiency. The long range of the Western Ghat mountains, on the west coast of India, forms a mighty wall 1500 to 2000 feet high, for many hundreds of miles. Against the crests of this natural wall, there beat the masses of vapour drawn by the sun's rays from the Indian ocean or from equatorial seas, accumulated during several hot and dry months, and propelled by the wind during the heat of summer. Of the vapours one portion is condensed on touching this high land, the first which is encountered, shedding rain in wonderful quantities, feeding the sources of great rivers, tearing up the hill-sides with torrents, or adorning them with cascades. The remaining portions pass onwards, with the driving breezes, to fertilize India. These are the phenomena which constitute the "monsoon" so familiar to all. Similar circumstances occur in the mountains flanking eastern Bengal and dividing it from Burma, in the eastern division of the Himalayan range, and in the littoral provinces on the eastern shore of the Bay of Bengal. The vapours, from the Bay of Bengal and from southern seas, are propelled by currents of air, and condense into a marvellous rainfall from contact with the highland which stops their aerial course. In the eastern section of the Sâtpura range which is the backbone of the Indian Continent, near the source of the Nerbadda river, the moisture-laden clouds, blown across the great plateau of the Deccan, are gathered together. They are hindered by the mountain summits from proceeding further, and are there changed into rain which supplies perennial moisture to the neighbouring regions. But with these, and perhaps some other, large exceptions, there is an abiding anxiety in most provinces lest the clouds should move on, without dropping fatness on their way.

In general terms (subject always to exceptions) the Sâtpura range, crossing the country from east to west, causes a climatic division of the empire. South of this range, that is in the Deccan and in the Presidencies of Madras and Bombay, the climate is equable, hot generally, but seldom reaching extreme heat, cool and slightly cold at some seasons, but seldom approaching severe cold; on the whole showing a high temperature on the average of the year. It may be described in southern India as equably hot all the year round except in mid-winter, when it is mild, and in mid-summer, when the constant breezes are cooled by the rains. North of the Sâtpura range, extreme degrees of heat are met with, and at some seasons at certain hours a degree of cold which appears acute to the senses. In the early part of summer the winds, heated in their passage across the western desert, rush over the inhabited plains with blasts like those of a furnace, from which the wayfarer will recoil as if smitten with fire. Even through the weary watches of the night the wind pursues its course. These are "the hot winds" so well known to many. Then it is that the earth becomes like iron, and the heaven looks like brass. In the centre of these phenomena lies the historic city of Agra, which is for a time one of the hottest places in the habitable globe; though it is almost rivalled by Delhi in this respect. But at these same places there is during the short winter a bright, cold, dry climate, and about new year's day there is frost at night. Further north, in the Panjab, the intense heat is nearly the same, but the winter is longer and colder. In all these provinces there is a rainy season of three months' duration, to mitigate the heat. The southern parts of the Panjab about Multan, and the province of Sind in the valley of the Indus, are almost rainless. From the proximity of the desert, the air becomes scorching. In the daytime, the people bear the rigour as best they may, crouching in their darkened houses; at night, when sleepless, they sometimes dash cold water over their bodies in order to obtain a brief repose. They are, however, re-invigorated by a cold, though short, winter. In the delta of the Ganges and in lower Bengal, the climate is quite different, being damp and much milder as regards both heat and cold.

North of the Sâtpura range, and in the Indus valley, the physical constitution of the Natives is decidedly superior. Their stature is taller, their thews and sinews stronger, their nervous force greater. Their character is more robust, and their temper more inclined to violence. South of the Sâtpura range, their physical frame is of lesser build, and their moral qualities less firm; with the exception of the Mahrattas, and some other hill tribes, whose resolution and endurance are seldom surpassed. In Bengal, their disposition is milder, but their mental faculties are more acute. The drought of northern India has been well said to be the "arida nutrix leonum," in allusion to the Sikhs whose cognomen of Singh has a leonine significance. The harder conditions of life, imposed by the extreme of dry heat alternating with considerable degrees of cold, nourish the sturdier races of men.

For Europeans, southern India offers perhaps more comfort, or less discomfort, than northern India, less liability to violent illness, with a better chance of long residence without specific ailment and without change of scene and air. To persons of enfeebled condition, obliged to live in the plains, the south will probably prove more favourable. But in northern India, the Briton, of average health and constitution, is stronger and healthier, more able to preserve the vigour which he originally brought with him from Britain. If a comparison in respect of violent illness should appear favorable to the Panjab, then it is to be remembered that, from the first, resort to the Himalayas has been easy for all whose health suffered in those plains. The autumnal season in northern India is very insalubrious, doubtless from the nocturnal chill setting in while the earth is still damp from the rainy season, and that is the time when all Europeans, who can, escape to the mountains. It may be doubted whether a European, residing uninterruptedly in the plains of the Panjab, would be as free from acute disease as he would be in southern India under like conditions. But in northern India, even those who have been most exhausted by the heat of summer are rapidly restored by the bracing and exhilarating winter. Opinion among Europeans, however, differs greatly respecting the relative advantages, or disadvantages, of residence in the north or south, in the east or west. Many Europeans will be found to praise those parts most in which they have lived the longest, and to disparage those parts of which they know the least. It is well that they should all cherish their respective views, which prove that they have enjoyed happiness in whatever part of India their lot may have been cast. They generally possess a faculty for accommodating their taste and preference to the external conditions amidst which they are thrown.

The diversity of these conditions may be exemplified by the different characteristics of the mountain retreats, where the Government of India and the several Local Governments spend the summer. For the Government of India, there is Simla with its oaks, firs and rhododendrons, and its distant view of the snowy range; for the Panjab, Dharmsala with its irrigated valley and near snowy hills almost overhanging the spectator; for the North-western Provinces, Naini Tâl with its fine lake embosomed in the mountains; for Bengal, Darjiling with its tree-ferns, creepers and semi-tropical vegetation, its cloud-effects, and its view of the grandest snowy mountains in the world; for Assam, Shillong with its green undulations, partly clad with pine forests, and its distant prospect of the Brahmaputra river; for the Central Provinces, Pachmari with its sandstone precipices, unfathomable rifts, and summer cascades; for Rajputana, majestic Abu with its darkling masses of granite; for Beluchistan, Quetta with its panorama of limestone formations towering aloft, barren and naked; for Bombay, Mahableshwar with its horizontal strata of igneous rocks cut into steep scarps, and its distant view of the sunset across the ocean; for Madras, Utacamand with its rolling plateaux and rounded summits, its botanic gardens and park-like drives.

Similarly, the finest and most celebrated views in the empire comprise a diversity of scenery, hard to be imagined, but still intelligible, when the degrees of latitude embraced, and the altitude of the mountains above the plains, are borne in remembrance.

In southern India, the western horizon of the sea is seen from mountains eight thousand feet high. The sun, descending towards his couch in the ocean, casts a sheet of light over the waters, which is visible from summits thirty miles off, and affords a sparkling background to the scene. For instance, let there be taken such a view as that which may be seen from parts of the Nilgiri or "blue-peak" mountains. The summits tower in the distance, with their violet hues which have given the name of "blue" to the range. In the foreground are verdant coffee-plantations, studded with bright houses and factories, in the middle distance are dark precipices of granite, and on the extreme horizon is the sheen of the sunlight glimmering on the ocean.

From a like position let the eye be turned towards the Wynaad country, a series of low hills and valleys. In the early morning, while the mists lie low and thick before they are lifted and dissipated by the advancing day, the valleys seem filled with vapours, as white and thick as wool, presenting a flat surface. The ridges of the hills rise up dark, as if islanded in a sea of clouds. Beyond them all, is the horizon of the distant ocean, not glittering this time, but cold and grey.

In further illustration of the same characteristic in scenery, let the view from Matheran, the summer retreat of the residents of Bombay, be considered. In the foreground there are plutonic rocks, bold and precipitous, yet fantastically shaped and grouped, also interspersed with vegetation. The middle distance consists of a plain, intersected in all directions by rivers, creeks and estuaries, terminating in the broad harbour of Bombay, which is surrounded by promontories and tongues of land, whereon the city of Bombay is built. Although the water looks dimly bright, and the land is too faintly grey for the city to be clearly discernible, still the knowledge that so teeming a population and so numerous a shipping are there, heightens the effect on the imagination. Beyond it all, there lies the shining ocean, almost merged in the sunset sky. Then the spectators realize what the poet conceived, when he sang of the sun setting,

> "Not as in northern climes obscurely bright,
> But one unclouded blaze of living light."

In the Himalayan regions a like effect is produced in another manner. The mountains rise abruptly to a great height, overlooking plains some thousands of square miles in extent. The traveller may see a grand view from an altitude of four or five thousand feet. He will behold it better by proceeding to the interior of the mountains, and ascending summits of ten or twelve thousand feet, near Simla, near Landour, or near Darjiling. The prospect is to be best enjoyed on one of the clear evenings which occasionally break the monotony of the rainy season, when winds have lifted the curtain of clouds and mists, when the atmosphere is transparent, and when all the hues and tints of the earth have been intensified by moisture. In the foreground are darkened rocks and forests, among which there float fleecy clouds lighted up by the sun with orange colour. In the middle distance the plain lies flat as a mirror, empurpled by the waning sunlight, and intersected by rivers, which wind across it, like serpents of supernatural glitter. In the extreme distance is the long horizon of the plains, resembling that of the ocean, and blending with the sunset-sky gorgeous with a splendour which can be displayed only in ethereal spaces, and cannot be matched on earth. The imagination is elevated by the knowledge that the lines of brightness athwart the plains represent famous and classic rivers, such as the Ganges, the Jamna, or the Satlej.

The scenery on the banks of the Indian rivers is at its best when they burst through clefts of the mountains, before spreading out into the plains. The Ganges debouches picturesquely from the Himalayas at Hardwar, the holiest of all the places of Hindu pilgrimage. The Godavery after passing through a tortuous defile, which has been well compared to the valley of the Rhine between Bonn and Bingen, is dammed up by a great dyke, whence numerous canals are drawn. The Mahanaddi pierces its hilly barriers by a series of gorges, before entering upon the plains of Orissa. Of the many river scenes in the country, two may be selected for their exceeding beauty.

Near Jabalpur in central India the river Nerbadda wanders for more than a mile amidst cliffs and bluffs of marble, from fifty to a hundred feet high, which enclose the narrow stream on both sides as with walls. The water, thus confined, has an immense depth and intense hues of mingled green and blue. Being very pure and still in the cold season, it receives perfect reflections from the snow-white rocks. The effect of the river, with the reflections from the marble on either side almost joining each other in the blue water, when viewed in perspective either by sun-light or by moon-light, transcends description. The voyager, rowing softly along the gentle stream, stops his little bark for a moment, and feels as if left alone with the Nerbadda in its marble palace.

On the western coast, the Gairsopa river, flowing from the Mysore plateau, falls over a sheer precipice of eight hundred and fifty feet, and leaps with one uninterrupted plunge from head to base of this great descent. If witnessed during flood, it is said to stun the senses, deafening the ears with its thunder, and blinding the eyes with its spray. When seen at its best during early winter, it divides itself into four falls, which can be combined in one comprehensive view, and which are named locally, the "Raja," from its stately and measured cadence, the "Roarer," from its sonorous impetuosity, the "Rocket," from the peculiar play of its waters as they shoot downwards, and the "Dame blanche," from the grace and elegance of its movement. The traveller, wending his way through the dark forest at eventide towards the famous cascades, finds his night's rest disturbed by the weird unearthly moaning of the waters as they fall. Emerging from the forest before sunrise, and facing the waterfalls, he sees nought but a thick sheet of mist and spray, hung like a white pall in front of the waters, from behind which he hears the resounding voice of the cataract. After the sun has ascended the heavens, the misty curtain is lifted, and the falling waters are displayed in all their variety of motion. As the sun descends towards the west, the spray rises, hanging around the waterfall like a thin veil of gauze, and receiving rainbow colours.

The Himalayan region displays, as might be expected, a rich scenery equal to that of the Alpine region in some respects, though inferior to it in regard to the lakes and other prominent features. Those travellers who reach the perpetual snows of the Himalayas have a much longer ascent to make, because, by reason of difference in latitude, the line of permanent snow is so much higher than in the Alps. They behold sights, in grandeur not superior to those beheld in Switzerland, though the summits are so much higher. It is doubtful whether, when range after range of mountains have been climbed, the superiority of the altitudes finally attained adds essentially to the effect upon the eye. The snowy ranges as seen from Simla itself are not remarkable, but from mountains in its neighbourhood, such as the Chore summit, the sacred sources of the Ganges and the Jamna called Gangotri and Jamnotri, can be seen, as represented by domes, towers and pinnacles of dazzling snow.

The town and station of Simla itself present a striking aspect, with their bright habitations of light and picturesque architecture, perched aloft on the heights, and serving as a crown to the cedar-clad mountain.

There are some points in the Himalayas which must be chosen for special notice. In the province of Kumaon at Bhinsa near Almora, the view of several groups of snowy mountains 26,000 feet high (above sea-level), at a distance of less than forty miles, is surpassingly beautiful. The middle distance is so fortunately placed, the atmosphere, in favourable weather, is so clear, and so little intervenes between the spectator and the stupendous masses of snow-clad gneiss or granite, that he is momentarily cheated into the belief that the soaring summits and the tortuous glaciers are close to his eye.

The view of Kinchinjanga upwards of 28,000 feet high, as seen from the station of Darjiling, is finer still. The low valleys, not more than 2000 feet high, are so situated that the spectator can look down into their very depths, from the same standpoint whence he looks up to the snowy summits. He thus can see, almost in one glance, a distance of 26,000 feet from depth to height. It happens, too, that at the moment when the summits are brightest, the shaded valleys appear gloomiest. To say that, during one of the very few perfectly fine days which occur in the year, these snowy summits are at sunrise tipped with fire, and are at sunset bathed in rose colour, would be to give but a faint description of the manner in which the mind of the beholder is impressed. Ordinarily, even in fine weather, among this eastern section of the Himalayas, which is so much more wet and verdure-clothed than the western, the clouds gather round about the mountains, and play over the vast landscape with graceful movements and in fascinating forms. All that has been eloquently written by travellers in other countries, regarding the clouds being suspended as gorgeous banners around the everlasting summits, is applicable to these scenes.

In the vicinity of Darjiling a still finer view is obtained by ascending the range 10,000 to 12,000 feet high, which divides Sikhim from Nepal. The spectator there beholds, on his right front the Kinchinjanga group, and on his left front the group of Mount Everest, of which the central peak, upwards of 29,000 feet high, is the highest known in the world.

In this quarter is situate the lake district of Sikhim, on the very top of a range from 12,000 to 15,000 feet high, bordering eastern Thibet. Of these lakes (which are six in number and lie near together) four are situated above the line within which vegetation can grow, being at nearly the same height as that of the loftier summits in Switzerland. The prevalence of tempestuous weather, during most seasons of the year, renders them difficult of access. When they are seen during the mid-autumn, the most favorable time, the sterile ruggedness of their craggy surroundings is sublime; the gneiss rocks having been riven and splintered by some tremendous explosive forces. In each lake the colour of the water is different, in one it is murky, in another purplish, in another turquoise-blue, in another amber-green. In the background there are the bare ochre-brown hills of Thibet, which from the effect of the atmosphere have a colour of aerial pink. Behind them there rises up the pyramid of Chimalari 25,000 feet high, draped in snow from the head to the base of its cone, and piercing the sky with a sharp apex.

Cashmir must be included in any notice of the Himalayan region, as it constitutes, if taken all in all, the most beautiful part of the whole empire. From the upper basin of the Jhelum river, which valley is Cashmir proper, there branch off many lovely valleys of the best Alpine character, still Alpine only. In Cashmir there are two lakes, of which one is fraught with poetic and historic associations, while the other is famed for having the snowy mountains mirrored in it. Still, these lakes may be equalled or surpassed by the lake region of northern

Italy, and with the lakes of Switzerland they cannot be exactly compared. It is rather the combination of divers elements of interest, the ruins and remains representing several distinct phases of civilization, the quaintness of the modern architecture, the picturesque approaches and surroundings, the great extent of the plateau, environed by snowy mountains on all sides and permeated by a navigable river, which constitute the peculiar charm of Cashmir, and which make it an object of desire to all men. If its merits be analysed and examined separately, each one of them may be matched elsewhere. But if they be regarded collectively, then in their beautiful entirety, they are perhaps unmatched in any country. Nevertheless, there are some objects in Cashmir which deserve, and will repay, special analysis.

The fountain of Vernâg, the source of the Jhelum, near the eastern extremity of Cashmir, is a sheet of water of an octagonal shape. Its colour varies from azure, to turquoise, to emerald, catching reflections from the surrounding architecture and foliage, yet tinging each reflection with the prevailing blue, like the Italian waters at Capri or Sorrento, and having a depth which the eye essays to penetrate but can never fathom. The autumnal tints of the umbrageous trees around make a foil to the dark-hued water, and impart vividness to the reflections.

From the temple-crowned summit of the Takht-i-Suleman, or "Solomon's throne," near Sirinagar the capital of Cashmir, a panoramic view is obtained of the whole valley. Far beneath the eye, lies the city of Sirinagar, like Venice founded amidst the waters, with the Jhelum river forming its main thoroughfare, and the branching canals its side-streets. On one flank there rises the citadel, on the other flank there stretch the poplar avenues where the national games and races are held. Hard by is the transparent expanse of the lake, catching the reflections of the rocky ranges around and of the floating clouds above. On its margin stand the groves of plane-trees, the royal gardens, summer-houses and fountains, where the poet laid the scene of Lala Rukh, and whence emperors, borne in luxurious barges over waters fringed with the lily and the lotus, issued mandates of war or peace to Caubul and to Delhi. Beyond the city, the Jhelum is like a silver streak, pursuing a serpentine course through the verdant plains, till it joins a line of broad light which represents the distant Walar lake. Along the horizon, on all four sides, there are snowy ranges, bounding the valley on the north, east and west, towards the Himalayas, and on the south separating it from India. At the end of summer, after rain, there are breaks in the long snowy line. At all other seasons the whole horizon forms a circle of uninterrupted snow.

Whether in the Himalayas, or in the plains and valleys of the Indian continent, the trees constitute one of the chiefest ornaments of the country. Many districts, and even some provinces, are characterized by sylvan beauty. Among the mountains the cedar forests, with their massive trunks and their umbrella-shaped foliage, make the ancient glories of Lebanon shrink into littleness by comparison. The cypress resembling, as the Persians say, the grace of the human stature, loves to grow out of the crevices of the rock or on the brow of the precipice. The fir, with its dependent branches and weeping leaflets, represents funereal melancholy. The yew grows thick in shadowy groves, where Druids might have worshipped. The lofty magnolia bursting forth with white blossoms seems sprinkled with newly fallen snow. The umbrageous plane still casts its shadow over the classic waters of Cashmir.

In the Indian continent, the teak, as the forest monarch, shoots up with an arrowy trunk, and a head crowned in summer with orange-coloured flowers. The "coronetted" palmyra, the feathery date-palm, the tapering bamboo, cluster in the fields, or around the homesteads. The casuarina whispers and murmurs when agitated by the sea-breeze. The pipal intertwines its roots with ruined buildings, till the masonry becomes enveloped like Laocoon in the folds of the Python. The banyan, with its tendrils drooping to the earth, forms trunk after trunk in rows like the supports of a Gothic structure, viewed in perspective, with arches of boughs and a leafy ceiling.

The effect of Indian scenery upon the mind is much enhanced by the aspect of the people, their costumes, their equipages and their surroundings. The complexion of all the Indian races is more or less dark and is, to that extent, uniform. The Caucasian type of head and cast of countenance prevail, the Mongolian being rare. In other respects there is extraordinary diversity. In physiognomy, in stature, and in all physical characteristics, the Bengali differs widely from the Sikh of the Panjab; the stately Rajput from the short Mahratta; the handsome Telugu from the dwellers in the Ganges valley; the rough Muhammadan on the Indus from his weaker but more refined and gracefully shaped brother of Madras. Opinions may vary as to the relative merits or demerits of the aspect of these several races. Among the Hindus, the Rajputs and the Sikhs will probably be thought the most picturesque, and the Pathans of the trans-Indus frontier, among the Muhammadans. In every part of India, both among rich and poor, often among homeless wanderers, subjects can be found well worthy of the artist's brush or pencil. The Indian costumes have a generic resemblance, though with many specific varieties. In some parts of the country, say near Benares, or Lahore, or Jeypore, or Madura, a gay crowd on festival days, with its sea of turbaned heads, will present a brilliant and varied mass of colour. After the sight of such comely multitudes, disappointment may be felt by visitors on meeting crowds at Calcutta or in Bengal where the dress is generally white; though even there, the light colours are often very effective in contrast with the rich greens of the foliage.

Among the upper and middle classes on gala occasions, the dresses are quite resplendent with gorgeous colours, recalling to memory the most ornate tales regarding the splendours of mediæval Europe. Yet the colours are not gaudy nor garish; though florid, they are not flashy. Nowadays in the costumes, the brightest fabrics of the west are tastefully mingled with the rich dyes and stuffs of the east. Though not versed in chromatic theories, the Natives are naturally gifted with an eye for colour, which renders their practice the theme of admiration, even among men of culture. This talent of theirs displays itself still more when the gentry, chiefs or princes hold civil and religious ceremonies, or institute festivities in celebration of marriages and other social rites. Then the most glowing descriptions of barbaric pomp and gold will fall short of the strange and curious reality. Much of the show will be solidly and substantially real, precious metals shining, and still more precious stones glittering. Much also will be the merest tinsel, spangle and finery. Yet the effect of tawdriness will be mitigated or removed by the general harmony of colour, under the all-pervading glare of the sun, or in the flare of the torch-lights. The embellishment of the equipages, once conspicuous in these spectacles, has been in part lost from the introduction of European vehicles. The elephants, however, and the camels are caparisoned and bedecked as of old. The favourite bullocks, constituting the very pink of animal beauty, are still to be seen drawing cars of antique build. If on any signal occasion large numbers of elephants are marshalled, with their ornamented trappings, and their gaily dressed riders, a noble spectacle is presented. When in former times the troops, or the untrained militia as they really were, of the Native sovereigns used to be reviewed, their gait, arms and accoutrements were attractive to the ordinary spectator, though perhaps not admirable to a professional eye. Nowadays these troops have a uniform and drill in imitation of the English army, whereby the picturesque effect is lost without an equivalent gain in warlike precision. Still, when a Native sovereign parades his state and dignity through his capital, scenes arise not far short of those described by historians. The gladdened eyes, the radiant aspect, the beaming faces of the people, on beholding their king issue forth, may afford scope for the reflections of moralists and politicians.

CHAPTER III.

OBJECTS OF BEAUTY IN ART.

Architecture under British rule—Interesting views at Bombay, at Calcutta, and on lines of railway—European churches and cathedrals—Beauty of Native architecture—Buddhist caves, rock-cut temples, pagodas and monasteries—Ancient frescoes—Sacred mountains of the Jains—Hindu or Brahminical structures—Mention of the finest temples—Mountain fortresses—Beautiful palaces—Excellence of Muhammadan architecture—Interesting remains at many places—Largest dome in the world—City of the dead—Mosque, palace and tomb of Akber the Great—Grand mosque at Delhi—Pearl Mosque at Agra—Matchless beauty of Taj Mehal mausoleum.

THE objects of beauty in Indian art, and especially of architecture, are equal to those in nature, like gems set in gold, where the jewels are worthy of their setting.

For a long time the British Government contributed little or nothing to the category of national architecture. Indeed, the style of many British structures was so erroneous or defective as to exercise a debasing influence on the minds of those Natives, who might be induced to admire or imitate it as being the production of a dominant, and presumably a more civilized, race. Most of the early buildings erected under British rule were, and many of the recent buildings still are, of a plain and uncouth fashion architecturally, however useful or commodious they may be practically. Of late years the Government has moved in an æsthetic direction, and at Calcutta, Madras and Bombay, fine edifices have sprung up in which the Gothic, Italian and Saracenic styles have been adapted with much taste and skill to the necessities of the east. A department of architecture has been established, from which the Native princes are beginning to obtain artistic designs for their palaces, colleges and civil structures.

At Bombay, along the shore of the bay, there is a long line of stately piles befitting a capital city in any country of the world, some of which were designed by Sir Gilbert Scott. The view of them as seen from Malabar Hill, with the blue sea before them, the city on their flank, the harbour behind them, the several ranges of Concan hills in the distance, and the Western Ghat mountains bounding the horizon, has often been compared with the scenery of the bay of Naples. It probably would rival the Neapolitan scenery, if only there were the transparent atmosphere and azure sky of the Mediterranean.

In Calcutta, the Eden gardens, rich in tropical vegetation, and embellished by ornamental water, form a fine foreground to the view of the State buildings. There, on a clear evening, the varied scenes, the semicircle of palatial structures, the foliage and serpentine water of the gardens, the tall masts of the shipping in the river close by, the moving crowd of horses and equipages thronging the strand, the guns of Fort William overlooking the whole like sentinels, combined with the ceaseless hum of voices, make up a marvellous effect.

Many of the largest public works under British rule, though not designed for artistic effect, do yet incidentally present a very handsome appearance and have surroundings fraught with interest. For example, the Bhore Ghat incline, between Bombay and Poona, where the railway ascends the Ghat range to a height of nearly 2000 feet, has very fine scenery in the rainy season, when the thunderclouds are blown away by the wind and display the precipitous and wooded mountain-sides, streaked in all directions with rain-swollen torrents, which leap in many series of cascades from the crests to the bases of the precipices. This spectacle, when seen to full advantage, is admitted by all railway travellers to be one of the most remarkable in the empire. In the Madras Presidency, the railway, as it rises from the Malabar coast at Beypore through a gap in the Nilgiri mountains, with the lofty granitic summits on either side, or as it ascends from the Coromandel coast through the wooded valleys to the central plateau, delights the traveller with the sights to be seen as he rapidly passes onwards. The views are striking and suggestive, from the pontoons which form a floating passage across the Hughli at Calcutta, from the railway viaduct a mile in length over the sandy bed of the Sone river near Patna, from the bridges across the Jamna at Allahabad and at Delhi, also from the lofty structure of iron-work, imbedded deep in the ground, which crosses the line over the Nerbadda at Broach.

The British Government has not yet constructed any sacred edifice which, in respect of ecclesiastical architecture, could be placed in any high rank. At many stations in northern India, however, handsome churches have been erected. The mementos at the "Bailey guard" in Lucknow, where so much of genius and bravery is buried, stir emotions in the breast of every Englishman. The memorial garden at Cawnpore, and the marble figure of the angel over the Well where the British victims of the massacre repose after their sufferings, attract the reverent and sorrowful regards of all beholders.

The Portuguese raised, at their chief settlements, cathedrals of much architectural pretension according to the style of the time. In the midst of the ruins of old Goa, is the church, whither congregations from new Goa occasionally resort, and where the remains of St. Francis Xavier are on great festivals exposed to the view of the faithful. At Bassein near Bombay, the Portuguese churches were ruthlessly unroofed by the Mahrattas for the sake of the timber: but the walls, arches, columns and windows still bear witness to the original grandeur of the structures. The ruins, interspersed amongst the dense foliage and dimly outlined by the moonlight, have a solemn and melancholy aspect.

Whatever be the estimation, favourable or unfavourable, of

European achievements, attention is at present centred and fastened upon the art and of architecture under Native dynasties, which were rooted for centuries in the country, making there as they hoped a lasting home, and were inspirited by political enthusiasm, social pride and religious fervour. The Natives are sometimes thought to be deficient in the sense of the picturesque; certainly they do not cultivate it as it is cultivated in Europe, and they seldom express it in words. But that they possess it naturally, is proved by their selection of striking and beautiful situations for their edifices. With almost all of their numerous structures, the beauty is increased by advantages of site. There is hardly throughout the whole continent a fine and effective position, on summit, eminence, river-bank, junction of waters or commanding point of prospect, which they have failed to occupy with some structure.

From the historic roll of these works, it is only possible to select those which have victorious beauty or consummate interest.

Buddhism as a religious reformation, and as a social and political movement, left grand traces of its handiwork. Of these traces many have been effaced, while some yet remain, though in a defaced state; many, again, having been carved in the hardest rock, are imperishable.

The "topes," or mounds, form an extensive class of remains. They were originally replete with beautiful ornamentation, which can now be recalled but imperfectly to the imagination. Their shape is that of enormous beehives raised hundreds of feet in height, as shrines enclosing relics, or as memorials of religious events.

The most conspicuous among them is the principal "tope" of the Bhilsa group near Bhopal. This mighty mound was originally constructed in masonry, coated with a thick envelope in cement, and surmounted with a structure on its apex; both structure and casing have long been lost. It is placed on the crest of a ridge of low hills, and when first reared must have gleamed from afar, like a beacon, to the inhabitants of the district. Around its base is a passage walled in with large slabs of stone, and divided into equal divisions by four lofty gateways, of which two, the northern and the eastern, remain standing. Of these two, the northern is the finest. It is a quaint and most suggestively beautiful remnant of the past. Over the entrance there is a façade consisting of sculptures in grey stone, representing elephants and various figures, together with the principal symbols of the Buddhist system. Immediately behind it, a tall tree has grown up, setting off, with its dark foliage, the hoary tints of the sculptures. A delineation of the form and details of the northern gateway has been prefixed to Fergusson's work on Tree and Serpent worship. Of these features, but little has been destroyed, and quite enough remains to enable the visitor to understand what the structure must have been. A plaster cast of the eastern gateway is in the Indian Museum at South Kensington.

Many of the rock-cut temples, or the cave temples, belong to Buddhism. The fondness for excavating their sacred places out of the mountain sides was a characteristic of the early races of India. Amidst the Western Ghat range of mountains especially, as at Nasik and elsewhere, also amidst the Eastern Ghat range, as at Khandagiri near Cuttak, in the hills which branch off from the Vindhyas towards the Ganges, and in other hill ranges, these interesting excavations are to be found. The total number of them, discovered as yet, amounts to nearly one thousand. Ofttimes, the traveller, arriving laboriously at the arched entrance of an excavation, peers curiously into the cavernous, and once holy, recesses. Turning round for a moment, he beholds the spreading landscape, the very prospect which Buddhists of old commanded, as they contemplated the wealth and civilization of the plains and valleys at their feet, whence the support of these national institutions was derived. In some of these places are inscriptions graven on the rock even as early as the reign of the Buddhist emperor Asoka, the shadowy outline of whose historic figure looms grandly through the mists that still obscure these times.

In the more modern of the Buddhist cave temples there is a stone figure, seated or standing, and sometimes colossal, of Buddha, with the ineffable calm of impassibility in the features. The forefinger solemnly points to warn men to look from mortality to immortality, from the seen things of time to the unseen things of eternity. The hand, holding a pinch of dust, indicates the insignificance of worldly greatness. The bearing and aspect are gentle and wise, yet grave, and in some degree severe.

Of the Buddhist caves and rock-cut temples, the finest group is that of Ajanta where, in a narrow and sequestered vale among the hills which branch off eastwards from the Western Ghat mountains, the trap rocks are almost honeycombed with the excavations. The valley, now an utter solitude shut in by mountain barriers from contact with the outer world, was once thronged with a community of priests, monks and worshippers living in seclusion. The pillars, capitals, doorways, shrines, seats for the priests, stalls for the monks and sculptures generally, are characterized by simplicity of design and execution.

Some of the walls were decorated with frescoes, well drawn and richly coloured, representing domestic scenes, secular and religious ceremonies, festivals during peace and after victory in war, royal and priestly processions. If these frescoes had survived they would have been inestimably precious relics of the past, but they have for the most part perished. Enough, however, of them remains to recall to life, before the imaginative eye, the people and things of that period. The process of decay can hardly be arrested; but the Government is causing copies to be made of some among them; and copies of others were made by their enthusiastic admirer Major Gill.

To the Buddhists belong many of the caves at Elura, a place which was signalized by the achievements of the Brahminists after the overthrow of Buddhism, and which will be mentioned presently.

Near the point where the railway incline surmounts the lofty crest of the Western Ghats, there is a single cave taking its name from the village of Karli. Its doorways and façades, its rows of columns with groups of elephants for their capitals, its roof arched and ribbed, render it, perhaps, superior to any one of the Ajanta caves, and constitute it the finest known specimen of a Buddhist excavation.

Near the city of Gya in Behar, there is at Buddh Gya a temple reared straight from the ground to a height of a hundred feet, in form resembling the Hindu temples dedicated to Shiva. It is a tower broad at the base and tapering towards the top, with an outer flight of steps at the basement. From the terrace at the top of the basement there still projects the withered trunk of the sacred tree, in harmony with the fate which has overtaken the structure. At Sarnâth near Benares, there are the ruins of a still grander fane.

In Sikhim near Darjiling there is a Buddhist population which enables the observer to study the modern and debased types of Buddhism. Their chapels and monasteries are placed in the midst of beautiful Himalayan scenery, overlooked by the snowy range, and surrounded by forests. The roofs are shaped like vast umbrellas with overshadowing eaves; the wooden pillars of the doorways are richly painted and the porticoes adorned with frescoes. At the entrances there pass in and out processions of high priests, abbots and monks, arrayed in vestments of red and purple. The large images of Buddha have the same mien and expression as the ancient sculptures. In one of the chapels the representation of Buddha assumes a threefold shape. In the centre of the group is the deity, or abstract wisdom, in whom no sex male or female can be distinguished; on the right is he who promulgated the faith, and who wears a sacred apparel; on the left is he who propagated it by arms and policy, and who has a martial garb; the figures being three times the life-size. The material of these remarkable images is terra-cotta of Thibetan workmanship; the figures are highly and tastefully coloured, and seen in the subdued light of the chapel, with some of the richly clothed priests in the front, produce an artistic effect. Sanctity attaches to the group; recently, an aged monk when alluding to his own end, was asked whither he was going; he replied, pointing to the figures, that he was going to meet those beings in another world.

In Nepal there are two large Buddhist pagodas of the Burmese type. One of these is on an eminence to which the ascent leads by a flight of steps. The traveller toiling up the stairs in the shade of the trees, casts a longing gaze at the brilliantly gilt apex of the pyramid, which seems so close above him, and yet so hard to reach.

In British Burma, living Buddhism may be seen to fair advantage. The forests supply the richest material, teak and other woods, for building, and suggest to the builders those designs which are derived from the shapes developed in sylvan growth. Consequently, the wooden structures and the wood-carvings in the Burmese pagodas are extraordinarily elaborate. The rich sombre and uniform colour of the wood and the shaded light, save the eye from being tired by the infinitude of detail in the pillars, ceilings, cornices and pinnacles. To these dark backgrounds, the priests, with their orange and saffron coloured vestments, give a graceful relief. At Prome, on the Irawaddy river, there is a cluster of low wooded hills, which are covered with numerous pagodas, rearing their pointed finials somewhat like the masts of shipping and surmounted by tapering structures cased with gilt copper. The architecture is in unison with the palms, plantain-trees and groves around. At Moulmein also, the heights are crowned with pagodas whence a noble landscape may be surveyed, with the city in front, behind it the plain watered by three converging rivers and the horizon bounded by the mountains of Siam.

At Rangun, the Shwe-dagong, or Dagon pagoda, is among the

chief ornaments not only of Burma, but of the British Indian empire. Placed on a wooded ridge, it rises to the height of near 300 feet with its towering structure, encased with burnished gilding, and narrowed gradually by a series of delicate curves towards an apex shaded by the sacred "htee" or umbrella. Seen from a distance, it seems to spring up from among the groves with a pyramid shining in the sunlight, and then to shoot up into the sky with an obelisk of flame.

The Jains possess many fine structures in different parts of India. The adherents of the Jain faith occupy the summits of the forest-clad Paras-nath which overlooks the plains of western Bengal, and of Abu which stands as a lofty outwork of the Aravali range. Their religious stronghold in the present time, is on the heights of the solitary Satrunj mountain, near Palitana in the peninsula of Kathiawar. The numerous cupolas, obelisks and spires, often bright with the whitest marble, seem to pierce the sky. The shrines are laden with the weight of gorgeous offerings, sent by the wealthy members of the sect from almost every populous city in the empire. From the terraces of the edifices, half temples half fortresses, is to be seen an extensive view of the rich plains, once studded with historic cities, of which the names alone survive, even the sites being untraceable. On the horizon are the waters of the Gulf of Cambay.

The Hindu, or Brahminist in contradistinction to Buddhist, remains are often, though not always, more recent than the Buddhist; they are therefore more numerous and better preserved.

The Brahminist Hindus excavated some of the finest of the rock-cut temples. To them chiefly belongs the series of excavations in the Deccan, known as the caves of Elura. Among this wonderful set of works, the temple of Kailas (or Hindu paradise) is pre-eminent. The architects first hewed, out of the trap formation of the hill-side, a broad passage all round a rocky mass, leaving this mass in the first instance a solid block. Inside this block, again, they hollowed out spacious chambers, on the interior walls of which they sculptured figures. On the exterior also of the block they carved a variety of devices. They then coated the whole with many-coloured pigments. Thus they produced a fane as large as a modern church, not built, founded or constructed at all, but excavated solid and entire out of the precipitous rocks of the mountain. Lastly, from the outer sides of the surrounding passage they excavated niches for sculptures. This train of operations renders the temple unique of its kind in the empire.

On the same side of the mountain with the Kailas temple are numerous rock-cut temples, of which the interiors are richly and elaborately carved, and which have made the name of Elura so famous.

The island of Elephanta in the Bombay harbour has some Brahminical caves of almost equal interest. The visitor, while gazing in the dim light at the gigantic sculptured figures, and the massive yet richly carved columns, looks through a vista stretching towards the bright landscape and the blue waters.

In the Hindu temples of recent centuries, in northern and central India, there is a want of height, size and expansiveness. Ingenuity seems to have been bestowed on ornamentation in detail, while the general proportions and dimensions were comparatively neglected. This fault, however, is not perceptible in the Hindu temples of the elder time, which are distinguished for breadth of conception, grandeur of design, correctness of proportion and subordination of details to the main features.

In Cashmir, the ruined fane of Martand (or the sun) is massive in construction and plain in ornament; the material consisting of huge blocks of dark stone. It has compartments somewhat like nave, transepts, aisles, and an extensive cloistered enclosure, of which the gateways were magnificent. The structure was meant to resist the ravages of time. The visitor, observing its broken arches, overthrown columns and leaning sides, perceives that some earthquake must have caused a destruction which is manifestly apart from the process of decay. Inspection disproves the truth of the tradition which attributes the mischief to Muhammadan iconoclasts. These ruins grey, with their background of Cashmir landscape and of snowy mountains, form an impressive object.

At Pâtan near Katmandu, the capital of Nepal, are the temples of the aboriginal Hindu dynasty which was overthrown by the Gorkhas. These fanes are still in good preservation. Their roofs, tipped with gilt copper cupolas, have overhanging eaves, somewhat after the Thibetan or Chinese fashion. Their masonry consists of bricks of great size, baked to a firm consistency and covered with a sort of pink enamel. Their blackwood carvings are set off with ornaments of burnished brass, resembling shields. They have considerable height with several stories. Their background also consists in part of snowy mountains.

At Brindaban on the river Jamna near Mathra and Agra, in the most classic ground of Hindu mythology, where the scene of the birth and childhood of the god Krishna was laid, there is a Hindu fane, having proportions and dimensions somewhat like those of a church, and built with grand material, the stone being of a deep red colour. The interior, fairly well-preserved, is the best example of Hindu art in the plains of northern India.

On the seashore of Orissa, stands the Black Pagoda, so called by mariners at sea who regard it as a landmark. It is a noble ruin, although what is now seen is only the vestibule of the great temple itself. There has been doubt felt by some as to whether the structure was ever completed, or after completion sank from failure of the foundations laid in a sandy soil; it probably was completed. If finished in the same proportions and detail with which it was begun, it must have been one of the most beautiful buildings ever raised by Hindu hands. The ruin inspires sentiments tinged with melancholy, standing as it does near the beach, with the billowy sands surging round it, and within sound of the sea waves.

At Mahabalipuram near Madras, masses of rock rear themselves up on the sea-side, protruding through the low-lying littoral ground or the sandy beach. Upon each one of these separate rocks the Hindu architects laid their transforming hands, hewing the shapeless masses into shapely forms of dome, cupola and convex top, and excavating stately interiors, based not upon artificial foundations, but upon the everlasting stone. The finest of these rock-cut fanes is second only to that of Kailas at Elura, already described. One temple in the vicinity is built in the ordinary way upon rocks jutting out into the sea, and the surf at high tide dashes up the steps at its entrance. It was near here that Southey laid the scene of his poem, "The Curse of Kehama."

In southern India, in this respect unlike northern or central India, the Hindu temples of recent centuries have imposing proportions as well as most elaborate ornamentation. The temple itself is usually lofty, and stands in the midst of a spacious courtyard, which is surrounded by walls and has one or more "Goparums" or gateways, often as many as four. Sometimes there are several enclosures, one within the other, each having gateways, in which case the number of gateways is multiplied. These lofty gateways have magnificent façades, reflecting honour upon the Hindu architects, and constituting some of the most noteworthy features in the country. Such are the gateways at Tanjore, at Srirangam, on the sacred island in the river Cavery near Trichinopoly, and at Madura. In one of the principal courtyards at Tanjore there is the figure of a sacred bull about twenty feet high, a granite monolith; men nowadays marvel how the vast block was carved and transported to its present site. Often the taste of the architects displayed itself in the construction of noble colonnades, such as that at Rameshwaram, on one of the islands of Adam's bridge, which almost connects India with Ceylon. At Madura, in addition to the fanes and gateways, there are numerous courtyards, aisles, corridors and colonnades, replete with figures carved in stone, and often presenting a fine perspective with a beautiful play of light and shade. The precincts are crowded with the busy and gaily dressed multitudes of those who buy and sell in the temple; the scene in its way is hardly equalled anywhere else in the empire.

Benares, in the north, which notwithstanding rival claims to pre-eminence, must be regarded as the most sacred city of Hinduism, has a host of temples, none of which are remarkable for their dimensions. The city, lining the high bank of the Ganges, can best be viewed from a barge, dropping gently down the current at sunrise, when the people issue forth to bathe in the holy river. Then is perceived the unequalled river-frontage of towers, lattices, porticoes, spires and cones. The palaces bear the names of all the principal Native sovereigns and chiefs of the Hindu faith in all parts of the empire. The structures are dedicated by Hindu piety to all manner of religious uses, with terraces and stone platforms, on some of which every earnest Hindu prays that his body after death may be burned to ashes as the best passport to a new and happier state. The steps, flight after flight, are thronged with multitudes eagerly pressing for immersion in the water which, according to their faith, washes away sin.

The architectural ambition of the Hindus was not limited to sacred structures, but extended to palaces and buildings for royal uses, to fortresses, and also to works of public utility, whereby the names of founders might live in the grateful memory of posterity.

The particular wells, known by the name of "Baoli" are contrivances on a laborious scale for ensuring a supply of water at all seasons in arid tracts. Enormous cisterns are excavated to a depth of a hundred feet or more, with broad steps leading down to the deepest part and with spacious galleries at various heights all round the reservoir, according to the rise and fall of the water at the several seasons so that there may be access to it always. The finest specimens of this remarkable class of structures are found in the province of Gujerat on the west coast.

Sometimes towers were erected of stone-work elaborately carved, in celebration of victories; of a shape resembling that of the Italian campaniles. Notable among these is the tower of victory at Chitorgarh in Rajputana, a monument which is placed on a celebrated hill and looks down upon the scene of some of the most gallant deeds ever performed by Rajput patriotism.

The fortresses of Gwalior on the confines of Hindostan, of Asirgarh in the Sâtpura range, of Daolatabad and Gawilgarh in the Deccan, of Gûty in the Madras Presidency, of Nandidûrg in Mysore, frown sternly from their beetling crags, and have features of rugged grandeur enhancing the effect of their historic associations.

The picturesque Mahratta hill forts, built on rocky eminences in the Western Ghat range, were the eyries whence Sivaji, like the eagle, used to swoop upon the plains, namely, Junîr, where he was born; Rajgurh, where he founded his predatory rule; Pertabgurh, where he openly rebelled against the Muhammadans and assassinated their envoy; Raegurh, where he held his court and controlled all western India till death closed his reign. The scenery around these places is in unison with the momentous events which occurred in them.

Little, save mounds and hillocks and the remnants of structures here and there, remains to mark the extensive site of the ancient city of Ayodhya, or Ajudhia, on the banks of the Ghogra. The splendour of this city is the theme of descriptive eloquence in the epic poetry of the Hindus. And every educated Hindu turns his thoughts towards its glory as the representative of the golden and heroic epoch of his nation.

Near Bijayanagar, in the Madras Presidency, where the

Hindus made their final, but ineffectual, stand against the encroachments of the Muhammadan conquerors, there exist the remains of magnificent temples, some of which are among the best memorials of Hindu art and architecture, while others have lofty, though gloomy, interiors. The ruins of the city cover an extensive area; the palaces and many-storied towers, the stone platforms raised for witnessing state spectacles, the fountains and conduits, the elephant stables, have a style of antiquated simplicity, which is most interesting. Here and there solid rocks are hewn and fashioned into gigantic and grotesque figures of divine incarnations. The site of the city is remarkable, in the midst of granite cliffs and boulders, watered by canals from the rock-bound stream of the Tungabadra. The scenery of the river, with its rapids, with its rocky barriers mirrored in the placid pools, and with the monolith pillars of the ancient viaducts still standing, is in harmony with the historic halo which surrounds the place.

The palaces of Hindu kings are often built on the margin of artificial lakes, in the midst of which are islets adorned with gardens and summer-houses. Such, particularly, are the celebrated palaces at Udeypur in Rajputana. Such, also, is the situation of the palaces at Ambair, the old capital of the Jyepur State, near the modern and well-planned city of Jyepur. The palatial summer-pavilion at Dig, near Bhurtpur, is of comparatively recent construction. It embodies many of the finest principles of Indian architecture, and is the most beautiful of the modern structures.

Amongst the old palatial buildings there may be noticed the palace of Mandla near Jabalpur in central India, specially remarkable as having been constructed by an aboriginal dynasty of Gonds, and of Chandragarh near Arcot in the south, where the native chief is said to have signed away to the East India Company the strip of what was then sand, but now is the site of the Madras city.

Foremost among the palaces of India is the palace built by Tirûmal Naik at Madura. Its courtyards and arcades, its vestibules, anterooms and halls of audience, its rotund chambers, vaulted roofs and arches lofty as those of a church, combine to excite the admiration of the beholder and to render the name of its founder renowned. A mystery enshrouds the memory of Tirûmal Naik, by reason of the generally received tradition of his tragic end. It is believed that searching for hidden treasure he was enticed into a subterranean chamber by some Brahmin conspirators, who suddenly closed the door, and left him to starve in darkness.

The Muhammadan architecture is one of the chief ornaments of the Indian empire, and has the highest claims upon the attention of Englishmen.

The Muhammadans in India can indeed boast of many secular structures of size and beauty, forts, palaces, halls of audience, summer-houses, colleges, caravanserais and market-places. But their highest efforts were given to religious edifices, mosques, shrines and tombs. Saints being much venerated, costly shrines were raised to preserve their example in the mind of the faithful. Though tombs were often built in affectionate remembrance of the departed, still it was sometimes the custom for sovereigns to build their mausolea in their lifetime, which accounts for so many tombs being so magnificent.

Some conquering dynasties have bequeathed more monuments of usefulness as signs of their occupation, but none ever left more beautiful traces of their conquest, than the Muhammadans. In boldness of design and breadth of idea they always equalled and often surpassed the Hindu art, and infinitely excelled it in respect of taste, in the most æsthetic and artistic sense of the term. They were in the very first rank of the architects of all nations, ancient or modern, respecting simplicity of form, adjustment of proportions, gracefulness of curvature, chasteness of ornament and quality of colouring. Some of their later structures were like poems, so artistic was the composition. The combination of these merits in the highest degree was hardly attained till the reigns of the Mogul emperors, and reached its zenith in the time of Shah Jehan. Still, it shewed itself almost from the very first; despite some crudeness or awkwardness here and there, and something of angularity, its progress may be traced from dynasty to dynasty, from province to province, from century to century. Nor did it suffer any deterioration till buildings were, in later days, erected at Lucknow. These edifices, however lofty or imposing, belong to an inferior style of art.

Thus, for example, the structures at Ahmedabad in the province of Gujerat near Bombay, may not present specimens which could be singled out for special mention, but nevertheless are replete with beautiful details of interest to every student of architecture. A similar interest attaches itself to the buildings, sacred and secular, at Bijapur, at Golconda, and at Bedar, all in the Deccan; to the ruins of Mandu in central India; to the remains of Toghlakabad and other cities, which were built near the site of the comparatively modern city of Delhi; to the mosques at Jounpur near Benares; to the ruins of Gour in Bengal, including the fine Adina mosque, which is, however, much overgrown by the teeming vegetation. Among these there are some structures which must be chosen for notice.

At Bijapur, the dome of the tomb of king Mahmud is the largest in the world, exceeding even the duomo of Florence. Its structural arrangements are well worthy of being studied by all architects. It is one of the most imposing, though hardly one of the most beautiful, buildings in the empire. In beauty it is surpassed by the mausoleum of king Ibrahim close by. At Golconda, near Hyderabad, the collection of domed tombs of the kings, at the foot of the frowning citadel, has caused the place to be named the city of the dead. It somewhat resembles the tombs of the Caliphs near Cairo. Near Delhi, the Kutab Minar, soaring aloft to a prodigious height, in shape somewhat like an obelisk, and covered with elaborate carvings, has excited the wonder and admiration of all beholders.

Of a later period, when the Mogul empire was first consolidated by Akber the Great, are the mosque and palace built by him as a country seat at Fatehpur Sikri, near Agra; also his tomb at Sikandra in the same neighbourhood. The design of these buildings is very fine, and the contrast of colour in the material afforded by the brilliant white marble, and the dull-red sandstone, is remarkable. The style in some respects recalls memories of Hindu architecture, while in other respects it displays nascent beauty, and affords promise of the architectural triumphs which followed. The emperor, though a Moslem, was imbued with cosmopolitan ideas respecting religion and philosophy, and had chosen one of his queens from a royal Hindu house in Rajputana.

The two mosques at Lahore, one built by imperial orders, and called "Padshahi," the other built by a minister, and called "Waziri," are in a more advanced style. The body of the Padshahi mosque is of red sandstone, while the three cupolas are of marble. The Waziri mosque is quite different, being adorned with exquisitely coloured glazing in floral devices.

The Muhammadan artists cultivated the art of fixing beautiful colours on earthy substances. The number of such men being limited, they died out during the wars and revolutions, leaving no successors in their art which has thus perished. Traces of the art survive, however, in the mosque at Tatta in Sind, which structure is the gem of that province. The Muhammadans also practised the art of mosaic with inlaid stones, imitating leaves and flowers with coloured stones, inserted in white marble. This art still survives among their descendants.

The "Jama" mosque at Delhi, of a later period, built by the emperor Shah Jehan, is in good preservation as one of the prime ornaments of the empire, and is probably the most beautiful mosque on a very large scale that has ever been seen in the world. Its vast dimensions, swelling cupolas and lofty arches;

its spacious courtyard, arcades, gateway, cloisters and flight of steps, produce ultimately an imposing effect. But even this is hardly perceived at first by the beholder, because his admiration is so riveted by the grace of its forms, the nicety of its proportions, the delicate adjustment of its component parts, and the harmony of its colouring. For the material of this noble structure the marble lends its brightness and the sandstone its finest red.

Besides the "Jama" mosque which, as its name implies, was built for the general attendance of all the faithful, special mosques were designed for the attendance of the emperor himself or of his immediate family and suite. In the palace precincts, inside the fortress of Agra, there is a mosque, built by the same emperor, of faultless construction, entirely in white marble. It was named the Moti Masjid or Pearl Mosque, and well it deserves that designation. It possesses many of the superb characteristics ascribed to the Jama mosque. It is inferior to the Jama mosque in size, but is superior even to that mosque in loveliness. It is carefully preserved by the State as one of the most precious gems of the empire.

The spectator standing in the courtyard of this Pearl Mosque with the gateway behind him, the arcades on either hand, and the mosque with its cupolas in front, beholds nothing but sky and marble. As he lifts up his eyes towards the dazzling white, the cloudless sky has an intense azure. The perfect contour of the cupolas strikes the vision, while the atmosphere behind seems to have infinite depth. Then, under the arches in the broad recesses of the building, there are the cool shades of the marble, diversified by the play of reflected lights, and affording grateful relief to the eye fatigued with beauty. A more lovely edifice for divine worship has probably never been erected.

The supreme effort of Muhammadan genius was the design and construction of the mausoleum erected at Agra by the emperor Shah Jehan in memory of his beloved empress Mumtaz-i-Mahal, whence the building has acquired the common name of the Taj

Mahal. Some Italian artists may have assisted in the details of the ornamentation. But to the Muhammadan alone belongs the imperishable renown of having reared this the peerless queen of all the structures in India, perhaps in the world. The British authorities, proud of possessing this unequalled treasure, maintain it in good preservation and adorn its gardens with all the choicest flowers of the West. People who have seen it constantly during the greater part of their lives, never tire of seeing it again and again. Artists despair of representing it on canvas; and in truth no drawing that can be made, no account that can be given, will do justice to it. There is almost equal difficulty in analysing the reasons why it appears so exceedingly beautiful. Doubtless, the colouring is one important cause. The marble which, in that dry climate, is but little sullied by the stains of time and at a short distance seems, in the sunlight, to be pure as a snow-wreath, the liquid blue of the sky in the cloudless winter season, the sombre green of the funereal cypresses, contribute to the effect, which every one feels but none can fully explain. There must, however, be other and higher causes; among these are the perfect proportions and the exact balancing of one part against the other. In support of this view it may be noted that in other places, imitations on a smaller scale have been attempted, with only slight deviations from the form and proportions of the original, but the effect is marred, the beauty gone, the resemblance lost. If the edifice be well-nigh indescribable when viewed by day, still more does it transcend description if seen by night, when the moonlight rests upon the marble, and by contrast deepens the gloom of the cypress shades. When all nature is hushed, a sentiment arises of solitude in the pale presence of the monument, until the historic dead ascend in dim procession before the imagination, and a feeling of awe mingles with a sense of the overpowering beauty of the scene.

CHAPTER IV.

EUROPEAN CLASSES, OFFICIAL AND NON-OFFICIAL.

Importance of the Covenanted Civil Service—Results of new system of competition—Interesting duties of civil servants—Historic names of Civil Servants in the past—Military officers in civil and political employ—Distinguished names among them—Several classes of covenanted officers—Medical officers—Military and civil engineers—The clergy—Eminent prelates—Uncovenanted European and East-Indian officers—Non-official Europeans—Mercantile firms—Chambers of commerce—Indigo-planters—Tea and coffee-planters—The Anglo-Indian press.

THE Covenanted Civil Service is the most important class in the country. It consists of 928 officers, of whom 7 are Natives, and the remainder 921 English; there are 623 in the Presidency of Bengal, 158 in that of Madras, and 147 in that of Bombay. It represents before the Natives the essential qualities of British rule, and personally symbolizes to them the mind and intent of the Government. It supervises the collection of the revenue, the repression of crime, the administration of justice, and the relations of the State with the people. There are some important matters, indeed, which are in great part managed by other official classes; such as the finances, the public works, the political and foreign relations, the higher education, the application of English law, the general legislation; though in these also the Covenanted Civil Service has a considerable share. But in so far as the action of Government concerns or affects the daily life, the domestic comfort and the ordinary affairs of the people,—the arbitrament for weal or for woe rests with the Covenanted Civil Service. The members of this Service, officially termed the Civil Servants, are generally too much absorbed in the work before them to reflect much on their own position. They are conscious of being representative men in the eyes of the Natives. According to their conduct, the character of England herself is measured by the mass of the Indian people. Even if some Englishmen in India evince unpopular qualities, they are seen but little by the population in the interior. But the disposition, temper, ability, demeanour, life and conversation of the Covenanted Civil Servants, are familiar to millions of men. Thus the Natives, when thinking of the government under which they live, and of the nation from which it emanates, judge mainly from what they see of the Civil Servants. It is well that England should be gauged by the standard of some of her best sons.

More than twenty years have elapsed since a fundamental change was made in the mode of appointing men to this Service, according to which they are admitted by open competition, instead of being nominated by the Directors of the East India Company. The Service enjoyed so much repute under the Company, and had won such historic fame, that the results of the change from nomination to competition have been awaited with some anxiety by English opinion. Whenever the conversation in English society turns upon India, the question is asked whether the new class of Civil Servants, who enter by competition, is equal to the old class of Civil Servants who entered by nomination, and whether on the whole the change is working successfully. The answer may be given in the affirmative without any hesitation. The change has not produced, and probably will never produce, all the benefit which its advocates and admirers predicted, but it is producing the benefit which might fairly be expected. The competition does not indeed allure the most successful alumni of the universities in the United Kingdom. Nor is that combination of ability and energy in unison, which amounts to genius, found more in the new Service than in the old, for this quality, which never has been, and doubtless never will be, wanting among British people in India, cannot be tested by examination and will not be ensured by regulation. But young men are procured, of more than average acquirements and more than ordinary industry. Under the old system of nomination, inferior men as regards diligence and capacity crept into the Service occasionally. Such instances, which must be specially harmful in a country like India, are not found under the system of competition. Some men will prove to be unsuited, by habit of mind or from physical failings, for the work of their profession; but such cases are infrequent. The predictions formerly hazarded to the effect that many men would be mere bookworms, inapt in horsemanship and other pursuits essential or incidental to an administrative career, have happily failed to be verified by the event. Formerly the mettle of the old Service was sorely tried in the pacification of newly annexed territories, or in quelling disturbances and rebellions. Recently the spirit of the new Service has been evoked by famine and pestilence menacing many millions of people. Its members have in these fiery trials displayed zeal, constancy, endurance, and energy not to be surpassed in Anglo-Indian annals. They are filling the office of Magistrate and Collector in almost all the districts throughout the empire; an office which concerns more immediately the welfare of the Natives than any other. Some of them are arriving at a position which entitles the holders to fill the higher administrative posts. They are entering the secretariat under the several Local Governments, and the secretariat of the Government of India; one of them has just obtained a seat in the Council of the Governor-General. Most of the district judgeships are now held by them, which offices also directly concern the welfare of the Natives; and soon some of them will be ascending the bench of the High Courts.

In general terms there are two branches in the work of Covenanted Civil Servants, the executive or administrative, and the judicial. Formerly in some divisions of the empire, the men were interchangeable between the two branches, while in other divisions they have long been kept separate. But at the present time, the plan almost universally adopted is in this wise. The young officers are, for a very few years, all employed in the executive or administrative branch, in order to become familiar with the vernacular, the ways and the customs of the people. They are then divided by a final distribution, some being assigned to the executive or administrative branch and some to the judicial, according to the needs of each branch; after that, they are not interchanged between the two branches. In this distribution, the aptitudes, acquirements and preferences of individuals are considered as much as possible consistently with the necessities of the service. Though many men from the first bend their minds towards the judicial line, yet with the majority the executive or administrative line is regarded as the more interesting of the two.

It is in the administrative line that a man as Magistrate and Collector receives charge of a district, with an area of 3000 to 5000 square miles, and a population of one to two millions. Looking at the great and varied interests entrusted to his keeping in relation to the revenue, the treasury, the landed tenures, the police, the magistracy, the prisons, the public education, the municipalities, the sanitation, the local funds and the works of material improvement; at the many contingencies and emergencies in which all his energies may be summoned for the preservation of the people from danger; at the relations which must be maintained with all classes of the Natives in a firm, judicious, considerate and conciliatory manner;—he comes to regard his district almost with the same sort of feelings with which a great landowner regards his broad estate. He learns to take a lively interest in the concerns of the district, in the industries of the people, in their manufactures, their productions, their trade, their festivals and their local customs. With many individuals among them, he will form a lasting friendship. One of the faculties he must cultivate is a discriminating insight into the character and disposition of those with whom he comes in contact. He will be surrounded by many Natives who are themselves endowed with this very faculty, and who intuitively perceive, or learn by subtle observation, the strong and the weak points in the character of every Englishman in authority. He will oft be surrounded by flatterers, and will constantly meet with those who desire to mislead, cajole or deceive him. In seeking for an expression of the sentiments, ideas, feelings and reflections of the Natives, he must be careful not to let his own view be perceived, nor to evince any sign of a foregone conclusion; for they are but too apt to chime in with the opinion of official Europeans, or at least to avoid indicating any contrary opinion. If he be not on his guard in this respect when conversing with Natives, he will find that instead of ascertaining their sentiments, he is only hearing an echo of his own. As they are very reserved in communicating their views to an official European, it is harder for him to probe their inner mind, than for a non-official European, before whom they have less reserve and with whom they will converse without fear of possible consequences. While incessantly watchful against wrongfulness concealed under specious and plausible masks, he must beware of the uncharitable insinuations against their neighbours, in which Natives are too prone to indulge and which are more dangerous than open accusations. There is nothing which good Natives, who do their duty incurring enmity thereby, dread so much as the risk of their conduct being traduced before him by covert suggestions, and of his mind being poisoned, as it were, and set against them.

While cautious not to allow interested persons to make separate or personal representations to him regarding matters under investigation, he cannot be too accessible to all sorts and conditions of Natives. In his own house, on certain days, at certain hours, or at any hour which his pressing duties may leave comparatively free, also during his drives and walks, he should be ready and willing to receive Natives, to talk with them, so as to catch the tone and feel the pulse of the people. His recreation in the cool hours of the morning will be to inspect the city or the station near his headquarters, promote sanitation, examine schools, inspect public works and form plans for material improvement. He will take the same pleasure in doing this as a landlord takes in going round his gardens, parks and farms and considering plans for the improvement of the property. His ambition is to leave behind him some useful work, as a mark of his sojourn in the place and a sign of his improving hand.

For nearly half the year, he quits his headquarters and marches with tents about the district. This camp life under canvas constitutes the most enjoyable part of his Indian career. He then has intercourse at all hours of the day with classes of Natives, who can hardly be observed with advantage at the central station of the district, and who can be best understood when met with at their remote homes. While he is riding through the fields, halting in the villages, shooting by the way, lounging after a march in the shaded anteroom of his tent under the spreading boughs, or warming himself by the bonfire outside his tent door on cold or frosty nights, he is on much more easy and familiar terms with the Natives than he could possibly be at his headquarters, where he is surrounded more or less with his staff and subordinates. Often he pursues the wild sports of the east; and then he learns many things about the district and the people which could not otherwise be learnt. At every turn his eye glances on picturesque objects, and sometimes it rests on sights of beauty and interest; all which help to endear to him the district where his lot for a time is cast. After some weeks or some months of marching and touring, during which time he has seldom heard the English language spoken, he returns to his headquarters with his physical frame invigorated, his mind refreshed, his imagination stored with new ideas and his will braced with fresh resolves. Many of the beneficent plans, which he then conceived, he proceeds to carry out, as he once more sits in his central office during the long hours of the summer days. In the hum and the heat of these close and crowded rooms, and amidst the whirl of never-ending business, he longs for the day to come round for him to travel once more in the interior of his district, at the season when nature decks herself with the dew that glitters on the rising crops, and when she is freshened by the health-giving breezes of an eastern winter.

Indeed, that part of the British administrative system, which directly concerns the majority of the Natives, is centred in the office of Magistrate and Collector. So long as these very important officers continue to be able and efficient, as they have heretofore been, the administration will be regarded by Native opinion as in the main successful. They are usually esteemed by competent observers as being among the best types of the English in the east. A prelate of the Church, acquainted with countries of the East and West, is said to have declared that as a class they are among the best men he ever knew.

The junior Civil Servants, in the executive or administrative branch, undergo in the districts a training to suit them for the life which has just been described. They pass examinations in the vernacular language or languages of the division of the empire to which they are attached.

A divisional Commissioner of revenue and police is the superintendent of the Magistrates and Collectors in several districts which make up a division. There are several such Commissionerships under each of the Local Governments (except Madras). The Commissioner is thus at the head of a province, or part of a province, and in several respects represents the Government. He is a high functionary in the eyes of the Natives, and the statements, just made regarding the Magistrates and Collectors, apply to him.

The District Judges, also Covenanted Civil Servants, form a very important class of functionaries. Their duties are not only judicial, consisting of the trial of original suits and the hearing of appeals from some classes of Native Judges, but are also in a considerable degree administrative.

The District Judge is the superior of the several Native

Judges who are serving in the district, and the visitor or inspector of the various courts established therein. He makes a tour from place to place inspecting these courts, examining their returns, testing their procedure, and learning the popular estimate of their character and efficiency. He is, in short, a sort of minister of justice for the district; upon his diligence and watchfulness the convenience of suitors, and the promotion of the many interests relating to civil justice, must greatly depend. The juniors in the judicial line serve as Assistant Judges, and so become trained for the office of District Judge.

It is from among the District Judges that men are selected for the bench of the High Courts; and many able and learned men have been thus obtained to discharge the duties of these tribunals.

It is impossible here to describe the varied work, besides district work, which is done by Covenanted Civil Servants in many capacities, as political Residents at Native Courts, as heads of fiscal departments, as Chief Commissioners of provinces, as Secretaries to Government, as Members of the Councils, as Lieutenant-Governors of divisions of the empire, and sometimes as Governors of Presidencies.

There is every hope that the historic traditions of the Civil Service in the past will be emulated by the Civil Service in the future. All the well-wishers of India will pray that the memory of good men departed may encourage the new Civil Servants, and that the spirit of the most illustrious of their predecessors,—of Warren Hastings, of Teignmouth, of Mountstuart Elphinstone, of Metcalfe, of Macnaghten, of Thomason, of Mertins Bird, of Edmonstone, of John Lawrence,—may ever rest upon them in their labours.

Next to the Covenanted Civil Service, there is a very important class of officers drawn from the army for civil and political employ. These officers used formerly to be taken from the European officers of the Native armies; they are now taken from the Staff Corps. The greater part of the diplomatic or political appointments in the country are held by them; also many of the civil appointments in several provinces, namely the Panjab, Oudh, British Burma, Assam, the Central Provinces, Sind and Berar. In these capacities their duties are the same as those of the Covenanted Civil Service; and all that has been stated regarding that Service, is applicable to them also. They have always been most zealous, able and efficient; many of them, having been originally chosen on account of their promise of talent, have become eminently distinguished. Some of the best and greatest names in Anglo-Indian history have belonged to this very important class of officers; such names as those of Clive, Munro, Malcolm, Alexander Burnes, Henry Lawrence, Mark Cubbon, John Low, James Outram, John Jacob, Herbert Edwardes, John Nicholson, Henry Durand. Of these, Munro became Governor of Madras, Malcolm Governor of Bombay, and Durand Lieutenant-Governor of the Panjab. Many of them survive, either in retirement, with names destined hereafter to be inscribed on the rolls of history, or in active service, with abilities capable of preserving the brightest traditions of their profession.

There are other classes which, though not having the official style of covenanted, are yet under covenant with the Government, having been sent out from England under this condition. These classes have of late years grown much in importance, and their members are now filling places of consequence in the public service. Such are the educational officers, generally graduates of the universities of the United Kingdom, to whom practically is entrusted the management of the national education. Such are the Civil Engineers, trained in the Royal College of Civil Engineering at Coopers' Hill. Such are the Forest officers, despatched from England, after having been professionally instructed in the forest schools of France and Germany. Such are the scientific officers, geologists, botanists, chemists, meteorologists, astronomers, appointed from England.

The Indian Medical Service has been in part employed with

the Native Army and its members have heretofore been military officers. But its largest and most important employment has been among the civil officers and employés of the Government, and among the Natives. One of its highest functions has been the education of the Natives as medical men and medical practitioners. At the Presidency towns of Calcutta, Madras and Bombay, its members have an extensive private practice, not only among their own countrymen, but also among the Natives. It furnishes to Government skilled advisers in every branch of sanitation. It contributes largely to the advancement in India of those sciences which are cognate to its own work; in botany especially it has held a distinguished place. It has raised the British character in the estimation of the humbler classes of the Natives, by reason of philanthropy scientifically directed in performing surgical operations, and in superintending charitable dispensaries. Its influence with the middle and upper classes of Natives is considerable. By recent arrangements it will be relieved of its military work, and will be devoted to those civil duties for which it is so signally qualified.

The several Corps of Engineers in India were separate bodies until the amalgamation of the forces of the East India Company with the Royal Army. They contained as high an average of talent and capacity, and as many shining lights of the public service, as any corps that ever existed. The names of some of its members will live in Anglo-Indian history, such names as Proby Cautley and Baird Smith in the North-western Provinces, Robert Napier (now Lord Napier of Magdala) and Alexander Taylor in the Panjab, Arthur Cotton and Anderson in Madras, Haig in the Central Provinces, Michael Kennedy and Fife in Bombay.

The position of the civil engineers under their covenants has been already mentioned. They now constitute the larger number of the officers serving in the Department of Public Works, a branch of the service which has grown rapidly of late years owing to the extension of canals and the construction of railways by the State. Although the Government is striving to educate the Natives for the profession of civil engineering, still at the present time, the employment of a large number of Europeans is necessary in this profession, and for an indefinite period the direction of the great public works must remain in European hands.

The clergy consist mainly of the Chaplains of the English Church in the service of Government who minister among the European soldiery, and among all the servants of the State both civil and military, also of Presbyterian Ministers and of Roman Catholic priests who attend to the troops and other establishments of their respective communities. They constantly visit the hospitals of the European troops, and accompany the forces into the field on active service. They also visit the numerous civil stations scattered over the country, but their scanty number is altogether too few for such extensive charges; consequently societies are formed for bringing out additional clergy from England. The Bishops of the English Church were three in number; two more have been recently added, as it was found necessary to strengthen the episcopate by reason of the growing needs of the community. The Bishop of Calcutta is also metropolitan in India. Among these prelates there have been several who exerted an elevating influence on the State and the community. The memories of Bishops Heber, Wilson, Cotton, Milman, and Archdeacon Pratt, are reverently and affectionately cherished.

There is a large class of European officials who are termed uncovenanted, to distinguish them from the covenanted. They are not so numerous as they once were, owing to the competition of educated Natives for the numerous ministerial appointments which may be designated as clerkships. And in situations superior to ministerial appointments, the policy of the Government is to employ Natives as much as possible. Still, Europeans, uncovenanted, are largely employed in several important branches, especially the Financial department, the

Police, the special branches of revenue such as salt and opium, and in many other miscellaneous capacities. Some of them have been employed in the administrative work of districts in the Panjab and other provinces, and have there sometimes won distinction. The rules regarding furlough and pension have of late years been greatly modified to their advantage.

The same remarks apply to the class of East Indians or Eurasians. Their home is in India itself, and they suffer more and more from the competition of the Natives. This disadvantage is quite inevitable; but they are striving to counteract it by improved education. They will doubtless succeed in maintaining their position in the country; but it is to be feared that the struggle will be hard. Many of them have served the State with usefulness and honour in various capacities; some of them have also been distinguished.

The description, thus given of the official European classes in India, would by itself convey but an imperfect idea of the European community, which consists largely of non-official classes.

Even those Indian regions most favoured by climate, such as the mountains of the Himalayas and of the Nilgiris, have failed, and probably will ever fail, to afford a field for British colonization. The British conqueror will never establish colonies of his countrymen in India, as Alexander established colonies of his Greeks in Asia. Repeated attempts at such colonization on the part of British people have proved unsuccessful. It seems doubtful whether the children, of European parents bred in India, could be reared at all after two or three generations. The climate is unfavourable to children, even of European parents bred in Europe, after five years of age. English parents are, as a rule, anxious to send their children to England for education. The circumstances of India are unsuitable to Anglo-Saxons as labouring men.

Still, non-official Europeans in India have been, and will continue to be, numerous and influential. The beginnings of

British rule in India were factories and settlements, not only at the three Presidency towns of Calcutta, Madràs and Bombay, but at many places in the interior. These establishments have been closed long ago, but the three Presidency towns have grown into centres of empire and of trade under the leadership of Europeans, and take rank among the populous cities of the world. It has been well said of these cities that, unlike so many Indian capitals in the past, they are not merely courts and camps which perish after a revolution, but are founded on the lasting interests of commerce. Although the Natives acquire a large and increasing share in the trade with foreign countries, still much of that trade remains in European hands. Though many of the new and advancing industries have fallen under Native management, many also are under European guidance; and the influx of European capital is constant. Notwithstanding the improvement in the stamp of Native lawyers and the rise of the Native Bar, the Native suitors still employ English lawyers and barristers in most of the important causes before the High Courts of Judicature. At Calcutta, Madras and Bombay the English Bar has always formed an important institution, and is rising into influence at several centres in the interior of the country.

Some European firms in the Presidency towns have succumbed to the disasters which appear to be of periodical recurrence in an age when speculation plays too great a part. Of those firms which remain, the heads and some of the partners reside in England more than formerly; and the business in India is consequently entrusted more to agents. The merchants of personal weight and individual eminence, though still happily numerous, are not quite so abundant as they used to be. It is commonly said that the race of merchant princes is diminished, although the number of Europeans engaged in trade has increased.

Nationalities, other than British, have always been represented in the mercantile community, and have of late borne an increasing proportion to the whole. The French are not so numerous as they once were; the Austrians, the Italians and the Russians appear but slightly; but the Germans are fast growing in importance and the Americans are rearing their front of enterprise. Added to these, the Greeks, the Armenians and the Jews now included in the English-speaking community, all enjoy much mercantile repute and entitle Calcutta and Bombay to the name they love to claim, that of the hall of all nations.

The Chambers of Commerce, long established at these great centres, are the principal organs of European non-official opinion in the country, and are repertories of commercial intelligence. They are represented in the several legislatures by members whom the Government chooses from their body. They express Native as well as European sentiments; they are the chief, though not the sole, interpreters of independent opinion to the Government; they raise their voice on many matters fiscal, economic and financial. The patriotism of their sentiments and the accuracy of their extensive information secure to them the willing attention of the Government. In grave emergencies, demanding the organization of public charity, they are looked up to as the leaders of independent action, and they unfailingly enact a worthy part.

In Bengal the European indigo-planters once formed a very important class, owning broad acres, possessing large leasehold interests and dwelling in fine country-seats. But the properties were vitally affected by the agrarian troubles of 1860, and the owners have for the most part passed away. In Behar, however, they still survive; their busy factories, extensive establishments, picturesque houses, gardens and parks constitute some of the most remarkable and interesting sights in that province. During the crisis of the famine which threatened the safety of the province in 1874, their services in obtaining transport for the importation of grain by the Government, for the support of the people in danger, was as beneficial to the public interest as it was honourable to themselves.

It is as tea-planters and coffee-planters that Europeans,

chiefly British, have happily increased in India. They have now covered, or are covering, with their plantations, the slopes of the mountains which hem in Assam, a portion of the hills bounding Bengal on the east, the territory ceded by the Bhotan State, the greater part of Darjiling and British Sikhim, much of the Kumaon province, the north of Hindostan, some of the Kangra valleys in the Panjab, and to the south many portions of the Nilgiri section of the Western Ghat mountains, including valleys, slopes and ridges in the State of Curg, the district of Wynaad and the kingdom of Travancore. In many of these plantations, they have introduced steam machinery and many scientific appliances. They offer a good occupation to young men from England, who are prepared to undergo a thorough apprenticeship in the business, and to master the details of the work. But experience has shewn that the management of the plantation, and the preparation of the tea or the coffee for market, constitute a difficult profession, and demand a professional training. It was the want of this knowledge, at the outset, which contributed to the many failures which occurred. Those, who witness the success which is now apparent, would little imagine, unless they studied the history of many concerns, how much capital was dissipated in the beginning, how many fortunes were impaired, how many hopes were wrecked. Many of these disasters, however, inculcated lessons from which those, who came after, have judiciously profited. It is to be hoped that in future these concerns will have an unbroken career of prosperity, educing many of the best qualities of the Anglo-Saxon, supporting the pioneers of civilization in regions previously unoccupied and affording an outlet for some of the superabundant and unemployed energies of England.

The Anglo-Indian newspaper press, as an institution, has always flourished. It circulates not only among the European community, but also among the educated Natives. Indeed from it, the Natives gather largely their ideas regarding public matters and political affairs. The Europeans also pay much regard to it, although they read the newspapers from England as well. It criticizes with the utmost freedom and independence the policy and proceedings of the government in India, and spares no pains to present information collected from all parts of the empire. It obtains contributions from all sections of the European community, including the official classes. Some of its contributors have held high offices under Government, as the State permits its servants to communicate their thoughts and their knowledge to the newspapers, on the condition that they avoid matters of a confidential or controversial nature, or topics that may be otherwise objectionable, and rather encourages them to publish compositions which may promote the cause of science or enlarge the bounds of knowledge. The press also endeavours with much success to lay before its readers all the newest intelligence of the day, in Europe and in other parts of the world, together with the substance of all the most interesting discussions and the best-reasoned opinions in the English prints. It exercises real influence, and is of much use and assistance in the governance and management of the country. Its editors enjoy political consideration, and among them there have been several, now either deceased or retired, who in their day were among the leading minds of the country and were ornaments of current Anglo-Indian literature, namely John Marshman, Meredith Townsend, George Smith, J. O'B. Saunders, Dr. Buist, Robert Knight, J. M. Maclean.

CHAPTER V.

NATIVE STATES.

Relations of the Native States with the British Government—Loyalty of Native sovereigns during war of the mutinies—Order of the Star of India —Imperial assemblage at Delhi—Visit of the Prince of Wales—Advantages to the empire from existence of Native States—Education of young Native Princes—Internal administration of Native States—Their military forces—Mention of largest States—The Nizam of the Deccan—Jammu and Cashmir—Protected Sikh States—Rajput Princes—Mahratta Princes, Sindhia, Holkar and the Gaekwar—The Princess of Bhopal—Travancore —Political importance of the Deccan—Mysore—Kingdom of Nepal—Khan of Khelat—Eminent Native Statesmen.

THE Native States constitute a political entity of some magnitude in the Indian Empire. In round numbers they have an area of half a million of square miles and a population of fifty millions of souls. The sum total of their revenues cannot be precisely stated, but may probably exceed fifteen millions sterling annually. Though sovereigns in their own dominions, they are all more or less under the control of the British Government, as suzerain and paramount power. In accordance with existing treaties, some of them are potentates enjoying much consideration, while others are hardly distinguishable from feudal barons. They have had the most diverse relations with England in past times. With some of them, the pure mirror of English friendship has never been dimmed or sullied from the beginning; with others, it has been at one time shattered, and its fragments have been afterwards reunited. With some, the English connection has been an unbroken series of alliances, services, rewards and concessions, all thankfully remembered. To others, former collisions with English power have left ungracious memories now lapsing into oblivion. Whatever their past circumstances may have been, they are all conscious that their destinies are linked with those of England, and that there is a community in interest, in peril and in safety, between themselves and the supreme authority.

When the mutinies suddenly broke out in 1857, the conduct of the Native sovereigns, and the attitude of their States, were watched by the English with anxiety. Had these Native powers turned against the paramount power, and sided with the mutineers, the flames of revolt, which blazed over so many districts, would have enveloped the whole empire. In that moment, though some of the States, as distinguishable from the sovereigns, did misbehave, though sometimes their troops joined the mutineers and their vassals rebelled, yet almost all the sovereigns personally, together with their relations and retainers, displayed a firm allegiance. Herein they acted according to the instinct of self-preservation, being convinced that they would be buried in the ruins of the British Government if it should fall. Nevertheless, it must be in generosity admitted that they gave full play to noble and loyal sentiments. They rendered a priceless service to the British cause, at the moment of its extreme depression. They deserved then, as they will ever deserve, to be esteemed as bulwarks of imperial stability, and as conservative elements in a country where subversive and explosive forces may at times burst forth. Enjoying an undisturbed existence under an all-protecting power, they are the natural foes of revolutionary disturbance.

They were once apprehensive lest the British Government should refuse acknowledgment of their right to adopt heirs and successors, in event of lineal descendants failing. As descendants are not unfrequently wanting in these old families, it became very important that the principle of adoption should be permanently recognised, because in the absence of such recognition, any State might, on the demise of the sovereign without male issue, revert or escheat to the paramount power. All fears on this account were set at rest by a decree of the British Government in 1858, sanctioning the right to adopt according to the Hindu and Muhammadan institutes. The decree was communicated to every Native State, and to every Chief who was held to be governing his own territories. This measure was carried when Lord Canning was Governor-General, and has caused fragrant memories to gather round his name.

The creation of the Order of the Star of India has produced a moral effect upon the Native princes and chiefs, which time will serve to strengthen more and more. This measure, so graciously intended, cements their relations with the British Crown, elevates them in the estimation of their subjects and associates them with the British functionaries, as members of the same Order, in a fraternity of honour. The favour of the Sovereign, respecting admission to the Order, is most highly prized among them; and its insignia are worn by them with pride on all public occasions.

The visit of the Duke of Edinburgh to India in 1870 was loyally accepted by the Native States, and by Indian British subjects, as a mark of favour shewn to the nation.

The fealty and loyalty of the Native States have been strengthened, their Oriental sense of grandeur gratified and their imaginative faculties stimulated by the addition of the imperial style to the titles of the British Sovereign, and by the gracious visit of the heir-apparent to the British Crown. The visit of the Prince of Wales was regarded by them as most auspicious, and produced great good among them and their subjects. It constituted, in their eyes, a fresh tie, binding them indissolubly to the British Crown and nation. The august proceedings, connected with it, will ever be remembered by them and their successors, with pride in the past, and with hopefulness for the future.

The State ceremonials at the Imperial Assemblage at Delhi on New Year's Day of 1877, were held before the largest gathering of Native sovereigns, princes and chiefs that has ever been seen under British rule. Probably that Assemblage was never equalled by any meeting of allies and feudatories around the emperor in the brightest days of the Mogul empire. It left a happy impression on the minds of all present, and will be a sunny spot in their memories. Its fame spread among the many nationalities of India, and confirmed the popular ideas regarding the final consolidation of the empire. It will serve as a landmark in the recollections of many millions of men.

The appointment of several Native princes to be Councillors of the Empress, in conjunction with some of the highest British functionaries, had an ennobling influence upon the Chiefs as a body. The selection of two among them to be honorary Generals in the British army was regarded as a high honour.

The creation of the Order of the Crown of India, to which Native princesses are admitted, will exercise an elevating influence socially, in a country where the need of such an effect was peculiarly felt.

The Native States supply some of the unavoidable deficiencies of a foreign rule, among a people with whom a versatile fancy, a passion for external display and a spirit of veneration for visible glories, are often predominant. The citizens and the countryfolk gaze with glistening eyes, eager looks and intense admiration, upon the glitter of chivalric pageantry and the pomp of eastern royalty. The middle and upper classes regard the regal or feudal spectacles with an enthusiastic pride which constitutes the nearest approach to patriotism of which they are, as yet, capable. It is noteworthy that these sentiments are felt as much by the Natives, who are British subjects, as by those who are subjects of the Native States. Considerateness and graciousness, on the part of the British Government towards the Native States, are popular in the British dominions. Harshness or undue severity, on the part of the British Government towards the Native States, would be unpopular in the British territories, and would excite unfavourable comment among the educated Natives especially.

The Native States operate as an imperial safety-valve to release several kinds of discontent which would otherwise be pent up in the British territories, and, failing to find any vent, might burst forth injuriously. Persons who cannot meet with any scope under a foreign rule, who are too proud to submit to a system fashioned upon modern principles, and are yet too innately active to remain without some employment good or evil, can always discover some congenial sphere under the Native rulers. Many intractable characters who, if restricted to British centres of political influence, would themselves become agitated and would communicate their agitation to others, may resort to Native courts and capitals, where, though not innocuous, they are not so noxious as they might otherwise have been. Thus, as it were, many acrid humours of the imperial body are drawn off from its vital parts to its remoter members.

In the golden age of the Hindu polity, many of the Native States were ruled on a patriarchal system with paternal benevolence, and were founded on filial obedience. Even the Muhammadan period was adorned by many instances of statesmanlike administration. But during the dark night of all-pervading disturbance before the dawn of British ascendency, these States, with scarcely any exception, groaned under utter misgovernment. Out of the chaos, hideous forms of crime, like Thagi, evolved themselves. Though the more salient of these evils were repressed after the establishment of British control, yet much misrule continued, the English being too much busied, in reducing their own political household to order, to note the administrative shortcomings of their feudatories. Of recent years, however, the Native States, though not actually forced to follow the lead of the paramount power, have yet felt the constraining power of moral compulsion, and have been moved by a worthy ambition to emulate improvements which are sanctioned by the highest example. Consequently they have imitated, with more or less fidelity, most of the reforms introduced by the British Government, for instance, judicial organization, education, sanitation and public works. In some respects, for instance, the management of the land revenue, they have followed the English in adapting the results of Western wisdom to the peculiarities of Eastern society. In arranging customs unions, accepting commercial reciprocity and relinquishing transit duties, they have evinced a laudable readiness to fall in with the ways of imperial uniformity. In stamping out barbarous and inhuman practices, like self-immolation of widows and female infanticide, they have obeyed the dictates of civilized morality.

Thus it has come to pass that many of the Native States are comparatively well-governed. Some of them, indeed, are indicated by economists as rivalling the British territories in prosperity, and by philanthropists as emulating the British Government in the diffusion of popular contentment. The praise, accorded with justice to Native States, has sometimes operated to the disparagement of British rule. If Native rule is so good, how, it is asked, can the British rule be evincing its superiority? In fact, however, it is from their contact with the British that the Native rulers have become what they now are. Nevertheless, if those independent Europeans who have long resided in Native territory, or those Englishmen who are cognizant of both British and Native rule, were to be questioned, there would be a preponderance of testimony in favour of the British system. The opinion of Natives would be still more valuable, were it not clouded with a natural and excusable partiality. However wide may be the popularity of the British Government, many of its subjects imagine that their lot would be happier and better under Native rule. There are many, who sigh for some regime that in its essence shall be national. Still, experience has shewn that whenever, in adjusting the boundaries of dominions, or in exchanging territories, the English officers have had to propose the transfer of villages or districts, from British to Native rule, they have received remonstrances from the Natives concerned. Sometimes these remonstrances have been couched in such language of dismay as implied the sincerest flattery of British rule.

The British Government wisely seizes every opportunity of educating under its own auspices, young Native princes. Several sovereigns, now reigning, have in their youth been thus educated. In the next generation, almost every prince will have been educated after the European method, either by private tuition in the palace, or at institutions established for youths of princely degree.

Some of these institutions, such as that at Ajmere for the kingly families of Rajputana, or that at Rajkot in Kathiawar for the chiefs of western India, have been dignified with a collegiate status. English has been spontaneously chosen by the Native States as the language for their diplomatic correspondence with the British Government. These circumstances induce the chiefs to regard themselves as alumni and the paramount power as the alma mater.

The Native sovereigns and their advisers are skilful in raising the utmost amount of revenue, with the least possible trouble to the people. The average rate of revenue per head of the population will generally be found higher in the Native States than in the British territories. This will be regarded by the admirers of Native rule as a proof of its superiority. It is partly due to the greater flexibility of the Native system, which quality is often more profitable to the exchequer than the rigidity of the British method. But it should be accepted as a proof that, at least according to an oriental standard, the British taxation is mild and moderate.

Many of the Native States, notably the Protected Sikh States, the Rajputana States, some of the Central India States, the Baroda State, and others have been greatly enriched by the British railways which pass through their territories; no demand having been made upon them by the British Government on that account. Some Native sovereigns, as the Nizam, Sindhia and Holkar, have furnished funds for the construction of railways in their dominions. On the other hand, it is to be remembered that the Rajput States made great concessions to the wishes of the British Government respecting customs arrangements with which the railways were connected. In cases where British canals have passed through Native States, such as the new canal from the Satlej, a contribution has been given by the States.

In civil expenditure, the Native States are for the most part careful and economical. They shew a politic profusion in all that relates to the functions of the priesthood, the religious observances and the popular festivals.

In their military expenditure they sometimes persist in an extravagance which is injurious to the commonweal. They generally employ a large number of untrained men, where a much smaller number of well-disciplined men would suffice. They sometimes maintain forces at a strength which might, under some conceivable circumstances, prove embarrassing to their own States as well as to the paramount power. Some few of them possess arsenals and magazines, also factories for making guns, powder, arms and ammunition. The armament of the Native States is a matter needing watchfulness, but is a very delicate subject for the paramount power to approach. The British Government does, however, what it judiciously can, in suggesting a policy of reduction. The Native States have some difficulty in reducing their military establishments, as such reductions are regarded as invidious, and are very unpopular with certain sections of their people. If such measures were hastily or harshly undertaken, some disturbance would probably ensue. Still, it would be well if these forces were fewer than they actually are. Experience has shewn that they cannot always be depended upon, when the British territories are seriously disturbed, even though their sovereigns and masters are loyal to the British cause. In the war of the mutinies, however, the troops of the Jammu and Cashmir State, and of the Protected Sikh States were loyal, and fought in the field on the British side. During the recent Afghan war, a considerable body of these troops, belonging to the Native States of the Panjab, were despatched into the field, and did much useful service on the north-west frontier. These Native States sent their contingents with the utmost alacrity, and the troops behaved well. The moral and political effect of this movement was considerable. The Native States, also, from all parts of the empire loyally offered to place their forces at the disposal of the British Government on that occasion.

Favourable as this picture of the Native States may seem, if compared with that of former times, yet it would be incomplete without some reference to each of the principal States.

The Nizam's dominions have, for nearly a whole generation, been governed by an eminent Muhammadan statesman, first in the capacity of minister of the late Nizam, and secondly as co-regent during the minority of the present Nizam. The amelioration effected within this time will hardly be realised by any, save those who are acquainted with the many cankers which eat into the heart of that hapless State. The Arab mercenaries, nominally the servants, but really the masters of the Nizam, professedly his guard, but in action his controllers, have been brought within a manageable compass. Rich districts have been rescued from the avaricious grasp of military chiefs, to whom they had been mortgaged in security for arrears of pay due to the troops. The Rohillas, who prowled about the country in herds like hungry wolves, are resting in enforced quiet. The mob at the capital, Hyderabad, once a seething and surging mass of devilry, has been cowed and quelled. A regular administration in civil affairs has been introduced throughout the country. There has been formed a class of Native administrators of independence in character, fertility in resource and vigour in conduct. Something is effected for public education, medical aid to the sick, and repairs of roads. Though a regular settlement of the land with its revenues and tenures, after the British model, has been but partially introduced, yet many steps have been taken in this direction, especially with a view of rendering the land-tax equitable and moderate. The artificial lakes for irrigation, which abound in some parts of the Nizam's dominions, and which attest the enlightenment of the Hindu dynasties preceding the Muhammadan conquest, have been repaired, imperfectly perhaps, but still with some degree of efficiency. The State ship was once water-logged with financial embarrassments, and was fast sinking beyond hope of recovery. From this catastrophe it was saved by the business-like firmness of its minister; and for a time its finances were on the high road to solvency. Of late years, however, there seems to have been some retrogression, partly by reason of the excessive strength of the military forces which are still retained. These forces are far beyond the real needs of a State, in which order is preserved by a British subsidiary force and a British Contingent, and which is environed by British territory as by a wall. The Arab element in this State should always be watched. The chiefs at the head of these Arabian bands were pure Arabs, of some ability and ambition. Their sons and successors, born of Indian mothers, have a quieter disposition and are well affected. The Arab troops, though not so formidable as they were, are still of importance in the Deccan, being superior in energy and courage to the inhabitants of that province. It is very necessary to prevent their being recruited by the influx of comrades from Arabia.

The sovereign of the combined State of Jammu and Cashmir is the son of Golab Sing who played a historic part in the wars that led to the annexation of the Panjab, and whose troops were ranged under British command during the memorable siege of Delhi, thereby producing a moral effect on north-western India. He possesses less statecraft, but more enlightenment, than his father. He maintains an army, sufficient but not overgrown, and was raised in 1877 to the honorary rank of a General in the British army. He succeeds well in the management of his fellow-tribesmen, the Rajputs of the lower Himalayan range; but is less successful with the Muhammadan population of Cashmir. He has long been associated with gracious and pleasant memories in the minds of hundreds of Englishmen, by reason of the hospitable facilities which he affords to visitors for seeing the sights of Cashmir. But, alas! the name of happy valley so affectionately given to Cashmir by countless admirers, can be applied nowadays to its scenery only, and not to its inhabitants. Of late years epidemic pestilence and desolating famine have wasted half the people to death, and driven the remainder to despair. Seldom has nature in such beauty looked upon man in such misery.

The group of principalities styled the Protected Sikh States, intervening between Delhi and the Panjab, were snatched by the British from the jaws of Ranjit Sing, when he threatened to devour all his neighbours. They remembered their deliverers who in turn were menaced with destruction at the outburst of the mutinies in 1857, and were among the very first to appear in arms on the British side against the mutineers. They declared that their swords should be drawn for that power under whose wing they had nestled for fifty years. In the chronicles of feudal chivalry there is not a brighter example of fidelity on the part of feudatories towards their liege, than that exhibited by some of these States, Pattiala, Jhind and Nabba, towards the British suzerain in the darkest days of 1857. Ties, destined doubtless to be indissoluble, were then formed between them. Subsequently these States have derived prosperity from the public works, railways and canals, of the British Government, and have consolidated their civil administration after the fashion of the Panjab territory, with which their own territories are so greatly intermingled. They maintain military forces adequate but not excessive, composed of those martial elements in which the valley of the Satlej abounds. Their situation, on the national highway of northern India, is a commanding one. If there be any Native States in which the administration is really comparable with British rule, they are here.

In the Himalayan region round Simla there is a group of Protected Hindu States. These suffered grievously under Nepalese domination upwards of fifty years ago, from which they were liberated by the British. They remember their liberators with a gratitude which finds expression even in the present time.

A large congeries of States is formed under the name of Rajputana or Rajasthan, of which the principal are Udeypur, Jyepur and Jodhpur. These Rajput chiefs have, next to the Brahmins, the purest blood in India. In antiquity of descent they rank peerless among the Native sovereigns; the pink and flower of Indian heraldry is acknowledged to be with them. During the earlier Muhammadan invasions they won imperishable fame by deeds like those of the defenders of Saragossa, of Antwerp or of Londonderry; and in their hill-forts were heaped up hecatombs of men slain for the fatherland. With the advance of the Mogul empire, their autonomy was established. They sheltered Akber the Great in his infancy; some of them gave sultanas to the imperial seraglios, and by marriage mingled their blood with that of succeeding Moslem emperors. The immunities, secured by them, were continuously enjoyed during the wars and treaties which terminated in the establishment of British supremacy. During the war of the mutinies they were steadfast in their allegiance to a supremacy in their eyes so beneficent. They retain to this day, more than any other Native States, the original image of Hindu polity, untouched by the defacing fingers of modern change. Their administration, partly patriarchal partly baronial, has a rough and rude efficiency. During recent years, they have endured some inconvenience and sacrificed some predilections in conforming to the British proposals regarding the revenues from salt and customs, in order to fulfil the behests of the paramount power.

The Mahratta sovereigns in Central India, Sindhia and Holkar, bear rule over alien clans and vassals, which difficult task they perform with much considerate circumspection and a fair degree of success. The Mahratta, however, in Central India has but a slight hold on the local Rajput chiefs and the indigenous tribes. In the event of any grave conjuncture arising, some trouble in that quarter is to be feared. Sindhia for a long time enjoyed the advantage of having his financial and territorial affairs managed by a very able minister. He devotes special attention to his military business; his troops, limited to the number settled by existing arrangements with the British Government, are maintained by him in a fair state of efficiency. In 1877 the honorary rank of a General in the British army was conferred upon him. Holkar is assiduous in personally supervising the management of his revenues and finances especially, and of his political affairs generally: there is no Native prince in all India more diligent than he in State business, for which indeed he possesses an aptitude developed by education and training. Both Sindhia and Holkar are much esteemed and respected by the Mahratta subjects of the British Government in the Deccan.

The Baroda State comprises some of the richest territories in the empire. After the death of Khande Rao the Gaekwar of Baroda, whose loyalty to the British Government was conspicuous, the affairs of the State fell under mismanagement, which led to the deportation of the late Gaekwar Malhar Rao, and to his detention as a State prisoner. An adopted son was placed on the throne, with the princess Jamna Bai as regent, and a very able minister, one of the best in India, was appointed to conduct the administration, which is accordingly prospering.

The State of Bhopal is well governed by a Native Princess, the head of a Muhammadan family whose loyal allegiance to the British Government has been conclusively proved.

Among the princes of Bundelkhand, the Raja of Pannah is known as an enlightened ruler, and as a man of broad sympathies. His territory is still famous for its diamond mines.

The State of Bahawalpur, on the bank of the Satlej, was carefully administered by the British Government during the minority of the Nawab, who, after having been duly educated in the Western manner, has been recently placed in full charge of his territories.

The kingdom of Travancore, in the south, has an area, very fertile, of coast and mountain, endowed with the choicest gifts of nature and possessing various commercial advantages. It includes many coffee plantations. Its affairs were well managed by the late Maharaja recently deceased; he had been liberally educated, and long had the services of a very able minister.

The State of Kolhapur, in the Bombay Presidency, has been managed by excellent Native officials, chosen by the British Government, during the minority caused by the lamented death of the late Raja while on a visit to Europe.

In western India there are several States of the South Mahratta country which are at present in a quiet and orderly condition. Some of them have at times been centres of political mischief; and in event of a general disturbance, attempts would probably be made to corrupt their fidelity.

It is to be remembered that these States adjoin the Deccan, where the mind of the people is affected by the past associations of Mahratta rule. The memory still survives of the Mahratta revolt against the Muhammadans. It is kept alive, in the popular imagination, by the sight of the mountains and fastnesses close at hand, which rendered that uprising practicable at first and successful at last, and which might, at any time, be made the basis of rebellious movements. Traditions of this nature are always apt to be perpetuated in mountainous regions. The British Government should continue to note the disposition of the Deccan mountaineers, and mark the features of the wild territory where they dwell.

The condition of the cluster of States, which form the Kathiawar peninsula, has been greatly ameliorated of late years, and order has been substituted for disorder. In some departments, such as the land revenue, these States adhere to their old ways; but in other branches they adopt all the improved methods of the time, and are thriving apace. The same happy account may be given of the neighbouring State of Cutch.

There are many lesser States in western India, Pahlanpur, Radhanpur, the Mahi Kanta, the Rewa Kanta and others, all in a satisfactory condition at present. In some of them, however, trouble has in former times arisen, and might again arise.

In north-eastern India, the uncivilized State of Bhotan has remained quiet, since its barbaric insolence was chastised during the last war. The Raja of Manipur has loyally co-operated with the British Government in dealing with the disturbances raised by the frontier tribes, and has received a British decoration. The Raja of Sikhim has become virtually a dependant of the British Government. The State of Cûch Behar has been managed by the British Government during the minority of the Raja, who has been well educated.

The Mysore State is shortly about to be placed under the administration of the Raja on his coming of age. The determination of the British Government to take this step, has had a good effect on Native opinion throughout the empire, and has been viewed with satisfaction by the Native sovereigns and chiefs. The British Government has managed the State for many years with all the advantages of an enlightened system, and has striven to train up a class of Native administrators who will assist the young Raja in managing his country. It contended in 1877 and 1878, zealously and humanely but without adequate success, against a severe famine, which afflicted this territory and was protracted beyond all precedent in the records of misfortune. It also advanced large sums of money to this State during that terrible time.

There are two Native States, bordering upon India, which by treaty have relations with the British Government, namely Nepal and Khelat.

The mountain kingdom of Nepal stretches from the malarious

forests fringing the base of the eastern Himalayas to the watersheds of perennial snow which divide India from Thibet. It has been within living memory the scene of dynastic broils and wholesale massacres. The tales of bloodshed at Katmandu the capital, on the succession to the kingship and the ministership, shock the ear of humanity. This State was for many years ruled by a Native soldier-statesman, Jung Behadur, with a rod of iron. With him discipline and order were the first objects, rather than equity and moderation. The former, however, having been permanently secured, gradually led to the introduction of the latter, until his regime became famed for its justice. In this instance, the old Native ways were followed, and no attempt was made to imitate the British model in civil affairs. But in military matters the British system has been copied with marked effect, so far as can be seen externally. If the qualities of the Nepalese army were to be seriously tested, its proficiency in the art of war would probably prove to be respectable. There is an air of self-reliance about the Nepalese officers of rank, which is seldom observed in the Natives of India in the present age. Such a demeanour is the natural outcome of the pride with which the limited, yet dominant, clan of Gorkhas remember that they subjugated aboriginal Himalayan races superior to them in art, industry and civilization, though inferior to them in war, policy and organization. But for the intervention of the British power they would have overrun north-eastern India; and in the event of any political convulsion they would re-assert themselves. They manifest jealousy of Englishmen visiting the outlying Nepalese territories. The valley of Katmandu, Nepal proper, where the British political Resident is stationed, is freely traversed by visitors of all nationalities. But the valley where the real Gorkhas live and which is regarded by them as the birthplace of their power and the nest of their warrior brood, is not to be beheld by European eyes.

The British relations with the Khan of Khelat have, of late, been drawn much closer than formerly. In past times, the Khan's dealings with his chiefs and vassals were unsatisfactory; disputes arose which threatened his authority with destruction and his realm with anarchy. Since the treaty of 1876, his external relations with the British Government have been satisfactory, and the dissensions in his territories have been happily composed. He and his chiefs have rendered loyal co-operation throughout the recent Afghan war. Without asking for the aid of British troops, they preserved security and order for some months in the Bolan Pass, a vitally important point in the British military communications with southern Afghanistan. Owing to their good arrangements, under the guidance of the Agent to the Governor-General, vast quantities of British stores and material were conveyed up the Pass, without any attempt at plunder being made, and even without any thefts occurring. The value of this service on the part of the Khan and his State will be appreciated by those who know the troubles which arise from the marauding in many parts of the trans-Indus frontier. His loyalty and the good conduct of his State, at that trying time, have been substantially acknowledged by the Government of India.

From this review it will be apparent that the Native States add strength to the eastern dominions of the English Crown, exert an influence upon the people of India, and are worthy members of the British empire. The general advantages to the country, arising from the existence of the Native States, have been already explained. There remains one special advantage, with the mention of which this exposition may conclude.

A class of Native statesmen is raised up, who have a better chance of showing originality of talent and force of character than they could possibly have in the territories administered directly by the British Government. Thus the ruling race acquires a far better idea, than it could otherwise have had, regarding the development of which Native ability is susceptible, and the part which Natives can fill when thrown on their own resources. Many Native statesmen have been produced of whom the Indian nation may justly be proud, and among whom may be mentioned Salar Jung of Hyderabad, Dinkar Rao of Gwalior, Madhava Rao of Baroda, Kirpa Ram of Jammu, Pandit Manphûl of Alwar, Faiz Ali Khan of Kotah, Madho Rao Barvè of Kolhapur, and Purnia of Mysore.

CHAPTER VI.

MATERIAL PROGRESS OF THE NATIVES.

Census of the population—Gradual growth of the people in numbers—Expansion of cultivation—Land can yet sustain increasing people—Cultivable waste in India itself—Emigration from India to British colonies—Sufficiency of food supply in India—Her wealth under British rule—Remittances of money, public and private, to England—Outlay of English capital in India—Wealth of former times as compared with the present—Capital largely accumulated by the Natives—Increase of cattle—Reasons why India is inferior to Western nations in wealth—Maintenance of the poor—Public opinion regarding material improvements—Industrial employments—General condition of the Natives.

THE aspect of the country, the principal objects of interest therein, the European community, and the Native States, having been briefly described, it becomes necessary to approach the very important topics relating to the condition of the Native population in the British territories.

Thoughtful Englishmen, though they can hardly be familiar with a country so distant and so peculiar as India, feel a conscientious and benevolent interest in the welfare of the Indian people. As they cannot become personally cognisant of a subject, so vast in its component parts yet so minute in its details, they are content to leave the management of it, for the most part, to responsible experts whose minds, from youth to age, are dedicated to this purpose. It is possible for them, however, to entertain, evince and express a determination that every effort shall be exerted for the good government, the advancement and the civilization of India ; and this they do effectually. Such a determination on their part produces an elevating influence on public opinion in England itself. It operates powerfully on the disposition of the Englishmen engaged and employed in India, spurring the slothful, firing the ambitious, encouraging the dejected. It affects the sentiments of the Natives, causing them to believe that there exists in England a gracious Sovereign, an august senate, a sympathetic people. It makes them feel that there are, in England, many who care for their fellow-subjects in the East, who listen to the cry of the distressed, who attend to any grievance that may be reasonably urged, who burn for any wrong that may be done. This belief is growing stronger year by year in the Native mind, promoting its contentment, settling its convictions and establishing its loyalty.

The thoughts, then, regarding India, which are uppermost in the minds of Englishmen, relate to the progress of the Natives. Such progress is mental and moral, as well as material. It may be considered first in its material aspect.

The population of India is much larger than that of any nation in Europe or America, and exceeds the population of any country in the world except China. Hence anxiety is often felt lest the resources of India should some day prove unequal to so heavy a pressure and so severe a strain, lest the people should grow too thickly on the cultivable land, lest pauperism should arise and spread. For the due consideration of this problem, some knowledge is essential as to whether the population during the nineteenth century is greater or less than during the preceding centuries, whether it is increasing fast under British rule, whether it is likely to increase in the immediate future and whether, in event of such increase, it will readily find subsistence within the limits of the country. Unfortunately, statistics of the population were never collected by the Native rulers in any adequate manner; and no proper light is thrown upon this fundamental matter by the archives of Native rule. At the commencement of British rule, the primary importance of numbering the people was never perceived or was quite overlooked. Generation after generation of English officials passed away, without anything being recorded beyond vague or imperfect estimates of the population. It was thought that to make a census of the empire, or even of a province separately, would excite the fears of a timid and suspicious people and might even cause some civil disturbance. The first steps towards making a census were taken twenty-five years ago in north-western India; the example was followed first by one province then by another; and in 1872 the first census of all British India was made. It was effected without any opposition on the part of the people. A retrospect of British rule during the nineteenth century causes us to wonder why so essential a measure was not adopted at an earlier time. Had such an enumeration been made in each province as soon as possible after its acquisition, and then for the empire as soon as the British conquests and dominions assumed imperial proportions, had also a fresh enumeration been made from time to time and its results compared with previous enumerations, so that errors might be detected, discrepancies reconciled and conclusions verified, we should at present possess a body of information valuable to the philanthropist, the administrator, and the economist. But in fact there are not in any large division of the country, excepting the North-western Provinces, and in parts of the Presidencies of Madras and Bombay, antecedent records with which the results of the recent imperial census can be compared with a view to testing its accuracy. A fresh census will shortly be taken, and doubtless the operation will be repeated after each succeeding cycle of years. This census may show that in some provinces the normal rate of increase has been arrested by the recent famines. A statistical basis having been obtained by enumeration, there will be a registration of births and deaths, so that the knowledge may be kept abreast of the progress of the population. Such a registration is attempted, and though very imperfect as yet, will improve year by year.

Recent enumerations have indicated little increase over the former statistics, in the provinces where the numbers had been well ascertained on former occasions, but a startling increase in those provinces where the numbers had never been properly ascertained before, as for instance in Bengal, and in parts of southern India. In their grand total for the empire, the numbers far exceeded all previous estimates. The remarkable excess may have induced some thinkers to apprehend that the people are multiplying to a degree which the resources of the land can hardly bear. This apprehension rose to a pitch almost of alarm when the famine of 1874 overtook some of those North-eastern Provinces where the census had shown so great an excess over former calculations. The nascent alarm has subsequently yielded to sober consideration.

Still, the question, so frequently and anxiously asked, whether the population has sensibly increased or is increasing, remains for the most part to be answered by conjecture or inference. In north-eastern India the population has certainly increased largely within the last two generations; perhaps also in some few other portions of the empire. Whether it increases in most provinces, is more than the best judges can pronounce. It is slightly but not materially increasing, on the whole, according to the latest information. But the correctness or incorrectness of this information will not be ascertained until enumerations shall have been made on several future occasions. Just before the commencement of British rule the population may have, owing to war, revolution and devastation, become less than at any time for many ages. It may have, owing to the maintenance of peace under British rule, increased somewhat and recovered its former standard of strength, without as yet exceeding what was the normal complement of people in the land. Doubtless, it is seen to be very dense in many places. There are, however, remains and monuments to show that in bygone ages it must have been at least as dense, perhaps even denser, in those very places. On the one hand, some districts have, within the time embraced by authentic history, been reclaimed from savagery or have been peopled within the memory of living men. On the other hand, some districts now abandoned to the wildness of nature, have indisputable marks and traces of a remote civilization which could be produced only by a flourishing people.

In a country where marriage is universal, where the ambition of raising up progeny is unchecked by those restraints which western civilization often imposes, and is encouraged by religious dictates, the children will be very numerous in the aggregate. But the marriages are too early to be perfectly fruitful, consequently the families are seldom large and often very small. Infantine mortality is occasionally deplorable, and the ravages of disease among the young children are almost constant. The death-rate among adults is higher than among European nations. In some of the most thickly inhabited districts, extreme damp, for several months in each year, reduces human vitality to a low ebb, and men sink away like candles burning to their sockets. The chilly damps of autumnal nights follow days when the pores of the skin have been kept open by heat. There are malarious exhalations when the air is hot, and the ground is still saturated with the moisture of the rainy season that has but recently ceased. Hence fevers prevail so largely that scarce a person in the whole population escapes. The accession of these fevers year after year must undermine the constitutions of many people. Crowds of pilgrims huddling together in a vast concourse at holy spots become infected with cholera, and fleeing in terrified bands, spread the pest far and wide. Though in some districts the population have pure water from streams for drinking and ample means for bathing, a great advantage in a hot climate, yet in many places their drinking-water is impure and directly provocative of disease, and their resources for bathing are scanty. Epidemics, varying in type from time to time, sweep away multitudes, and famines, more or less destructive of life, recur periodically.

Thus, as regards population, the existing influences tend in some respects towards expansion, and in other respects towards repression.

From the want of agricultural statistics at the outset of British rule, it is impossible to test the extent to which cultivation has increased within the nineteenth century. There is, however, a consensus of testimony as to the magnitude of the increase. The shrinking of the area, affording cover to wild beasts, has been noted in the traditions of one generation of sportsmen to another. Within the past forty years, the records of the settlements of the land revenue in many parts of the empire, and the known rent-roll of estates in other parts not subjected to settlement, have afforded positive evidence to the same effect. In some districts the latest settlement records prove that the increase has proceeded apace. The expansion of cultivation, then, clearly indicates increase of rural population. It has been said indeed that the land, becoming poorer, sustains fewer people, and that consequently an increase of population need not be inferred from an expansion of cultivation. But if the land has become poorer, as may be the case in some districts, still the deterioration must be very gradual, and not enough to affect any inference regarding the increase or decrease of population.

Inasmuch as, despite all drawbacks, many tendencies point towards improvement, the population may increase. Reflective persons will be anxiously considering whether the country can support a much larger people than that which it now contains. In respect of density or of sparseness, the population varies extremely in different parts of India. In some parts it is either full near to overflowing or is manifestly too full; in other parts it is thin or manifestly too low and needs recruitment. A comparison, of the total population with the whole cultivated area, would not be a satisfactory test in an empire so vast and so diversified. If made, it would show an average density, not excessive according to standards accepted in other parts of the world, and not beyond the sustaining power of the land. In general terms, India, though on a wide and general average fairly well peopled, is too thickly peopled in some parts and too thinly in others. National benefit would arise if the people were to migrate from one centre of industry to another, according to need. But this would be an undertaking contrary to their disposition, and certainly beyond the power of any government. Though some classes are migratory, yet the people in the main are domestic and home-abiding. They are attached to their ancestral rights in land, are fond of the fields they till, and cling to the humblest of their homesteads. The subdivision not only of the property in the land, but even of its occupancy, is generally considerable and sometimes too minute, though as yet it has hardly anywhere passed the limits of reasonable endurance.

If, however, the people were stirred by the colonising impulse which moves hardier and sturdier races, there is still, within the bounds of India itself, a vast quantity of arable land awaiting the invasion of the plough. Some observers, noting the wonderful aptitude with which in many places the Natives of India utilise for cultivation every available piece of ground, may naturally conclude that culture has already approached its possible limit throughout the empire. In such places indeed this limit has been reached long ago. In other places, however, when enquiry is specially turned towards the cultivable waste, outlying lands are found, some here and some there, the grand total of which would be anticipated by few except statisticians or surveyors. Adjoining India and now incorporated in the empire, British Burma offers a practically immense scope for the immigration of farmers and farm labourers. Large numbers of agricultural labourers find employment in Ceylon. During the crisis of the famine of 1874 in Bengal and Behar, a consideration of the density of the population, subjected to danger, induced the authorities to take stock, as it were, of the available waste. It was soon perceived that within two hundred miles at the utmost, and often within a few miles, unoccupied land existed enough to afford an outlet for the overflow of people. There is a large expanse of cultivable waste in the centre of the Panjab; and similar instances might be readily adduced. If then, any national peril of this nature should begin to threaten, there is a safety-valve within India itself. When, in any district or province, landed property is so much in demand that it cannot be bought, and tenants can no longer obtain fields, then the pressure of circumstances will drive agricultural capitalists and cultivators to the nearest of the untilled and untenanted tracts.

Irrespective of the land yet to be brought under cultivation, the land already cultivated may be made to yield much more than at present. In some respects, the skilful and elaborate husbandry of the Natives strikes competent observers with admiration. The manuring and preparation of their crops are sometimes found to be better than has been commonly supposed. The harvests, which in autumn and spring wave over the land in expanses apparently unlimited because unbroken by hedgerows, convey the idea of a natural fertility to which some justice has been done by industry and practical knowledge. The sight of hundreds of square miles of land, tilled and cropped without rest or cessation during many centuries, yet remaining rich and productive, seems to forbid the apprehension that any process of gradual exhaustion can be going on. Though most of the agricultural products are of ancient origin, yet many products are of comparatively recent introduction, and scarce a decade passes without some new product rising into prominence. The irrigation from the wells sunk deep into the ground, having ingenious water-lifting machinery which relays of men and bullocks ply day and night for many weeks consecutively, impresses the spectator with a notion that the bounties of nature are fully applied by art to the use of man. The canals for irrigation in India are magnificent, dwarfing by comparison the modern system of irrigation in any country of Europe, or of Asia, except perhaps China, and all the ancient canal systems save that of Mesopotamia.

Notwithstanding these favourable symptoms, however, it may be admitted that, in some parts of the country a slight deterioration of the soil is probably setting in. With many products the crop is not nearly as heavy and valuable as it ought to be. Eleven bushels of grain per acre are produced in India as compared with thirty in England. Fresh examples are frequently observed of virgin soil yielding crops which are not equalled in succeeding years. Such facts indicate that the productive elements drawn away from the ground are not artificially replaced. The husbandry is in some respects, primitive and imperfect. The materials for manuring are often very defective. Despite the canal system, much rain-water, to be reckoned by millions of cubic feet, rolls year after year wasted to the sea. It is not mere dreaming to hope that practical and technical education will teach the husbandmen to improve their culture and will counteract the otherwise inevitable exhaustion of the soil, that new products will be introduced and irrigation extended, and that thus the land may be enabled to sustain even more people than the teeming millions of persons who now stand upon it.

The countries adjoining India, being poor and mountainous, cannot receive immigrants. But heretofore some of the colonies of England have offered a field for immigration, under climatic and social conditions favourable to the Natives of India. Thousands of Indian families have been willing to emigrate. The stream of emigration from India to the Mauritius, to Natal, to the West Indies, and to Guiana, began many years ago, and became quite brisk from 1873 to 1876. It subsequently slackened, partly owing to fluctuations in the sugar trade. The emigrants came chiefly from the mid valley of the Ganges, that is the provinces of Behar and Benares, and from the northern parts of the Madras coast. They appeared in numbers enough to stock the labour markets of the colonies, but not enough to produce any perceptible effect on a dense Indian population. Of those who emigrated, some stayed in their colonial home, but many returned to India greatly improved in circumstances. Much care was taken by the Government for facilitating emigration and for ensuring the welfare of the emigrants. The matter really depends on the colonial demand for Indian labour. That demand is at present too fitful and uncertain to favourably affect the prospects of India. But if it ever shall be steady and continuous, and shall promise wages much higher than those of India, then there will be plenty of emigrants to found new Indian provinces in the tropical regions south of the equator, and even in parts of Australia. There is not, however, practically, any chance of emigration to the colonies becoming, even at the best, sufficient to relieve any over-peopled Indian province.

Irrespective of future contingencies, anxiety has been expressed lest the supply of food for this vast population should fall short on some dire occasion. Indeed in 1877, when it seemed likely that the Madras and Bombay famines would be prolonged over a second year and that a new famine would appear in northern India, a thought of this kind did flit for a moment across the minds of the authorities. The transient fear, however, passed away. Although the twelvemonth between the summer of 1877 and that of 1878 was the most formidable year in respect of famine that has passed over India during this century, there was not any protracted anxiety as to the food supply failing, nor was there any failure whatever. In 1874, when severe famine hung over many millions of people in Bengal and Behar, there was much exportation of food-grains from Calcutta; it was proposed that this should be prohibited, but the Government of India declined to issue such prohibition, and the exportation went on. In ordinary times, and even in times of partial famine, India is a food-exporting country, and nothing short of a general and severe famine would stop this exportation. Such a famine, though within the bounds of possibility, is unprecedented in the annals of calamity, and in reference to the several climatic zones and the many degrees of latitude and longitude comprised in India, is extremely improbable. When Bengal was afflicted in 1874, Madras and Bombay had propitious seasons; when Madras and Bombay suffered in

1877, Bengal was prospering. Under all circumstances, the coast provinces of British Burma and the delta districts of the Ganges, which regions export edible grains by hundreds of thousands of tons, have unfailing seasons. The area under irrigation from canals, though as yet insufficient relatively to the total area, is considerable and is nearly, though not quite, beyond the reach of failure. The internal grain-trade of the country proved most active during the crucial trials to which it was exposed in the middle of 1874, in 1877 and 1878; and there was not any deficiency in the total supply within the empire. The anxiety related, not to the quantities of grain available, but to the means of transporting it, and these means were for the most part supplied by the railways. There was indeed one notable exception when, in the beginning of 1874, the Government was obliged to despatch grain in vast quantities to north Behar. Even then, however, there was grain within the limits of the empire; the difficulty consisted in placing the food within reach of the famishing people.

The experience gathered during several generations, and the records now collated of many precedents of calamity, establish beyond doubt the periodicity of famines, not indeed in any fixed cycle or rotation, but of sure recurrence after intervals longer or shorter. Strenuous efforts have been put forth by the Government, with chequered success, for mitigating the consequences of these visitations. Doubtless, the lives of large multitudes have been thereby saved, and the sufferings of still larger multitudes have been alleviated. Notwithstanding these exertions, considerable mortality has occurred. In the face of these facts, few administrators will affirm that mortality can be, or will promise that it shall be, prevented. The strictest enquiry has been made regarding the practicability of such material works being undertaken, or such other measures being adopted by the Government, as may stop the accession of famines; but as yet no such possibility has been discovered. The material improvements which have been, or may yet be introduced, can at the best only diminish the area, or mitigate the consequences, of drought. Even in prosperity, then, famine is like an apparition warning people of doom, and as a skeleton pointing its finger to apprise the nation of a danger which is ever impending and cannot be warded off.

It is often debated both by Europeans and Natives, whether the material prosperity of India is increasing or decreasing under British rule. Many educated Natives apprehend that it is decreasing, and probably notions to that effect find popular acceptance. Certainly any Native agitator would choose for his discourse some assertions of this description, as likely to be believed. He would also add another assertion, namely this, that the national wealth is decreasing partly because the English draw it away to England. This argument indeed is urged by some of the Native newspapers against the English Government and nation. Similar views, regarding the abstraction of wealth from India, seem to be held by some continental nations, and have been propounded by some English authorities whose dicta command attention.

Formerly it was believed that profits and indirect tribute were drawn from India by the East India Company. Since the assumption of the government of India by the Crown, attention has been turned to the annual payments made by the Government of India to that of England. To these payments the misnomer of tribute has been unfortunately applied. Coupled with these are the remittances to England of the savings made by officials from their salaries, and of the profits realized by merchants, bankers and traders in their business. The payments by the Government have, indeed, of late years grown to formidable dimensions and are still growing. But they are legitimate and natural, consisting of the price of articles imported into India by means of Government, which really pertain to the import trade, of the interest on capital which is fructifying within India itself, and of the remuneration of services rendered to India. In a country where the

Government, the administration and the trade are controlled and in part carried on by foreigners, it must needs happen that a portion of the income made by them in India will be spent out of India. Whereas, if their places were filled by Natives, the income made in the country would be almost entirely spent there. The pension system has been created, or at least greatly developed, under British rule. Thus the Native pensioners spend their pensions in India, while the European pensioners spend theirs in England. Under Native rule the social splendour of the places where the officials congregated, and where the courts and camps were formed, lives in the pages of many histories, and is exemplified in some degree at the capitals of the Native States nowadays. That splendour arose from expenditure incurred mainly, though not entirely, in purchasing indigenous articles, and in encouraging local manufactures. The modern capitals of the Viceroy and his lieutenants, of the Governors and administrators throughout the empire, are also splendid. But the splendour is of a different kind, and does not equally develop the Native industries. Consequently some, though not many, of the old Indian arts or manufactures, especially those of the more delicate description, have shrunk, decayed or perished. The labour of the persons, whose hands and minds were employed therein, has been turned into other channels. The employment afforded in older days to enormous numbers of soldiers, retainers, orderlies and dependants, is much reduced in these times. The drawbacks to the material progress of the Natives, which arise from these limited facts, may be admitted.

Under Native rule, the State expenditure was governed by ideas different from those which prevail under British rule. It was incurred largely for personal grandeur, lavish display and refined luxury; but seldom for purposes of general utility. It was usually devoted to the production of articles which were consumed once for all, and to things which did not lead to the production of wealth or to the accretion of capital. The sovereign, his relations, his nobles bearing the proud title of his pillars of state, lived chiefly to while away time by every amusement which the culture of the age could suggest, and to enjoy life with every device which the resources of the country could afford. In their suite were many idlers, born only to consume the fruits of the earth. Numerous establishments were entertained to support an ostentatious dignity, and to employment for those who did not care to work in productive industries.

Under British rule, extravagance is curbed, and frugality, in matters relating to the pomp or circumstance of State, is carried so far as to constitute a political disadvantage in the eyes of many. Establishments are kept at the lowest scale consistent with the efficiency of the public service. Not a man is idle; on the contrary, every one is actively engaged in some pursuit, and the highest functionaries live a laborious life. Expenditure is applied by the Government, not to perishable articles of luxury, but to things of real usefulness, and to works, which, being remunerative, lead to further production. This policy induces people to save, and fosters the growth of capital, which widens the field for lucrative labour. Some Native States followed, in certain respects, a policy similar to that which the British Government adopts generally, and in so far as they did this, they were much to be commended. But the opposite notions, which have generally regulated the Native and the British systems respectively, must cause a difference to be perceptible on the face of the country. Such difference is not necessarily in favour of the Native system, but will be thought by many to be in favour of the British Government. Many of the educated Natives, however, who turn their attention to current politics, give scant credit to British rule for diverting expenditure from unproductive luxury to reproductive improvement. They will charge the Government with undue profusion respecting the very establishments and the very works, which European opinion usually indicates as conducive to national prosperity.

Such views will probably dissolve as the light of civilization advances.

Further, under British rule, the Natives sell to nations beyond the sea vast quantities of raw produce, and some manufactures, for prices which would have astonished the mediæval traders. In part return for these exports, countless articles of domestic use or consumption are imported, cheaper in price and better in quality than anything which could be made locally. Fresh products are introduced and raised in extensive areas; new manufactures are established, employing tens of thousands of families. Machinery is imported, multiplying the mechanical forces of the country and the motive power of the people. Capital, saved and accumulated in foreign countries, is employed to the amount of hundreds of millions sterling in India, affording to her an incalculable benefit which she could not possibly have obtained without the security of British rule. The unproductive multitudes of soldiers and retainers, once so overgrown, are reduced to the minimum of establishments needed for defence and administration, whereby untold numbers of men are transferred to employments producing national wealth. In these ways, the unavoidable disadvantages of foreign rule, in respect of material prosperity, are compensated by many advantages. Whether the loss is more than counterbalanced by the gain, is a matter for discrimination.

Thus it happens that the probability of the visible and tangible wealth of the country having increased or decreased under British rule, is a subject of frequent discussion both among Europeans and Natives. Such a discussion, however interesting, cannot be decided with the certainty that would follow a similar disquisition regarding some European countries, such as Great Britain, France or Belgium, where the immeasurable augmentation of wealth is manifest. For India, in her own fashion, has been wealthy during many ages. Her wealth indeed never has been, and is not yet, great relatively to her size and to the numbers of her people, but is on the contrary small. It has, however, been regarded as great absolutely, and thus has struck the imagination of mankind. One reason for this is the peculiar aptitude, which she used to possess, for gathering her riches together at a few centres of attraction and so displaying it most effectively. The historical accounts of the plunder, realised after military or political catastrophes, may seem fabulous, but are nevertheless well founded, despite rhetorical exaggeration. There never has been a country where wealth was so much concentrated, or so little diffused, as the historic India. Hence the traditional ideas of eastern wealth have indefinitely exceeded the reality. Besides these central accumulations of goods and property, there must have been much wealth collected in divers lesser places. No economist can study the story of the Mahratta conquests, wherein statecraft was chiefly devoted to the organization of plunder with unparalleled skill and audacity, without wondering how the country could have endured visitations so long protracted and so oft repeated. Here is proof, however, of the national habit of collecting, hoarding and secreting property. Descriptions of accumulated wealth occur in the histories of the wars of the present generation, for example, the verified accounts of prize at Hyderabad in Sindh in 1842, at Delhi, Lucknow, Kirwi and other places during the war of the mutinies. During many years past, even up to this very day, the dacoities or gang-robberies which occasionally break out, tell the same tale of wealth collected in rural as well as urban homes, to an amount which might not otherwise have been suspected. Large amounts of gold specie or bullion are transmitted by the Natives through the Post-office. The circulation of notes has risen to many millions sterling, within a few years after the introduction by Government of a paper currency. The money-order system is extensively used, and the popularity of the savings-banks is rising. All these facts point to a like conclusion regarding the national wealth. At the modern capitals, such as Calcutta and Bombay, the Native wealth, though much less dazzling and ostentatious than in the capitals of historic renown, is much more useful and substantial. It is devoted to plant, mechanism and machinery, instead of the brilliant trappings and luxurious articles of other days, and thus it may appear by comparison to be less than it really is.

But if the wealth of India be less concentrated now than formerly, and therefore not so easily measurable or computable, it is much more diffused. A signal proof of such diffusion is found in the almost universal substitution of metal for earthenware in the domestic utensils of most of the humbler classes within the last generation; the replacement of thatched roofs of the cottages by tiling; the use of foreign piece goods to some extent instead of the coarse country-made cloths; the employment of wheeled carriages instead of pack animals; the superior construction of the carts engaged for trade and agriculture; the improved breeds of draught cattle. The bedizened equipages, caparisoned elephants and prancing steeds of the rich man are rarely to be seen. But the poor man, with his cart and pair of bullocks, rides to market as he seldom rode before. All this evidence, not flashing before the vision like the manifestations of former ages, but being obtained only by penetrating and far-reaching observation, perhaps receives less of popular consideration than it deserves, but will nevertheless be appreciated by the statistician and the economist.

The outcome of these complex considerations may be summarized thus. The growth of material prosperity among the Natives is not so great as might at first sight appear from the statistics of trade and production, if a comparison be instituted with former times. The national wealth, though real and expanding, is less discernible than formerly, being so much more diffused.

Touching the wealth of the Natives, there is the question whether capital is saved and accumulated, as much as might be expected under the peaceful circumstances of British rule. Some authorities apprehend that the people have become too poor to save anything of material amount, or to accumulate much that would be worthy of the name of capital. It is remarked that the Natives do not subscribe largely to the State loans which are raised nowadays, nor hold any large portion of the public securities. Doubt is expressed whether the proportion of the national debt held by them is as great as it formerly was. There are, it is alleged, few objects, patent to European observation, which could be indicated as the points whereto Native capital is directed. The peasantry are said, in general terms, to have no capital. Such apprehensions, if substantiated, would give birth to misgivings in regard to the future of the country.

It must be admitted that the accumulation of capital among the Natives is far from being what economists would desire to see, or what statesmen might expect, after two generations of internal peace unbroken save on one great occasion, and after the introduction of so many material improvements. Nevertheless, there is some saving and accretion in progress throughout the country, and there exists an accumulated store, which is absolutely great, though small in relation to the numbers of the people. The Natives do not hold the stock of the Guaranteed Railway Companies, which is held by shareholders in England. Nor do they hold what is called the sterling paper of the Government securities, which is held by Europeans. But of the rupee paper, as it is termed, which is held largely, though not wholly in India, a considerable portion, about 18 millions sterling worth, is held in the names of Natives. In other words, out of the national debt of India, held partly in India and partly in England, which may be set down at 138 millions sterling in all, about 18 millions, or one-eighth, is held by Natives. This proportion is not very considerable; still the amount of eighteen millions is something absolutely. In the absence of detailed information for the earlier times of

British rule, there is no knowledge whether the proportion is materially less now than formerly; it probably is less, however. But inasmuch as in those days the debt itself did not exceed thirty millions, and as Europeans then held some part of the debt, it is clear that the Natives could not have held essentially more than they now hold. The reasons for Natives not holding more than they do, are these, that the rates of interest have been gradually lowered, and that Europeans obtain possession of the securities. The loans have been for the most part raised in England for many years, because the funds could be obtained more cheaply and advantageously there than in India. In other words, the Natives have been driven quite legitimately out of a part of this field by the competition of European capitalists. Some considerable portion of the municipal debentures, issued by corporations on the security of town revenues, is held by Natives. Some of the capital of the Presidency banks, which have special relations with the Government, belongs to them. The fact is that the Natives can find many safe investments which yield more than the 4 or 4½ per cent. obtainable from the public securities. In former times, it was hard to find any secure place wherein to put their money save in the Government treasury, but in these times there are many such investments. The Government, again, finding the money market in London so conveniently resourceful, resorted to it. Had there been no such resources available, then the Queen's Government on assuming the direct administration of India would have obtained money by loan from the Natives, in the same manner as the East India Company used to do, but upon less favourable terms, and at higher rates of interest. Still, with these abatements, money would have been forthcoming in India year by year, and in greater sums than in the time of the East India Company. Even now, this very course has recently been prescribed in the raising of loans for material improvement. It has been repeatedly ascertained that two to three millions sterling can be obtained in this manner at comparatively cheap rates of interest. More could doubtless be obtained if higher rates of interest were offered. Up to a very recent date the financial credit of India, as indicated by the rate of interest on the national debt, has been one of the best in the world, second only to that of England herself. One reason, among many others, was this, that the London market furnished so much of the resources. Without these resources the Government must have paid a higher rate of interest, and according to this standard its credit would have stood lower in the financial quotations of the world.

Meanwhile the capital of the Natives has continued to increase, and questions arise as to the objects to which it is applied. In the first place, the external trade is partly in the hands of Native capitalists, though a large part is in the hands of Europeans, and the Native share of the trade requires a considerable amount of capital. In the next place, the internal trade of the country passes through the hands of Natives, and here again much capital is employed. In visible proof of this, there are the Native bankers of all grades, spread throughout the empire, leaving no place whatever in it unoccupied. There are the vast numbers of carts and draught-animals engaged not in agriculture but in transport, and the equally great numbers of boats for inland navigation. The capital thus employed must be held to have imposing proportions. The silver and gold coin in circulation, reckoned at many millions sterling, chiefly belongs to Natives. The large imports of gold and silver have mostly passed into their hands. The hoarded specie and bullion, also reckoned at many millions sterling, is in their possession. Of the Government notes in circulation, a portion is believed to be retained or secreted, and that belongs to Natives. The deposits in the State savings-banks amount to nearly two millions sterling, of which much belongs to Native depositors. To the Natives pertains a part of the capital employed in the local industries of cotton and jute, which are conducted after the European fashion. Lastly, since the recognition by the State of a marketable property in land, an enormous amount of Native capital has been lent out on landed security to landholders great and small.

The moneyed classes among the Natives are readily observable by Europeans, when a survey is made of Indian society. These classes exist everywhere, both in town and in country; they are said to be even elbowing the Europeans out of the trade at the Presidency cities. Their capital really represents a part of the savings of the nation, and they receive high rates of interest for their money as they lay it out. These rates used to be usuriously high under Native rule, 15, 20, even 25 per cent. and were in some degree justified by the want of security, or by the weakness of such security as was offered. They have become lower and lower since the introduction of British rule, owing partly to the improvement of securities, and partly to the competition of capitalists, great and small, among themselves. They are even now comparatively high, varying greatly according to circumstances or to localities, and ranging from 7 to 12 per cent., though they may sometimes be even lower, and not infrequently higher. It is reported that Native merchants now lend money to each other at 6 per cent. The fact of the rates of interest being occasionally high among the Natives, may perhaps be considered by some as an unfavourable symptom, indicating that the material welfare of the country has not been promoted, as much as might have been hoped, by the long peace under a settled Government. On the other hand, the circumstances that the rates have of late years been so considerably reduced, and have in some cases fallen to 7 and even 6 per cent., may be accepted as a proof not only that security of investment has improved, but also that the quantity of Native capital has increased.

It is thought by some authorities in England that the poorer classes in India are becoming gradually depressed, but this view would hardly strike employers of labour on the spot. Labour for private enterprises or for public works cannot always be obtained; it is comparatively abundant only in the hot season when domestic or agricultural work is slack. It is becoming more scarce than formerly, and has to be remunerated more highly. Even for service in the Native army, once the most favourite of all employments, it is becoming difficult to obtain recruits; and one main cause of the difficulty is this, that the men are better off at home, and do not care so much as of yore for the military wage.

It has been thought by some that the cattle generally have decreased and are decreasing; incidental dicta of eminent men have been cited to the effect that it is more difficult now than formerly to obtain good animals; statistics of the settlement department are quoted to prove the fact of decrease in the Deccan of western India. These particular statistics in the Deccan have not, however, been accepted by the principal authorities on the spot, and their result is opposed to known facts which point to a decided increase. In the Deccan the cultivation has spread greatly and the local trade has expanded; consequently the cattle both for ploughing and for drawing carts must have multiplied in an equal degree. The same consideration is applicable to most other provinces of the empire, and especially to the Madras Presidency. Therefore it is highly probable, indeed practically certain, that the agricultural cattle have largely increased almost everywhere. Similarly, the number of draught cattle must have risen in most districts, while in some districts, near the railway lines, it may have declined, their employment being superseded by the use of the rail. Trustworthy statistics of cattle can hardly be secured, and there are not sufficient data for making an exact comparison between the present and former times. Those who are best able to take a comprehensive view of the matter, will not believe that any decrease on the whole can possibly have occurred, but on the contrary will expect to find an increase. Of late there have been signal instances of draught cattle being easily obtained in large numbers. During the famine of 1874 there were 202,000 draught bullocks in excellent condition collected within six weeks in the northern districts of Behar and Bengal, for the transport of grain by Government. About the same time 10,000 draught bullocks were purchased for Government within a fortnight in the North-western Provinces for a similar service, and large additional numbers could have been immediately procured. In 1879, there were 9000 bullocks bought in Sind for military service at the shortest notice, and the people offered to produce any additional number that might be required. Regret was felt in Khandesh, near the Deccan, that distance from the seat of war prevented some of the purchases of bullocks being made there. Whenever animals are wanted for transport in war, it is notorious that if camels and ponies shall fail, there is a practically unlimited reserve of bullocks.

Such expectation of increase, however, will relate only to the serviceable cattle. Among a Hindu population, averse to destroy these animals, numberless unserviceable cattle are preserved in ordinary times, and in seasons of drought are left to their fate. Thus, during the recent famines, many thousand head have perished, which were of no value except for their horns, hides and bones. The loss of such creatures, however, does not affect the agricultural or locomotive power of the country. The working cattle, being stall-fed, were preserved through the drought, as was proved by the briskness of the grain trade, and the undiminished area of cultivation, for all which things the labour of bullocks was essential, to a more than ordinary extent. Nevertheless, the condition of the cattle is far from being all that might be desired. From July to December there is plenty of herbage for grazing in the plains throughout the country. During the rest of the year, the grazing is scanty in those provinces to which there are no hills adjacent, and it is from such provinces that instances are drawn of cattle suffering in the hot season. The peasants do not indeed raise special crops, as they might, for fodder, but the stalks of several of the cereals supply a nutritious substance, which is carefully stored for feeding the cattle during the dry season. But in the many provinces where hills are near, pasturage, often of excellent quality, is available, and the herds are sent periodically to the valleys for grazing. Still, it must be admitted that the increase of cattle is checked and the pastoral wealth, which naturally should belong to the country, is diminished by destructive murrain and epidemics.

In proportion to her size and population, India emphatically is a poor, a very poor, country, in one, at least, of the ordinary acceptations of the term poor.

The labour of the people is not strenuously nor successfully exerted, and man to man, an Indian does much less work in a given time than a European. Human employment is held cheap, and has heretofore been abundant, so the wages are low generally, though they have of late years risen in many places, and have doubled at some centres of industry. In rural localities, however, they are still very small and, where received in kind, may even be relatively less than they were. The average of food consumed per head is somewhat small in quantity and comparatively innutritious in quality; under these mild skies there is little craving for nutritious diet. The ordinary wants are simple and easily satisfied; the artificial needs are few, and those which exist are inexpensive. The climate does not, by augmenting the necessities of clothing, lodging and firing, drive people to self-help, therefore on the whole, the inducements to exertion are but weak. Consequently the average income is very small, and the margin of surplus, for anything beyond the wants of bare existence, is narrow. In Europe and North America the working power and motive force of the people are multiplied by mechanical means and scientific resources. But such appliances are as yet wanting for the most part to the Indians, who have been well described as being essentially un-mechanical. It comes, then, to this, that some two hundred and fifty millions of men in India work less, make less, produce less, indeed very much less, than an equally large population in Europe. Let a certain result be assumed as a symbol of what is accomplished in a year by the whole people of India. Certainly half, possibly even one-third, of that number of Europeans would accomplish as much in Europe. Whether, however, they would accomplish the same in India is another question, regarding which doubt may be felt. But a consideration of the circumstances immediately shews that the Indians are, and must be for a long time to come, comparatively poor.

In another sense of the term poor, however, the case is different. Those who, having comparatively much, yet not enough for their wants, are said to be poor, and those who, possessing little, have yet enough for their slight and modest needs, are held not to be poor. In that view of the matter, the Indians are not so poor as might at first sight be supposed.

Apart from famines which occur periodically, the poor in India do not dread absolute hunger in ordinary times, nor do they suffer from rigours of climate, though many of them are but scantily fed. There is no hard winter before their eyes, no poor-law, no poor-rate, no call for the community being legally compelled to maintain the disabled and the destitute, nor any considerable pauperism. There is little of the slow-wasting penury, the cankering care, the sense of pinching insufficiency, which, irrespective of absolute destitution, are so often mentioned in the most advanced and civilized countries; a mouthful is somehow found for all. Some classes of indigent beggars by profession exist, quite apart from religious mendicants who form a large and anything but needy class. Infirm persons are to be seen among the villages, in numbers which range in a certain proportion to the population of each village. These are supported by private charity, of which the stream never runs dry in ordinary times, and which the villagers afford without the least difficulty. They are well known to the relief officers of the Government in times of famine, for they then fail to receive support from the villagers who need all their little means for themselves. Thus, they are the first to come on the State relief. But as soon as the famine abates and some prospect appears of returning plenty, they are immediately thrown back on their villages or parishes, and receive the same voluntary sustenance as before. Here, then, is a sort of self-acting voluntary system, a creditable sign of the popular character, and a satisfactory symptom in respect to the circumstances of the country.

A proof of the comparative poverty of India is afforded by the experience of the income-tax. If such a tax of one per cent. were levied in the same manner as the English income-tax, touching the same sort of incomes in India as those touched in England, with as near an approximation as can be had relatively to the different circumstances of the two countries, the yield would not with careful administration exceed one million sterling. This at the best represents the income of the nation, assessable to income-tax, at one hundred millions sterling. Yet the corresponding income of the United Kingdom is several times as much, notwithstanding that its population is only one-fifth of the Indian population. But as Great Britain is abnormally rich, let a comparison be instituted on the same assumed data with any European country, and the comparative poverty of India will be apparent.

The feeling for art which characterizes even humble handicraftsmen in India is ascribed by Dr. Birdwood, one of the best authorities on this subject, in his recent work on the *Industrial Arts of India*, to the men being in easy circumstances. According to him, they know nothing of the struggle for existence, living in comfort and serenity, and are thus enabled to attend to their work with contented minds, taking in it that pride and pleasure which are essential to artistic excellence. He ascribes these happy circumstances to the landed tenures. And though evidently alive to any faults which may be found in the existing order of things, he concludes his description with the following picture, the truth of which will be recognised by all who know the Deccan, and which may serve as a foil to the descriptions which represent the peasant's life as a round of grinding care. He writes thus,

> "For leagues and leagues round the cities of Poona and Sattara there stretch the cultivated fields. . . . Glad with the dawn, the men come forth to their work, and glad in their work they stand all through the noontide, singing at the well, or shouting as they reap or plough; and when the stillness and the dew of evening fall upon the land like the blessing and the peace of God, the merry-hearted men gather with their cattle, in long winding lines to their villages again. . . . Thus day follows day and the year is crowned with gladness."

Critics sometimes fasten upon the poorest districts in the country and generalise therefrom; and it is well that the authorities should be reminded of the weakest parts in the beam of the State. Still it is desirable also to observe some of the finest parts of the country, such as the tracts around Dacca in eastern Bengal, the district of Calicut on the Malabar coast, the delta of Tanjore, the cream of the Gujerat province near Bombay, the valleys near Kangra in the Panjab, and many other places.

Having regard to the admitted poverty of the nation, some well-informed persons are beginning to express doubts whether the material improvements and public works are not being pressed on by the Government, at a cost which the people cannot bear, and at a pace in advance of the needs of the country. Certainly, monitions of this description are never misplaced, for there is ever a fear of embarrassment arising in a subject country from over-zeal on the part of the ruling race. It is necessary that the Government should shorten its improving arm, in reference to its own financial means and to the immediate needs of its people. But within the memory of many surviving administrators, a cry arose of an opposite description. The East India Company was charged with being, in its solicitude regarding military, political and administrative affairs, somewhat neglectful of material improvement, which was accordingly much urged on its attention by most organs of public opinion.

In truth the great Company did its utmost for material improvement, as for every other good thing, according to its lights, means and opportunities. Since its time, material improvement has advanced with a speed which, though creditable, is not at all great as compared with that of Western countries. There is now perhaps a tendency in public opinion to restrain the action of Government, lest a new danger should arise from too much forwardness. If, however, any signs of undue backwardness were to become perceptible, the same cry as of yore would probably arise, to the effect that justice was not being done by the Government to its vast estate and its noble heritage. In India there are still some who complain, with seeming force, of the insufficiency of existing improvements, advanced as they are, to meet the wants of the country.

Many thoughtful men, reflecting on the extinction of some Native industries as already mentioned, the partial substitution of foreign for indigenous manufactures, the augmented attention bestowed upon the raising of raw produce for exportation and, as a consequence, the increased dependence of the population upon the land, have therefrom derived anxious forebodings. The extinguished industries were chiefly, though not entirely, of a refined and delicate description, employing a number of hands, which, though large, was not important relatively to the population. On the other hand, employment is afforded to tens of thousands of persons by the new industries and manufactures, which have been, and still are being, introduced. The greatest of all industries next after agriculture, namely the industry which provides clothing for the mass of the people, is as yet almost intact, or but slightly affected, notwithstanding the importation of English piece-goods. The indigenous looms and spindles for the coarser fabrics ply as much as ever in every village, and in every town. The finer textile fabrics, if not quite what they once were, are still considerable and famous. The use of metal implements and utensils has enormously increased. While much of the material is imported from abroad, these articles are largely, though not wholly, manufactured within India itself. Though the non-agricultural and industrial population in some of the old cities in the interior of the country has decreased, yet three great cities, Calcutta, Madras and Bombay, have been created, having an aggregate non-agricultural population of nearly two millions, and being as populous as any cities that were seen in the brightest days of the Mogul empire.

This brief account of the material condition of the Natives, while stating unreservedly every ground of apprehension, shews that there are yet many causes for congratulation. Though the average of sickness and death-rate is high, still the population has increased and is increasing. Though the people have grown in number and are generally poor, still they are neither pauperized nor unemployed. Their area of cultivation has expanded, their industry has developed itself, their trade, foreign and domestic, has advanced at a steady pace, and their spirit of enterprise has been encouraged. Though their needs are few and their condition humble, still their clothing, dwellings and domestic utensils have improved. Though the poorer classes depended for many weeks consecutively upon State assistance during famine, they shewed themselves, after the cessation of the calamity, to be superior to the temptation to pauperism. Though the manufacturing and labouring industries have, to some limited extent, declined in refinement, they have become larger in bulk. Though the national wealth is not so visibly concentrated as formerly, it is more diffused among the masses of the people. Capital, though accumulated less in a few hands, is saved as much as ever, and is scattered more among whole classes of the population. Though the agriculture is backward on the whole, still in several respects it is practically good. As the staple industry of the country, it not only feeds the teeming millions, but also enables them to store reserves of food, and to export in these times vastly more produce than at any previous era. Though large sums are annually remitted to England, still India receives a price for what she sends away, greater than that which is paid for what she buys from other nations; and she has long enjoyed the benefit of foreign capital largely expended within her limits. Though there are dangers ahead, there are also springs of progress and elements of security. If taken all in all, the condition of the people is found to be improving materially, in a manner which may fail indeed to fulfil the expectations of Western economists, but is still in accordance with the best examples afforded in the East. The recent calamities of season have given a pale cast to the national thoughts and imparted a gloomy tinge to public opinion. But, when the natural bounties of rain and moisture shall be again vouchsafed, then will the land burst forth with fertility, and the people will press onwards in the path of improvement.

CHAPTER VII.

MENTAL AND MORAL PROGRESS OF THE NATIVES.

Effect of British rule on the character of the several classes of the people—The peasantry—The aboriginal tribes—The temper of the Muhammadans—The Parsis—The Native nobility—The landlord-class—The traders—The priesthood—The educated classes—Their mental improvement, moral conduct and religious belief—Their loyalty—And their political aspirations — Native munificence — Culture of physical science — Vernacular press and drama—Advancement of Natives in the public service—In other professions—Good effect of Natives visiting England—State of the Native mind and disposition generally.

THE mental and moral progress of the Natives is in part connected with the material conditions, which have been summarized in the preceding chapter. But it must also depend on divers circumstances, some of which are within the control of the British Government. The peace and security, introduced and maintained by the strong arm of power, afford, as it were, air, light and space for the growth of some of the best human qualities, and suppress or eradicate many evil habits which in troublous times spring up with rank exuberance. But the operation of the same causes must close many avenues against restless ambition, shut off many careers of enterprise and adventure, wither the self-reliance, stifle the aspirations, and deaden the energies of many. With such persons, a foreign Government is unavoidably unpopular, however much it may strive by far-sighted policy to avoid unpopularity. Their number, once great, is much less nowadays, but will still remain considerable, and must be reckoned among the motive forces of the country. Nevertheless, if it must be feared that rapine, violence and disorder during the declining years of Native rule had a brutalizing and debasing effect on the national character, it may be hoped that peace, order and security under British rule have an elevating and humanizing effect. Heinous crime of all categories, though still too prevalent, has very much decreased. In many other countries it has been remarked that while crimes of violence decrease, crimes of fraud increase. Happily this is not the case in India; for there the crimes under both these heads have decreased. But while the gentler virtues are fostered, the ruder merits are stunted. While ability is systematically cultivated, original talent is less developed. It must be remembered that a foreign rule, though conducted with the utmost liberality and enlightenment, cannot but exercise some depressing influence upon the character of the people. On the other hand, it may produce many vivifying and purifying influences, which can be perceived only by a review of the various classes into which the nation is divided, and such an examination, in brief, will now be attempted.

It can hardly be said that the effect of British rule upon the character and disposition of the humblest or labouring classes, in the rural or remote districts, has as yet been marked or decisive. These poor people have still the reserve, shyness, and undemonstrative habits characteristic of races long subjected to exaction, servitude, and the necessity of slavish obedience to the will of their superiors. But they are now free from the old exactions and from the custom of forced labour. They have the right to refuse their labour according to their own interest or convenience, and to demand for it its worth in wages. Their carts and cattle are not liable to impressment, save for war. They know that there are tribunals, before whom all British subjects are equal, and by whom oppression can be stopped. These immunities must impart to them some sense of free citizenship, some idea of the dignity of humanity. The invitation for their children to enter the State schools, and the attention bestowed inside the schoolroom upon the poorest, as upon the more fortunate, child, must afford some encouragement.

Near the capital cities and the centres of industry, the labouring classes are no longer humble. On the contrary, they are becoming intelligently conscious of their improved status, independent in giving their labour, observant of the terms in their engagements, and tenacious of their claims to remuneration; and these qualities in them become more and more strongly marked according as their labour rises from unskilled towards skilled grades. They are growing in numbers and in strength year by year in every part of the country. Such growth is a thing almost unknown in former times, and is directly attributable to British rule.

The peasant proprietary and yeomanry of British India exist in all the divisions of the empire except the provinces of Bengal and Behar, and constitute a mainstay of the nation. They have from time immemorial evinced, under every form of trial and trouble, many distinctively excellent qualities, such as self-reliance, courage in defence of home and family, mutual dependence among brethren, aptitude for village or parish organization, fraternal cohesion among the members of communities, instinctive perception of the nature of property, tenacity in assertion of proprietary right, veneration for ancestral custom, endurance of hardship and enterprising industry. If it be held that the gold of these sterner and more robust virtues is best tried in the fire of war and revolution, there may be fear lest, during a time of peace and security, the character of this peasantry will not improve, and perhaps may even deteriorate. Still, many of their most useful qualities are preserved, under British rule, by the equitable settlement of the relations between the State and the peasantry as payers of the land-tax, by the recognition of a heritable and transferable right in landed property and by the record of all rights in the land.

In the peasantry there are to be included the cultivators and tenants, who were all much oppressed and harassed in former times. Many among them have, under British rule, risen in status and condition, and feel a sense of security and comparative independence, which their forefathers never could have felt. Some among them, however, are still in an insecure and unsatisfactory condition; and in particular provinces, such as Behar, the whole class is in a depressed state.

It is from the peasantry that the armies of all Native Governments, and of the British Government, have been drawn. The peasants used to be proud and glad to enrol themselves for military service. Their martial impulse, aptitude for war, and readiness to serve under the standards, were once renowned. Within the last two generations, these qualities have much declined, though the men are still counted among the good soldiers of Asia.

The predatory spirit, and instinct for the fray, were once prevalent among them. These tendencies have been much repressed, but experience even up to recent dates has indicated that they would break out again, if the bonds of civil order were ever to become seriously loosened.

It must be acknowledged that the improved security of landed property has encouraged peasants to borrow and money-lenders to lend. This indebtedness, which was always common, has become more rife than ever. And in so far as it prevails, it saps away the manly sentiments, and fosters the extravagance to which, in their way, the peasants have ever been prone.

It is to the peasantry that the educational efforts of the State are largely directed. Some authorities advocate a liberal expenditure of public money on superior education among the middle and upper classes; others deprecate it. All authorities are agreed that there should be no stint of expenditure on the education of the peasant proprietors and of the cultivators. But despite all the benevolent efforts that have been put forth, the progress of education among these people is as yet slow, the proportion of them who can read and write is small, and the great majority is still rude and unlettered.

As might be expected, so great a class comprises many of those castes into which the Hindu nation is divided. Under British rule so many tribes, formerly devoted to trade, military employment or mechanical industry, but not to agriculture, are now acquiring so much of interest or property in land, that in some districts statisticians find it hard to specify what should properly be termed the agricultural class. The mass, however, of the men, devoted entirely or almost entirely to agriculture, still belongs to the humblest of the four great groups into which Hindu castes are arranged. It was to this group that the hardy Mahrattas of Sivaji, and the staunch Sikhs of Ranjit Singh, belonged. The Rajputs were once potent and widespread throughout northern and central India, and extended even down to the south. Within the last few centuries, they have been sorely thinned in numbers, by reason of their patriotic resistance to foreign invasion, during which the stories of their self-sacrificing heroism are not surpassed by the annals of any nation. Higher in the scale are those Brahmins who follow secular pursuits, apart from their brethren of the priestly orders. Their influence in landed concerns is comparatively slight in northern India, but is considerable in eastern, western and central India and almost dominant in many parts of the country.

The peasantry also includes many aboriginal tribes, Gonds, Bhils, Kols, Sontals and others, inhabiting the mountainous tracts in the interior of the continent and peninsula of India, and not professing any formal religion, though following religious observances of a primitive description. These are excitable by nature, and ever ready to fight against any wrong that may be attempted or on behalf of any right that may be threatened. When thus excited, they swarm like bees after leaving the hives. They are gradually falling under the sway of Hindu, or rather Brahminical, proselytism. And they seem likely to become ere long Hindus, unless in the meantime they shall, as appears possible, be converted to Christianity by the efforts of the missionaries. Large numbers of them, indeed, have already been thus converted.

Aboriginal races of a like character, Lushais, Nagas, Duflas and others, inhabit the forest-clad mountains on the north-eastern frontier which separates India from Burma and China. They frequently bring themselves into collision with British power, and it cannot be said that as yet any beneficial effect upon their character has been produced. The tribes dwelling in the Himalayan region are, with the exception of the sturdy and self-reliant Gorkhas of Nepal, Hindus of a mild type of character, flourishing under British auspices. On the great western frontier from Karachi to Peshawur, inhabited throughout by Muhammadans, the amelioration of the character of the tribes has been decisively marked in the southern or Belûch section, but is less perceptible in the northern or Pathan section, though even there, despite the frays, forays and internecine fights, much improvement has been effected.

A survey of the Indian peasantry would not be complete without some reference to the Muhammadan population. No eastern sovereign has so many Muhammadan subjects as the Queen-Empress of India. Of the Indian Muhammadans, the greater number live under the Lieutenant-Governor of Bengal, who alone has in his jurisdiction as many millions of Moslems as the Sultan of Turkey and twice as many as the Shah of Persia. The Indian Muhammadans are met with on all the coasts or in every port of India, and are emphatically the sailors of the Indian seas. In the interior of the country they are urban rather than rural, employed in some branches of commerce, in retail dealing, in skilled and refined industries, in the army, in public and private service; but seldom connected with agriculture save in the capacity of landlords. In Sind, however, the agricultural population is Muhammadan, both landlords and cultivators. In eastern and northern Bengal, in the region comprising the basin of the Brahmaputra river and its affluents and in the united delta of the Ganges and the Brahmaputra, the tenants and cultivators are also Muhammadan, while the landlords are Hindu, with the exception of some prominent and meritorious gentlemen of the Muhammadan faith. These districts are among the most productive in the empire and export great quantities of raw produce. Several articles, much used in the manufactures of Great Britain, are raised by the Muhammadan hands of Bengal. By the same hands is the water traffic conducted in the wonderful network of Bengal rivers. These people were Hindus of humble castes, and have been converted within historic times to Muhammadanism. They have their religious services performed generally in the Bengali tongue, and have probably less acquaintance with the phrases of Arabic, the sacred language of their faith, than their fellow-religionists in any other country. Their social condition is so low that the institution even of matrimony is lax; endeavours have, however, been recently made by special legislation to give validity to their marriage rites.

Elsewhere in India, the Muhammadans, being scattered, do much to leaven the mass of Native opinion. Besides the discontent engendered among them by historic memories, there is one special circumstance affecting their contentment. Under Native rule they enjoyed a large portion, perhaps the lion's share, of the State patronage, and at the outset of British rule were found in the front everywhere, whereby they continued as before to be largely employed in the public service especially in its higher grades. But nowadays they are beaten by Hindus in the open competition of mind with mind. Their youths in the schools and colleges are surpassed by the Hindu youths and are consequently placed at a disadvantage when entering a profession or contending for advancement in public employ. It is to this that the Muhammadans themselves attribute the fact that they are falling in wealth and status while the Hindus are rising. Though not refusing to join schools of Hindus and of mixed nationalities, they prefer to have institutions of their own exclusively, where Arabic and Persian literature constitute a prominent feature. The Government has of late co-operated with them in establishing institutions on this principle. Some Muhammadan gentlemen, for instance the late Nuwab Amir Ali, Nuwab Abdul Latif of Calcutta, Syed Ahmed of Aligarh, Muhammad Ali Roghè of Bombay, Synd Idrus of Surat, and others, have shewn an enlightened desire to imbue their countrymen with ideas of civilized progress.

The temper and disposition, politically, of the Muhammadans form one of the many sources of anxiety in India. Some years ago, the religious revival commenced by the Wahabis in Arabia, the breeze of fanaticism which ruffled the surface of the Muhammadan world, and other causes difficult to define, excited the Indian Muhammadans considerably. Plots were discovered and state trials instituted; some grave and melancholy events occurred which need not here be recounted. Within the most recent years, however, the Indian Muhammadans have become comparatively well affected. Be the reasons what they may, the symptoms of disaffection among them have of late abated.

The Parsis deserve some special mention; they maintain intact the religion of Zoroaster, and the social customs which they brought with them from Persia, after heroically resisting the Arab invasion. They preserve, unmixed by marriage with any other race, the qualities which carry them to the van in the march of life, and to the front in every arena which they enter. As men of business they are unsurpassed in India, and in many mechanical industries they are distinguished. Though they are still comparatively small in numbers, their importance must be measured rather by their resources and their capacity for work. They are loyal and devoted to the British Sovereign and nation, and there is no class more contented. Their influence, however, can not be regarded as national, as it would hardly be acknowledged either by Hindus or Muhammadans.

The great landlords of India (known by the names of Zemindar, Talukdar, and other titles) are chiefly associated in the public mind with the provinces of Bengal, Behar, Orissa, and Oudh. They are to be found, however, in almost all parts of the country, even in those parts where peasant proprietorship is the prevailing tenure. Some of these Native gentlemen apply capital to the soil, reclaim the waste, conciliate their tenantry and in all respects show forth a bright example. Others again, though falling short of this standard, exercise their territorial influence beneficially. In Bengal, if the landlord or zemindari tenure was created by the British Government in order that, among other things, capital on a large scale might be applied to the land, then it must be admitted that no such result has been attained. The principal Zemindars or landlords form a lettered and refined class, having a great stake in the country, possessing leisure which is much given to the consideration of political affairs, and exerting on the whole a salutary influence on Native opinion. There is probably no class in India more loyal than the Zemindars of Bengal, certainly there is none whose position rests so much on the stability of British rule.

During the long minorities, which occur frequently in estates of all sizes, the Government exercises its legal power of educating the infant heir, of placing him in the Court of Wards and of managing his property till he comes of age. The amount of business, thus undertaken by the State on behalf of the landlord class, is quite enormous. Many fine properties are saved from injury, debts and encumbrances are cleared off by good management during the minority, and many young landowners are inducted into their hereditary positions with all the advantages of nurture and instruction.

In many parts of the empire there is the scattered remnant of a Native nobility, consisting of men who are unavoidably in worse circumstances under British rule than under the preceding Native rule. Some of them are still able to maintain their station, dignity and reputation. Many, however, are drifting into embarrassment, or sinking under the weight of trouble till an Encumbered Estates Act affords some relief from the pressure. Many of them still enjoy, by the grace of the British Government, a part of the emoluments they received under the Native rule in return for service, although they are now excused from serving. Such men, living in uncongenial quiet, cannot but meditate on the wealth, power and honour, which their immediate ancestors possessed two or three generations previously; and this brooding meditation must produce discontent and restlessness. They will chafe under the restrictions which a civilized system necessarily imposes. These disquieting reflections spread to their relations, retainers and dependants. The policy of the Government has been, by all the legitimate means in its power, to arrest the decadence of these old families, to prevent the disruption of their estates and to preserve their territorial influence. With this view several enactments for the relief of encumbered estates have been passed; but the process of decay can hardly be stopped.

The mercantile, trading and banking classes continue to show the enterprise, acuteness, methodical habits and business-like aptitude, for which they have been so long famed. Formerly they were much esteemed for rectitude, trustworthiness and fair dealing with all men, their credit standing proportionately high. Their name has of late years been occasionally tarnished by the failures, collapses and disasters incidental to an age in which speculation is so rife. On the whole, however, their reputation and credit are still good. They are ever ready, perhaps too ready, to lend money to the landowners great and small, and but too often draw intentionally or unintentionally, both gentry and peasantry into the vortex of extravagance and the meshes of indebtedness. Although, by thus affording credit, they provide a resource most useful in the transactions of the nation, they are often regarded as grasping and extortionate. In some places, odium has been incurred by them as being indirectly the cause of civil troubles and disturbances. On such occasions they have been objects of exaggerated condemnation, and have been called the Shylocks of the age, or harpies preying on the vitals of the people. Their natural intelligence, transmitted through many generations, is still further fostered by education, and their sons are conspicuous for proficiency in all the educational institutions. Their profession is largely composed of Hindus belonging to the caste which is by the Hindu system devoted to this calling, among whom the Marwaris of Rajputana have always been eminent and are still growing in wealth. They also comprise several sections of the Muhammadan community, many of the Parsis and some of the Brahmins. They are amenable to many of the best influences of the English administration, and bear a hearty allegiance to the foreign Government under which they flourish. Having in their hands the capital and the financial sinews of the country, they constitute one of the bulwarks of British rule.

The priestly classes are still numerous throughout the empire. The Hindu priesthood includes only those Brahmins who follow religious callings, and not those who are engaged in secular pursuits, though a certain sanctity is attached also to them. The influence of the priesthood has among Hindus been as potent as in any nation of the world at any epoch. With the Mahrattas especially it is in full vigour, and is politically an element of unrest. It survives with the mass of the Hindus, who still flock in countless multitudes to hallowed bathing-places, still approach inner sanctuaries of idols with heartfelt awe, still load the shrines with offerings, still brave the toils and often the fatal hardships of their pilgrimages. With the worship and the observances in some places there are, no doubt, still mingled many of those practices which have been justly regarded by Western observers as immoral. In some parts of the country, among the establishments attached to the temples there are hapless classes living degraded lives. In certain exceptional cases, the records of the courts of justice have contained surprising revelations of customs shocking to civilized humanity.

With the educated classes of Hindus, the priestly influence is sinking fast towards its final decadence. There remain indeed some Hindus of culture and learning, who stand by the ancient faith and its observances. But as a rule, educated Hindus pay little more than an outward respect to the forms and to the ministers of that national religion which is so intertwined with the social institutions and the civil laws of the people. Possibly, this effect is not as yet perceived by many of the lesser priests who officiate among the humbler orders of Hindus, nor by some of those priests who dwell in learned seclusion at the many holy places in the country. But it must surely be recognised by many of these keen-witted and clear-sighted men. Proud as they are of their race and lineage, strong in the faith of their divine origin, persuaded of their own sanctity, conscious of their own intellectual superiority, they cannot but regard with indescribable sentiments the new empire which crushes prejudices, superstitions and antiquated ideas, as the Jaganath car of their own traditions crushed its victims of yore. Still the aspect and bearing, the lofty brow, set features, imperturbable countenance and erect stature indicate a pride not to be lowered by outward defeat. Although defeated, they will not surrender to the victor their unconquerable will, for they look upon themselves as endowed with a nobility which worldly puissance cannot confer, nor modern civilization bestow.

The influences of the age tend to weaken the barriers which the ancient system of caste sets up between the several classes of the people, thereby restricting the mutual sympathy which ought to exist according to the dictates of nature. With many of those who have received a broad and liberal education, or travelled much by railways and steam-ships or visited foreign countries, the distinctive feelings which gather round the idea of caste have become deadened. Even they, however, are usually obliged, on their return to India, to conform to the ceremonial procedure necessary for restoration to the status pertaining to caste. Some men, whose sense of the fitness of things rebels against the notion of caste, prefer to remain outside the charmed circle. But with the great majority of the people, the sentiments relating to caste still hold full sway.

The Jain religion, though at first sight apparently cognate with Hinduism, is separate and distinct. It has saints of its own, and promises an absolute repose approaching to annihilation, as the consummation of bliss. Its most salient feature is an excessive tenderness for animal life, carried to a degree of superstitious absurdity. A devout Jain will not harm even the smallest reptile; he fears lest he should inhale the minutest insect that floats imperceptibly in the air. This faith, however, has among its adherents many of the most hard-headed and actively business-like Natives in India; that is to say many of the traders and bankers of Rajputana, Gujerat and Cutch, and other members of the mercantile caste, scattered throughout the empire. Its devotees are strict and zealous; its shrines are among the richest in the country. Its adherents, though ready to defend their sacred places pugnaciously against encroachment from the Hindus, are free for the most part from fanaticism and are to be reckoned among the loyal and contented classes of the population.

The Lingayet sect is widely spread in the lower portion of the Deccan, and in southern India. It originally professed to constitute a reformation of Hinduism and to inculcate a pure morality in consonance with that of olden times. Its adherents are numerous among the commercial and agricultural classes and form one of the respectable sections of the community.

The Sikh faith always was in close relation with Hinduism. A man was admitted into the sect by special ceremonies, one of which was called the baptism of the sword; unless admitted by these means, he remained, as he was born, a Hindu. This faith, originally promulgated with much simplicity and purity of doctrine, was subsequently established by force of arms in northern India. It had sacred books, a separate language, a learned priesthood, religious edifices, and somewhat fanatical devotees of its own. It numbered among its adherents many warriors and statesmen, and whole tribes of resolute and strong-handed men. It played a considerable part in the modern history of India and, but for the intervention of the British power, might have been dominant in other quarters of India besides the northern. While it was the representative of political force and the symbol of military power, not only were the sons of the old adherents admitted to the ancestral faith, but also fresh applicants for admission were numerous. After national triumphs in war and policy, the new disciples flocked to the temple gates for admission. Since the annexation of the Panjab to the British empire, these influences have disappeared, and the sect is probably not so large as it once was. Though fewer applicants may now be seeking admission, and though some Sikhs may not care to have their sons baptized into the faith, still the majority are steadfast, and the constitution of the sect is maintained. Sikhism, though quiet and loyal at present, is one of those inflammable things which a spark might kindle into fire. Its idiosyncrasy and susceptibilities are thoroughly understood by the Panjab authorities, and its fidelity to the empire is well preserved. It would stand proof against many trials and temptations, but if tried over much, it would reassert itself, and would assume the headship of a national movement. Meanwhile the priests, as a class, are well disposed, but outbursts of proselytizing zeal may occur from time to time, on the part of persons claiming saintly or prophetic functions, who are not really connected with the Sikh sect.

The fanaticism which smoulders in the hearts of some among the Muhammadan priesthood, like embers ready to be fanned into flame, is one of the great political forces in the country. Nothing that the Government can do will mitigate it, but many things, which the Government might inadvertently do, would aggravate it seriously. In recent years it has been an element of mischief; at the present moment, however, it seems to be quiescent.

The educated class is drawn from the several sections of society which have been already mentioned. The education of this class is for the most part derived from the national instruction introduced by the British Government. There are, indeed, some educated men, whose instruction has been obtained purely from indigenous sources, independently of aid from their foreign rulers, has been kept strictly within the ancient grooves, has been conducted in rustic cloisters, monastic establishments or the shade of sacred groves, and is directed chiefly to religious objects. These men, though still numerous, must be decreasing gradually throughout the country. Men of business are still to be seen, who have been educated only in the old style, and whose practical talent and acuteness have not been developed by modern instruction. They are, however, becoming more and more rare, and will soon pass away without successors of the same type, for their sons are all educated in the new style.

Thus, the only educated class that need now be observed consists of men brought up under British supervision, for whose mental and moral condition the British Government is responsible. These men follow other professions besides the public service, such as the bar and other legal pursuits, private practice in medicine, commerce and banking, civil engineering, mechanical industries and the like. But many of them enter the public service in its various grades from the lowest to the highest. They thus become members of one homogeneous profession which equals, probably in magnitude and certainly in importance, all the other professions taken together. It is this dominant and leading profession which most readily admits of specific observation, and in which the results of the national education can be best tested.

That the natural intelligence of the educated men is sharpened by rigid method, and that their mental stamina are strengthened by discipline, will be surely assumed. That their minds are opened to the reception of new influences, expanded into a larger growth, drawn towards wider spheres, raised into higher regions of thought, and fixed in grooves of stricter accuracy, may be reasonably expected. That they are steadier officers, cleverer men of business, abler administrators, better workers and apter learners, from being thus educated, is easily conceivable. The harder questions relate to the effect of the education on the conduct of these men, on their trustworthiness and integrity, their loyalty to the British Sovereign, their gratitude to their foreign instructors, their attachment to western civilization and their sentiments in regard to the existing order of things. The answers to such questions, if thoughtfully rendered, will be found quite as satisfactory as could be fairly anticipated.

In the first place, a due and proper standard of rectitude among the Native officials of the upper and middle grades has been obtained. Such men are now regarded as gentlemen in the best sense of the term, that is as men of honour. Their character is not impugned, their rectitude is trusted by public opinion, corruption on their part is not suspected. In this description, as in all general descriptions, there must be reservations and exceptions, but such is the tone pervading these bright parts of the picture. Of the numerous changes which have of late years arisen in India, this particular change is among the most noteworthy. For many authorities, still surviving, can remember the time when such Native officials were not regarded as men of honour, when their uprightness and integrity were constantly impugned, when their conduct was frequently distrusted, when imputations of corruption were bruited abroad. One cause of the moral improvement, now perceptible, springs from the better organization of the public service. The men are, by the concession of adequate salaries, placed in a position superior to temptation. They are embodied in regular departments, which have grades ascending like the steps of a ladder, offer scope for ambition and open out prospects of promotion to be seen through the vista of coming years. Thus they are so situated that they shall have everything to gain by fidelity, and everything to lose by misconduct. Another and a higher cause of the improvement is traceable to the influences of Western education, the moral teaching imparted by European culture, the practical ideas of duty thereby infused, the virtuous principles thus instilled, the companionship of English instructors and the association with them in the daily life at school or college. It is to these two main causes that the Natives themselves attribute the amelioration which is happily perceived.

In the lower grades of educated Natives, however, misconduct is still common and but too frequent even in the middle grades. Still it will be found to exist almost exactly in proportion as the advantages, moral and material, allowed to these grades fall short of those beneficently granted to the upper grades.

Together with the public service, the profession of the law has advanced pari passu. This great profession is for the most part a product of British rule, and is divided, as in England, into two branches, like those of barristers and solicitors. Admission to the Native Bar is regulated by tests and examinations, which ensure the possession of high qualifications by those who apply for it. An almost equal improvement is visible in the Native barristers as in the Native judges, and a standard of professional etiquette prevails, formed on the English model. The standard was much lower in former days, when advocates but too often connived at or participated in malpractices and even in frauds. Any remnants of these evils, which may still linger in the profession, will ere long be eliminated. As now constituted, the Native Bar is fast becoming a power in the country; its independence of demeanour, freedom of speech and sympathy with the people, are raising it daily in public estimation. Its conduct fosters the salutary belief, which is settling down in the minds of the Natives, to the effect that the British system of civil justice constitutes a real palladium of their liberties and privileges. Its loyalty will be true towards the Government which is its foster-father. Improvements, similar in kind but much less in degree, are taking place in the profession of the Law, which branch includes attorneys, solicitors and all other legal practitioners. These Native practitioners formerly had a very evil repute for stimulating wrongful litigation, promoting fraud and poisoning the moral atmosphere around the precincts of the Courts. Of this mischief, much has been removed by the improvements in the Native Bench and Bar, and by the operation of public opinion; but much, unfortunately, remains.

As an instance of the mental and moral progress of the Natives, the expansion of the Post-office may be mentioned. The Government has adopted the principle of all the reforms which have proved so successful in England. By amalgamating under one administration the imperial and local post-offices in the various provinces of the empire, postal facilities have been placed within reach of every large village throughout the country. The increase of letter-writing and of postal business has been remarkable. Within the last fifteen years, the number of Post-offices has increased from 2200 to 5500, the length of postal lines from 48,000 to 58,000 miles. The amount of receipts in cash from the public has risen from £401,000, to £660,000 per annum, exclusive of official postage; and the number of covers delivered from 59 millions to 131 millions annually. A portion of the increase in correspondence is due to the Government and its servants, also to the non-official Europeans; but the mass of it is due to the Natives, under the influences of education.

The foreign Government in India must be prepared to realise the fact that the hearts of educated Natives are deeply stirred by the Western education, and that an active process of mental fermentation is setting in. These men are from their youth instructed in matters concerning the rise, progress, zenith, decline and fall of empires; the relative dimensions, population and resources of the several great powers of the world; the constitution, legislature and privileges of States monarchical, constitutional, despotic, republican; the territorial arrangements consequent on modern warfare; the various nationalities of which kingdoms are composed. It follows that they will observe current events whether peaceful or warlike with an appreciative insight, and will speculate on the effect which such events may produce on the fortunes of England. A competent knowledge of the recent history of their own country will shew them how often the commerce and the fortunes of India herself have been affected by events occurring in distant regions, for example by the civil contest in America, by the wars in the Crimea, China and Turkey. An extensive vernacular press is growing up which offers brief summaries of the political affairs and occurrences of the world. The English press in India presents daily, full extracts of all the best news and opinions of the press in England, together with comments suited to the currents of public thought in India, and is read by the English-speaking Natives with as much attention as by the English themselves. Native trading firms have their headquarters or their branches in the United Kingdom or on the continent of Europe, and will ere long have them even on the other side of the Atlantic. For these reasons, England must, whenever she engages in affairs of world-wide importance, be prepared to reckon with a mass of Native opinion instructed to a degree heretofore unknown. The lights are various in which Natives regard alternatives of peace or war. If in any conjuncture it should appear that, on a fair consideration of her own interest and honour, England ought to fight and yet holds back from fighting, then the Natives would be quicker than ever to draw the gravest inferences. If after anxious suspense, the English standard, ever to Eastern eyes the symbol of victory in the end, is unfurled, it is followed by the hopes and prayers of the majority of the Natives.

More than once of late, when the inevitable moment seemed near, utterances of loyalty and god-speed arose from the organs of Native opinion in all parts of the country. Still, as a rule the Natives raise their voice decidedly for preserving peace, not at any price, but at some sacrifice, rather than for incurring the risks of war, with the certainty of special taxation in the present and the probability of the public burdens being augmented in the future. They certainly are adverse to an aggressive, and favourable to a pacific policy.

The educated Natives are also moved by aspirations for self-government, for political power, and even for representative institutions, the concession of which does not at present fall within the range of practical politics. Such ideas have been mooted in former times, but have never been so fully defined, nor so openly declared, as they are at present. The reports of Parliamentary debates, concerning India and the East proximately or remotely, are scanned by the Natives with anxious interest. The utterances of English orators or statesmen vindicating the character, conduct, status and interests fiscal and financial, of the people of India, are welcomed by the Natives with a gratitude as deeply felt as it is fervently expressed. The name of any member of either House of Parliament, who by word or deed espouses the cause of the Natives, soon becomes a household word among them. Although benevolence is admitted by them to be a prominent feature of British rule, still after having been for so many centuries the sport of despots, the prey of conquerors and the victims of revolution, they have an ineradicable fear that the English nation may prove to be not wholly an exception to the rule of selfishness and harshness which has so often prevailed with foreign and absolute rulers. They seem always glad to be reassured by responsible and influential persons regarding the kind and good intentions of England, and such assurances cannot be too often repeated. There has been of late a tendency with some Natives to rely for sympathy and support specially on particular parties or sections of parties among the politicians of England. But this tendency is deprecated by the best organs of Native opinion, on the manifest grounds that Natives are the very last persons who should encourage the notion of India ever becoming a battle-field for party strife in England, and that all political parties ought to be urged to co-operate for the object of benefiting their Indian fellow-subjects.

Thoughtful Englishmen may remember that self-government among the Natives is one of the goals to which many of the administrative arrangements of India are tending. Natives are appointed members of the legislative council of the Governor-General for all India, and of the local legislatures of Madras, Bombay and Bengal. They are honorary magistrates in the interior of the districts; they serve as jurymen, as assessors to aid the judges in criminal trials, as members of arbitration tribunals and of conciliation courts in civil causes. They take part in the administration of the funds raised by the road cess and other local cesses, in the management of schools, hospitals, dispensaries and other institutions. They furnish the great majority of the commissioners in the municipalities, which exist in the capital cities, and are scattered over the length and breadth of the empire. They thus become the responsible trustees, administrators or controllers of the rates for levying the local taxes. In Calcutta and Bombay especially, and in some other central places, they enjoy as ratepayers the electoral franchise for the election of members of the municipal corporations. The system whereby, in so many parts of the country, village communities are constituted, or village headmen are vested with petty powers in police matters, is the very embodiment of the principle of self-government in the rural districts.

Native associations are formed for the avowed purpose of representing their views, wishes or grievances to the authorities. Several of these bodies, such as the British Indian Association of Calcutta, the Anjuman of Lahore, the Sarva Janik Sabha of Bombay, can make their voice heard, not only in India, but even as far as England. Such societies are regarded by the

Government, as affording the means for legitimately and temperately representing or vindicating the opinions of the Natives. Their memorials and addresses, though sometimes transgressing the limits of propriety, are, as a rule, fully reasoned and moderately expressed.

Personal kindness and charity have always been among the most loveable characteristics of the Natives. These sentiments have induced men to support not only their female relatives and their aged or helpless connexions, which is well, but also their able-bodied and idle male relatives, which is not well. Many a rising man is weighted in his career by listless persons who hang about him, instead of shifting for themselves. This tendency, which has been heretofore excessive, is diminished by the influences of education. Virtuous and most commendable sacrifices are often made by Natives, who stint and pinch themselves in order to afford a good education to their young relations. The youths thus educated generally recompense their friends for these sacrifices, by evincing a resolute spirit of self-help.

The sympathy of Natives, also spreads beyond the circle of relations, friends or dependants. It extends to the miserable wherever met with, to the living community at large, and to the needs of posterity yet unborn. The charity of Natives is, indeed, often misdirected, but is generously profuse. Every Native, who makes a fortune, immediately gives away a part of it to works of public usefulness or charity. Every city in the empire is improved, endowed or beautified, by the benevolence or munificence of individual citizens. In prosperous years the sums, thus nobly dispensed, are enormous; and even in the worst years, the source of this bounty never runs dry. In the interior of the country, works of public utility, on the roadsides and in many other spots, attest the spirit of philanthropy which prevails among wealthy Natives. In many provinces the Government wisely publishes a list of the works of public utility constructed by individuals; these publications redound to the credit of those concerned.

The Government always delights to honour the Natives who thus devote a portion of their substance to the welfare of their countrymen. Patents of Native nobility are discriminately granted to meritorious persons. Successive Viceroys of India have studied the unwritten rules which govern the constitution of Native nobility, and have granted Native titles judiciously and considerately to persons recommended for their good deeds by the several Local Governments; a moral force of some potency is thus exercised. British decorations of the Star of India are bestowed upon Natives; knighthood not unfrequently has been granted to them, and in rare instances a Baronetcy has been conferred; the new Order of the Indian Empire has many Native members. The effect of these measures upon Native sentiments is to encourage loyalty and public spirit.

Sound as the national education may have been in respect of history, literature, practical morality and political philosophy, it has been and still is defective in respect of the physical and natural sciences. Yet, scientific study, the value of which is now recognised in all countries, has in India a special importance. It qualifies the Native youth for professions in which they have hitherto had but little place. It diverts from the elder professions, namely the law and the public service, some of the students who would otherwise overcrowd those professions. It displays before the Natives fresh ranges of thought and new modes of thinking. It tends to correct some of the faults which are admitted to exist in the Native mind, while educing and developing many of its best qualities and faculties. In two of the most immediately important among the scientific professions, namely medicine and civil engineering, the Government has done for the Natives everything that could reasonably be expected. Hundreds of Native engineers, architects, physicians and surgeons have been and are being sent forth into the world. In respect of other sciences also something has been effected, but the greater part of what is needed still remains to be accomplished. The important step which the Universities in India have recently taken, by granting degrees in Science, will essentially affect the standards and aims of the national education.

Reflection upon all these things will lead thoughtful persons to inquire what are the religious tendencies of the Natives. In the first place, the faith of the Muhammadans does not seem to have received any shock from Western education and civilization. Nor has the Hindu faith been shaken with the mass of the Hindus, who follow the ancestral idolatry with the same simplicity as of yore. The faith is dubious with Hindus who have some tincture of education and who probably regard their national religion with half doubt and half belief, much as the Greeks and Romans regarded the gods of their fathers. But among highly educated Hindus the faith is dead or dying. With some it has been shattered well-nigh to the very base, while from the minds of others it has already vanished like the fabric of a vision.

Many educated Natives have long cast away the last shreds of their belief in the mythology, the sacred story and the future world of Hinduism. But they do not become irreligious men, nor atheists, nor materialists. They believe in the immortality of the human soul, in the existence of abstract principles of right and wrong, in the omnipresence of a Supreme Being, who is the creator and preserver of all things, who is absolutely just and good, to whom all men are accountable after death for deeds done in this life. They adopt a morality resembling that inculcated by Christianity, and sometimes expressly derived from the Christian Scriptures. Occasionally they listen to sermons preached from texts in the New Testament. By some they would be called deists or theists. They call themselves Brahmos or Adhi-Brahmos, members of the Brahmo-Samaj or of the Prarthana-Samaj, and quite recently they have assumed the name of Theosophists. The spread of the Brahmo sect, first in Bengal and then in other provinces, is one of the phenomena of the time in India. Keshab

Chander Sen, a man of high qualities and gifts, is among the best known of its leaders. Its nomenclature signifies the believers in the one Creator of all men and things. Its growth is understood to have been recently checked by some internal dissensions, but is probably destined to expand further. Its marriage rites have formed a subject of special legislation. The divine origin of certain castes is discarded by it, and caste is regarded merely as a human institution, like the social grades of civilized countries.

But, with all these changes, it is remarkable that educated Hindus are bestowing more attention than has ever yet been bestowed in modern times on the ideas, ethics and primeval religion, which prevailed in the prehistoric period of their ancestry. They cast a reverential retrospect towards the dawn of Hindu time, when the dayspring of genius visited their race, before mists arose to obscure the truth, or fables were invented to mar the simplicity of natural religion, or errors grew up to mislead the conscience and to sully the intuitive perceptions of right and wrong. The writings thus studied are comprehended in the name of Vedic literature, which name has now to educated Hindus the same sacred significance that Scripture has to Christians. Thus, as a result of Western education, the later and more elaborate writings of the Hindu priesthood are disregarded, while the earliest literature of Hinduism is studied with renewed veneration.

There is frequent discussion in India regarding the operation of these influences, moral and mental, upon the loyalty of the educated Natives towards the British Government and nation. Fears have been expressed lest unsatisfied ambition, want of suitable employment and habits of criticizing unreservedly the existing order of things, should gradually undermine the loyalty and gratitude which these men ought to feel. Such fears, though not fully justified by the facts, have been aroused by divers symptoms deserving attention, and have been aggravated by the conduct of at least a portion of the Native vernacular press, consisting of newspapers published in the various languages of the country.

Of the Native newspapers published in the English language, as yet few in number, some are distinguished by loyalty and good sense as well as by cultivated ability, and are creditable products of the new education; as for instance the 'Hindu Patriot' of Calcutta. Others are notable for a latitude of criticism which, though extreme, does not transgress the limits ordinarily claimed for journalism.

The vernacular newspapers, 203 in number, have a circulation of about 57,000 copies and exercise some influence. Of these many are signally and consistently loyal, while preserving independence in their thought and freedom in their criticism. Others again have been disfigured occasionally by writings which, though not actually seditious or treasonable, are objectionable in their political tendency and likely to have the effect of causing ill-feeling against British rule, whether that effect is intended or not. Some few contained treasonous passages calculated to excite hatred against British rule. It was the occurrence of these passages from time to time which induced the Government of India to pass the Vernacular Press Act, empowering the executive authorities to check the publication of such matter. This Act was generally, though not universally, approved by English opinion in India, was for the most part disapproved by educated Natives and was much discussed in England. It was not framed with any intention of repressing the free play of sentiment, fettering liberty of thought or preventing legitimate criticism of men and measures. Nor has it really been attended by any such consequence. The good sense of the Native journalists has generally spared the authorities the necessity of enforcing the Act, the procedure of which has been used only in one or two instances. The appearance of passages politically objectionable, indeed, has not entirely ceased, but has become rare and slight.

There remains, however, in too many Native newspapers a

disposition to find fault with everything and to be pleased with nothing under British rule, to form inflated notions and to ventilate impracticable suggestions. Such manifestation of discontent, though affecting the reputation of the Native press, though pointed at by its critics and regretted by its friends, should not be taken to mean more than it really does. Allowance must be made for some vagaries of thought in a nation which is being exercised in new ways of thinking. The state of the country and of the people often invites or demands criticism on the part of the Natives, it is in every way desirable that their sentiments and opinions should be unreservedly made known to the ruling classes, and such outspoken frankness should never be mistaken for disloyalty or disaffection. Though the Native vernacular press is in some degree important, yet its importance should not be exaggerated, for while it is read more or less by most of those who have any education, still its circulation is very far from reaching the mass of the people. The best and ablest Natives read chiefly the newspapers published in English.

The Indian drama is an ancient institution and still has a place among the popular recreations; though it has never obtained the same hold upon the minds of Hindus as upon the ideas of some Oriental races, the Burmese and others. There are Native theatres at the capital cities of the empire, and the plays are acted with some histrionic ability before large audiences. The pieces often relate to the classic times of Hindu history or legend. In 1876 some pieces were produced of which several portions were calculated to excite contempt for British people and disaffection against the Government. An Act was passed by the legislature empowering the executive authorities to stop the evil. The theatrical managers, however, ceased immediately from misbehaviour, and spared the authorities the necessity of putting the law into force.

There is danger of discontent being engendered in the minds of educated Natives if adequate and suitable employment does not offer itself to them in various directions. As all the arts and sciences, which have helped to make England what she is, are offered for, even pressed on, the acceptance of the Natives, it must be expected that those who do accept these advantages, will be animated by hopes and stirred by emotions, to which they were previously strangers. They will evince an increasing jealousy of any monopoly of advantage in any respect being maintained in favour of Europeans. They are already raising a cry louder and louder, the purport of which is India for the Indians. They discern, or think they discern, undue liberality in some, and unwise parsimony in other branches of the public expenditure, in reference to Native interests.

The fulfilment of these ideas is only in part within the power of the Government, being dependent on the progress of affairs in the country at large. In so far as its means permit, the Government is bound to attend, indeed has attended and is constantly attending, to this subject which is so essential to the mental and moral progress of the Natives. The most effective means at the present time consists of advancement in the public service. It is towards this that the ambition of educated Natives is too exclusively directed, and regarding this that complaints are too frequently preferred. No well-wisher of the Natives considers that the Government has yet succeeded in doing nearly all that needs to be done in this cardinal respect. Still, every candid observer must admit that the story of the measures taken by the Government for gradually improving the pay, promotion, privileges, pensions and official prospects of the Natives in all grades of its service, forms one of the brightest pages in the annals of British India. Natives have been raised to some of the highest spheres in the country, such as the legislative councils and the High Courts of judicature. The regulations have been improved, and the facilities enlarged, for their admission to that covenanted Civil Service, which is mainly filled by the highest class of European officials in the country. The improvement of the emoluments of Native officials must be gradual, and the fact of its being so gradual may diminish the sense of its real magnitude. Some of it is due to the necessity which the Government felt of remunerating its servants more highly when the money value of everything rose, and when the remuneration of all sorts of private employment increased. There remains much, however, that is attributable to the well-meaning desire of the Government to do its duty by the educated Natives. The Government is not able to provide careers for all the Natives who become educated. There is danger lest the youths from schools and colleges should resort too exclusively to overstocked professions such as the law and the public service. Graduates of a University may be seen applying for lowly-paid appointments, wandering from office to office or struggling for the practice of a petty practitioner. It were better far that such men should make careers for themselves not only in trade, business or private employ, but also in other professions which spring from the applied sciences. Such professions are in India fast expanding in connexion with civil engineering, mechanical industries, medicine, practical chemistry, botany, arboriculture, horticulture, scientific agriculture, geology, art principles applied to manufactures, and the like. But for the successful pursuit of careers, in some of these departments, more educational facilities are needed than any which as yet exist. It is in the gradual supplying of such needs that the Government can best co-operate with the enterprise of individuals or with the collective efforts of the Native community.

All tendencies towards good are assisted by the private societies, such as the National Indian Association, which shew the Natives that they are cared for, and thought of, by benevolent people, ladies and gentlemen, in England. Lasting friendships are formed in English circles by Natives who visit England, and these men communicate to their countrymen happy impressions regarding society in the centres of English life. It is especially desirable that Natives should be encouraged to finish their education in England, and for such an education the ancient Universities afford the best and highest opportunities. It was for this purpose that the Indian Institute has been recently established at Oxford through the kindly solicitude and the unremitting exertions of Professor Monier Williams.

Of late, certain symptoms of disloyalty manifested by some limited sections of certain educated classes, have caused reflections to be made against the effects of education upon Native loyalty. But that disloyalty was traceable to social and traditional circumstances quite apart from educational causes, and was checked, not fostered or encouraged, by education. There doubtless will be found disloyal individuals among the educated classes, as there are among all classes in a country subjected to foreign rule. Nevertheless, a well-founded assurance may be entertained that those Natives who have learned to think through the medium of the language, and are imbued with the literature and the philosophy of England, will bear towards the English nation that heartfelt allegiance which men may feel without at all relinquishing their own nationality. The Natives certainly are anxious to be considered loyal. Nothing wounds and irritates them more than imputations of disloyalty; and nothing gratifies them more than a frank and cordial acknowledgment of their loyalty.

This review of the mental and moral progress of the Natives shews many gleams of sunshine, as it were, in the national prospect. The peasantry retain the moral robustness for which they were famed in troublous times, have new virtues which are developed in an era of peace and security, and are, at least passively, loyal to the British Government. Some of the humblest classes are beginning to feel sentiments of independence unknown before. The trading and banking classes, though not always free from the charge of grasping usuriousness, are full of enterprising energy, and are actively loyal to the political system under which they thrive. Though, in some provinces, the upper classes are unavoidably depressed grieving over the decay of their territorial influence and fretting under the restraints of a civilized administration, they yet form in other provinces a wealthy and lettered class, whose interests are founded absolutely on the stability of British rule. The moral effects of the national education are clearly perceptible. The educated classes are happily advancing in rectitude and integrity, and are striving for self-improvement. Though the field for their employment has not yet been widened so much as they may have expected, and though the existing professions are becoming over-crowded, still their status and prospects have been greatly improved, and new professions are arising in many directions. Many of these men have divorced themselves from the superstitions by which their race had been so long enthralled; and though their religious state is far from that which is to be desired, still they have not inclined towards infidelity or materialism. They are indeed moved by political aspirations, but still feel thankful for the many improvements already effected in their condition, and hopeful for future benefits. Though intelligently alive to the import of passing events among the great powers of the world, they yet trust in the might of England to preserve her empire. Though there are occasionally symptoms of discontent and disloyalty here and there, still there is every assurance that the great majority of the men, whose minds are formed by the language, literature and science of England, will remain faithful to the British Sovereign and nation.

CHAPTER VIII.

NATIONAL EDUCATION.

Educational policy declared in 1854—Present number of scholars considered relatively to the population—Educational resources financially, both private and public—Government policy regarding superior and lower education respectively—Primary schools—Village schoolmasters—Middle schools — Want of technical instruction — Normal schools — Vernacular literature—Superior education—Universities in India—Affiliated colleges —Characteristics, moral and intellectual, of Native graduates—Instruction in medicine—In civil engineering—Degrees in science—Agricultural instruction — Schools of art — Ethical teaching — Female education— Zenana missions—Education of European and East-Indian children.

NATIONAL education, in the English acceptation of the term, was scarcely known to the Hindu polity. Much public education, indeed, there was, but it related to the national religion or to legendary history and philosophy as connected with religion, and was managed by the priests. The antechambers of the temples, the cloisters of the monasteries and the sacred groves, all had their classes of students. Private education, also, existed for the sons of the rich in the courtyards of their fathers' mansions and for the young traders in the verandahs of the ancestral counting-houses. In some of the towns and villages, unlettered schoolmasters kept private schools. Under Muhammadan rule, similar circumstances existed; and in the precincts of every mosque, the Moslem youths were instructed in the formulæ of their faith. Muhammadan kings erected, in the plains of India, collegiate structures after the fashion of Baghdad or Isfahan.

The earlier educational efforts of the East India Company were wanting in definite aim. Among the pioneers, David Hare should be honourably mentioned; his philanthropic devotion has caused his name to be a household word among the Natives of Calcutta. Formerly there was fear lest the British officers should work upon the old lines of Native education. This was dissipated by Macaulay's famous minute against the teaching of false science, false history, false philosophy. The first effective efforts to diffuse real education among the peasantry were made by Thomason, the Lieutenant-Governor of the North-western Provinces. It was, however, the despatch of Sir Charles Wood (now Lord Halifax) in 1854, which formally prescribed a system of public instruction, and which is regarded as the magna charta of national education in British India.

Twenty-five years have since elapsed, during which time some considerable progress has been effected. There are now about two millions of scholars. This number, if taken by itself, may seem to represent a grand educational result. It is, however, found to be small, if compared with the number of those who must be of a schoolgoing age, in a population of 190 millions of souls. With the great majority of the present scholars, too, the instruction is only rudimentary.

The grant made yearly by the Government in India for education, amounts to £800,000, or about one-fortieth part of the net available revenues. This, however, by no means represents the total of expenditure incurred jointly by the State and the people for education. There are local cesses and rates levied for educational purposes, contributions by municipal corporations and other bodies, subscriptions and donations from private munificence, also the fees levied from scholars of all degrees. A considerable sum is exacted as the condition upon which the grants in aid are given by the State. The primary schools are in part supported by small subscriptions collected from the villagers; this private income may be small for each school, yet for so many schools, nearly 40,000 in number, it must be large in its aggregate. There are many schools, nearly 23,000 in all, which though inspected by public officers are not aided pecuniarily by the State, and for these there must be a large expenditure of unknown amount. Lastly, there is much private tuition, of which no returns are received. Thus if the total expenditure, incurred by the State and the people together on education, be computed, its aggregate must be greatly in excess of the State contribution of £800,000 and may be nearly double that sum. Still it must, even if it should mount up to two millions sterling, be regarded as small for so great a country.

Encouragement may be derived from the fact that the numbers of schools and scholars has heretofore shown a satisfactory and unfailing progress year by year. The progress has, however, been arrested in many provinces by the recent famine and pestilence, and is not likely to improve essentially for some time to come in those districts which have been so grievously distressed.

Much controversy has been raised respecting the relative claims upon the State, of primary and of high education. Many argue that it is the duty of Government to bestow its educational grants upon the humbler and more helpless classes, leaving the middle and especially the upper classes to defray their own charges for instruction. These regard with jealousy the sums spent on superior teaching, and would desire to see a part of them transferred to the primary schools. Many persons, including probably a majority of educated Natives, urge, on the other hand, that the grants allowed for high education ought not to be diminished. These expect that the enlightened few will scatter light among their fellow-countrymen, as the rays of the rising sun first touch the mountain-top and rest there for a while before penetrating to the dark valleys below. The Government, however, does not lean unduly towards one side of the argument or the other. It fosters all kinds of education, whether superior, primary or intermediate, according to the needs or circumstances of each. It considers that they are almost inter-dependent and that they should be made to co-operate and concur in action. Primary education supplies material for secondary education which leads up to superior or high education, which again elevates the tone of everything below it, and supplies the fittest instruments for all other sorts of instruction. Indeed, without high education, it would be impossible to find the means of teaching efficiently the schools of the lower grades.

Doubt has been expressed in many quarters from time to time whether the Government in India is not relying too much upon its own direct efforts, and too little on the grant-in-aid system prescribed in Lord Halifax's despatch of 1854. Certainly the principle, of employing the State contribution as much as possible in the development of grants-in-aid, is fully understood by the authorities in India. The observance of it, in respect to the higher education especially, will be more and more complete as the Natives become better qualified for self-help in these matters. Meanwhile the agitation, which sometimes springs up respecting this subject, proves highly beneficial, as keeping the attention of the authorities fixed on the fundamental maxim laid down in 1854.

Objections come from the same quarters regarding the expenditure upon the upper grades of the educational establishments. Such outlay is, however, incurred chiefly for inspection by European officials, an object absolutely essential in the present condition of the national education. Without such inspection the schools would deteriorate and the teaching would lose its thoroughness.

The national education has three branches, I. primary, II. secondary or middle, and III. superior. As the State has accepted the responsibility of guiding the public instruction, its first duty relates to the determination of the standards for the three branches.

By the method known as "payments by results," both masters and pupils are induced to follow any standard which may be prescribed. If the master be a salaried servant of the State, he receives greater or less remuneration according as greater or smaller numbers of scholars pass according to the standard. Thus the masters are obliged to attend to the scholars of moderate or indifferent ability; and the welfare of the weak pupils is guarded as well as that of the strong.

Scholarships are offered for competition among the scholars, which are stipends virtually affording to the holders the benefit of a free education, and which are tenable in schools of a grade superior to that of the schools in which they were won. Thus a chance is offered to a poor boy of genius to raise himself by power of mind, which was never afforded under Native rule. A gifted peasant-boy may, while in a primary school, win a scholarship tenable in a middle school, may there again win another scholarship tenable in a superior school, where he may acquire a stipend which will carry him through the University course.

Primary schools have now been organized in almost all parts of the empire. Generally there is a school of this kind for every large village, and in localities where the villages are small, for each little group of hamlets. Thus it may be said that a school exists within reach of nearly all the peasants. Nevertheless, a vast number of poor children grow up in ignorance, never entering a schoolroom; and in localities where one school is now to be found there ought to be several. Many well-informed and benevolent persons think that the Government should redouble its efforts in this direction.

Primary education, in its humblest form, should be adapted to the rudest minds among the peasantry, so as to gather into its fold as many hundreds of thousands as it can. As it takes root and grows, some additions to the instruction are cautiously made, enough to enable the children to improve themselves in their own sphere of life and to become more efficient in their humble calling, as they have but a short time, during their tender age, from their fifth to their twelfth or thirteenth year. Within that time must be learnt what they ever are to learn from books, before the day arrives when they go forth to help their parents in the daily toil.

But to impart even this small modicum of instruction, within so short a space of time, to young children of lowly capacity, there must be schoolmasters much better than any who can be ordinarily found in the Indian villages. Therefore the State undertakes the training of village schoolmasters, and insists on their possessing certificates of competent qualification. The rustic teacher in India represented a time-honoured institution, but he was dull and uninstructed. Nowadays the ancient office is filled by men of a new stamp, and the production of such men is among the first fruits of the British system.

The instruction in the primary schools is imparted solely in the vernacular. In the secondary or middle schools, it is imparted partly in the vernacular and partly in English.

These secondary schools exist for the middle classes of the people, including the small landholder who should learn mensuration in his fields and should master the village accounts, the trader who should be practised in arithmetical calculation, the clerk who should qualify himself for subordinate employment in a private or public office, the better sort of artisan who should acquire the knowledge necessary for success in his craft. These schools are in a tolerably satisfactory condition; and are regarded by the general public, probably also by the educational authorities, as the best among the British Indian schools.

Some technical schools have been commenced at different places in each division of the empire, where Natives may learn in their youth the theory and practice of useful trades, as young men are taught these things in Germany or Switzerland. Still, it is greatly to be regretted that so little has been done as yet in India for technical instruction. There are European manufactures, in which mechanical appliances are much used and for which a knowledge of mechanics is needed in the subordinate employés; there are railways where many subordinate places might be filled by Natives if they were technically educated; there are many scientific departments wher

Natives might be well employed if they were but qualified. All this ought to convince both the Government, and the Natives themselves, that if young Natives were to receive technical education they would find new employment, and that such employment would be developed from the very fact of Native talent becoming available. Of late years the Government has obtained a more practical grasp than formerly of this important subject, and in various parts of it progress is being made.

It is acknowledged that when English instruction is offered to the Natives, they should be thoroughly grounded in their own language. While many learn English, the more the better, still many can obtain their education only through the medium of their vernacular. Hence a new vernacular literature has to be created; and such a literature will be among the most enduring monuments of British rule. Some Natives make translations in the vernacular of the ancient Sanscrit poems; others compose original verses of considerable merit. On various branches of useful knowledge books have been, and are being, written in the vernacular languages, some of which are abstracts while others are translations *in extenso* of English works. Original works are brought out by Native authors, who, having mastered a subject for themselves, expound it in oriental mode of thought and expression, for the benefit of their countrymen. Another object, set before Native authors in the vernacular, is the preparation of text books in the physical sciences, and of science primers on the model of those which are prepared in England by some of the best living writers.

The normal schools, or training institutions for vernacular schoolmasters, form a part of the secondary education. These institutions become colleges for cultivating the vernacular languages. The resources of Sanskrit, the ancient language of India, with its copiousness, precision and flexibility, are adapted to the diffusion of modern knowledge among the Natives. The dead languages of elder times are used to preserve purity and expressive vigour in the living dialects. The Natives are taught that in order to speak and write their own language well, they must have some acquaintance with the classic tongue of their ancestors.

Superior education, mainly in English, is controlled by the three Universities of Calcutta, Madras and Bombay, incorporated by enactments of the Indian legislature. An institution exists in the Panjab also, which exercises functions like those of a University, and to which the status of a University will probably be ere long accorded.

A University in India is a body for examining candidates for degrees, and for conferring degrees. It has the power of prescribing text books, standards of instruction and rules of procedure, but is not an institution for teaching. Its governance and management are vested in a body of fellows, some of whom are ex-officio, being the chief European functionaries of the State. The remainder are appointed by the Government, being generally chosen as representative men in respect of eminent learning, scientific attainment, official position, social status or personal worth. Thus the fellows, being a mixed body of Europeans and Natives, comprise all that is best and wisest in that division of the empire to which the University belongs, and fairly represent most of the phases of thought and philosophic tendencies observable in the country. The fellows in their corporate capacity form the Senate, a meeting of which is styled a convocation. The affairs of the University are conducted by the Syndicate, consisting of a limited number of members elected from among the fellows. The business of the Syndicate is performed by a certain number of Faculties, consisting of persons elected from among its members. The Faculties ordinarily pertain to the subjects in which degrees are conferred, namely literæ humaniores, law, medicine and civil engineering; a degree in natural and physical science has recently been added. There are degrees of Bachelor of Arts and Master of Arts, and corresponding degrees in medicine and civil engineering.

Although the University exercises the functions assigned to

it by law quite independently, still much influence in its affairs pertains to the Government. The head of the Government, its members and its principal officers being ex-officio fellows and all the remaining fellows being chosen by the Government, the governing body is necessarily in harmony with the policy of the State and in consonance with its principles. It is desired that shades of reasonable opinion should be duly represented in the body of fellows, and the relations between the Government and the several Universities are excellent.

Certain schools, some belonging to Government others to private bodies, are designated as qualified to prepare scholars for passing the examination for entrance to the Universities, and these are generally styled high schools.

Certain colleges, some maintained by Government others by private societies, are authorized by the Universities to prepare candidates for the examination for degrees, and are thence declared to be affiliated. There are several of such colleges in each division of the empire. An affiliated college may either receive undergraduates only, that is those who have passed the entrance examination of the University; or it may receive classes of scholars for other standards, in addition to the undergraduates. Thus some colleges are schools with college classes attached to them, that is, classes consisting of students for degrees: while some possess solely a collegiate character, having none but undergraduates. At the several capitals of the empire, the Government maintains collegiate institutions with principals almost always European, and professors partly European and partly Native, all highly qualified. The several religious communities, Roman Catholic and Protestant, also maintain excellent collegiate institutions, all, however, receiving grants in aid from Government. There are, as yet, no examples of collegiate institutions maintained by Natives without any assistance from the State.

The fact that the Government in India maintains colleges

of its own at all, is the subject of complaint in some quarters. It is urged that the efforts of the State in this direction should be confined to making grants-in-aid to the colleges belonging to private societies, that these private colleges are suffering from the competition of the Government colleges and that the Government colleges at the Presidency cities of Calcutta, Madras and Bombay ought to be closed. Doubtless the Government would gladly be relieved of the task of affording the higher kinds of education, as soon as the country could perform that duty for itself. The opportunity of such relief may arrive some day, but is apparently yet distant. Meanwhile, liberal assistance is given to the private colleges, missionary or other, which are both numerous and flourishing. It is not probable that the Government would be willing at present to close its colleges, some of which in the interior of the country occupy ground which would otherwise be vacant. The authorities at the Presidency colleges do not attempt to undermine the missionary colleges by charging lower fees, on the contrary they charge somewhat higher fees than those of any private institutions. The missionary bodies, together with other sections of the general community, are duly represented in the senates of the several Universities. Nothing can be more desirable than a liberal encouragement on the part of the State to all private institutions, including missionary colleges. The complaints made or the recommendations urged, in reference thereto, will prove beneficial, as causing the eyes of the authorities to be turned towards the changes which may be gradually introduced.

The number of the Natives who enter the Universities, after passing an examination, is satisfactorily large; but the number of the Natives who take degrees is unsatisfactorily small. It is considered by Natives that a man, who has entered the University, is fully a member of it, and that such membership is sufficient. The Government itself has often failed to discourage this notion, and has even sometimes encouraged it by according a certain status to those who have passed the entrance examination only. Of those who enter, not more than one-fifth prosecute their studies in order to obtain degrees. An intermediate examination between the entering and the taking of degrees, called the "First Arts examination," was instituted by the authorities with the view of testing the progress of the undergraduates after passing the entrance. Thereupon many Natives contented themselves with passing that examination alone, in the belief that by so doing they had taken a sort of degree. Still, many Natives yearly do take the degree of Bachelor, while a few only obtain that of Master. It is detrimental to the position of the Universities that their alumni should consist mainly of undergraduates. The authorities ought to insist that the ultimate object of these great institutions, namely the taking of degrees, shall be attained. If the fulfilment of this object shall continue to be delayed, the remedy is to a great extent in the hands of Government. Greater precautions than heretofore should be taken to prevent an educational status being accorded to undergraduates, and to reserve for graduates only (with certain specified exceptions) the admission to the higher grades of the public service. A policy of this description has to some extent been adopted, and if it be persevered in, a marked increase will ere long be observable in the number of candidates for degrees.

The intellectual and moral characteristics of the alumni of these Universities, who now form a numerous class in Native society, are worthy of observation. It is allowed on all sides that these young men possess refined faculties, retentiveness of memory, power of intense application, aptitude for receiving and expressing ideas. Above all this, they follow an improved standard of rectitude and integrity, as already explained in the foregoing chapter on mental and moral progress. But it is perceived by their critics and acknowledged by their friends that they have several salient faults, such as immaturity of thought, fondness for rhetorical exaggeration, substitution of borrowed ideas for original reflection, subjection of the reasoning power to the imagination, inaccuracy of observation, and the like. These faults, which are common more or less to the youths of all nations in the world, have in India grown and expanded from special causes operating for a very long time, and will not be speedily cured. Consequently many persons apprehend that much of the higher education is superficial where it ought to be fundamental, and airy where it ought to be substantial. This apprehension probably renders employers of intellectual labour less anxious, than they might otherwise be, to have recourse to the young Natives who belong to the Universities. The authorities would do well to impress on the alumni of the Universities the conviction that a general education, if it be really efficient, should enable a man to apply himself to the acquisition of any sort of knowledge, however novel or alien it may be, and to assimilate into his mental system the ideas peculiar to any profession he may enter. If the young men will act up to these maxims they will be more competent than heretofore to turn their abilities to profitable account. But if they continue prone to imagine that, after having learnt so much at college they have little or nothing more to learn in life, they must fail to reap the fruits of their laborious education.

One of the means for correcting these faults is an increased attention in the Universities to pure science and applied sciences.

It is a happy circumstance that two of the sciences, medicine and civil engineering, have been successfully cultivated in all the Universities.

The three medical colleges of India, namely those of Calcutta, Madras and Bombay, are truly noble institutions, justly to be regarded with national pride. In the wards of the hospitals attached to the colleges, the clinical instruction is nearly all that can be desired, and the anatomical instruction is thorough.

The chemical instruction, though not enough to lead the student into the higher walks of the science, is practical so far as it goes. The botanical instruction is efficient in a like degree, and is given partly in botanic gardens. The instruction in ophthalmic surgery and in midwifery is given in wards specially constructed for these branches of the profession. Besides the theoretical physiology taught in the lecture-rooms, practical physiology is explained by trained demonstrators. Theoretical pathology is well taught, while practical pathology is in some of the colleges taught by trained demonstrators, but not fully as yet in other colleges. The Natives who pass through these colleges and receive university degrees, being styled licentiates, are medical men in the professional sense of the term.

Besides these fully qualified Native medical men from the medical colleges, there are Natives from the several medical schools who are certificated as hospital assistants. Several such medical schools exist in each division of the empire and they are very largely attended. The alumni are not indeed educated completely, but they are competently instructed up to a certain point and their professional training is so far efficient. They are grounded in surgery, medicine, and materia medica; and they have received clinical instruction. They are wanted as assistants to medical men everywhere, being especially useful in the interior of the country where medical men cannot be expected to reside, and where the sickness and the medical needs, in so great a population, exceed the powers of any medical staff that could possibly be provided. They can do much to dispense medicines for ordinary ailments among the rural poor, and can apply the known remedies which are needed when epidemics prevail or pestilence breaks out.

The Natives, both the medical men and the certificated hospital assistants, educated in the medical colleges and schools, have already acquired the confidence, and are still further rising in the estimation, of their countrymen. They are extensively employed not only by the Government, but also by municipal corporations and local committees separate from the State. They are fast obtaining a private practice, of a large and lucrative character, superseding the ancient profession of medicine according to the Oriental method. There is not as yet any regulation prohibiting men from practising medicine unless they possess diplomas from British authorities, and thus the practitioners under the Oriental system are still free to practise their art. These indigenous practitioners, though generally unskilled in surgery and ignorant of anatomy, are often skilful in the discrimination of disease, and are always well acquainted with the uses of medicinal herbs.

In civil engineering also, the State education has met with considerable success. The extension of public works throughout the Empire has created a large demand for Native civil engineers, and also for engineering assistants and overseers. There are colleges and schools for civil engineering in every division of the empire. Among these is included the college at Rurki on the Ganges, named, after its founder and promoter, the Thomason College of Civil Engineering. The college of Poona, besides teaching all that relates to civil engineering, affords instruction in other scientific branches, and is fast becoming a college of science for Western India. These colleges afford excellent instruction for both the superior and the subordinate grades of the profession. Extensive workshops are attached to them, in order that the instruction may be practical. For the same reason, the pupils undergo much professional exercise in the field. The Natives prove to be competent surveyors and very good draughtsmen; in some of the higher branches of the survey department, they have acquired distinction. That they will be most useful as assistants to European engineers is already manifest. Some of them have become civil engineers in the best sense of the term. Others, again, have failed when tried by the hard and critical labours incidental to the construction of public works. It would be premature to state the extent to which Natives will in the future be employed for the severer duties relating to these operations. They will certainly fill a place which, if not the highest or the most difficult, will be replete with opportunities of usefulness.

It has often been recommended that the Universities should confer degrees in other scientific branches, and should re-arrange the educational courses with this object. This view has at length found favour with the Universities, in which the literary and philosophic element has hitherto been stronger than the scientific. It was argued that a Native cannot do better than obtain at college a thoroughly good general education as a groundwork, that with this he may go forth into the world with his mind braced and disciplined, and may then prosecute with advantage any profession, scientific or other. In answer thereto it was urged that this system may doubtless be efficacious for some important professions, such as the public service, the law, and many sorts of private employment, but is not equally suitable for those who are to follow scientific professions, as botanists, chemists, mechanical engineers or scientific agriculturists. This would be proved by the analogy of the plan pursued with medicine and civil engineering; and if the future profession of the student is to be science in other branches, he must make use of his time in college for this purpose. The collegiate course, as prescribed by the Universities, comprises five years; under any circumstances these are the only years in a man's life which can be devoted to superior education, and much of them must be given to science if he is to become really scientific. This time is the spring season of his mind, when the faculties are most elastic and the memory most receptive, which should be partly employed in science and should be enjoyed while it lasts, for to him it will never return. In respect to the discipline of the mind, scientific pursuits afford an excellent general education, as training the faculties to habits of order, observation, method and classification. The dictum of Faraday may be quoted to the effect that "the study of natural science is a glorious school for the mind."

Instruction in scientific agriculture remains to be added to the system of State education. The Government of Madras has set an example in this respect, by employing a gentleman trained in the Agricultural Institution at Cirencester, Mr. Robertson, to found and establish an agricultural school for southern India. This school is furnished with apparatus and appliances, sufficient land is attached to it for experiments, and many students from the agricultural community are attracted to it. Some of the best students, who pass the examinations in this school, are appointed to be teachers in agricultural class rooms in other parts of the country. The Bombay Government has followed this example, by attaching to the scientific college at Poona a class for superior instruction in agriculture with suitable examinations, and by establishing classes for the same instruction in a lower degree at several places in western India. A department of agriculture has for some years worked well in the North-western Provinces, but does not seem to have attended particularly to agricultural education. Whatever steps have been taken in southern and western India, are but the small beginnings of what ought to be a widely diffused system. There is no branch of study likely to be so useful or so popular with the Natives. Interesting experiments in agriculture are made from time to time and prove futile; model farming is undertaken, and after a brief existence sometimes fails in a manner which discredits science and repels, instead of attracting, the attention of the people. These misfortunes arise because there are not enough persons to conduct the experiments, or the farms, to a successful result. Even if success were attained, the neighbouring peasantry would not be intelligent enough to appreciate it or to imitate its processes. The Natives themselves are awakening to a sense of the importance of improving agriculture, the staple industry of the country, and would willingly follow the guidance of the Government in this direction.

Schools of Art for the Natives have been established in the several divisions of the empire, and have been superintended by competent artists obtained from England. This branch of education received a great impulse from the exertions of Sir Bartle Frere when Governor of Bombay. Many young men thus receive artistic instruction and some æsthetic culture, all which proves most helpful in several professions followed by them as portrait-painters, photographers, lithographers, engravers, wood and ivory carvers, ornamental designers and draughtsmen, and more especially as architects. Thus, the art class rooms are well filled. The instruction embodies the principles applicable to art in all climes and the practice most approved in European art; but does not disdain the Native art. It encourages the student to fix his gaze on the antique remains of Indian art, which flourished at times when the national imagination was in its prime and its finer faculties soared highest; when Asoka graved on the rocks the edicts of duty and the Buddhists hewed sacred chambers out of the strata on the mountain sides; when the Brahminists covered their fanes with carvings which make bygone races of men live again; when the Muhammadans reared the tall minarets for prayer and the domes in memory of the dead. It aims at explaining the causes of the surpassing beauty of these old works, so that the same principles may govern the efforts of the present generation. It recognises the fact that inferior European art has sometimes been incongruously introduced into India, the effect of which, though meant to be elevating, must really be debasing and injurious to the opening faculties of the Native mind.

Above and beyond all the sorts of instruction, which have yet been indicated, is the instruction in ethics, or the science of human duty. While the Native youths are taught human duty comprising the relations of man to man, they are necessarily taught something of their duty towards God, although the teachers are precluded from adverting to religion. One of the effects of good teaching in history or literature must be to inculcate, always incidentally and often directly, much of the general duty of man. Thus, happily much is effected in this most important direction. The instruction might, however, be better systematized than it now is; sometimes text books are prescribed for it and sometimes not; in some institutions it is as an obligatory subject, in others it is optional. These variations in practice are found only in the Government institutions; the subject is obligatory in the missionary institutions. It were well if the several Universities should see fit to take up the matter in an uniform manner. Their action determines the teaching in the colleges and high schools, the example of these superior institutions is sure to be followed by the middle-class institutions, and ultimately by the primary schools, until a system of national instruction in ethics is established. The Natives will certainly be the willing subjects of such teaching. Many of them, while thankfully acknowledging all that has been done in this direction, do yet lament that a more systematic effort is not made to unfold before the minds of the young those eternal principles of right and wrong, which serve as beacons for the due conduct of life, and which ought specially to be included in an educational system that unavoidably excludes religious teaching.

Female education among the Natives is receiving much encouragement from the British Government; the matter is a delicate one, and any undue haste or even the semblance of pressure might, by rousing opposition, cause retrogression instead of progress.

Under the system of seclusion which has always been enforced in respect of Native ladies, it is difficult to ascertain what their intellectual condition is in the present, as compared with the past. By all accounts, they were generally uneducated in former times: some educated ladies there doubtless were, but such instances must have been rare. Nevertheless, in historic times, queens and princesses have signalized themselves by patriotism, by heroism, and even by statecraft. The empress Nur Jehan, immortalized by the poem of Lala Rukh, was not a creation of fancy, but an important historical character. The Roshanara Begum, sister of an emperor, long exercised great influence over State affairs. The noble conduct of the princess Chand Bibi of Ahmednagar has been the subject of a historical romance. When the Rajputs died fighting for their country, the conduct of the women was as brave as that of the men. Among the Mahrattas, the women of rank were generally conspicuous in political affairs. For instance, the widowed mother of Sivaji incited her son to deeds of daring for the sake of the Hindu faith. In later days some of them were famed for charity and good works, for example, the princess Ahalya Bai in Malwa, a devout and benevolent lady. Recently in Bengal, the person foremost in good works, in the dispensation of the noblest charity, in liberal consideration towards tenantry, retainers and dependants, in times of difficulty, was a woman, the Maharani Surnomaye, who has been honoured not only with Native titles but also with a British decoration. The Muhammadan princess of Bhopal has in time of danger proved a loyal adherent of the British cause and in time of peace a capable ruler. Every British officer who is accredited to princely houses among the Natives, knows that in the palace there are Native ladies who, though unseen, exert a real influence upon all negotiations, and faithfully uphold the dignity and interest of the families to which they belong. In short, it is manifest that the women, though by the Hindu social code declared to be dependent, and by the Muhammadans hardly acknowledged, are yet almost as influential in India as in other countries, even though they be uneducated. And this reason besides all other reasons, points to the desirability of their being educated. The fact of so many Hindu widows (Satis) having, up to comparatively recent times, immolated themselves on the funeral pyres of their husbands, a practice which would still be followed by many, were it not prohibited by British laws, proves a force of will, and a power of self-devotion to a principle, which may be productive of happy results if guided aright by education. As yet, the influence of the women has been but too often adverse to enlightenment, and favourable to retrogression. In most households, the female apartments are reputed to be the very home of ignorant superstition. The circumstance of a young Native having been brought up too much in the "Zenana," that is, under the tuition of his female relations, is proverbially regarded as a sign that he will prove illiberal and bigoted.

It is probable that a great improvement has taken place, in these respects, throughout Native society, and is moving onward with increased speed year by year. Instances are, probably, common of educated Hindus, whose mothers were quite unlettered, and whose wives can barely read and write, but whose daughters are being fully educated. In the upper and middle classes, the mothers of the last generation were mostly uneducated, those of the rising generation are educated partly, and those of the next generation will be educated altogether. At all the capital cities in the empire, there are female schools of a superior description, at which girls of the Brahmin caste attend, setting an example likely to be followed by other castes. The name of Drinkwater Bethune is honourably associated with an institution at Calcutta, for the education of Native girls. The Muhammadans as yet are less disposed to send their daughters to school. The Parsis, however, are zealous in this respect, indeed hardly less solicitous than Europeans. Among the Parsis, Mr. Manockji Cursetji has been most zealous in establishing the Alexandra Institute at Bombay. With all these institutions there are committees of Natives, gentlemen of various nationalities, whose social position carries weight with the community and whose presence proves that the movement does not solely originate with Europeans. There is much private tuition, and in many houses instruction is being given at home to the girls who by social customs are prevented from receiving it in class rooms, or from joining any educational institution. It was to aid in this work that the Zenana missions have been established, in which many highly qualified European ladies are engaged. It is only by such agency that the quality of this domestic education can be improved or be prevented from degenerating into a formal and torpid state. The highest importance is attached to the enlightened efforts made by European Associations in this direction, without which many well-born girls in influential stations would remain without real education being extended to that age when the mind is most receptive of knowledge. Female schools are springing up in the interior of the country; there are, probably, few towns without a school of this description. These schools are attended in the first instance by girls of high caste, whereby popularity is ensured; if they had been attended only by girls of humbler castes, they would never have gained influence. Here again co-operation is obtained from Native gentlemen, who prove their sincerity by sending their own daughters to school. In the primary schools of the humblest description, classes are opened for peasant girls of a tender age; and although such instruction may not amount to much, it produces some effect upon the peasantry.

For the diffusion of female education, the first care of its supporters, with the countenance or assistance of the State, has been to found normal schools for the training of Native schoolmistresses. Some of these institutions are, with the help of private societies, proving very successful, and sending forth many mistresses yearly, whose services are immediately engaged on good salaries for schools at other places. The social or religious prohibition of the re-marriage of Hindu widows, which is not yet removed or has been but slightly relaxed, consigns to an aimless and objectless existence many women, who are now beginning to find a suitable career in the educational profession.

On the whole, female education, though not as yet represented by large statistics and numbering only some tens of thousands of pupils, has made a real start, and will shew progress yearly. The happiest national effect has been produced by the example of those Native ladies who have individually evinced talent in general literature, and in poetic composition.

An equally potent influence is exercised by the European ladies who in their well-spent lives shew to their Indian sisters the visible blessings of enlightenment, and the elevation to which the female mind can rise when enjoying educational advantages. Prominent among these was Mary Carpenter, upon whose monument it has been written that "Taking to heart the grievous lot of Oriental women, in the last decade of her life, she four times went to India, and awakened an active interest in their education and training for serious purposes."

A review of national education in India would not be complete without some notice of the instruction which is being afforded to European and East Indian children. The introduction of railways and of various industries, in which many Europeans are employed, has caused the number of these children to increase greatly of late years. The parents often succumb to the illnesses incidental to tropical climates, as they are unable to obtain the changes of scene and air which prove so restorative to their more fortunate countrymen. Thus, there are many children, either orphans or bereft of one parent. A fatherless or a motherless European child in poor circumstances, if it cannot be sent to England, is, in India, exposed to grave dangers. The disadvantages which surround closer and closer the position of the East Indian section of the community, till it is quite beset with difficulty, have been already mentioned. Thus, there are several classes of Europeans or East Indians, who are domiciled in India, and must make it the home of their children, or who are unable to send them to England for education, or who, for some special reason, prefer to keep them in India. Among the children thus situated, there are many helpless ones, who if not cared for by the State or by the public, would grow up in ignorance. If such cases were to become numerous, some discredit would be reflected upon the ruling race in the eyes of an alien population. Humane considerations have always prompted the Government and the British community to make provision for the education of those who, from their birth or extraction, have peculiar claims upon European sympathy. The several Christian communities, therefore, both Protestant and Roman Catholic, have established schools for the children of their members, whether boys or girls. Originally these institutions were placed at the capital cities and at the principal stations in the interior of the country, and most of them are still maintained there. At the instance of Bishop Cotton, schools were established at the European settlements in the Himalayas, such as Massuri, Naini-Tâl, Darjiling and elsewhere, so that the children might benefit by the cool climate and escape from the heat of the plains. A similar principle has been followed in the Presidencies of Madras and Bombay. The Guaranteed Railway Companies have also performed their share in the good work. All the institutions receive grants-in-aid from the Government. At the colleges maintained at Calcutta, Madras and Bombay, by private societies, Europeans obtain an excellent education and study for the University examinations. They are also admitted to the Government colleges, though these colleges are maintained for the sake of the Natives. At some places also, technical schools have been established where Europeans learn useful trades and handicrafts. Thus, there are many flourishing institutions, supervised by the clergy of all denominations, reproducing in a strange land the happy scenes so frequent in England. The untiring efforts and powerful advocacy devoted by Archdeacon Baly to this humane cause will long be remembered with gratitude.

Nevertheless, the future of the rising generation of the white people in India and of the East Indian has moovd the sympathy and excited the anxiety of many excellent persons, clergy and others, whose opinions are entitled to respect. Statistical enquiries have been made by the Government at the capital cities, and it has been found that although few children of pure European birth are absent from school, still a number of East Indian children are in a degraded and neglected condition, the parents belonging to very humble classes. The Government has taken the case of these children into special consideration and has urged the several communities of Europeans to supply the need, promising them grants-in-aid. It would be difficult for the State to directly undertake the gratuitous education of such children, as the social circumstances do not admit of rates being imposed and school-boards established after the English model. But the existing institutions belonging to private societies are, with the State assistance, able to provide education if the parents will but exert themselves to obtain it.

Thus, the natural education is exercising an almost universal influence over the upper classes of the Natives, is producing a considerable effect on the middle section of the community, and is slowly though surely spreading among the mass of the people. Still, the extension of primary education among the peasantry continues to be one of those needs which cry out for sustained efforts on the part of the State. The instruction in some branches of applied science is successful but in pure science is inadequate; while technical education is in its infancy. The English language is being spoken more and more by educated Natives with purity of pronunciation and colloquial fluency. The general education is yielding fruit in respect of rectitude in conduct, zeal in performance of duty, and faithfulness in loyalty. During the visit of the Prince of Wales, the Natives rendered the worthiest homage to the royal presence by founding, in various parts of the country, educational institutions in memory of that gracious occasion.

CHAPTER IX.

RELIGIOUS ESTABLISHMENTS AND MISSIONS.

The State Church in India—Maintenance of religion by Native rulers—Their religious endowments in part maintained by the British Government—Religious establishments of the Portuguese—Attitude of the British Government respecting religion—Christian missions in Native States—The Roman Catholic Church in India—Protestant missions—Unabated efforts of religious societies—Approximate statistics of results—High authorities in favour of missions—Character of Native Christians—Prospects of Native Church—Special missions from Oxford and Cambridge—Moral effect of missions generally.

FOR duly appreciating the religious establishments it is desirable to consider the position of Christianity in India, in comparison with that of other religions. Attention in England is sometimes drawn to the State Church in India, as being an institution maintained, for the benefit of Europeans, from the public revenues. It seems to be thought by some that the maintenance of the Church from these funds involves an injustice to the Natives. The Native rulers, however, always accepted the duty of giving substantial support to religion; each dynasty maintained its own faith, besides allowing maintenance to the other forms of faith it found existing in the country.

For the due discharge of its practical duties, the British Government is bound to care for the spiritual needs of its servants as well as for their bodily safety. Medical establishments are maintained, and that measure is always deemed to be right and needful. The ecclesiastical establishment stands on the same footing. The servants of the Indian Government are peculiarly situated; they are, for the most part, isolated, and are unavoidably migratory, being moved about from station to station according to the exigencies of the public service. It would be impossible for them to sustain a religious establishment, and if that were not provided by the State, they would be left without any religious ministration. Apart from the clergy who minister to the European troops and the military officers, the clerical establishments are on the lowest and most economical scale, compatible with supplying the wants of the European community even in the matter of marriages and baptisms. It would have been a scandal if the Government had omitted to provide facilities for the rites common to all civilized societies, which facilities cannot, under the special circumstances of India, be otherwise provided. The cost amounts to only £150,000 a year for the whole country.

Perhaps it is not sufficiently remembered that several religions have from time to time immemorial, received endowments from the Native dynasties, which endowments are in part maintained under British rule.

In ancient times the Buddhist monasteries of India, some of the most widely extended monastic institutions that ever existed in any age or among any nation, absorbed a large portion of the public revenues. When the Buddhist system was finally subdued, and superseded by the Brahminical system throughout the country, the religious property and the conventual wealth lapsed to the Brahmins, a priestly class with unbounded influence in secular affairs. The Hindus, having abjured Buddhism and embraced Brahminism, continued the practice of bountifully endowing the Hindu religion. Temples were raised in every quarter, with numerous establishments. These were supported in part by voluntary offerings of devotees, but in part also by public revenues assigned to them by the sovereign and derived from land. Ecclesiastical charity was dispensed to the destitute and miserable of all castes; but especially to the needy of the priestly caste. The duty of feeding Brahmins was incumbent on every pious Hindu; but it was among the most sacred of the kingly duties of a Hindu prince. For this purpose also public revenues were assigned. Ultimately in every rich parish or village the revenues of some fertile fields, leviable by the State, were transferred to the priests. Thus it came to pass that a considerable amount of land revenue, the mainstay of the State income, was alienated in favour of the priests and the temples, avowedly as an endowment of religion.

The Muhammadans, on their conquest of India, respected for the most part the State endowments of the Hindu religion. Despite the Moslem hatred of Hindu idolatry, they dreaded the fanaticism and unpopularity which would be aroused among the idolaters by any attempt at interference. They sometimes did, however, commit deeds of violence against idolatry. In so far as they acted thus, they struck deep at the root of their own power. Then they proceeded to endow their own Moslem religion in the same manner; the mosques arose in all quarters with land revenue assigned for their support, by way of endowment. Then sprung up the adoration of saints and the canonization of royal and distinguished dead. Thus saintly shrines and domed mausolea arose; and these also were endowed with assignments of land revenue.

When upon the decline and decadence of the Mogul power the Mahratta empire arose, its founder Sivaji incited his followers by recounting such religious grievances as could be alleged on the part of Hindus, and promised them that the endowments of the Hindu temples should be augmented and that the State maintenance of Brahmins should be more liberal than ever.

The British Government, on its accession to power, found in existence a multitude of endowments, granted by its Native predecessors for the services of religion, and consisting mainly of assignments of the land revenue. It maintained these endowments, to some extent, regarding them as the property of religious institutions. It investigated the origin, the title-deeds, the method of management and application of the funds, in all these cases, so as to guard the State against fraud or imposition. This investigation was elaborate and embraced tens of thousands of cases. Its result, as might be expected, was that some of the assignments were disallowed for want of sufficient authority, and others were contracted or reduced, as being in excess of the original authorization. Still, many of the assignments stood the test, and they now exist under British guarantee. For some time British officers continued to supervise the management of certain among these institutions, following the practice of their Native predecessors. But as such supervision was open to obvious objections, it has been discontinued. The conduct of the British Government in these matters was actuated not only by sound policy but also by a true spirit of Christian charity and toleration. Nor have its motives in this respect ever been misconstrued by the Natives, though many of them would doubtless be pleased if the Government were to do more than it actually has done in this direction.

In the seventeenth and eighteenth centuries the Portuguese had in India flourishing settlements, where much wealth was accumulated in churches and in conventual establishments which comprised great numbers of persons, European, Native and half-castes. Some of these institutions were formally endowed, and much of their possessions partook of the nature of endowments. It is probable that if a European government, of a proselytizing disposition, had been permanently established throughout western and southern India, if it had invited the Natives to profess Christianity as the State religion, if it had endowed the Christian priesthood, churches and convents, and if missionaries had arisen of extraordinary zeal and energy like Saint Francis Xavier, a large portion of the Native population would have become Christian and would have remained steadfast in the faith.

This brief retrospect shews that there is nothing unusual in an ecclesiastical establishment being maintained by the British Government in India. The cost of this establishment is comparatively small annually, as already seen. The Government would have only been following the precedents of its

Native predecessors if it had gone further and founded some substantial endowments in favour of Christianity.

While previous rulers of India have promoted their forms of religion by endowment, the British Government has contented itself with providing for the spiritual necessities of its servants. It has scrupulously abstained from directly or indirectly inviting its Native subjects to profess Christianity, from offering inducements to any one in view of such profession, from conceding any peculiar advantages to professing Christians and from acknowledging any secular or temporal difference between Christians and others. It pursues this course not only from motives of worldly policy, but from its assurance that Christianity is of no avail unless embraced from pure and sincere conviction. It protects Christian missionaries and ministers when exercising their sacred vocation, in the same manner as that in which the ministers of all other religions are protected. It assists Christian Missions with grants-in-aid for educational purposes, under the same regulations as those by which similar assistance is given to all educational agencies whether secular or religious.

This example, too, is followed in the Native States, where Christian Missions receive the same protection as in the British territories. Indeed some of the most interesting among these missions are conducted under the very shadow of Hindu and Muhammadan rulers.

Under these circumstances the Christian Missions have become numerous and diverse, constituting in their aggregate, a noteworthy feature in the empire.

The Roman Catholic Church has real vitality in India and counts among its sons, not only Europeans and people of mixed blood, East Indians and Eurasians, but also Natives; many of the Europeans being of Portuguese extraction. Its work is extensive in the three Presidency cities of Calcutta, Madras and Bombay, at all the principal stations civil and military, in the empire, and in many rural districts. It has a hierarchy of

Archbishops, Bishops and Vicars apostolic and a numerous priesthood of various nationalities, French, German, Belgian, Dutch, Swiss, Italian, Portuguese, more than English or Irish. It possesses establishments of Lady Superiors, nuns and sisters. It has cathedrals, churches, chapels, convents, colleges, schools and orphanages, at the principal places in the country. It opens its collegiate doors and its class rooms to the members of all religions without distinction, and while preserving for its own members its services, ordinances and ministrations, it does not appear to press these upon others. Its education is afforded largely to Protestant Christians, boys and girls, and its attitude towards the Natives is very considerate. Its two Colleges dedicated to Saint Xavier, one at Calcutta, the other at Bombay, are among the best private institutions in India; they receive Europeans and Natives alike. Its principal orders are represented in India, especially that of the Jesuits. It has priests attached to many of the European regiments, and these ministers of the Roman Catholic soldiery receive salaries from the Government. The Roman Catholic priests bear a high repute in India, whether as ministers in their own religious community, as pastors among the ignorant, as teachers of the young, as instructors of the educated, as visitors of the sick, as dispensers of charity among the miserable. The best parts of the Roman Catholic system shine to special advantage in a country like India.

Nor has Protestantism, with its multiform development, been a whit behind in running the good race. The Church of England is represented by two of its principal religious associations, namely the Church Missionary Society and the Society for the propagation of the Gospel, both of which, though operating in many countries, have laid in India the scene of their largest operations. The Presbyterian community has contributed the missions of the Established Church of Scotland, of the Free Church of Scotland, of the American Presbyterians. In effective zeal and ability and in devotion to the cause of missions, no religious community in Christendom has surpassed the Free Church of Scotland. The Independent community has furnished the London mission; there are also the missions of the Wesleyans and the Methodists. The Baptist community was among the ablest pioneers of missionary enterprise and continues its exertions. The religious communities of Germany have sent forth several missions. Every one of these communities has according to its means and resources contributed munificently to the work, and has produced a roll of distinguished missionaries.

In the early part of the nineteenth century and even before that time, high hopes prevailed in the Christian world regarding the conversion of the heathen in India. Glowing visions floated before the imaginations of pious and enthusiastic men. It was with all the fresh bloom of such enthusiasm that many great missionaries, whose biographies now form part of the history of their age, entered on a life of labour in a strange land. Such men were Schwartz, Ziebenbalg, Carey, Marshman, Ward, Martyn, Judson, whose names are embalmed in the affection of all Christian men, and whose memory is enshrined even in the minds of the heathen.

It is now seen that the conversion of the heathen, though steadily continuous, will be comparatively slow, and that Christian teaching must, with education as its handmaid, wend onwards a persevering way, through not only the thick masses of heathenism, but also the new and many-sided beliefs which advancing knowledge and civilization may be expected to produce. Some disappointment has been felt by many, at the check which the progress of Christianity may seem at first sight to have suffered. Many persons looking to what they suppose to be the poverty of visible result, may have doubted whether the energies of the religious societies are not being wasted and their resources expended in vain. Some depression may have occasionally weighed down the spirits of the missionaries themselves. Adverse opinions and unfavourable anticipations have been declared by persons who had resided long in India, which declarations may tend to enfeeble the force of sentiment in England respecting Indian missions.

The friends of missions have, however, rallied from time to time, both in England and in the East. Missionary conferences are held at home and abroad; the funds and subscriptions, though perhaps not increasing commensurately with the growth of the national wealth, are yet large and afford such an income as may prove a powerful engine for good. A comparison of the statistics of missions in the past and in the present, and a sober estimate of possibilities, convince the missionary societies that a blessing does rest upon their labours. Men in sufficient abundance for the work have come forward, and among them many have employed, in their Master's cause, talents and gifts equal to those displayed by their illustrious predecessors.

It is hardly possible to state precisely the total expenditure incurred by all the missions in India, but, computed from data of the known expenditure of some of the principal societies, it can hardly be less than £300,000 per annum. It may even exceed that sum, if the educational grants-in-aid, earned by the missions under existing regulations, be added. The results, measured by available statistics, are not incommensurate, according to the standard of comparison adopted in secular administration, though they may fall short of the hopes of earnest men. If the total number of labourers, of all nationalities, school-teachers, catechists, lay preachers, Native missionaries and others, with the reverend clergy, European and American, at their head, be reckoned up, it will not be less than five thousand. The number of Native Christians is not less than 400,000 souls, of whom a fair proportion consists of communicants. To these may be added, as coming under the influence of the missionaries, all the school-children who, though not professing Christianity, attend mission schools where Christian instruction is obligatory. This addition will raise the total to between 500,000, and 600,000 souls. Nor has the number risen suddenly, and then stood still with tendency to fluctuation or retrogression ; it has steadily and gradually moved onwards. A similar result in secular affairs obtained by like resources would not be regarded as otherwise than satisfactory.

That the standard of personal worth, merit and capacity among the missionaries has been adequately maintained, will be manifest on recalling the names of those who have laboured in India within the present generation—the names of French, Sargent, Caldwell, Speechly, all four of whom have been raised to the office of Bishop; of William Smith, Leupolt, Thomas (of Tinnevelly), Bailey and Baker (of Travancore), Pfander, Welland, Hughes, Clarke, James Long, Vaughan, Mullens, Sherring, Wenger, Alexander Duff, John Wilson, Hislop, Nesbitt, Anderson, Murray-Mitchell, and others. Some of these, like William Smith, have become household words throughout large districts as teachers and evangelists. Some, like Pfander, have been distinguished scholars. Some, like Alexander Duff and John Wilson, as authors, as speakers, as authorities upon all Indian questions, have been among the foremost men of their day at Calcutta and Bombay and have left much posthumous fame. Some, like Hislop, have been cut short in the midst of a career bright with the prospect of usefulness.

No doubt, some Englishmen in India of long experience and much information, dispute the usefulness of Christian missions, and deprecate the devotion of so many energies and resources to labours which will bear little or no fruit. It does not, however, follow that local English opinion in India is adverse to missions. For the English in India subscribe considerably to the missions; appeals to their religious liberality always meet with response; and in proportion to their means they contribute as much as their countrymen anywhere. It is true also that some high functionaries have felt themselves unable to believe in the utility of missions, and their view ought to be taken into consideration by those who desire to master all the bearings of the case. On the other hand, nothing can be more emphatic than the testimony repeatedly given in favour of the missions by some of the very first among Anglo-Indian authorities, by such men as John Lawrence, James Thomason, Bartle Frere, Robert Montgomery, Donald Macleod and William Muir.

Sometimes blame has been cast on the missionaries for interfering in secular matters beyond their proper sphere and for taking part in popular agitation; and high authorities have occasionally considered that such blame has been in some measure deserved. On the other hand, a missionary is so situated that he has better means than any one else can have of knowing the real sorrows and anxieties of the people; and such knowledge conduces to lively sympathy. Thus a mutual confidence exists between him and his Native neighbours, who will open their hearts and lay bare the realities of their lives before him, with a frankness which they would not adopt in conversing with an official person. In representing these matters to the proper authorities he may possibly be accepting too unreservedly the points raised by the people, but will probably be urging considerations which no wise administrator would disregard, and affording information which the ablest officers would be thankful to receive from so trustworthy a source. Many a timely warning has thus been given, and many an evil has thus been seasonably brought to light, which might otherwise have remained undiscovered till it broke out in some worse form. If any oppressor or evil-doer among the Natives shall have been thus unmasked, he, and others like him, will condemn the interposition of the missionaries, which, however, will be regarded with gratitude by the majority of the humbler classes. On the one hand the missionaries should be watchful to inform themselves regarding the inner life of the people among whom they conduct their ministrations, and should be fearless and instant in apprising the authorities of impending evil. On the other hand, they should be on their guard against falling into error from hearing only one part of a story without its counterpart; and should be cautious in not lending themselves to the aggravation of popular excitement.

The character of Natives converted to Christianity is generally good. Though they do not possess all the Christian graces that might be desired, still their new religion does exercise a decisive influence on their life and conversation. Though they may not display all the firmer virtues of Christianity they must have some of such virtues. For they must have cast out with an effort many superstitions deeply imbedded in their mental constitution, have dedicated their thoughts to truth alone, have broken some of the ties which are dearest to humanity, and have borne the reproaches of those from whom reprobation is hardest to bear. Despite many temptations, the instances of apostasy have been very rare. On the other hand during times of rebellion and danger there have been instances of courageous adherence to the faith notwithstanding the severest threats.

Such difficulties, however, no longer exist for those Native Christians who have been born in the faith and nurtured by parents themselves sprung from Christians. Of these the number is considerable and constantly increasing, especially in southern India. With them the faith has become hereditary, and is held with some of that pride and tenacity with which Natives cling to everything ancestral. They are beginning to evince a laudable willingness to render their Church self-supporting, to sustain a Native ministry, and to bear some of the burdens incidental to ecclesiastical organization, according to their humble means. It was the growing need of episcopal authority and supervision for the admission of a large number of Native candidates to the ministry in its several grades, that caused the governing authorities to nominate three Missionary Bishops in southern India. There is much in the bright and happy condition of Native Christian villages in southern India, which makes the names of Tinnevelly and Travancore sound pleasantly in the ear of Christendom, which animates the breasts of all well-wishers with hope and thankfulness and which is fraught with auspicious augury for the future of the Native Church in India.

Many missionaries have done much for Oriental literature and for the enlightenment of public opinion regarding the nature and essence of Oriental religions, thus labouring in the closet and in the chamber, as well as in the schoolroom and in the thoroughfare. Most of them are nowadays engrossed in the administrative business which the ever-widening operations of the missions produce. They have by elementary instruction to prepare the minds of a large number of simple people for the reception of truth, and to maintain the moral discipline of the pastorate among large flocks. Thus their leisure and their opportunity for abstruse study are becoming less and less. Nor is the study of the subtle parts of the Oriental religions always necessary, as such matters are beyond the comprehension of the humble classes which form the mass of Native Christians. The qualities most needed for ordinary missionaries are an adequate knowledge of those religious points which can best be argued before Natives of plain minds and of average intelligence, a power of bringing truths home to the hearts of men, and an aptitude for establishing a moral control over multitudes, together with a trained faculty of insight into the mental standpoints of a strange and alien people. It is the consciousness of possessing such qualities that probably induces young men in England to offer themselves for mission work, and it is in regard to such capacities that they are chosen by the missionary societies. The missionaries do by their proceedings prove themselves to be thus qualified at least, while many of them evince additional qualifications.

The missions have by their religious preaching, in combination with the State secular education, and with the progress of general civilization, contributed to the overthrow of the Hindu religion among the majority of educated Hindus at the chief centre of Hinduism. These Hindus, when abandoning their own religion, do not generally embrace Christianity, but fly off to various kinds of philosophic belief. Their conduct no doubt influences large numbers of their fellow-religionists, whose faith has been shaken, and who might otherwise be looking to the Christian Bible for religious guidance. Thus there has arisen a leading and enlightened class of men who are Hindus in nationality only and not in religion, who not only fail to guide their less enlightened countrymen towards Christianity, but actually draw them away from it and towards other paths of belief. They believe that original truth was revealed to men on the banks of the sacred Ganges. They remember that there the religion of Brahma arose; that thence sprang the religion of Buddha and spread till it overshadowed India, Ceylon, Siam, Thibet, China and Japan, and that these two cognate religions have had more adherents than all the other religions in the world taken together and have been followed by seven hundred millions of souls. They apprehend that the Hindu religion is declining because it has been encumbered with mythology, overlaid with superstitions and defaced by corruption; and that if the Buddhist religion shall fall it will owe its decadence to the same causes. They gather from their historical studies that Christianity has been endangered by similar lapses and errors; and that it has been sometimes so disfigured as hardly to be recognised as the religion delivered to mankind by its Founder. Therefore they strive mentally to retrace their erring steps towards the undefiled sources of primæval truth, and aim at restoring the religion of Brahma and of Buddha in its pristine purity. Such is probably the main line of their thoughts, though there may be other lines parallel or divergent; and it is hard for foreigners to probe accurately the delicate and sensitive minds of men like these. Thus, in this increasing class, the missionaries find new opponents, more subtle and more formidable than any yet encountered, whom also the missions themselves have helped to raise up. If the encounter is to take place with any chance of success on the Christian side, it must be conducted by missionaries specially skilled and learned who shall be relieved from the public teaching, the school work and the administrative business, ordinarily undertaken by their missionary brethren.

Such missionaries are those who have been despatched by the Cambridge mission to Delhi, and are being despatched by the Oxford mission to Calcutta. They will meet with Natives highly educated in the Western manner, into the recesses of whose thoughts some entrance must be won by a careful and gradual approach. They may set forth the broad facts of the first spreading of Christianity, not only among wild races, but also among nations possessing some of the finest forms of philosophy that ever emanated from the human brain. They may shew how Christianity has shed its improving influences abroad, until the nations professing it have become the most civilized yet seen on earth. They may indicate how manifold corruptions, of which the existence must be acknowledged, have been removed in parts of Christendom, so that the real beauty of Christianity may be unveiled for worship. They may prove that, besides giving the highest conceivable sanction to the abstract principles of right and wrong, Christianity establishes relations between man and his Maker, and the personal accountability of every human individual to an omniscient Judge for the issues of this life and of eternity. They will have to vindicate these all-important positions in the face of acute and polished criticism.

The argumentative difficulties will be even more severe if Muhammadans as a body shall begin to cease believing in their own religion. There are no present signs, however, of that conjuncture arising; though there are some eminent Muhammadan converts to Christianity. Some Moslem priests do endeavour to answer the missionaries with argumentative skill. The Muhammadan generally, if pressed, would point with much effect to some portions of his religion, for example the definition of the attributes of God, as being of indisputable excellence. Whether that religion was better than the religions of Brahma and of Buddha, when originally promulgated, may be a matter for discussion; perhaps it was better. Certainly it has been much less corrupted; and being more definite in its dogmas and more specific in its commands, it is more likely to retain the allegiance of robust and vigorous nations.

The fact that the need of these special missions has been so practically recognised by the two ancient Universities of England, is of some importance in the history of Christianity in India.

There is often discussion as to whether the effect of religious missions in India is good, and if it be, then in what respects. It may be pronounced really excellent, with only such a minimum of drawbacks or abatements as must be incidental to all human arrangements. The Natives will regard the missions as proving that despite the allurements of temporal success, the temptations of imperial ambition, and the distractions of national life, the ruling race is still devoutly loyal to its own religion. They will expect that a race, which is loyal in this cardinal respect, will be just, faithful and honourable in all other respects. They feel no jealousy of the attitude thus assumed by the ruling race, seeing that the power exerted is from private societies and not from the State, and that a change of religion from secular motives is contemned as worthless Thus the reputation of the British nation is raised in their eyes; a fact of moral value and of political moment. The Natives must inevitably perceive some alloy in British virtue; there is much which they think blameworthy in British conduct. It is well that in the religious missions they should behold something of which the merit is unalloyed, and with which no fault can reasonably be found.

The missionaries themselves display an example the brightness of which is reflected on the nation to which they belong. They are to be heard preaching in every city, and almost in every large town, throughout the empire. They are considerately attentive to every enquirer and listener. They are held to be among the best teachers and schoolmasters in the country, even at a time when the educational staff of the Government affords a model of organization. They receive heathen children in the mission schools, not withholding Christian instruction, and yet retaining the unabated confidence of the heathen parents. They are trusted as benevolent advisers by their Native neighbours. They are known as friends in need, and as being ready to advocate temperately the redress of wrongs or the removal of oppression. In seasons of pestilence and of famine, they have been vigilant in forecasting evil consequences and instant in dispensing aid. They have been among the foremost in the voluntary bands of relief. They have often afforded to the Government and to its officers information which could not have been so well obtained otherwise. They have done much to elucidate before their countrymen and before the world, the customs, the institutions and the feelings of the Natives. They have contributed greatly to the culture of the vernacular languages. Many of them as scholars, historians, sociologists or lexicographers, have held a high place in Oriental literature and have written books of lasting fame and utility. They have, with the co-operation of their wives and daughters, accomplished much towards establishing and promoting female education, and have exemplified before the Natives the sphere of usefulness that may be occupied by educated women. They have enabled the Natives to note the beauty of British homes, which shed abroad the light of charitable ministration and diffuse the genial warmth of practical philanthropy.

CHAPTER X.

LAW AND LEGISLATION.

Constitution of Indian Government by Parliamentary enactments—Sacred character of Hindu and Muhammadan law—Administration of justice under British rule—English law in India—Councils in India constituted for legislation—Law Commission in London—Civil courts in interior of India—Their popularity—Public confidence in the High Courts of Judicature—Special legislation regarding indebtedness of the peasantry—Arbitration—Patriarchal rule—Non-regulation system—Answer to charges of over-legislation—Need of continuity in administration.

A COMPLETE stability belongs to the fundamental institutions of British India. They have a legal status which was conferred not by any authority in India, but by Parliament in a long series of statutes. The Supreme Governments, the Local Governments, the several Executive and Legislative Councils, and the Covenanted Civil Service derive their constitution from Acts of Parliament. The origin of the judicial system has a parliamentary charter. These statutes have been enacted by a chain, as it were, of legislation, each link connected with the other; and they were passed on the recommendation of committees of both Houses made after taking the evidence of the most experienced experts.

With the people of India, whether Hindu or Muhammadan, the national laws had for the most part a sacred origin derived either from the code of Manu and other scriptures or from the Koran. Obedience to them was not only enforced by the secular arm but also was constrained by the fear of divine authority. No ancient writing indeed has the absolute sanction for Hindus as being the word of God, which the Koran has for Muhammadans. Nevertheless there is a body of Hindu writings which, on the whole, are considered to have a religious sanction.

Under Native rule there were Hindu law officers and Muhammadan law officers to whom reference was made for deliverances on difficult points of their respective systems of law. These deliverances were regarded with much popular veneration, but the degree of respect, accorded practically to them by the executive power in a Native State, depended on the condition of the State itself. The restraint of law was faintly acknowledged by the sovereign and but slightly felt by those who conducted the administration even at the best, while at the worst it was ignored altogether.

Therefore the Natives admired the spectacle of the British Government binding not only its subjects, but also itself, by positive enactments, establishing courts of justice in which persons, considering themselves aggrieved, might bring suits against their fellow-subjects and against the Government, and where the acts of the very highest functionaries of State might be reviewed by judicial officers of comparatively humble grades. The admiration may have abated from subsequent familiarity with the system. But the confidence in British justice thus engendered still remains with the mass of the people, and lies close to the foundation of that regard and respect which cause acquiescence in, and acceptance of a foreign rule.

Originally the main objects of the regulations of the East India Company were to lay down an exact system of civil procedure for the guidance of the courts, to provide for the judges having recourse to the Native law officers in matters touching the social institutes of the country, and to leave matters not embraced by these institutes, to be determined either by the analogy of English law or by equity and good conscience. The Supreme Courts, separately established in the three Presidency towns, Calcutta, Madras and Bombay, administered the English law, which law came thus to have an important influence on civil justice, as so many important causes arose in these three towns where the trade of the country centred. Still at each Presidency town, and also in the North-western Provinces there were superior Courts, styled Sadar, in which the Indian regulations were observed, and which supervised all the civil courts in the interior of the country.

In this system, several defects were found to exist after the experience of two or three generations. The regulations, though prepared with the utmost care and with anxious thought for substantial justice, were drawn up by administrative and executive officers, and not by men who had in England made the law their profession, nor with the assistance of any regular draughtsmen. The civil procedure proved to be tedious or over-elaborate and failed to keep pace with the progress of legal science. There were in each division of the empire two tribunals of the highest authority, the Supreme or English Court, and the "Sadar" or Company's Indian Court. The Hindu law, which still governed all matters relating to the social institutes of the people, was found to be often conflicting, indeed consisting of several different schools of legal doctrine. That great division of law which relates to mercantile affairs and to dealings between man and man, was imperfectly comprised by the Hindu and the Muhammadan law, and was yet increasing constantly in size and importance, consequent on the growth of the country in wealth and civilization. It was deemed hardly practicable, and certainly inexpedient, to apply to India, in all cases except certain categories relating to Native institutes, the system of English law absolutely, a system which has its difficulties even for the English people, and which would be too difficult for such a people as that of India.

These faults have nearly all been remedied of late years either by the Government of India, or by the controlling authorities in England, or by the British Parliament.

The Government in England determined in 1833 that, besides the judicial system already established, a body of substantive law, criminal and civil, should be framed in a manner suitable to the people of India and conformable to the best notions of jurisprudence. A high commission for this purpose was appointed to sit in India and a law member was added to the Council of the Governor-General. At the head of this legislative department was placed Mr., afterwards Lord, Macaulay. The first fruit of the labours of himself and his colleagues was the preparation of the Penal Code, which after many years of consideration was passed into law. In 1853, a Legislative Council was formally constituted in India consisting entirely of servants of Government. In place of this, one supreme legislature for all India, and several legislatures of secondary rank for certain divisions of the empire, were established in 1861. These consist partly of Government servants and partly of non-official gentlemen, European and Native, nominated by the Government. The supreme legislature is the Council of the Governor-General, legislating for all matters which affect the Indian empire at large, and for all provinces save those under the Local Governments of Madras, Bombay and Bengal, which have legislatures of their own. The secondary legislatures are the Councils of the Local Governments of Madras, Bombay and Bengal, which legislate for all provincial affairs within their respective territories.

In 1861 a Commission was appointed in England to prepare drafts of law for the assistance of the legislature in India. It consisted of men high in position and authority, Lord Justice James, Justice Romilly, Justice Willes, and Mr. Robert Lowe (now Lord Sherbrooke), and sat from 1861 to 1870. It prepared drafts of several important and comprehensive Acts, such as the Civil Procedure, the Criminal Procedure, the Succession Act, the Contract Act, the Evidence Act, the Negotiable Securities Bill, the Transfer of Property Bill. Recently a commission has been appointed in India to consider further the Bills regarding negotiable securities and transfer of property; also to report upon Bills which have been framed regarding alluvion (land thrown up from rivers), master and servant, easements and trusts. A complete law of torts is by common consent considered necessary and will doubtless be framed. An excellent law of limitation has been passed. With these measures, and some few others which may be devised, there will be ultimately a code of substantive law for British India, scientifically constructed with all the light of the age, and so comprehensive in its scope as to be a boon to the empire and a standard of national ethics.

In addition, there has been much legislation for the many matters which arise in so extensive and diverse an empire. The old regulations have for the most part been superseded by Acts scientifically drafted. Respecting several important subjects, the many scattered laws have been combined into single consolidated laws resembling codes. This process of consolidation or codification will probably be continued for some time.

The legislation, thus produced, may claim a high degree of excellence according to the standards prevailing among the most advanced nations. It is the joint work of English lawyers, Anglo-Indian administrators, non-official Europeans residing in India and Natives chosen for character and intelligence. It embodies the best principles of English jurisprudence with adaptations suitable to the peculiarities of India. It is adjusted to the general wants of the empire and to the particular needs of provinces. It is conducted with long deliberation and with due regard to public opinion, European and Native. Some of the enactments passed by the Government of India are, as pieces of legislative workmanship, equal to the best achievements of the kind in any country.

A legislative department has been established as an integral part of the Government of India. It collates information from every part of the country regarding law and legislation. It causes professional reports to be made of the leading cases decided in the chief courts of justice. It has been presided over by English lawyers and jurists of eminent position. The names of Henry Sumner Maine, of James Fitzjames Stephen, of Arthur Hobhouse, constitute the highest guarantee to the public for the excellence of the legislation, and command the entire confidence of the community in India. Whitley Stokes has rendered service to the country by drafting the laws so clearly as to be understood by the Natives, and yet so accurately as to stand the test of practical use.

The Hindu and Muhammadan codes of law are still observed in all matters relating to marriage, inheritance, adoption, partition of property, testamentary disposition, management of religious institutions and the like. It is impossible to overcome the difficulty arising from the various and sometimes conflicting precedents and rulings of the several schools of Hindu law. Much more attention is, however, devoted now than formerly by the English and Native judges to these abstruse matters; exclusive reliance is no longer placed on the legal dicta of Hindu and Muhammadan law officers.

The functions of some of the ancient executive officers of the Native law officers, such as the Kazis, around whom so much of popular reverence and of ancient tradition is gathered, are carefully maintained respecting the solemnization of marriage, obsequies and other social rites.

For the administration of the laws, thus enacted, the judicial system has been improved and rendered uniform in principle for the whole empire, though there are some differences in detail as between the several provinces.

To ensure unity in the supervision of the civil justice, whether at the Presidency towns or in the interior of the country, the old Supreme and Sadar Courts have been amalgamated and formed into the existing High Courts, in which the Chief Justices and some of the judges are English barristers, while the other judges are members of the European judicial services of India, or are Natives selected for character and ability.

In the interior of the country, the object has been first, to place courts at all the principal points, so as to be within a few miles of the homes of the great majority of the people, next to render the proceedings inexpensive to the suitors and the decisions speedy. The administration of justice can be secured only by laws being judiciously framed, and by competent judges being appointed. The Government has done and is doing, its utmost in both these respects. The Natives shew acumen, discrimination and carefulness as judges; they are considered to shew more natural aptitude for the judicial department than for any other. Their high repute, in the present time for uprightness and integrity has been already described in a previous chapter on mental and moral progress.

There have been discussions whether civil justice, as now administered, can properly be deemed cheap and speedy. It has sometimes been reprobated as costly and slow. Still, on due allowances being made, it may be considered as not unduly expensive, nor for the most part tardy. The expensiveness is partly under the control of the State, which does its best on behalf of economy by simplifying the procedure and keeping the stamp duties moderate. It is partly beyond the control of the State, and is in the hands of the public, in so far as it consists in the remuneration of lawyers and advocates.

The profession of the law which formerly had an unfavourable repute, has grown and is growing, both in moral worth and in mental capacity. The Government cannot control or influence the emoluments of a profession which has its value in the market of intellectual labour. But the Government can provide that if the people do pay highly for legal advice, the advisers shall be persons of trained qualifications. This provision is effectually made by the tests to which men are subjected before admission to either branch of the legal profession. The character and status of the Native Bar has also been mentioned in the previous chapter on mental and moral progress.

It is difficult to ascertain whether suits are on the average of long or short duration, because in most provinces some few causes from special circumstances, sometimes preventable and at other times unavoidable, remain pending for an extraordinary length of time; a few such causes make the average swell so much that any conclusions which may be drawn from it become invalidated. If such cases be excerpted, then the average duration of ordinary suits will in most provinces, be found moderate and in some provinces satisfactorily short.

One reason of expense and delay in the final disposal of cases is the privilege of appeal which has been formerly much abused, which has in some respects been judiciously modified, but to which the Natives still cling pertinaciously. The importance of an appeal is not always to be measured by the value of the property in dispute, because a question of small pecuniary amount may involve a principle of consequence. After allowance has been made for this consideration, it will still be found that many trivial appeals, preferred from litigiousness, are occupying the time of highly paid and dignified tribunals. A considerable remedy has been applied by the establishment of Courts of small causes throughout the empire. These tribunals, despite their name, hear causes of certain kinds for large amounts, and with them the right of appeal is strictly limited. Additional limitations of appeal, in other kinds of cases, have been under the consideration of the legislature. And if appealing is yet regarded as an evil by some European authorities, it arises from the disposition of the people, and not from the policy of the Government. Any attempt to suppress it or to impose limitations, essentially stricter than those which now exist, would be very unpopular.

The popularity or unpopularity of the Courts in the interior of the country has been the theme of frequent controversy. That the Courts were formerly unpopular with many classes of the people may be admitted. They are still disliked by some classes, landlords and others, who after making undue use of their landed security to run into debt, find themselves confronted with their creditors before the judge. They are yet condemned by many executive authorities who find themselves checked by judicial action, and even by some non-official Europeans. There are some eminent persons who, notwithstanding all recent improvements, believe that those who thought to establish a system of civilized jurisprudence in India, have actually planted an Upas tree. Some Natives also may share this opinion, and the Courts may be less esteemed in some provinces than in others. Nevertheless, those who are cognizant of Native opinion as a whole throughout the empire, doubtless perceive that the Courts are, despite their shortcomings, amongst the most popular and most trusted institutions in the country. In some provinces they are more esteemed than any other department or authority whatever, and are regarded as the embodiment of what is best in British rule.

The Europeans at the Presidency cities and at other great centres, and the Natives also, regard the several High Courts with sincere respect and implicit confidence. Indeed there is nothing in the empire to which all classes, Europeans and Natives, are more attached than these august tribunals, though even in them practical defects are known to exist.

The Natives of India are, as a people, litigious; many of them seem to find in litigation under a settled rule that excitement for which under an unsettled rule they would seek in contests of other kinds. In reference to the probable wealth and resources of the country, the number of suits is large and their aggregate value considerable.

In the procedure, the most marked defects during recent years have been the difficulty in obtaining a proper execution of decrees. Often the interposition of delay and obstruction has been harassing and vexatious. Sometimes property has been sold inconsiderately without proper precautions for realising its value, in satisfaction of decrees for comparatively small amounts. These faults will be fully remedied if the provisions of the recently amended civil procedure are duly carried out.

In the dispensing of justice one fault has been the manner in which bonds which, though duly executed, were manifestly given by ignorant debtors the victims of usurious creditors, were admitted by the Courts as conclusive without sufficient cognizance of the original merits of the claim and of its subsequent augmentation. A well-meant and carefully considered attempt has been made by special legislation to remedy this fault in the province where it most prevailed, namely the Deccan. It remains to be seen whether this legislation has been sufficiently thorough to prove successful; and it were vain to suppose that the same defect does not continue to prevail in several other parts of the empire.

The ancient "Panchayet," which means an arbitration court consisting of five members, has for the most part vanished into the past, from which it will but rarely emerge to revisit the land. Nothing would have pleased the Government better than to maintain, develop and dignify this institution, if the people would but acquiesce, but they will not. In the Panjab persistent efforts were put forth to naturalize this institution under the British arrangements and to induce the suitors to resort to arbitration, but the people would not have it. Their preference for standing tribunals, with judges appointed by the State, is remarkable. The law provides for suitors resorting to arbitration, and they do resort to it occasionally, but not often. In some places, such as Poona in the Deccan, an arbitration court sits regularly, and affords satisfaction to the public. Elsewhere such an arrangement, whenever practicable, receives encouragement from the Government. But the substitution of arbitration for regular judicial trials would in most parts of the empire be unpopular, and could not be attempted in the present temper of the people.

For the prevention of forgery, fraud or fraudulent alteration of papers, it is essential to establish a system of public transfers by means of registration. The practice of tampering with unregistered documents of private transfers has been a blot on the social life of the Natives, and though probably much diminished, it still exists. The authorities have still to be on their guard against it. They have therefore long looked towards the excellent models of public transfer afforded in some of the countries of continental Europe. In respect of real property the land revenue administration supplies, as will be seen in a future chapter, almost as perfect a registration as could be devised for landed tenures, and for mutations of ownership and occupancy, by succession and by transfer, for most provinces of the empire. Beyond this, no adequate measures for notarial registration generally were for some time undertaken. Since 1867, however, a department of registration has been legally constituted and completely organized throughout the empire. Registry offices have been established in every town, and are gradually being extended to the villages, so that the facilities for registering may be augmented. Muniment rooms are provided in every office for the safe keeping of documents. Besides the registering clerks, there is an inspecting staff, and in every division of the empire a responsible functionary is at the head of the department, so that the Native public may feel confidence in its management. Fees are levied on the registration, enough to defray the cost of the establishments and of the management. The scale of fees is arranged in order that the department may be self-supporting, but not with a view of its yielding any fiscal profit to the State. The law renders the registration compulsory for certain sorts of documents, such as those relating to immovable property beyond a certain value. For other documents, notably those relating to wills and to personalty, it leaves the registration optional. The tendency of legislation is to enlarge the category of the documents in which the registration is compulsory. Meanwhile the country is studded with notarial offices; and numbers of documents to be reckoned by hundreds of thousands are registered year after year. The result must be to clear and purify the moral atmosphere in many social quarters.

"Patriarchal administration" and "personal rule" were once phrases of much currency in India; they embodied ideas which had practical effect at one time, but which have now, however, disappeared. Men of eminence and ability may be met with who deplore the gradual, and now complete, substitution of the reign of law for the reign of individuals. Still every nation, as it advances in wealth and civilization, demands to be ruled, not by the will of persons, who however able and well-meaning will be sure to differ one from the other in a manner sometimes seemingly capricious, but by a fixed system to which all men can steadily look, and on which they can reckon when forming their plans. India constitutes no exception to this tendency, which is indeed irresistible. Although the Natives are apt somewhat inconsistently to speak of over-legislation, they yet desire that there shall be laws for almost every matter, to which they can appeal either as against the executive or in conflict with their neighbours. They have a dread of the unrestrained eccentricities of authority. On the other hand, the scope actually afforded nowadays to executive authorities, though different perhaps from what it used to be, is yet very great. The executive heads of districts and of provinces still wield enormous powers for good or for evil.

Sometimes it has been imagined that in the Native States substantial justice is more successfully dispensed than in the British territories. This view will be entertained only by those who are better acquainted with the flaws and shortcomings of their own system than with those of the system in foreign territories. It will not be held by those who have acquaintance with affairs in the interior of the Native States.

The name of the "non-regulation system" still haunts the memories of many whose experience and knowledge deserve every respect. It originally meant this, that into some newly annexed or freshly conquered provinces, the regulations pertaining to the older provinces of the empire were not introduced, while instead of them executive orders were issued by the authorities on the spot. These executive orders differed indeed from the regulations, were somewhat more simple and followed better the light of recent experience. But they were just as well considered, as precisely drawn up and as strictly prescribed for observance, as the regulations of the older provinces. The result, then, was merely the substitution of one set of rules, perhaps an improved and simplified code, for another set. The provinces thus governed, of which the Panjab was the chief, were styled "non-regulation," in contradistinction to the old, or "regulation" provinces. As laws, with scientific legislation, came to be passed for the "regulation" provinces, they were one after another ordered by executive authority to be observed partly or wholly in the "non-regulation" provinces. Some important laws were passed by the legislature for all the provinces of the empire without exception. Then legislative acts were passed for each of the principal "non-regulation" provinces, specifying what particular laws or parts of laws, and what executive orders, were to be legally regarded as having force within it. In each province a chief tribunal was appointed, of which the judgments would be independent of the executive government, as in other countries, and which would supervise, according to law, the proceedings of all the subordinate courts. Unless specially enacted otherwise, or ordered otherwise under authority of law, the Acts now passed by the legislature are operative in all provinces alike. Thus the reign of law has irrevocably spread to the "non-regulation" provinces, nor would the mass of the population in those provinces desire to revert to any former system.

Still, the Government has power by statute to remove any tract from the operation of the laws, and this power is occasionally exercised in the case of wild and uncivilized territories.

It is feared by many that a strong current of opinion has set in against scientific and systematic legislation for India. Nevertheless, the more thoughtful persons, European and Native, are convinced that there must be such legislation. The ancient laws and prescriptive rules leave unsolved countless matters which arise nowadays between man and man. The establishment of a foreign rule, the diffusion of trade and the infiltration of new ideas by means of education, must cause the oldest things of the former civilization and the newest things of the modern, to be placed in juxtaposition. For most of the cases arising out of such conjuncture the indigenous system cannot possibly provide, and new phases of contention appear. A sense of being wronged arises among the Natives, who are quick to feel injury and urgent in obtaining redress. If the jurisdiction, under which they live, proves so defective as to leave them smarting and brooding under a consciousness of injustice, they will even shed the blood and burn the houses of their fellow-subjects the oppressors. If the judges are to follow justice and equity they will find it hard to determine what is just and equitable in complex cases. In the absence of legislation there will be gathered together a mass of judge-made law. The judges will themselves deprecate the virtual formation of law by such a process. They know that with it the establishment of principles must be casual, that under it a comprehensive view of social expediency can hardly be taken, and that by it doctrines become declared with much delay and great cost to the suitors, which ought to have been declared beforehand by the State. The only remedy for this is legislation. Then, the legislation must be scientific, representing the best moral thoughts and social ideas of the nation which is being developed under British rule. The language, while indisputably clear and easily intelligible, ought to be formal. Otherwise there will be an ambiguity about fundamental terms which is specially embarrassing, and the law will be more intricate and bulky than it need have been.

Complaints are loud in India regarding the evils of quibbling, chicanery and misplaced ingenuity. These evils are caused or aggravated by an indefinite condition of the law, and the only remedy for them is definite legislation. As Sir James Stephen said, "To try to avert these evils by leaving the law undefined and by entrusting judges with a wide discretion is to try to put out a fire by pouring oil upon it. Leave a judge with only one of those leaden rules which may be twisted in any direction and every sort of topic is left to the advocate. Homœopathy is the only system by which the malady of litigation and quibbling can be treated. The real antagonist of the pettifogger is the legislative department."

The Natives well know that the profession of the law must exist, unless the Government is to be conducted by sheer physical force, and according to the arbitrary will of the ruler of the day. They have been instant in remonstrance whenever by any project of law it has been proposed to transfer a matter from the judgment of tribunals to the discretion of the executive authorities. They object to those Acts which contain only general provisions and empower the Government to make rules for practice, on this ground that such Acts delegate to executive discretion what ought to be prescribed by law.

Again, if recourse were not constantly had to legislation English law would gradually creep over the country, like ivy over a wall, entwining itself with all social affairs and relations. In doubt as to what they should do, or how they should decide, the judges would follow the precedents or analogies of that law, the English, to which they could most readily refer and in which the chiefest among them had been trained. Thus a nucleus of judge-imported law would be formed, around which a mass of decisions would gradually be gathered. This very consummation was at one time likely to be brought about, as a consequence of British rule, and was averted only by the legislation which has been undertaken.

The law in India declaring the liability of debtors for their debts has often been reprobated. Its abolition has even been recommended as a panacea for much suffering. The idea of such legislation is apparently supposed to have been borrowed from English law. It is as old, however, among the Hindus as their ancient lawgivers, and is a part of the prescriptive law of the country. Among Muhammadans it is as definite as in any civilized nation. Its importance has been augmented under

British rule by the growth of transactions, commercial and other, in number and magnitude.

It is sometimes urged that a centralized system of legislation for so wide an empire will cause undue interference with the customs and unwritten laws of the Natives, will injuriously affect the constitution of Native property and will subject the inhabitants of one part of the country to laws unsuitable to them, though suitable to the inhabitants of other parts. As already shewn, it is amply provided that the Natives shall have the benefit of their own law in all the departments of social life to which they will naturally desire its application. So far from overlooking the constitution of Native property, the English officers have investigated it with infinite pains and evince a jealous care to vindicate and conserve it. They have formed a voluminous literature on the proprietary tenures among the many nationalities of India. Now that men are entering more and more into transactions ramifying through several divisions of the empire, it is necessary that the subordinate contracts should be governed everywhere by the same law and procedure. In many branches of substantive law, therefore, the legislation must be uniform and centralized. For those matters where peculiarities exist, extending to certain provinces or localities, provincial legislation has been provided, as already seen, by the establishment of local legislatures.

In short, the objects of the legislation have been elucidation and simplification. No law has been passed without necessity, or before it was necessary, therefore there has not been anything which could be justly described as over-legislation.

The principle that all rules for the governance and administration of the country shall be fixed by legislation, is vitally important to the good government of the Indian empire at the present time. By these means the vagaries to which even the best and ablest men are liable, are stopped, and there is no possibility of radical changes being made without due deliberation and without adequate demonstration of their expediency.

After the experience of three-quarters a century, crowded with discussions, experiments and revisions, an administrative system has been formed, sufficiently uniform for imperial necessities and yet sufficiently variable for provincial peculiarities, securing the confidence of the people who desire to live and labour under a settled system, preventing the abuse of power by those whose well-meaning zeal outstrips their discretion, and yet affording room for the exercise of all the talents which even the ablest men can display. The improvements, suggested from time to time, ought to be sanctioned and defined by the legislation, for which several legislatures have been established on the spot. Under any circumstances there are matters which legislation cannot reach, but which executive authority can control. But if individual administrators were allowed to modify fundamental or widely important principles according to their personal judgment, then confusion, perhaps even disaster, would arise. Such men will generally be energetic, and will have independent and resolute minds. Then they will necessarily differ in opinion; one man would move the hands of the national clock rapidly forward, the next man would put them back again. In paraphrase of the classic proverb, they would pull down and build up, they would change square things to round. Continuity of principle, practice and conduct is essential in the position at which the empire has now arrived; a continuity not too rigid to be slightly diverted or deflected, according to expediency, but still strong enough to preserve the general line of its direction. The ship of State may tack about, indeed, according to the winds of circumstance, but her general course should be determined, and she should steer upon it as much as possible.

CHAPTER XI.

CRIME, POLICE AND PRISONS.

General character of crime in India—Good conduct of the people—Thagi, its horrid characteristics, its repression—Self-sacrifice of Hindu widows by burning, its suppression—Female infanticide—Regulation of marriage expenses—Political import of dacoities in Deccan—Gypsy tribes—Occasional occurrence of serious riots—Penal code and criminal procedure—Regular police—Its former faults—Its reorganization—Condition of village or rural police—General regulations regarding arms—Prisons under British rule—Recent improvements therein—Juvenile reformatories—Convict settlements.

THERE are some peculiarly dark deeds which have disfigured the Indian annals, otherwise the crimes of India do not essentially differ from those of other climes. Possibly the people of India, having, with some exceptions and reservations, a sober, orderly and law-abiding character, may be compared favourably in respect of crime with the people in more advanced countries.

The rise and spread of Thagi has left a stain upon the history of the eighteenth and nineteenth centuries in India. The crime was in its perpetration simple, it consisted of the waylaying and strangling of travellers on lonely roadsides for the sake of the money and valuables they carried about them. Its dire characteristic was the secret formation of gangs banded together for its purposes, operating by combination in widely separated parts of the country, maintaining complete inter-communication, obeying leaders of various degrees, having formulæ for the admission and the swearing in of members, enrolling them as the devotees for life of a murderous profession, and possessing a vocabulary of watchwords. It attracted to itself a superstition amounting to a horrid and unnatural religion. It arose from the disregard of human life, caused by scenes of incessant bloodshed during wars and revolutions, and from the demoralizing effects of the ruthless system of spoliation established by the Mahrattas and continued by the Pindaries. Though its existence was suspected, yet its real proportions and its shocking extent remained long unknown. Its discovery was followed by repressive measures, which ended successfully after a comparatively brief time, through the unaccountable readiness with which so many of the Thags became approvers and informers. The information given by them would have been incredible but for the subsequent verification of particulars, whereby certainty was obtained regarding the distressful numbers of the victims, and the extraordinary accumulation of murders committed by individual murderers. The fulness of their disclosures would almost indicate that they were conscience-stricken, were it not for the callousness of their demeanour when recounting the damnatory narratives. The psychology of these criminals is worthy of study, because it shews that there are some baneful tendencies inherent in the Native mind, which will not be eradicated in one or two generations, and would surely manifest themselves again, if repressive action were to be relaxed.

Sometimes instances of the systematic poisoning of wayfarers have given warning to the magistracy that Thagi under another form is ever ready to spring into life again. The cases of other dark murders now and then point to the same inference.

The old crime of Sati, whereby Hindu widows were burned alive on the funeral pyres of their husbands, has ceased long ago throughout the British territories. The ideas from which it sprang have no longer any hold upon the minds of the highly educated classes. Possibly the practice would revive among the less educated classes if the British prohibition were withdrawn. The monuments always erected on the spots, where the dread rite has been observed, are regarded with popular reverence. The same prohibition exists generally in the Native States and is fully obeyed; if any instance occurs in these days, it must be very rare.

Female infanticide has been largely practised among certain tribes of Rajputs, who are imbued with an austere pride in their lineage, who find it most difficult to provide for their marriageable daughters in any manner consistent with the rules of their caste, and who regard an unmarried daughter as a slur upon their family. The Government has for many years set itself to suppress this most inhuman practice by various measures legislative and executive, with some considerable success at least, though probably not without some failure. Perseverance will doubtless conquer this crime ultimately, but it is extremely difficult to reach either of the two roots of the evil, namely, the pride of caste and the excessive scale of marriage expenses. It is probable, however, that the undue expenditure on marriages has been somewhat reduced.

Some Native reformers have formed associations for the regulation of expenditure on marriage solemnities, an expenditure which is the fruitful parent of many evils besides infanticide. In this way some effect has been produced on public opinion among the Natives, in respect to matters where interposition on the part of foreign rulers might do more harm than good.

Dacoity or gang-robbery has always been reckoned among the plagues of India. It has thriven by reason of the fierceness and audacity which distinguishes some classes and the timidity and submissiveness which characterize so many other classes. It has been always one of the first evils with which the British Government had to cope. In Bengal proper, especially, it was a crime with an extensive organization, having professional ringleaders followed by gangs of enrolled men. This organization was encountered by a still stronger administrative machinery under British authorities, and so became broken up and dispersed. The crime continues, however, to break out from time to time in a milder form in several provinces, and many persons are still at large whose chief occupation is the planning of overt robbery, with more or less of violence according to the resistance which may be offered. It is one of the earliest symptoms of impending scarcity, political excitement or any social trouble.

Gang-robbery assumed an ominous shape and troublesome dimensions in the Deccan near Bombay during 1879, by reason of the ferment in the public mind during a time of war, following a long protracted series of hard times. The services of two regiments of Native infantry and one regiment of Native cavalry had to be employed in its suppression, by reason of the difficult ground in the midst of the Western Ghat mountains where the events took place. The trouble lasted for three months, despite the efforts of the authorities to terminate it speedily. Considerable amounts of property were robbed, with much violence, in villages lying within a short distance of the mountains. The robbers used to betake themselves with their booty to mountainous positions difficult of access, and shewed resolute courage when attacked by the Native soldiers and the police. The plague would have spread indefinitely, if the Government had not taken numerous precautions and availed itself of many means of repression. The Brahmin leader and his immediate adherents were avowedly forming a conspiracy against the Government, though his followers were actuated by the ordinary desire for plunder. Some of his colleagues in mischief probably entertained political views of some sort. The number of men engaged in these plundering gangs was quite small, but a nucleus was formed by them, around which badly-disposed persons might gather. Their proceedings were watched with a strange interest by some sections of the Native community and with an equally strange apathy by others, while among some classes a lively alarm was excited. An incendiary fire in the old palace of the Peshwas at Poona was lighted about the same time under suspicious circumstances.

In the prompt suppression of this evil, Major Daniell, of the police force, signalized himself by his skill and vigour. Though the attempts thus made by evil-minded persons proved futile and abortive, and though any exaggeration of the importance of such silly and clumsy designs ought to be avoided, still these occurrences demand the thoughtful attention of politicians.

Rioting and disturbance are uncommon in India, but occur now and then, as if to warn the Government of the many dangers which lurk in so vast and varied a country. In 1872 an attempt was made by fanatical means to stir up rebellion in the Cis Satlej territories of the Panjab. In 1873, a serious conflict occurred between the Parsis and Muhammadans in the city of Bombay. In 1873, some agrarian disturbance, not severe, occurred in North Eastern Bengal. In 1875 the Sontals, who had broken out in rebellion, caused some trouble in the heart of the Bengal territories. In 1878 some serious riots, not destitute of political import, broke out in the city of Surat on account of the licence-tax. In 1879 there were some troubles in the hill region of Rampa in the Madras Presidency. Events of this nature shew that even in a time of general peace, the authorities must preserve a vigilant attitude and be prepared to enforce order on the instant that necessity arises.

There are in most parts of the country certain persons who live without any ostensible means of livelihood, who abide sometimes in one village for a time, and sometimes move about from village to village, and who are well known in the neighbourhood to be thieves by profession. The villagers, with that feebleness of public spirit which is unfortunately common, refrain from disturbing these people, so long as the depredations are carried on elsewhere. The palpable existence of this evil has induced the legislature to arm the magistracy with a stringent power for calling upon such suspected persons, when duly brought up by the police, to shew that they have some means of livelihood, and, in default of that, to give security for good behaviour, detaining them in custody until the security is given. The power needs to be sparingly and cautiously exercised, lest an undue power should be indirectly placed in the hands of the police. It is exercised, however, in many cases greatly to the benefit of rural society.

In several provinces there are nomadic gypsy tribes who, having a quiet demeanour externally, are yet skilful and daring thieves. They wander about, and settle down like a small flight of locusts, on any piece of waste ground that may be available; and the neighbours soon find their property slipping away from them bit by bit. Here again the legislature has wisely empowered the executive to take effective steps for restraining these criminal tribes, for reclaiming them from predatory habits which they follow because they know no better, for settling them down in fixed dwellings on cultivated lands and for practically teaching them the lessons of honest industry. These measures have already been blessed with some results, and may with considerate persistency be crowned with full success ultimately.

The kidnapping, purchasing or otherwise obtaining of children of both sexes for vicious and wicked purposes, being discovered to prevail in some places, the Government and the legislature were constrained to adopt special measures for eradicating or at least for checking this hateful evil.

Forgery was once a common crime, and was regarded by Natives as comparatively venial. It still exists, though doubtless diminished, as improvements in the judicial and executive administration restrict the opportunities for its commission. Of late years extensive forgeries of the Government currency notes have been perpetrated with extraordinary skill and boldness.

Adultery among the humbler classes is not uncommon, and is punished by the criminal law under British rule, but not with the same severity as under Native rule. Probably the Natives blame the Government for not inflicting severer punishments, forgetting that excessive severity is seldom efficacious in offences of this description. The revengeful anger aroused by conjugal infidelity, leads to many murders, more perhaps than any other cause.

In places where the herds graze loose and wander over extensive tracts of waste, cattle-stealing is rife, as might be expected, and is one of the plagues of rural society. Necessity of detection produces a race of professional trackers, who, with acuteness almost equal to an instinct, will hunt the tracks of stolen cattle for many miles, judging from marks not distinguishable by the ordinary eye.

Perjury was formerly a flagrant evil in the courts civil and criminal. It is still very frequent but will gradually decrease as the social standard, and the administration of justice, improve. The curious ordeals and forms of oath which used to be practised have been stopped.

The penal or criminal code is in full operation throughout the empire. It is declared by one of the highest of living authorities, Sir James Stephen, to be the best system of criminal law in the world, and it adds renown to the illustrious name of Macaulay. It is supported by an equally excellent criminal procedure, which has been revised from time to time, and is worthy of the great repute of Sir Barnes Peacock and others who laboured for its design and completion.

The police of India has from time immemorial been divided into two parts; first, the regular police, appointed and paid by the State and in all respects forming a part of the civil establishments of the country; secondly, the rural or village police, holding office by a quasi-hereditary tenure, not appointed by the State, but recognised by authority, and paid, not from the public treasury, but by emoluments drawn from the villages, and constituting a local institution of great antiquity throughout the empire. The police has been maintained in this double form under British rule.

The character of the Indian regular police for inefficiency and corruptness was, for many years, the subject of constant regret and anxiety to conscientious Englishmen concerned in the administration of the country and interested in the welfare of the Natives. With Englishmen, outside official circles, it was a theme of reproach against the Government. The Natives lamented the evil, which was a matter of common notoriety, but were more sparing in their reproaches. They had never known any higher standard for comparison, and were better acquainted with one of the principal causes of the evil, namely the timid unresisting disposition of their own people ever ready to offer encouragement to corruption and temptation to inefficiency. Despite the improvement in its organization during recent years, the police is still very far from being what it ought to be. On the introduction of British rule the Government formed its police on the model of that existing under Native rule, which would, it was hoped, prove suitable to the peculiarities of the country. In fact, however, police administration was one of the weakest parts of Native rule, and the instrument, formed on its pattern, broke to pieces in the hands of the British magistrates. Service in the police has always been unpopular with Natives of superior stamp, and men of character avoided entering it. Men of ability rarely entered it, except with the intention of making an unlawful fortune within a short time, risking the chance of such detection as would lead to personal punishment, but quite prepared for dismissal. The chances were that when a man had reaped gains during a brief sunshine of impunity there would be enough of detection to warrant his discharge from the service on moral conviction of dishonesty, but not sufficient proof for bringing him to judicial punishment. When the heads were thus evilly inclined, the body of the police was corrupt throughout, each man being bad after his kind. They committed divers acts of oppression, and they sometimes extorted confessions by torture. The scale of pay was low, being much the same as that which had prevailed under Native rule. It was not sufficiently remembered that if men of inferior status possess power and are lowly paid, they are sure to eke out their income by illicit gains.

There were but very few European officials in the country, and it was impossible to detach any of them for the supervision of the police alone. Elaborate rules were framed for regulating the conduct of the police in the repression and detection of crime. But such codes of rules were like skeletons, destitute of any capacity for vital efficacy; it was impossible to make these dry bones live. In a large and populous district there were one or two European magistrates who had a general supervision over the police administration among many other things; they did their best, but that was little indeed under the circumstances. The people were apathetic in demanding redress for injuries, in reporting crime and in bearing testimony. They would condone even grievous wrongs, disavow the losses of property which they had suffered, and withhold all assistance from their neighbours in similar plights, rather than undergo the trouble of attending at police offices and criminal courts. A similar disposition was evinced by the landowners, who were specially charged by law with the duty of assisting the regular police and without whose support it was difficult to enlist the hearty co-operation of the village police. During the troubles through which the country had passed antecedently to British rule, the landowners would first band themselves together to resist robbery and plunder. Next they learnt to regulate the mischief, to take it into their own hands and to become abettors, protecting themselves, but conniving at the spoliation of the general public. These habits, even if checked on the introduction of a settled rule, still survived for many years. The British officers found that criminals had friends not only among the police but also among the landowners. Some crimes were so overt, like murder in broad daylight, or the descent of armed ruffians upon a village, that they could not fail to be reported. In various ways much crime was brought to light, and of that a certain proportion was proved and duly punished. Many criminals were brought to justice, enough to fill, even to crowd, the jails. At the best, however, much crime was undetected, many criminals were at large, and many bad characters with no honest livelihood, and no profession except that of crime, lurked about all parts of the country. Many an earnest English officer, struggling in vain to rectify these evils, felt like a buffalo ramming its horns against a wall, or a bird beating its wings against a cage.

The first efforts at reform in organization were made in the cities of Calcutta and Bombay. European officers of status and capacity were appointed to the sole duty of supervision; superior grades of Native officers were instituted, and a complete constabulary was organized. The area under the city police is limited in extent, but is densely peopled; affairs are conducted very much under the public eye, and are exposed to the gaze of enlightened criticism. Hence, the conduct of the police is tolerably good, and its administration comparatively satisfactory.

A reform on a large scale, however, was made by the Madras Government, who organized the police for the whole of their territories after the best English model, appointed a Native constabulary with superior grades, and placed European officers to command them in every district. In these proceedings Mr. (now Sir William) Robinson took a distinguished part. Subsequently in Oudh similar steps were taken under the active supervision of the late Colonel Herbert Bruce. Then a commission was appointed to sit in Calcutta, consisting of selected officers representing every division of the empire, to prepare a scheme for the reorganization of the police everywhere. There were discussions whether the new force should not be independent of the magistrate of the district, but the police was ordered to be a department, separate indeed, still under the control and at the command of the magistrate. This system has been for some years in force throughout the empire. The regular police is a constabulary with much the same designations as those current in England. It is a department with many European officers, one or two of whom are stationed in every district. The magistrate has thus at his elbow a qualified European officer, whose attention is devoted to police affairs, and who can proceed instantly to the scene of every grave occurrence that may be reported. It is the presence of the officer on the spot immediately after the events, which ensures detection and prevents malpractices. The superior grades consist of Native officials well trained, fairly educated, and comparatively highly paid, who look to promotion, have character and repute to maintain, and dread losing their places. Below them are grades of Natives, among whom the best men have some motive for serving well and faithfully, namely the hope of being chosen for advancement to the upper grades. When the superior Native officials are comparatively free from corruption, the subordinates become so of necessity.

The general character of the police force is not at all military, and the authorities have been anxious to maintain its civil status. The men are subjected to some sort of drill and wear uniform but do not usually carry arms, some of them, however, are regularly armed, and guard jails and treasuries. At some points on the frontiers there are special bodies of police with a military organization. In the country generally the police cannot be depended upon to fight, when any serious disturbance threatens, and on such occasions some troops must be called into action.

Although much improvement has resulted from the new organization, it were vain to imagine that the old evils and objections, already described, have disappeared; they have, in fact, been only mitigated. The pay of the constables, though not liberal, is yet as much as can be afforded in reference to the pay of the Native soldiery. The salaries of the superior Native police officers, though much better than formerly, are not sufficient to procure Natives of the best type for the work. The service in the police is not so much esteemed as that in the fiscal and administrative departments. The Native police officers, though much raised above the former standard, are not yet equal in character and status to the corresponding grades in other civil branches. Although some meritorious Natives have received considerable promotion in the police, the superior appointments demanding the exercise of promptitude and energy, must for the present, as a rule, be filled by Europeans.

The village police or watch was not for the most part so innately vicious as the old regular police. Being men of the villages and holding office usually by an hereditary tenure, the watchmen had some understanding with, and some fellow-feeling for the villagers. But they sometimes became the actual agents in crime when the landholders being badly disposed began to collude with criminals. In such cases the village police were nothing but an additional evil to a much vexed neighbourhood. Their dues were imperfectly regulated and their little income was precarious, so that they were obliged to eke it out by other work, to the detriment of their proper duties. Often their subsistence depended on a piece of land, allotted to them in virtue of their office, and much of their time would be spent in cultivating it. Thus the police service rendered by them was often little more than nominal. On the whole, this rural police, though of ancient origin and containing the germ of a valuable institution, was for many years inefficient. During recent years, however, measures have been taken to remedy these defects in the village police in every province of the empire, and to place it by law on a permanent basis and in a state of efficiency. Its emoluments are fixed and secured, its duties are defined; it is kept separate from the officials of the regular police, but is bound to fulfil their behests, and to co-operate with them in every possible way. It is required to make reports of every crime or unusual occurrence with due punctuality. Though very far from the degree of efficiency which might be desired, it is still much improved. Its conduct is of much importance to the well-being and comfort of the rural population.

The British Government in India has always found it necessary to regulate the possession, manufacture and importation of arms, in its own territories, for obvious reasons relating to the public safety. On the conquest or annexation of provinces, one of the first measures usually adopted was a requisition to the people to give up their arms, which they did without demur. The disarming, as it was termed, has been effected with tolerable completeness throughout the empire. Many arms are, however, still secreted; they are occasionally forthcoming, though rusty from disuse, whenever trouble threatens, and would be largely produced if any general disorder came to pass. No restrictions are imposed in the Native States, save such as may have been arranged by diplomatic negotiation. Many Natives of rank, British subjects, are licensed to carry arms; many also of humble station are allowed arms for destroying wild beasts. Europeans, sportsmen and others, have arms in India as elsewhere. Under all these circumstances, it became necessary for the Government to carefully revise the law respecting the importation, the transport and the bearing of arms.

The importation of European arms into India by sea, for Native States, involved several serious considerations. Those Native States, which require such armament, have to make special arrangements with the British Government. All those who need firearms, for legitimate purposes, can obtain them without difficulty. The revised legislation seemed at the time to excite some dissatisfaction, but at present no particular complaint arises. The Government desires to take only such precautions as are necessary, and to carry out even those with all the considerateness that can reasonably be expected.

Reference having thus been made, first to the prevailing crimes, next to the police agency for the repression and detection of crime, it remains only to follow the convicted criminals to their prisons.

The institution of prisons in the modern sense of the term

was but little known practically under Native rule. Many Native States nowadays have prisons in imitation of British rule. But few States, if left to themselves, would have any prison worthy of the name, though they might have dungeons or bastilles. Indeed, resort was had as little as possible to long-termed imprisonment as a form of punishment for ordinary crime. Short confinement with flogging, fines of various sorts, compensation to relatives of murdered men, and mutilation in cases of grave robbery, were the descriptions of punishment usually in vogue. Capital punishment, though not unknown, was seldom inflicted.

On the introduction of British rule, a prison was established in every magisterial district, and was constructed according to the lights of that time, much on the model of Native houses and structures which always are wanting in ventilation. The prisoners were received into what seemed better accommodation than free men of their class possessed, and their diet was fully equal to that of the ordinary poor. Fetters and shackles were used to prevent them from overpowering the scanty guards. They were brought daily beyond the prison precincts in gangs, to work in road-making, and for many years the local roads near the principal towns and stations were maintained by prison labour. In the arrangements for cooking and for messing a reasonable consideration was shewn to caste prejudices. There was no special sanitation, yet there was neither misery nor squalor. The magistrate of the district was solely responsible for the prison, but no professional and scientific supervision was undertaken. Little was attempted in the direction of the numerous humane refinements and reforms, which are now deemed indispensable in the management of prisons. There was nothing to cause scandal, and there was no distressful hardship beyond that which is incidental to crowded and ill-ventilated wards in a hot climate. Life prisoners were transported across sea to the straits of Malacca and other settlements beyond the confines of India. The voyage across "the black-water," as the ocean is called, had for many years an ominous though salutary sound to the ear of the evil-doer.

Gradually public opinion, in India as elsewhere, awoke to the belief that for prisoners something more than mere incarceration is morally obligatory. And within the present generation, reforms have been introduced into the prisons of India, which, though still lagging behind, are advancing towards the same end as that to which prison reformers in England and elsewhere look forward. The district prisons have been improved in construction, especially as regards ventilation. Many central prisons have been erected on the best-known models, and to them have been drafted from the district gaols all prisoners save those sentenced to short terms; some of these prisons may be fairly designated as fine structures. The outdoor labour on the roads was considered injurious to the health and discipline of the men, liable to petty abuses, and wasteful in respect to the labour of the guards with the scattered gangs, therefore, indoor labour within the prison precincts was substituted. The men were concentrated upon organized industries and upon manufactures by hand or by machinery according to opportunities. At most of the prisons the entire clothing of the inmates is now made; many useful articles, not ordinarily produced in the neighbourhood, are manufactured for local consumption, and even for exportation. The prison-made carpets, for instance, both of the rougher and of the more ornate sorts, have some reputation in the market. In some of the larger central prisons, machinery is extensively worked for manufactures in cotton and other fibres; printing, lithography and other practical arts are carried on. The sale proceeds of prison-made articles defray a considerable portion of the expenses of the prisons. Next, the scale and composition of the diet were further improved, and a liberal allowance of warm clothing, to obviate the effect of the chills and the changes of temperature incidental to hot climates, was ordered. The rules for ironing and fettering were revised in a considerate spirit. A careful distinction was observed between those sentenced to hard labour and those not so sentenced, and a partial attempt at classification of the prisoners was made, in order that persons imprisoned for light offences might not be made worse by contact with hardened criminals. Rules were made whereby the prisoners might, by good conduct, obtain a slight reduction in the terms of their imprisonment and so have some motive for self-reformation. Arrangements were made to afford elementary education to all prisoners who could in any way be made to learn. A complete system of sanitation was enforced and medical officers were placed in executive charge of the prisoners under the supervision of the magistrates. In every province of the empire an Inspector-General of prisons was appointed to ensure uniformity of practice.

The prisoners, sentenced to transportation for long terms or for life, are now concentrated at the settlement of Port Blair in the Andaman islands in the Bay of Bengal. From the first, arrangements were made in that convict settlement to afford the men some opportunities for colonizing in the island. It became apparent, however, that the conditions of colonization were being rendered too easy, and were liable to abuse, as impairing the deterrent effect of transportation. Special measures have subsequently been taken to ensure that the men shall undergo a course of complete discipline as prisoners, before being admitted to any privileges.

Reformatories are established at central places for the moral reformation of juvenile offenders who have been sentenced to terms of imprisonment. But the further and equally important principle that the magistracy should have the power of taking up and sending to reformatories, children of the class known as "street arabs," who are without parents or relatives or ostensible guardians and are manifestly growing up in vice and crime, is not practically carried out, though in theory its justice and expediency are recognised.

There are, however, many faults, still perceptible, which must be removed before the prisons in India can be approved by reformers. In many of the prisons the mortality is occasionally lamentable; in few would the sanitary returns and the statistics of sickness indicate permanent salubrity; and the general death-rate among the prisoners in the aggregate must be regarded as high. The ventilation, despite all the attention which has been bestowed upon it, is still defective in many prisons; the sleeping wards are generally too full at night and sometimes are quite overcrowded. The classification of the prisoners, according to the character of their crimes or offences, is carried into effect during the night in the wards, but not during the day when the people are at their labour, or at the best is observed imperfectly during the working hours. Solitary confinement is but rarely enforced as a necessary part of the course to be undergone; though it is sometimes ordered as an additional punishment for breaches of prison discipline. It has not as yet been found possible to provide that the prisoners shall sleep each man in a separate compartment. This reform was earnestly advocated by Mary Carpenter during her visits to India. Though many prisoners, while in prison, learn much that may be useful to them in leading an honest life after their release, still the arrangements for their education and their moral discipline are defective. At the best their physical condition will not appear good, if judged by the standards prevailing in advanced countries. While many prisoners gain in weight and strength during their incarceration, many on the other hand languish and sicken under the sense of constraint and confinement, so distressing to their nature.

CHAPTER XII.

LAND-TAX AND LANDED TENURES.

Nature of land-tax—The tax is a portion of the rent, and a percentage on gross value of the produce—Immense work of field survey and record of rights—Property in land created or recognised by British Government—Value of such property—Fee-simple estates belonging to Europeans—Permanent settlement in Bengal and elsewhere—Importance of village communities in northern India—Tenures in Madras and Bombay—Antiquity of village officers—Indebtedness of peasant proprietors in some districts—Tenant-right—Privileges of occupancy tenants—Tenants at will—Protection accorded to cultivators.

THIS main branch of the Indian revenue embraces questions of interest, social, moral or economic, which may be discussed quite apart from fiscal details.

Controversy still hovers round the definition of the land-tax. After protracted discussion whether this tax is of the nature of rent or of revenue, and after disputation affecting the nomenclature more than the essence of the case, the best opinion is that the tax really consists of a certain portion taken by the State from the rent. The accepted definition of rent is the profit of the cultivation after the cost of husbandry has been defrayed, and after the subsistence of the cultivator and his family has been provided. Thus out of the rent there is a portion taken by the State, usually much the smaller, while the remaining portion, usually much the larger, remains with the people. That portion which is taken by the State may be regarded as revenue. The same principle doubtless obtained in theory under Native rule and in well-ordered Native States received observance. But in many of such States, as foreign or intestine troubles caused depletion of the treasury, the ministers would absorb more and more of the profit or rent, till nothing but bare subsistence was left to the landowner. Whatever may, or may not, be the shortcomings of the British Government, it has set up on unshakeable foundations the principle that the land-tax shall absorb only a moderate percentage of the rent or profit of the cultivation. In the vast majority of instances this principle has been followed; there may yet be some instances where too much of the rent is taken for the State; but such instances when discovered are gradually rectified.

Calculations have been made which tend to shew that too narrow a margin of profit remains to the peasant proprietor. It is difficult to frame detailed calculations of this nature, which involve so many small particulars of peasant life. But revised calculations indicate that the proper margin must really exist. The value of the produce of the different sorts of land is known; and a reference to this and to other broad considerations shews that the land-tax represents but a small percentage of the proceeds. The following table, taken from a recent publication by Mr. H. S. Cunningham, embodies the best information recently collected.

Provinces.	Percentage of land revenue on estimated gross value of crops.
Panjab	5·6
North-western Provinces and Oudh	7·8
Bengal	3·9
Central Provinces	3·8
Berar	4·6
Bombay	7·6
Madras	6·3

In all the provinces of British India excepting Bengal and Behar, the Government has undertaken to make a detailed settlement, consisting of an assessment of the land-tax either upon every field separately, or upon each village or parish after a detailed examination of all the fields in it. For this purpose a scientific survey has been executed of the outer boundaries of every village or parish and of all physical features within it. Further, a survey has been executed of every field, in some provinces rough but approximately accurate, in other provinces with something near scientific accuracy. Regarding every field, there are entered in a register the names of the owner, the occupant, the subowner, the lessee, or any one who has an interest in it, superior or inferior, also the rent, and the revenue if separately assessed. Regarding every village or parish there is a summary or abstract of the tenures, the rights, the customs, the rent-roll, the land-tax. This minute and comprehensive operation is termed the "Record of Rights;" it shews varieties according to diversity of circumstance in the several provinces, but in its main features it is uniform for them all. It is thus the Domesday-book of British India; its proportions and details probably exceed those of any similar work undertaken by any Government in any age or country, so vast is the cultivated and cultivable area to which it relates, so numerous is the population which it affects. It constitutes the most laborious of all the tasks essayed by the British in India, and this enormous work has been accomplished within forty years, that is between 1835 and 1875, or in a space of time hardly exceeding one generation of men. To it has been devoted some of the best civil talent at the disposal of the Government, and its successful accomplishment sheds lustre on the memory of several eminent men departed, on the names of Mertins Bird, Thomason, Lawrence, Wingate, Goldsmid, Priestley.

Not only has the initial work of the field survey been so vast, but the keeping up of such a survey, and the revising of it yearly according to the personal changes of ownership or occupancy, to the reclamation of the waste or to other changes in the cultivable area, even to modification in the boundaries of fields,—represent a never-ceasing round of work. Thus the constituted village accountant is the notary for all transfers temporary or permanent and for all devolutions of property in land. The village accounts revised annually and filed in several public offices constitute a notarial register for every village. From this system, however, are excepted the territories of Bengal proper and Behar where landed property is very valuable, and where transfers offering temptations to fraud are often effected.

It is upon a consideration of all the circumstances, elucidated by this field survey, that the land-tax has been assessed. The assessing officer duly considers the varieties of soil so numerous and yet so well known to the peasantry, the crops raised in rotation upon every plot of ground, the value of the produce according to the average of yield and of prices, the presence or absence of artificial irrigation, the distance or the proximity of markets, the advantages or disadvantages in respect of roads and communications, the fiscal history of the neighbourhood, the habits of the people, the bearing of the calculations thus educed upon the previous assessment, with the view of determining whether the landowners can, or cannot, bear enhancement and whether they are, or are not, entitled to reduction.

There may be discussions whether the technical designations of the various forms of property which exist in the empire have been rightly rendered under given circumstances, whether the British Government is correctly or incorrectly styled the universal landlord, in all the provinces with some exceptions, whether it has inherited from preceding dynasties a manorial and seignorial position or whether it has receded from such position. There is no doubt, however, that the Government has either conferred *de novo* on the people or else recognised authoritatively as belonging to them, something which is equivalent to property in land. There may be dispute whether under Native rule such a property did exist, or whether if existing it was formally recognised. Certainly it was but too often beaten down, battered and defaced in troublous times, like standing crops by hail or thunderstorm. Still the best opinion is that it struggled on with an unbroken though a precarious existence. At all events under British rule it has been either created afresh, or confirmed by a recognition which has resuscitated a more than pristine vitality. Throughout the empire the land is possessed by men who can inherit, lease, transfer, sell or otherwise dispose of it, subject only to one condition, namely that of paying the land-tax. The property, with its privileges and liabilities, then devolves on the transferees, without any question on the part of the State. So long as the people pay the tax, which is payable in cash, they are absolutely free from any interference on the part of the State respecting the raising, reaping or storing of the grain, and they make their own arrangements uncontrolled. They have the benefit of any improvements effected, or of any capital laid out by themselves. They present the money due from them and no enquiries are made regarding their affairs.

Certainly, their land is liable to be sold by the State in order to meet arrears of unpaid land-tax or other cesses upon the land. But, after all, this is no uncommon proviso, for in the case of other taxes, the property taxed is liable to seizure in event of default. Sale of the land is, however, enforced only in the last resort; personal property, excepting always the implements of agriculture, is first attached, temporary leasing to another party is tried, so that the property may have a chance of recovering itself, in practice sale is very rarely ordered. When the process is adopted, it is fenced round with numerous provisions, prescribed by law, and framed in order to ensure that the owner shall receive due notice, and shall be otherwise protected; and he has his legal remedy if any one of these provisions shall be neglected.

Notwithstanding the creation or recognition of such property, the arrangement may be vitiated if the land-tax be fixed so high as to render the property valueless, or even to impair its value. But the land-tax is not so fixed; on the contrary it is assessed at such rates as leave a margin of real profit to the owner. If by any chance it is found to have been fixed too high according to this principle, steps are always taken for its reduction.

Although the generic features of landed property, as above set forth, are much the same throughout the empire, there are yet several specific varieties. The most perfect form is that which has been accorded by the State to European owners in the Himalayas and in the Nilgiris, tea-planters, and coffee-planters. In these cases the land-tax is either "redeemed" by the owner, that is, compounded for, on the payment of a certain sum down, or else is fixed in perpetuity at what is called locally a "quit-rent," that is an almost nominal rate. The owner then considers himself to have what is called locally the "fee-simple." These designations are here given as they are actually used, without reference to their correctness, or otherwise, according to the English law whence they are drawn. There may be other varieties in this tenure; but on the whole the European owners will probably admit that they have a complete and satisfactory title.

The next tenure is that where the land-tax is fixed for ever, without any possibility of enhancement, by what is termed locally, "the perpetual limitation of the demand." This prevails throughout the provinces of Bengal, Behar and Benares. With it also may be classed the separate "Zemindaris," or estates existing in several parts of the empire. The owners, who hold under this tenure, resemble landlords in the United Kingdom. Their land-tax is generally light and their property is valuable, being made the subject of large pecuniary transactions, in the same way as in the most advanced countries. It is by means of such transactions that European indigo-planters have become possessed, either by ownership or by long leases, of so many extensive estates. As the families of the Native landlords have increased, and as subdivision is still the prevailing rule of Hindu inheritance, primogeniture being the exception, the allotment of shares among the members has often proved difficult and troublesome. The process is known locally by the name of "partition," and has formed the subject of elaborate legislation. Where, as in parts of eastern Bengal and northern Behar, the tax, originally moderate, has become extremely light when spread over the cultivation which has increased within the limits of the estates, these tenures are but little inferior to the "fee-simple" tenures just described. The landlords have under them tenants with many varieties of tenancy.

Resembling them in most respects, save one, are the landlords of Orissa, of Oudh, of Sind, of the Central Provinces, and of other "Zemindari" estates in several parts of the empire. The point of difference is this, that the land-tax is fixed not in perpetuity but for a long term of twenty or thirty years. The landlords of the Central Provinces are for the most part petty in degree, though still above the rank of peasant proprietors.

The next tenure is that of the peasant proprietors of the greater part of the North-western Provinces and the Panjab, whose land-tax is also fixed for long terms of twenty or thirty years. In their case there is a peculiarity in that they are, for the purposes of land revenue, grouped together in villages or parishes. As the men are usually descended from a common stock and form a cousinhood, they are legally held to be a "village community," or a "coparcenary" consisting of "co-partners," or, as they call themselves, a "brotherhood." The manner in which this form of society arises in India and in other countries is described in Sir Henry Maine's work on village communities. The village was originally the proprietary unit throughout India; though in some parts it has subsequently disappeared. The compact front it presented to martial invasion and to armed spoliation has been the theme of much eloquent description. The State assesses the land-tax upon the village in the aggregate; the members of the brotherhood then assess upon themselves their quotas of the assessed amount, each man according to his share or holding, with the sanction of the assessing authorities. If any member shall thereafter fail to pay his quota, the other members are liable for it, with the proviso that they may take up the holding of the defaulter.

There is thus a solidarity between all those who belong to the fraternity; and this is the arrangement so well known in northern India by the name of "joint responsibility." It is condemned by some, as leading to hardship and other complications. By other authorities the hardship has been denied and the advantages to the brotherhood have been urged; the practice is defended in respect of these considerations and in deference to established usage. It has the effect, among other consequences, of keeping the lands of each village in the hands of a certain clan, and renders the ingress of strangers very difficult. In many places the communities will not allow any of their members to transfer holdings to strangers, while transfers to members of the village clan or of kindred clans are common. Nevertheless, holdings have often been transferred to strangers, especially Native bankers who acquire possession under mortgages; and sometimes such transfers give birth to feuds. On the whole, the property is effectively valuable, in proof of which, among other signs, may be adduced the fact that moneys, large in the aggregate, are advanced, year after year, by Native bankers to these landowners on the security of their proprietary tenure. The men are peasant proprietors cultivating a part at least of their holdings, leasing the remainder to cultivators as tenants.

Each of these village communities has a quantity of waste land included in its area, which waste is the property of the brotherhood. Every member of the brotherhood has an interest in this common waste according to his share or his holding. In the densely peopled parts of the country, as the territory between the Ganges and the Jamna or the upper part of the Panjab, the waste entirely belongs to the village communities. In other territories, as the central Panjab, where the waste is extensive, the communities have a liberal allowance of such waste made to them; and the remaining waste is reserved to the State.

Resembling these northern proprietors in many respects, are

the men who hold under the ryotwari, or ryot's, tenure in the Presidencies of Madras and Bombay; in which category also may be included the landholders of many parts of British Burmah and of Assam. The "ryot" of the State, as he is technically termed in Madras and Bombay, is virtually a peasant proprietor of the land he holds. He cannot be interfered with in his tenure while he pays his land revenue, and he has a heritable and transferable right therein. He may have some waste land also allotted to him; he has facilities for giving up to the State any field he does not care to keep and for obtaining fresh plots from the State; otherwise the unallotted waste belongs to the State. Lands are, however, assigned by the State to the ryots, as grouped into village communities, for pasturage and for woodcutting. The land-tax is assessed not on the village in the gross, but upon every field or upon every holding in detail. Each "ryot" pays separately his land-tax to the State, without any concern in the affairs of those who own lands in the same village with him. That the tenure amounts to property in land and comprises a valuable security, is in the Bombay Presidency attested by the fact of large sums of money being lent by Native money-lenders and bankers to the "ryots" on this security, which practice has grown greatly during the present generation since the introduction of the current settlements made for thirty years, and has in part conduced to the indebtedness of the peasant proprietary of the Deccan.

In northern, western and southern India, alike in those provinces where "joint responsibility" prevails and where it does not, the ancient organization of the "village" is preserved. There is the village headman, who is the medium for collecting the quotas due from each landowner in the village, who in some districts is vested with petty police powers, whose office is usually hereditary, whose position is officially recognised, and who has legally defined responsibilities for the reporting of crime and for assisting the police. There is the village accountant, much better trained and educated at present than he ever was under Native rule or during the earlier times of British rule. There is the village watchman forming part of a rural constabulary of which the status and emoluments have been much ameliorated. There are also village servants, the blacksmith, the shoemaker and harness-maker, the weaver, the barber, the potter, who are members of hereditary trades, and are very interesting to all who study the industrial arts of India.

The indebtedness of the peasant proprietors in some parts of the empire has caused and still causes anxiety. Nothing can be more disappointing to those who have done their best to assess the land-tax moderately, and have so assessed it according to all available data, in order, among other things, that the peasant proprietors may live in manly independence, untrammelled with debts, than to find that these men are nevertheless but too often burdened with these obligations. At first sight it will be inferred that the land-tax must be too high, but enquiry generally fails to shew that such is the case. The fact is that many of these men have a thriftless and improvident disposition. On occasions of marriages and social festivities they habitually incur expenses beyond their means, and the village-banker is at hand to offer temptation. The commonest experience in the world shews that any one may become involved in debt if once he begins to incur charges which he cannot immediately defray. It is in this way that these men become indebted, once they yield to the seductions of the money-lender. In seasons of drought, they may reasonably obtain assistance and then the money-lender exercises a useful function; and at most times they may reasonably obtain some accommodation, the amount of which is speedily cleared off. But once they go beyond this point, they are snared in the toils of the money-lender's books, and as he prefers to keep them there, he takes care that they shall not easily escape. He charges interest simple and compound till the victim becomes confused, and signs a fresh bond for the renewal of the debt, principal and interest together, with but little insight into the method by which the account is made up.

In the Deccan, the peasant proprietors having been first rendered somewhat extravagant by some seasons of inflated prosperity and then reduced by some unpropitious years, ran largely into debt from which extrication was difficult. In their embarrassment they turned violently upon the money-lenders as the authors of their misfortune, and some disturbance ensued. Enquiry, by a special commission, shewed that the evil had not proceeded to any irremediable length and that not more than one-third of the peasantry had become seriously involved, two-thirds being still comparatively free. Legislation was undertaken for removing the evil which, after all abatements, was proved to be considerable. Additional facilities are afforded for the settlement of the debts; conciliation courts and arbitration tribunals have been established. Authority is given to the judges to examine, more closely and equitably than before, the particulars of which the debts were composed, to separate the principal from the interest, which is to be reduced to a fair and moderate amount. Those peasants who became seriously involved, have suffered much misery which has evoked the kindly sympathy of philanthropists and reformers in England, and has been eloquently described by Florence Nightingale.

The regret felt respecting the indebtedness would be mitigated if the debts had been incurred for agricultural improvements, such as the construction of wells for irrigation; but they are generally not incurred for such purposes. The Government, however, has always made advances in cash to peasant proprietors for the construction of wells, and other small works of irrigation. The people do not largely apply for these advances in ordinary times, but whenever they do receive such accommodation they are punctual and honest in repayment. In times of drought, however, they are forward and eager in applying for advances, which are readily granted by the authorities. Some thousands of wells, in various parts of the empire, have by these means been constructed during the recent famines. Recently there has been legislation for the purposes of facilitating the grant of advances by the State for agricultural and other material improvements, upon a large as well as a small scale. In some cases landowners have availed themselves of these advantages, but generally the landholding community has been backward and hesitating in this respect.

The liability to enhancement of the land-tax, after the expiry of even a long term of years, does detract somewhat from the value of the property. Lands of which the tax is settled for thirty years, though valuable, are not nearly so valuable as lands where it is settled for ever. Still, the landowner, seeing the carefulness and moderation with which the assessment has been made, and understanding the data on which it is founded, feels confidence that the same principles will be observed at the next assessment. He knows, indeed, that after enjoying for at least the term of settlement the entire benefit of all improvements he makes, he may have to surrender some portion of it to the State at the next settlement in the shape of enhanced assessment, still he is assured that the greater part will be left to him. Nevertheless, there are undoubted evils in the system of periodical revision; as the end of a current settlement draws near, the people are anxious and doubtful, and their energies are somewhat impaired. The progress of improvement is retarded for a time, as the outlay of agricultural capital is postponed till the new assessment shall have been completed.

These and other considerations have moved the Government to debate whether the principle of the permanent settlement of Bengal should not be extended to some parts of northern India. At one time a measure of this character seemed very near to promulgation; the Government paused, however; arguments on the other side were urged; and the prospect of any such extension seems now to be remote. It is felt that in some parts of Bengal and Behar the permanently settled land revenue has become extremely light and almost nominal, having been assessed for ever on lands then imperfectly cultivated, but subsequently brought under complete cultivation. A rate of incidence, which may have been reasonable at the time, is now unreasonably light; thus it is felt that there has been an unwarrantable sacrifice of the State income. This is no reason for infringing upon the permanent settlement, which is inviolable wherever it has been made. But it is a reason for hesitating to introduce such a settlement into any tracts, save those which are cultivated to the utmost, so far as can be reasonably foreseen. The question then arises as to whether any, and if so, what, lands are thus cultivated at present. There may indeed be few or none such, regard being had to the effect of railways and other works of material improvement. Hence the Government may doubt whether, having respect to the imperative interests of the public revenue, it can afford to extend the permanent settlement, much as that extension might on other grounds be desired. Endeavours, however, have been made, perhaps are still being made, to educe some principles whereby the future revisions of assessment shall be regulated, so that the landowners may know as nearly as possible beforehand what to expect on these occasions.

Tenant-right, by which is meant the status of the occupant or cultivator, below the grade of peasant proprietor, has formed a vexed question in several parts of India. The permanent settlement in Bengal is held by some authorities to have made either no provision, or very inadequate provision, for the status of tenants, occupants or cultivators subordinate to the landlord. Under the circumstances of Bengal there long existed a body of opinion adverse to tenant-right, though this feeling has probably abated of late years. In the North-western Provinces and in the Panjab there has always existed a sentiment in favour of tenant-right. In Oudh the question has been keenly contested and, after some controversy, much has been done for the tenantry. In the Central Provinces, their position has been gradually improved step by step. In Sind their status is still under consideration with a view to improvement. In the southern and western parts of the empire, that is in the Presidencies of Madras and Bombay, no very large questions of this nature have arisen, except in the Concan, where the disputes between the Khote landlords and their subholders have been recently determined by legislation.

In Bengal twenty years have elapsed since a legislative enactment was passed, with which the name of Edward Currie will ever be honourably associated. Thereby the principle was established that a tenant, who had been uninterruptedly in occupancy for twelve years, shall not, in the absence of specific agreement, be liable to have his rent arbitrarily or summarily enhanced, and that if the landlord shall demand an enhancement to which the tenant does not agree, such enhancement shall not be enforced without an order of a court of justice. In other words, a landlord cannot ordinarily enhance the rent of such a tenant without bringing a suit; and this necessarily operates as a check upon the landlord and a protection to the tenant. It is theoretically possible for the landlords to evade this enactment by not allowing any new tenant to remain as long as twelve years, or by removing tenants as their respective terms of years approach termination, but practically this, if it has happened occasionally, happens rarely. Generally the landlords allow their good tenants to run on undisturbed, and thus to rise, one after another, from the status of a tenant at will without rights to that of an occupancy tenant with rights as above described. Already the number of such occupancy tenants in Bengal is considerable, and will increase from time to time.

In Behar, the same law prevails; the people, however, avail themselves of it but little. From various local causes, the tenantry though physically active and industrious, are morally depressed; they probably have not the spirit, certainly not the power, to assert their rights. Among these causes are the density of the population, and the multiplicity of the people demanding to cultivate upon any terms, however meagre, which they can obtain. Thus the peasantry in Behar are for the most part tenants at will, without any rights; their condition is not worthy of the fertile and thriving territory which is cultivated by their industry, and has called forth indignant remarks from some officers of much local experience. The circumstance has caused anxiety to the authorities; improvement was retarded by the famine, but some measures of amelioration will doubtless be found practicable, though the evils, however manifest, are difficult of speedy remedy. Beneficial changes, however, in their condition have of late been brought about.

In the North-western Provinces and in the Panjab, when the settlement of the land revenue was made for terms of twenty and thirty years and when the rights of all the proprietors were recorded, special consideration was given to the status of the tenantry, who form a considerable class, notwithstanding that the country there is so largely held by peasant proprietors. The tenants were broadly divided into two main classes, first those who had rights on the presumption of their having had possession for a long time, or from father to son, whence they were locally called "hereditary;" secondly, those who had not such a status, who were tenants at will, being locally called "non-hereditary." The "hereditary" tenants were held to possess much the same rights as the occupancy tenants above described, and they comprised a large proportion of the entire tenantry. Subsequently, questions having arisen regarding the operation and the validity of these settlements in the Panjab, an enactment was passed by the legislature which virtually confirmed these arrangements. Laws of a similar nature regarding the relations of the agricultural classes towards each other have been enacted for the North-western Provinces and Oudh. But in Oudh it seems to be held by some authorities that there yet remains more to be effected before full justice is done to the peasantry.

Thus, the position of a considerable portion of the tenantry in northern India has been hedged with many safeguards. The occupancy tenant is effectually protected against undue exaction and from interference or eviction, so long as he pays the customary or the stipulated rent. It is generally admitted that he may inherit the lands, but not that he may improve, sell, transfer or sublet them without the consent of his landlord. Custom, however, varies in many localities, and instances may be found where he can do all these things, and where he differs but little from a sub-proprietor. Probably, as time advances, these several points will be cleared up in his favour; and the logical sequence will be to promote him gradually to the position of a sub-proprietor who may do what he sees fit with the land, having the benefit of all improvements, so long as he pays the stipulated rent, the landlord retaining a voice in all improvements or alterations, lest the land should be in any way injured. In any case, it appears to be necessary that the superior proprietor should have at least this much of concurrent authority over his own land.

There remains, however, for the "occupancy" tenants a difficult question which seems to be still far from solution, namely this, can the landlord enhance their rents? and if he can, then what principle is to guide the enhancement? In some places, for instance eastern Bengal, these tenants once affirmed that their rents should not be raised. They even stirred up agrarian disturbances and agitation, in support of claims which really were to that effect. The landlords claimed, and will probably continue to claim, some share in the proceeds of the increased value and yield of the produce of their estates, which is locally termed "the unearned increment." Such disputes may be carried before the courts of justice; but the judges can decide only by the custom of the neighbourhood, often a moot point, or by other dubious data. It is much to be desired that some principle should be evolved, commanding the acquiescence of all concerned, and be embodied in a legislative enactment. The Government in Bengal has for some years been engaged in paving the way for such legislation.

Whether the measures in favour of occupancy tenants be considered sufficient or not, there remains a class of tenants, numerous in many provinces, and numerically preponderating in some provinces, who are tenants at will, in the technical sense. In some places such men are of long standing on the estate; in many places they are migratory persons who do other work besides cultivation, and who are free to move and to change. Even their position, however, has been guarded by many just provisions; their rent may be enhanced indeed, but not during the currency of the agricultural year, nor without adequate notice. If they are to move, timely notice and warning must be given them; they may be evicted for failure to pay rent, but the eviction must be regulated by a procedure framed for their protection against oppression. If process of distraint or attachment be issued, their implements and plough-cattle are exempted.

Under Native rule the rent was very often paid in kind, because the revenue itself was so paid; where the revenue was paid in cash, rents came to be paid in the same way. Under British rule rents are still sometimes paid in kind, but more often in cash, and the tendency towards this mode of payment becomes strengthened from time to time.

Opinions will differ regarding the merits or demerits of what has been, or is being, done regarding tenant-right. At the greatest centre in the empire, Calcutta, the landlord influence, both European and Native, is strong. Many of the Native landlords have evinced a considerate and conciliatory spirit towards the tenantry. Those who incline towards the landlord's view, will probably deem that the law has done enough in this direction. Irrespective of them, however, the majority of the Native community will probably be in favour of the tenantry, and would perhaps welcome any further legislation in the direction of tenant-right. Official opinion may not be unanimous on the subject, but would probably support the same view. Some European officers, of ability and of special knowledge, consider that all the cultivators, now regarded as tenants at will, should have their rents determined for a long term of years and should not be liable to eviction so long as they duly pay such rent. In Mr. Irvin's interesting book upon rural affairs in Oudh, recently published, and entitled 'The Garden of India,' opinions of this tendency are fully explained and vindicated. It is possible that opinions of this nature may find acceptance more and more, and that the tendency of future changes and of coming legislation will be in this direction.

The Indian Famine Commission in their recently published report clearly indicate an opinion that further legislation is required for the better protection of both occupancy and non-occupancy tenants.

On the whole, the management of the land-tax is the most satisfactory, as it is the most important, part of the administration of British India. Whatever faults may exist in it, they are slight as compared with the merits; whatever shortcomings may still be perceived, they are small relatively to the vast and undoubted achievements. Property in land has been recognised throughout the empire with a practical efficacy unknown before. It has been rendered valuable by equity and moderation in taxation; its devolution has been secured by all the forms and processes exemplified in the most advanced nations. Tenant-right has been established for the better classes of husbandmen, and has been so dealt with that its growth and diffusion among the humbler peasants may be promoted. Thus, the landed system becomes a mainstay of the national stability, and a foundation of popular contentment.

CHAPTER XIII.

REVENUES.

Land revenue—Average rates of its incidence—Tributes and contributions from Native States—Excise—Assessed taxes—Customs—Abolition of import duties on English piece goods—The salt tax—English salt imported—Opium revenue—Objections to it discussed—Stamp revenue—Total of general revenues—Government receipts as contradistinguished from revenue proper—Taxation for local and municipal purposes—Projects for new taxes deprecated.

THE nature of the land revenue has been explained in the preceding chapter. Its average yield may be set down at 21 millions sterling per annum; though in some years, owing to recovery of arrears, its receipts have exceeded this sum. Its incidence per acre varies considerably, as might be expected, in different provinces, but averages in most parts of the empire, 1¼ rupee or 2*s.* 6*d.* per acre unirrigated, and 4 rupees or 8*s.* per acre irrigated. The best calculations shew that it falls at the rate of four shillings per annum per head of the landowning population.

Some authorities have apprehended that it is a heavier burden in the present, than it was in the past, generation, and in proof of this, the fact is adduced that its total amount has nearly doubled during this time. Had such an increase occurred with the same population and the same cultivated area, it would indeed be remarkable. But during the time, fresh provinces, with 36 millions of people and 242,000 square miles of territory, have been added to the empire, to which circumstance alone 6 millions sterling of land revenue are attributable. The area of cultivation generally is ascertained to have increased by more than 50 per cent., while in some provinces under the Madras Government it has amounted to 100 per cent.; and the prices of agricultural produce have risen. To these causes some legitimate increase may be ascribed, but in no instance is any increase due to an augmentation of the share claimed by the State in the rent or profit of the cultivation. On the contrary, the share thus claimed has everywhere diminished, and in some provinces, especially the North-western, the diminution has been remarkable. In the Panjab the lightness of the British land-tax, as compared with that of the Sikh Native Government, is notorious and has brought about a great increase in the value of land. Calculations have been made which seem to shew that when the Permanent Settlement was made in Bengal, the total rental of the Zemindars amounted to only a few hundred thousand pounds annually and that it now amounts to several millions sterling. In the Bombay Presidency the area of cultivation has so greatly expanded that, notwithstanding a reduction in the rate of assessment per acre, there has been a considerable augmentation of the land revenue. Thus the best information goes to prove that the land-tax is becoming relatively lighter. Certainly the Government and all its officers earnestly desire that this tax should be really moderate, believing that such moderation affords the surest basis of popular contentment under British rule. Except in seasons of drought, the demand is punctually paid and easily collected.

It has been sometimes suggested that the British system of collecting this tax is too rigid and unbending and that a greater degree of elasticity and flexibility of method is needed, according to circumstances of drought and other calamity. Now, British rule is more rigid in this respect than Native rule; there must necessarily be more of such rigidity on the part of the British, between whom and the people a settlement or compact has been made, than on the part of Native rulers, between whom and their people no such arrangement had been effected. The essence of a settlement is that the people should, in the main, take the poor years with the good. In bad years, however, the British authorities invariably shew consideration, notwithstanding the settlement, giving the men time to pay, suspending the demand till the seasons improve, and sometimes remitting a portion of it altogether. These lenient measures are adopted to a large extent in all provinces.

Some authorities have thought that in certain places, or under certain circumstances, the Government might advantageously revert to the old Native system of collecting the land revenue in kind, instead of the existing system of collecting it in cash. But the prevailing opinion would be wholly adverse to such a measure which would be regarded as retrograde. Such a method of collecting is contrary to the genius of British rule. It would give rise to the inquisitorial interference which British policy has been so careful to avoid, and it would impair or destroy that sense of manly independence and spirit of self-help which the British administration has striven to foster in the people. It would resuscitate a host of abuses which the British system has extinguished, and it would, in all probability, prove unpopular in practice.

The tributes and contributions from Native States amount, on the average, to nearly three-quarters of a million sterling. They represent an item of income which, in times free from political disturbance, may be regarded as fixed and certain.

The excise amounts, on the average, to upwards of two millions and a half sterling; if perfectly well managed throughout the empire, it amounts to three millions sterling. It is levied on spirits made locally from various sources, the wild fruits of trees and the like; and on drugs, prepared from the opium poppy, from some sorts of hemp, and so on. It is not liable to evasion on any of the items of which it consists, except opium.

As a tax upon opium grown and consumed in the country, it is quite distinct from the revenue derived from the opium exported to China. It is subject to evasion because, in the province of Behar and in Central India, great quantities of opium are produced for exportation. But while the exportable opium pays its full duty without any unlawful abatement, the persons concerned in the production of the drug contrive to secrete a certain proportion, small doubtless as compared with the total quantity produced, but enough for the private consumption of themselves or their neighbours, sufficient also to affect the yield of the local excise. In the province of Gujerat, in the peninsula of Kathiawar and on the western coast, adjoining the opium-growing districts of Central India, there is a large consumption locally which for the most part evades taxation. Some progress has, however, been made towards prevention; and constant attention is directed to the subject.

There have been doubts felt regarding the moral effect of the system of excise on spirits. Farming this branch of the exciso, does indeed prevent evasion, for the farmer and his servants become ex-officio preventive agents with vigilance stimulated by self-interest. On the other hand it sustains a class of influential publicans who have every incentive to encourage drinking among all those who are inclined to this indulgence. At one time the farming system was found to be coincident with aggravation of drunkenness among some of the mountainous tribes, and a modification of that system was followed by moral amelioration in this respect. In several provinces the system has been re-arranged so that it should be freed from any possible reproach on the score of encouraging intemperance. There is indeed in the great capital cities, the large central stations, and many other frequented places, an excess of drinking, which might not perhaps excite surprise in northern climes, but which is more than would be expected in warmer latitudes. The sight of this may give to some observers the impression that under British rule drinking prevails more than under Native rule. Wider observation will, however, prove that the Indians, if judged by the standard of advanced nations, are sober and temperate in the main; and that despite any defects which may still lurk in the excise system, the British taxes do operate as some check upon insobriety.

The assessed taxes at present consist of a licence tax on trades imposed since the famine of 1877, with a view of ensuring a surplus of income over expenditure, and so enabling the State to execute works of material improvement for the prevention of famine. It is held that the mercantile classes are but little taxed otherwise, and bear less fiscal burdens than other classes of the community. This licence tax is not assessed upon a consideration of the income of each taxpayer, like an income tax. The taxpayers are grouped into classes, according to incomes above and below certain amounts, and for each class one rate is fixed for all who are placed therein. The tax may therefore be described as a rough income tax upon traders, without the inquiry into the affairs of individuals which is apt to be unpopular in India. If not so productive as an income tax, it is considered to be less objectionable. It cannot be said to have escaped unpopularity, but it has been collected without difficulty and with as little discontent as could be expected. There have been proposals to extend it to professions, and so to bring it still nearer to the principle of an income tax; these met with some disfavour at Calcutta but with some favour at Bombay and Madras, they have not, however, been carried into effect. If financial requirements necessitate the imposition of direct taxation, then a licence tax on trades with an approximate and easy assessment upon graduated classes, is much the best, or the least objectionable, form of tax. Such a measure does tend to remedy the acknowledged flaw in the fiscal system, namely the fact that the mercantile classes for the most part escape taxation by the State; they pay municipal taxes, indeed, but no appreciable taxes to the Government. In England it were easy to show how the merchant contributes to the public revenues; but it would be difficult to prove anything of the sort in India, in the absence of any assessed taxes. If the measure, however, goes beyond a rough licence tax on trades, it must gradually grow or merge into an income tax.

There would be grave objection to the re-imposition of an income tax at the present time, if that could possibly be avoided. A few years only have elapsed since the Government of India, after long and careful discussion, decided to abandon this tax. There was much to be said both for and against the tax, all which was urged publicly and officially. The decision for relinquishment, having been formally taken, ought to be respected and not disturbed except under overwhelming necessity. The arguments for the tax were much the same as they are in England, save that in one respect they were stronger, inasmuch as, in India, the measure embraces taxable classes otherwise little included in taxation, while in respect of productiveness, they were weaker. The objections against it were much the same as in England, save that they were stronger in respect to the facilities for evasion, and much stronger in respect to unpopularity. It was the comparative unproductiveness on the one hand, and the inevitable discontent on the other hand, that weighed so much with the Government of India, when, on striking the balance between conflicting considerations, the abandonment of the measure was determined.

The Customs have yielded in recent years two millions and a half, even two millions and three-quarters sterling; but are yielding less now, and are likely still further to be diminished. One principal heading in the import tariff, namely the duty on English piece goods, is seriously attacked, and may be abolished altogether. One large item in the export tariff, namely the duty on grain, is held by some to be not sound in principle, incapable of standing against the objections which might arise from any change in the rice markets of the world, and likely to last only so long as the Indian rice maintains its present position in the European trade. The list of dutiable exports has been rendered short: but the list of dutiable imports, though reduced and modified from time to time with the view of saving trouble to the trade and to the people, is still long; all its items, however, are levied without causing difficulty or discontent.

The question of abolishing or retaining the import duties on

English piece goods has excited and still excites much discussion in India. The duties on the particular articles in this category, which were most immediately exposed to competition from Indian manufactures, have been abolished, while the remaining, or most of the remaining, duties are indicated for abolition as soon as the financial circumstances of the country may permit. For the abolition it is argued that there is a growing competition between English and Indian manufactures respecting many of the articles which constitute the clothing of the population of India. The margin is becoming more and more narrowed which determines whether the British manufacturer or the Indian manufacturer shall obtain the custom and patronage which such a population can bestow. The import duty may be light, still it becomes important where the trader's profit is so slender as to be appreciable only when the trade is large, and where so slight a difference in price may turn the scale for or against the circulation of the English goods in the interior of the country. This competition is intensified by the fact that while the mass of indigenous fabrics is still made by hand without the advantages of steam and of machinery, some of these fabrics are now being made on the spot, at Bombay and elsewhere, with all these very advantages and often with English capital and under European supervision. It is natural that the British manufacturers should look upon the import duties with jealous eyes, and should apprehend that they are protective of indigenous, to the exclusion of English, manufactures. The very fact that those who produce manufactures on the spot with machinery, are opposed to the abolition, shews that they believe the duties to have a protective tendency. The circumstance that the importation of those piece goods on which the duties have been remitted, has proportionately increased since the remission, affords proof that the duties did operate protectively.

These and other similar views find some echo in India, but are there frequently controverted. Stress is laid on the fiscal loss which at present the finances cannot properly bear; while the loss caused to the English producer by the retention of the duties, and the gain to the Indian consumer by their abolition, are held to be less than has been often supposed, and too slight to be really appreciable. The cause of English piece goods not making their way into the interior of the country, is not the existence of the duties, but the fact that they cannot be laid down in India as good in quality for the same price as the indigenous goods. The repute of the English goods, it is said, has been injured by sizing and other questionable processes. The English manufacturers would do better, it is argued, if they attended to maintaining a good quality at a cheap price, rather than to agitation against the duties. The welfare of India is so much bound up with the State finance, that whatever is financially injurious operates directly on the condition of the people.

The salt tax yields on the average nearly seven millions sterling, and is one of the few taxes, perhaps it is the only tax, affecting all classes. Though imperceptible to the upper and middle classes, it is in some degree felt by the poorest classes, but then it is the only tax they pay, and represents the only contribution which they make towards the expenses of the State which protects them. Its incidence per head of the population is computed at 7*d.* per annum. It used to be designated a monopoly of the East India Company; and the general rule still is that salt shall not be manufactured in India except by the agency, or under the supervision of, the Government. The whole seaboard of the empire, including the Malabar and Coromandel coasts, the deltas of the Ganges and Indus, the shallow and nearly dried arm of the sea named the Rann of Cach, the Salt range of the Panjab, and the salt lakes and saliferous basins and tracts of Rajputana and Central India, produce salt enough for the vast population of the empire. All these tracts are still made to yield salt, except the delta of the Ganges and the upper coasts of the Bay of Bengal. In these excepted tracts, the manufacture of salt, once so extensive, has been suppressed in order that an import duty might be levied on the salt imported from England, and the expenses of local manufacture be saved; thus the salts of Droitwich and Chester alone are seen in the markets of Calcutta and of Bengal.

The people of Bengal proper have long borne, without murmuring, a high rate of salt tax, higher than that of any other part of India, nor have any striking facts been elicited to shew that the tax appreciably affects consumption. At one time the rates in the Presidencies of Madras and Bombay were much lower; of late they have been raised, though they are still lower than that of Bengal, which, on the other hand, has been slightly reduced. In the North-western Provinces, and elsewhere also, there have been signs indicating that the tax, if raised too high, would affect the consumption of salt by the people and would deter them from giving it in sufficient quantity to their cattle.

In northern and central India a remarkable change of system has been recently introduced. Formerly, the salt, made in the jurisdiction of the Native States of Rajputana, used to be despatched by a long land transit to the markets of the North-western Provinces and of the Central Provinces, and was taxed on crossing the British borders. For the purpose of this taxing, a preventive line, manned with Native sentinels at intervals all the way, under the command of European officials, stretched for about two thousand miles, beginning from near the Satlej in the north, and passing through Central India down to the Godavery in the south. This line was indeed necessary so long as no other means could be found of protecting the salt revenue. Still it represented a waste of power; also it inevitably operated as a trouble to the people and an impediment to trade. But, with the loyal and praiseworthy co-operation of the Rajput States, the management of the salt-works in their jurisdiction has been entrusted to British supervision, and the railway passes by the works on its way to the British territories, so conveying the salt to the marts. Thus, the salt being controlled at the very source of supply, the preventive line can be spared. The line was accordingly abolished at a great saving in cost of establishment and to the satisfaction of all concerned.

Together with the salt tax, duties used to be levied on this same preventive line, on sugar chiefly indigenous, and were relinquished when the line was abolished.

The opium revenue fluctuates considerably according to the ranges of prices in the Chinese markets. It yields on the average upwards of nine millions sterling gross and upwards of six millions sterling net, after defrayal of all expenses. It is levied in two ways; one, on the eastern or Bengal side, by opium, made in State factories from poppy cultivated under State supervision, and sold by auction at Calcutta on the State account to merchants who export it to China; the other, on the western or Bombay side, by an export duty levied on opium made by private manufacture from poppy grown in Native States.

Objection has been raised to the method adopted on the Bengal side, as directly connecting the Government with the manufacture of a drug which is regarded by many as deleterious. These operations are, however, undertaken by the Government only as a means of securing the revenue. It would be possible to substitute for them the system which prevails on the western side, and which would be free from this particular form of objection. But as the Bengal system has been long established and is thoroughly understood by the numerous persons concerned in it, the authorities have hesitated to make any change, lest some loss should thereby accrue to the revenue. Nor is the argument really affected by the fact that the opium department makes advances in cash to the cultivators who raise the poppy. For the cultivation would exist equally whether the Government supervised it or not; its profits would immediately attract the capitalists who abound in that part of the country, and in the absence of the Government many others would make the advances. Whichever method be adopted, the eastern or the western, the opium will be exported to China.

The real and important argument is that which attaches blame to the Government of India, because opium is exported from India for the consumption of the Chinese. Now, in effect the Government of India adopts towards opium the same attitude which the Government in England and in other countries preserves towards spirits, that is, it taxes the drug heavily. If opium flourishes in India, when thus weighted, it would flourish as much or more if lightened by the relief from fiscal burden. There cannot, then, be any objection to the taxation, as it falls upon an article which is a luxury and which, if it be useful in extreme moderation, is most deleterious if used in excess. To abandon the taxation would be to injure the treasury, leaving no check upon the consumption of the drug, but rather giving some encouragement thereto. Whether those, who object to the existing opium system, would go so far as to recommend the absolute suppression of poppy cultivation may be doubted. Inasmuch as the culture is very profitable to thousands of cultivators, and as the exportation is still more profitable to traders and capitalists, any attempt on the part of- the State at suppression would be futile, and would only lead to dangerous abuses. Nor do the British territories comprise the only area fit for poppy culture, for as already seen much of the best soils for the poppy are in Native States. The question, too, is not confined to the opium exportable to China; the Indians consume opium to some extent, though much less than the Chinese. At present the drug is taxed for the Indians as for all others, a check being thus imposed on the local consumption. In this respect, then, the Government plays, as levying a tax, the same part in respect to its own subjects as the Chinese. There remains, then, only the moral question as affecting the Chinese, which is very difficult of adequate discussion in a work relating to India. In China there are apparently two parties to be considered; one the people or consumers, the other the State. In respect to the people of China, there are certain broad considerations which must be as applicable to them as to all other nations. They are evidently fond of the Indian opium, are determined to procure it if they can, and are willing to pay a very high price for it. Nor is their desire at all lessened by the circumstance that their own Government is understood to be opposed to the use of the drug. They grow great quantities of opium at home for their own consumption, notwithstanding the efforts which their Government is understood to make occasionally for the suppression of the culture. Nevertheless, the Indian opium continues to be consumed in China as much as ever, because it is of a quality much liked by some classes, is not equalled by the indigenous drug, and therefore still commands a high price. It is not found, then, on examination that the Indian revenue from opium does any harm either to the Indians or the Chinese. On the contrary, the levying of this revenue must effect some good indirectly in checking the consumption of the drug. It seems, however, to be held by some authorities that the Chinese Government, objecting on moral grounds to the consumption of opium, desires to prohibit the importation of Indian opium into China, but is prevented from so doing by the existing commercial treaties and other arrangements with England. This is a point hardly to be discussed in a work relating to India. It is manifest, however, that if the Chinese Government shall ever attempt to prevent the importation of an article of luxury much desired by the people, it will be essaying a task which has rarely been undertaken by any Government with success anywhere, and which the Government in most civilized countries does not attempt. There may be other important points relating to China which can be best explained by the authorities who are cognizant of its affairs, and whose views will doubtless be received with due deference. The only object of the foregoing remarks is to explain the conduct and the position of the Government in India.

The stamp revenue now yields three millions sterling, and its growth has for many years been steady and satisfactory. It is a fiscal heading new to India since the introduction of British rule, and its profitable character is often a marvel to the Natives, who regard it as an instance of Western ingenuity.

Although objections are raised against some parts of it, still on the whole it is far from being unpopular. The stamps are grouped under two categories, namely those which are levied on judicial documents and those on commercial documents. The judicial stamps are free from evasion, and are realised easily. They are by some condemned as being taxes on justice; this objection is not indeed destitute of weight, though it is counterbalanced by the fact that litigation flourishes, and that the petty classes of suits are specially numerous with a slight tendency to increase. The commercial stamps are rarely made the subjects of complaint; but they are probably evaded to a great extent, notwithstanding all the precautions which the authorities can take; but, persevering vigilance will gradually prevent this evasion, with a corresponding advantage to the revenue.

The several heads of revenue thus described make up on an average a total of 43½ millions sterling thus,

	Millions sterling per annum.
Land	21
Tributes	¾
Excise	2½
Assessed Taxes	½
Customs	2¼
Salt	7
Opium net	6½
Stamps	3
Total	43½

This total of 43½ millions may be regarded as the revenue proper of the Government of India, a sum much less than the totals which appear rightly in the published accounts on the receipt side. The total of receipts stood at 50 millions sterling some years ago, then it rose to 55, and now stands at 65 millions. Nevertheless, the revenue proper is not more than 43½ millions really; and by some authorities has been reckoned at even less. The fact ought indeed to inspire the authorities with a spirit of caution, and prevent them from being led away by the thought that an empire, of which the annual accounts shew receipts of 65 millions sterling, must be able to afford a liberal expenditure.

There is a difference between receipts and revenue, as technically understood. While the Government possesses a large revenue proper, as already described, it has also large receipts which must, under a sound system of national account-keeping, be entered in the same statement and on the same side with the revenues. There would be danger in having two accounts, or in allowing the financial authorities to decide on their discretion what items should be included or excluded, and whether headings of revenue should be exhibited gross or net. The rule followed is this, that on the receipt side all bonâ fide receipts from whatever source shall be fully exhibited, also all items of revenue gross, and not net, no abatement being made for expenses; that all bonâ fide charges for whatever purpose, whether for defence or administration, for concerns managed by the State, or for the raising of the revenue itself, should be exhibited on the expenditure side. Thus the fact that while the revenue proper stands at 43½ millions only, the revenue and receipts amount to 65 millions, represents no discrepancy and involves no error whatever.

On the principle above explained, it comes to pass that the land revenue is shewn gross; a large expenditure is indeed exhibited against it, 2½ millions sterling, much of which is really devoted to the administration of the affairs of the land. The opium revenue is also shewn at 9 millions gross, although in the total of 43½ millions given above, it is shewn net at only 6½ millions. There are some departments instituted for special purposes of administration, which yield receipts indeed, but have a large expenditure; such as the receipts of the forest department which is established for the preservation of the forests; of the post-office and the electric telegraph, which are established for the sake of postal and telegraphic communication. There are recoveries in some of the greatest of the spending departments, as receipts from sale of stores, and various dues, in the departments of the army, the marine, the public works, the State education. Lastly, there are large receipts from national concerns, in which the State has incurred a great outlay, or for which it has advanced considerable sums of money, or on account of which it has heavy liabilities to discharge. Such receipts are the interest on loans and advances, the income from canals, the earnings from State railways, the net traffic receipts from the guaranteed railways. There are other items of receipt, which it would be tedious to specify, and which contribute to swell the grand total of receipts. It is further to be noted that while from one period or one decade to another, the total of receipts including revenue shews a continuous and considerable augmentation, this result is largely due to the growth of the receipts as distinguished from the revenue proper. There has been augmentation also of the revenue, but that is partly due to the increase of taxation.

There have been a natural growth and a spontaneous expansion of the revenue itself also; all the branches of revenue may so far be described as prospering. Still there is, at the best, but too much ground for the apprehension, so often expressed by some authorities, that the revenue is not elastic in the English sense of the term, for it seldom grows with any rapidity and it never springs forward.

It is to be remembered that besides the taxation for the purposes of the State, there are rates levied on the land for local purposes, amounting to 2½ millions sterling annually.

Octroi or town duties are also levied in most of the municipalities throughout the county. In many places these duties were found to operate as transit dues to the injury of trade, and the requisite remedy has been applied.

Of the total of the revenue proper as above shewn, 43½ millions, only 36¼ millions are really paid by the people of British India; of the remainder, 6½ millions are paid by the Chinese and ¾ million by the Native States. The sum of

36¼ millions sterling distributed over the 190 millions in British India would give an average of 3*s.* 9*d.* per head per annum, which will doubtless appear very small. The average is, however, too general to be very suggestive. The real incidence of taxation on the several classes of British subjects has been well described thus by a recent writer, Mr. H. S. Cunningham:

> "The landowner pays for land revenue, an amount ranging from 3 to 7 per cent. on the gross produce of his lands, and a further fraction by way of provincial rates. If he goes to law he may contribute something to stamps; if he drinks, to excise; and if he prefers English to native cloth, to customs; but when he has paid his land revenue, his only imperative tax is 7*d.* (per annum) for salt. . . . The owner of personal property, though a millionaire, may under like conditions of abstinence from the luxuries of drink, litigation and English cloth, contribute nothing but the 7*d.* for salt, to the expenses of the State. . . . The artisan's position is the same. The trader when he has paid his 7*d.* on salt and, if his gains are over £50 per annum, his licence tax, may go free of further taxation. The only imperative tax on the agricultural labourer is the annual 7*d.* for salt."

It would be difficult to shew how the people of British India are to be taxed at rates more moderate and light than these, if they are to be taxed at all.

There have been schemes devised at various times for raising additional items of revenue, such as those relating to a tax on tobacco, to fees on the solemnization of marriages, to a rate on houses. But the prevailing opinion has been, and is, adverse to fresh taxation, if it can possibly be avoided. The popular contentment, resulting from lightness of taxation and ease in the collection of the revenue, has long been regarded as one of the many pillars supporting the fabric of British rule. The Government in its capacity of paramount power has induced the Native States to forego vexatious imposts, and transit duties hampering commerce; having itself first set a good example in this respect. The grace of this policy would be marred, if the Government were to strike out a fresh line of fiscal development, in the very direction which it had previously deprecated.

CHAPTER XIV.

CANALS AND IRRIGATION.

Canals for navigation and for irrigation—Canals in Asiatic countries adjacent to India—Irrigated and unirrigated tracts in India—Irrigation from wells —Native works of irrigation—British system of canals—In Hindostan—In the Panjab—In Behar—In Orissa—In the deltas of the Godavery and the Kistna—In Tanjore—From the Tumbadra river—From the Indus in Sind —Lakes for irrigation in the Madras Presidency—In the Bombay Presidency —Principal rivers from which canals have been drawn—Rivers from which canals remain to be taken—Different plans of constructing canals— Proportion of irrigated or protected lands to the whole cultivated area— Canal water-rent—Financial returns from the canals—Indirect benefits— Navigation of the canals—Immense value of canal irrigation to the country.

THE term canal signifies to the ear of an Englishman a means of navigable communication and to the ear of an Indian a means of irrigation. In the thoughts of Indians and Anglo-Indians canals are associated partly with navigation, but mainly with irrigation. Some authorities have indeed recommended that, even for communication, reliance should be placed mainly on canals to the supercession of railways, but such views, however, have not prevailed nor are likely to prevail. Still, in India, although irrigation is regarded as the primary work of a canal system, it is recognised that a good canal ought not only to supply the fertilizing element for production but also to bear on its bosom the freights of produce for distant markets. Many of the largest irrigating canals are designedly adapted for navigation; and in some of the best irrigated districts they render service to communication as well as to production.

Some Asiatic countries adjacent to India, such as Persia, have from time immemorial depended on irrigation conducted from springs by ingenious contrivances (called karizes). The ancient canal system of the Tigris and Euphrates has shrunk to a scarcely recognisable likeness of its original self. The irrigation in Central Asia survives, impaired, indeed, but still effective, after so many political revolutions. Some of the territories to which the eyes of statesmen turn, such as Bokhara, or Khiva, are really oases of canal irrigation in the heart of desert steppes, like jewels set in the midst of sand. There the fierce and rude races have no rains in due season whereon to depend; their irrigation is their staff of life, without which they could not hold their native country for a single twelvemonth; if an enemy obtained possession of the canal sources and heads, the inhabitants must surrender at discretion.

In India, however, irrigation, though very important, does not possess such overwhelming importance. Whole regions, such as the Gangetic delta, the littoral region of the western coast or the inland valley of the Nerbadda, have an abundant average rainfall on which mainly their agriculture depends. The inhabitants of the fluvial districts of Bengal, like the people in England, sometimes dread immoderate rain rather than drought, and their anxiety is not so much for irrigation as for drainage. The great rice harvest, the jute fibre and the safflower of Bengal, most of the cotton and millets of Hindostan, are produced without artificial irrigation. In most parts of the country, too, where irrigation more or less prevails, there are extensive crops, raised from the rainfall alone, and called the "dry" crops, in contradistinction to the "wet" crops raised from irrigation. In the oft-recurring times of drought, these "dry" crops are the first to wither, still, they seldom fail, save in extraordinary seasons. And in every cycle of years there are copious and seasonable showers which render the "dry-crop" lands excessively productive, bringing the cheaply cultivated soils into temporary competition with soils cultivated at considerable expense, and sometimes even causing the markets to be glutted with grain.

In ordinary language, the term irrigation is probably connected with canals and watercourses only. In Europe, a well is mentioned only in reference to purposes of drinking. But in India, irrigation is conducted from wells as well as from canals. In the villages there are some wells for drinking only, but the vast majority of the tens of thousands of wells in India, though they serve for drinking, are sunk mainly for the purpose of irrigating. It is to this well-sinking that the peasants in most parts of India devote some of their little capital, not caring generally to seek assistance from the State in this respect, save in times of famine. The well-irrigation is considered to be supplementary to the rainfall and is needed, in the case of many products, to render the yield abundant and profitable. For instance, the wheat of Northern India, the poppy of Behar, the sugarcane and the vegetables in most parts of India, are grown with the essential aid of irrigation from wells. Some of the very best, though the most expensive, cultivation in India, such as in several of the northern districts of the Panjab, is from wells.

The works of irrigation represent so ancient an institution in India, and the Natives have often shewn so much cleverness in constructing such works, that a reproach has sometimes been unjustly cast against the British Government as being inferior to its Native predecessors in this matter. In truth, however, the English have entered, and are entering, the lists in this noble contest, renovating or enlarging the best of the old works, compassing new works, and overcoming difficulties which no preceding Government could have attempted to encounter.

The Muhammadans constructed many water-works of beauty and celebrity, but these were undertaken for conducting the water to parks, pleasure grounds and palaces. They did not usually in India bend their constructive genius towards agricultural irrigation, as they so often did in other lands with such masterly effect.

The Hindus have fairly established a claim to historic fame by reason of their exertions in this beneficent line. Commencing in the lower Himalayas, the earliest Indian domicile of their nation, they stemmed and deflected the mountain streamlets and babbling brooks, so as to lay them all under contribution for the wealth in water. As they spread southwards into the mid-continent of Central India, where mountainous ranges ramify in all directions, they searched out the valleys embosomed in the hills, where the rainfall of the wet season can be gathered together by closing up the natural outlets of the drainage, and so stored in reservoirs, which, though partly natural, are mainly artificial. Thus, by erecting dams of massive masonry, firmly welded together with structural skill, they formed reservoirs, which, though bearing the modest name of tanks, are really lakes, and which by their picturesque beauty, their historic interest, and their economic value, have challenged the admiration of many generations. Each of these works gives life and wealth to many townships, sometimes to scores of villages. Such favourable sites, arising from extensive geological formations, are discovered not singly but in groups and series. Consequently, if one lake is successfully completed, others will be constructed in the neighbourhood, and thus the district or province, which has been adorned by these works, is correctly called a lake region.

Migrating further southwards to the southern peninsula, they still constructed lakes and tanks in the same fashion. They also essayed bolder efforts in construction, and grappled with some of the large rivers which, rising in the Western Ghat ranges, run due eastwards to the Bay of Bengal. These rivers they stemmed at points where the waters first begin to divide themselves into deltaic ramifications. The dams thus built were named "anicats"; and the name "anicat" has become classic with British engineers. Above the "anicat" the river waters are stopped so that canals may be taken therefrom, and conducted over the surface of the country like veins and arteries charged with the very life-blood of prosperity to whole districts.

At first the British Government was too much busied in the consolidation of its conquests to take up so difficult a matter as the origination of a canal system. But for many years before its abolition, the East India Company gave its best attention to works of irrigation on a great scale, and with some success. Since that time, that is for nearly one generation, these beneficent operations have been prosecuted, and the result is that the canals of India are now amongst her most remarkable characteristics.

The canal system which the British Government in some degree adopted from its predecessors, but in the main originated and worked out for itself, may be described in this wise.

In northern India, one great canal is drawn from the Ganges at Hardwar, the point where the river debouches from the Himalayas, and another from the same river lower down its course. Thereby a part of the available water supply of this great river will be carried off for irrigation during the summer and autumn, and nearly the whole supply during the winter when the crops greatly need water. From the river Jamna the old canal constructed by the Muhammadans on the right bank for the sake of the imperial demesne at Delhi, has been improved and enlarged for the sake of irrigation; and another canal has been drawn from the river on its left bank. From below Delhi, a new canal from the same river has been constructed, running towards Agra. By these means, the available supply of the Jamna water, in the cultivating season, will be diverted for irrigation. Thus the middle of Hindostan, the very heart of India, ever regarded as the empress province, is now an extensively irrigated tract.

In Rohilkhand some lesser canals have been projected or constructed, from the rivers which issue from the Himalayas to join the Ganges.

In the Sirhind district of the Panjab, from the point where the river Satlej debouches from the Himalayas, a great canal is taken, drawing off nearly all the winter supply of water from that river for irrigation. From the river Ravi north of Lahore, another great canal has been taken, utilizing the winter supply of the water, for irrigation in the country around Amritsar, the home of the Sikh nation. Further south, in the territory between the Satlej and the Ravi, many lesser canals are drawn, watering comparatively rainless tracts down to the vicinity of Multan; also in the Derajat territory, trans-Indus. These are called locally "inundation" canals, because they receive their supply of water when the rivers rise during the summer and the rainy season.

In the province of Behar, a great canal is taken from the Sone river, for irrigation in the territory near Patna. In the district of Midnapur south of Calcutta, a lesser canal has been constructed which, though drawn from a small river with a comparatively scanty supply, is yet very useful.

In Orissa, the river Mahanadi, after leaving the Eastern Ghat mountains, is dammed up at a suitable point near the city of Cattak, whence the stream is diverted, supplying considerable canals on both banks of the river. Near here, the Muhanadi has branches forming its delta; other rivers flow parallel with it from the Eastern Ghat mountains to the sea: from which canals may be taken in a series connecting Orissa with the districts around Calcutta.

Southwards on the east coast, at a point where the river Godavery debouches from the Eastern Ghat mountains, the river is dammed by a mighty dyke or "anicat," whence is drawn a series of canals covering with a network of irrigation the rich deltaic district to the seashore. Further south, the river Kistna or Krishna issuing from the same range, is stemmed in a similar manner, whence a like system of canals is derived, for irrigating the delta of Masulipatam.

Below Madras, in the southern peninsula there are drawn from the rivers Cavery and Colerun near Trichinopoly, large canals which, running eastwards, have many branches near

Tanjore, and intersect that district with numerous channels, causing it to be regarded as the most richly watered region in the empire.

From the Tunga-badra, or Tumbadra, river which divides the Nizam's dominions from the Madras Presidency, a large canal has been commenced and conducted for some distance but not completed.

The province of Sind, with a population of two millions of souls, depends, for its cultivation, upon the Indus, as Egypt depends upon the Nile. The irrigation is drawn from numerous canals, which were constructed by the Muhammadan rulers, but have been improved and enlarged by the British Government.

In the Madras Presidency, many large artificial lakes for irrigation have been constructed by the British Government, of which the enumeration would be tedious.

Several similar lakes have been constructed in the Deccan districts of the Bombay Presidency, from which much irrigation is derived. The masonry dam of Lake Fife, near Poona, is one of the finest in the world. Some minor canals have been constructed, in the Deccan also, from the upper courses of the rivers Tapti and Kistna or Krishna, and a canal is being constructed from the river Nira.

Canals have been proposed or projected in general terms or designed more or less in detail, but not yet undertaken, to be derived from the following rivers,

the Chenab in the Panjab,

the Sarda in Oudh,

the Gandak in Behar,

the lower part of the Pennar on the east coast north of Madras,

the Periar stream which issues from the Travancore mountains near Madura in the southern peninsula,

the lower part of the Tapti, on the west coast north of Bombay,

the lower part of the Nerbadda in the same quarter,

the Wardha, the Wynganga and lesser streams in the province of Nagpur,

the upper course of the Mahanadi in the eastern extremity of the Central Provinces,

the Chambal in Central India,

the Betwa and the Kene in Bundelkhand, and

the Jamna to carry off surplus water of the rainy season towards the arid tracts east of the Satlej.

Artificial lakes and several canals, greater or smaller, have been projected in the Deccan districts of the Bombay Presidency, which works have, however, not yet been undertaken. There are probably other projects or proposals in different parts of India, for thoughtful officers are constantly busying themselves with plans, whereby the drought so much dreaded in most parts of the empire may be averted.

From this review it will be apparent that the following great rivers have by the British Government been placed under contribution more or less, for the fertilization of provinces or districts in India,

the Ganges,

the Jamna,

the Sone in Behar,

the Satlej,

the Ravi in the Panjab,

the Indus,

the lower part of the Mahanadi and some lesser streams in Orissa,

the lower part of the Godavery on the east coast,

the lower part of the Kistna or Krishna,

the Cavery and Colerun in the southern peninsula,

the Tunga-badra or Tumbadra in the Deccan,

the upper courses of the Kistna and the Tapti,

and many other lesser rivers and streams, for the formation of artificial lakes, which it would be tedious to enumerate.

The following rivers are known to be capable of affording water for irrigation, but remain yet to be dealt with for this purpose,

the Gandak in Behar.
the Sarda in Oudh,
the Chenab in the Panjab,
the lesser rivers in Orissa,
the lower part of the Pennar near Madras,
the Periar river near Madura,
the lower part of the Tapti on the west coast near Bombay,
the lower part of the Nerbadda on the same coast,
the several rivers in the Nagpur province,
the Chambal in Central India,
the Betwa and the Kene in Bundelkhand.

There are lesser rivers and streams from which reservoirs may be formed for irrigating the Deccan districts of the Bombay Presidency. The only remaining rivers of note are the Jhelum in the Panjab, from which a canal might perhaps be taken; some smaller rivers which flow through Native States and of which the capabilities are not known; the rivers in the humid regions of lower Bengal where it is drainage that is wanted rather than irrigation; and the Brahmaputra river and its affluents, the Megna and others, which are not likely ever to supply canals for irrigation.

In the construction of these works two main principles are adopted, which differ from each other according to the variety of physical circumstance, and which have at times been subjected to much professional controversy.

In the north, the rivers are fed from sources arising in the perpetual snows of the Himalayas, and have in the winter season, generally called the cold weather, a volume of water which, though much shrunken in comparison with the summer supply swollen with the rains and the melted snow, is yet considerable. It is this volume of water which the engineers desire to carry off almost in its entirety for fertilization, using only a portion of the summer supply according to convenience. At the points where the river issues from the mountains and enters upon the plains, the ground is undulating, or even somewhat hilly and often has a rapid slope. Unfortunately for the engineers, the Himalayas have not great lakes at their base, like the Alps on their Italian side, which serve as natural reservoirs of water whence canals can be drawn. Therefore the engineers excavate the channel in the steep banks and sides of the rivers, carrying it across the rugged beds of tributary torrents. These operations relate to what are called "the head-works." The river is thus led into its new channel, which, passing through the rough ground for some miles, enters at last the more level portions of the plains. Then branch channels begin to be constructed in order to distribute the water for irrigation. As may be imagined, these head-works present very striking features. The channel is conducted by tunnels and by viaducts, sometimes above, sometimes below, the torrent beds, sometimes piercing, sometimes rounding, the spurs of the hills.

All this occurs in localities where the surrounding scenery adds the beauties of nature to the wonders of science. The "heads" of the Ganges canal at Hardwar, of the Satlej canal at Rupar, of the Ravi, or Bari Doab, canal at Madhupur, are almost as interesting to the artist and the tourist as they are to the engineer. In the foreground are the massive stone works, the noble arches and piers, and the canal flowing clear as crystal, in the middle distance are the lower hills looking purple in the eastern atmosphere while the horizon is bounded by the everlasting snow. For the first few miles of its course, the Ganges canal consists of a series of works which are triumphs of skill and science. There are few localities in the whole empire whence more pleasure and instruction can be derived than from the course of the Ganges canal, between Hardwar, the celebrated place of pilgrimage, and Rurki, where the engineering college and workshops are established.

Experience shewed, however, that the Ganges canal had been

constructed at too steep an incline in the lower part of its course and was beginning to tear up its bed and banks; this defect has been remedied, though at great cost. Insalubrious swamps were formed from the obstruction of the surface drainage by the canal works, and the public health was consequently affected in several places; endeavours are being made to remedy this defect also. The subsoil percolation, near the course of the high-level canals, causes a saline efflorescence in some places, which is detrimental to cultivation; for this, too, remedial measures are under consideration.

In the south, and with all the rivers except the Himalayan, the waters are not snow-fed, but are sustained by the moisture of the rainy season. There is an overwhelming volume of water in the summer, but in the winter scanty streamlets meander over broad expanses of sand and debris. Some suitable locality is chosen at the head of the delta, often near the base of a mountainous range, where, by the construction of dams or dykes, of great dimensions, the waters of the rivers can be stopped, and diverted so as to supply large canals on both sides, with subsidiary channels ramifying over the deltaic region, much like the branches of the rivers themselves.

There is also the practice already mentioned, whereby the volume of streams is dammed up and collected during the season of floods, so as to form artificial lakes to be used as reservoirs whence canals can be drawn. That which nature has done for the Italian engineers by the lakes at the southern base of the Alps, science effects for the English engineers in southern India. Every Englishman who travels in India must be struck as he beholds the lakes near Poona, near Arcot, and at many other places, filled to the brim with summer floods, where engineering science has followed nature's truest model. Nor is the visitor astonished by only a few artificial lakes of unrivalled proportions; for almost the whole of the Madras Presidency is studded and dotted over with lakes large and small, attesting the ability and resources which the Madras Government have applied to this subject, so vitally important to the people.

With the northern practice the name of Sir Proby Cautley will be handed down to the grateful remembrance of posterity, and with the southern practice, that of Sir Arthur Cotton. Of the many benefactors of India in recent times, there are few who have done more material good than Sir Arthur Cotton, during this generation. Both he and Sir Proby Cautley have raised, or contributed to raise, a school of hydraulic engineers, whose deeds have shed lustre on the public service in the Presidencies of Bengal and of Madras. Also the name of Fife is similarly associated with the irrigation works of the Bombay Presidency.

Notwithstanding the magnitude of this system of irrigation from canals, the greatest of its kind in the world, the proportion of the whole cultivated area in the country, thus protected from the effects of drought, is not so considerable as might be at first sight expected. Some deltaic districts such as those of Tanjore, Kistna and Godavery, are for the most part well protected even in seasons of drought, some outlying tracts only remaining unprotected. In most of the districts in the Madras Presidency, too, a considerable part of the cultivated area is irrigated in ordinary seasons. But in seasons of great drought the lesser lakes, and even some of the larger lakes, fail altogether, or lose a part of their supply. Thus, while the best of the irrigation works can be depended upon in time of famine, many of the second-rate works cannot, though they render assistance more or less ; and at the same time many of the lesser works must be expected to fail partially at least. In the Bombay Presidency the area thus protected is relatively very small, and the works are subject to the same conditions as those of Madras. An exception is formed by the province of Sind, which is almost entirely irrigated, and where the anxieties arise not from drought but from floods. In the north, the great canals can be depended upon in time of famine; but the tracts protected by them form only a small percentage of the total cultivated area. Still this percentage comprises the very cream, so to speak, of the territory, and those lands which are the most productive, yielding much more than any other land. Consequently where ten per cent. or even five per cent., of the land, can be thus protected, that protection is a very much larger factor in the national welfare than would appear from a mere consideration of the percentage.

The State, having constructed the canals, receives water-rent from those who benefit by the irrigation. The mode of assessing the water-rent varies in different provinces, but is everywhere regulated with scrupulous regard for the convenience of the people, so that they may have every facility for ascertaining what will be due from them. Sometimes the amount is fixed for long periods, together with the settlement of the land revenue. Where one person is the owner, and another person the cultivator, the water-rent is levied, partly from the owner by what is termed the owner's rate, and partly from the cultivator, by what is termed the cultivator's rate. Where the same person is both owner and cultivator, he pays a combined, or consolidated, rate.

It may seem strange that in some parts of the country the people should at the outset hesitate to make use of the water from the canals for irrigation. In the south, where irrigation has been practised for centuries, and where the British system is an expansion or development of pre-existing Native systems, the people make full use of the water, being willing to pay for it, and anxious to obtain it at the price fixed. But in the north, the husbandmen previously unaccustomed to canals, often regard the canal water only as a last resource in time of drought to save the crops, and not as a permanent means of preserving and also of improving the cultivation in ordinary years. When drought threatens, they will defer incurring the cost of taking the water, in the hope that, after all, the rain will descend in time to save the harvest; and such postponement is often so protracted that the opportunity is lost. After hesitating for weeks, they are sometimes seized with panic and press in multitudes at the gates of the canals, like terror-stricken creditors making a run upon the banks. In Orissa, where the rainfall happened to be unusually copious and seasonable for several years after the opening of the canal, this unwillingness has been especially manifest, but will gradually be overcome. It has appeared also in northern India and in the Bombay Presidency. Whenever drought occurs, there is a sudden expansion of canal irrigation which shrinks again when the danger is overpast, but of which a part remains and forms a permanent augmentation of the irrigated area. These circumstances tend to prove that there was unnecessary dilatoriness on the part of the people in availing themselves of the water. Thus it comes to pass that their lives and property are protected against destructive drought, by means of works constructed by the State, at a cost which falls not upon those who are specially protected but upon the whole community. In other words, these people are furnished with an important and costly insurance at the expense, not of themselves, but of their fellow-subjects. It may be argued that if canals are vitally important, if the State cannot afford to construct them unless it recovers from the people enough receipts to defray the interest charges on the outlay, and if the finance of the canal system is to be placed on a sound basis, then those people, who might take the water and yet fail to do so from their own default, ought nevertheless to pay some special rate or cess to defray the cost of the insurance by which they benefit. These considerations have induced the legislature in India more than once to enact that such a rate or cess shall be imposed on those lands which are proved to be well within reach of the canals. But such measures have always been opposed, as constituting a dangerous precedent. Some official authorities, notwithstanding the cogent arguments in its favour.

S 2

feel repugnance to a compulsory rate upon people for canal irrigation of which they have not seen fit to avail themselves. The Natives especially object to any plan of this description, alleging that it encourages the Government to embark on comparatively unremunerative projects, in the assurance that in any event there will be receipts from the special rate or cess. In the end, the opposition has prevailed and the legislation has been disallowed by the controlling power in England.

There has been unavoidably some room for difference of opinion as to what are, or are not, the bonâ fide receipts of the State from the canal irrigation, irrespective of the land revenue. The difficulty of discriminating between the water-rent and the land revenue has been enhanced by the arrangements, made to save the people from inconvenience, whereby the payments on both accounts have been settled together, or else virtually consolidated. In some provinces the barest return of water-rent has been taken, without allowance for the improvement in the land revenue by reason of the irrigation, and the financial return from the outlay on canals seems unduly low. In other provinces, besides the water-rent, the greater part of the land revenue has been taken into account, and the return seems perhaps excessively high. After making all due abatements for these several considerations, it may probably be said that in the south the canals yield a large return for the outlay incurred on them, exceeding the interest chargeable on their capital, and that they will ultimately pay off the capital itself. In the north, they are slowly and gradually beginning to yield returns equal to the current interest on their capital account, while they have much retrospective interest to defray on account of the years when they yielded but little. In some places, as Orissa, in the Sone valley, and parts of the Deccan, they have hardly begun to defray even the current interest, though they do yield something. On the whole, the financial returns, recently revised, shew that the net income from the canals more than covers the current interest on the capital outlay, and that in the aggregate the canal system of British India is paying six per cent.

The canals in India are mainly for irrigation, and although after satisfying the needs of such irrigation they have sometimes but little water to spare for navigation, still they are generally constructed so as to be navigable. In the north they are navigated to some appreciable extent, and in some of the canals between Calcutta and Orissa the navigation constitutes a large item in the business. In the south the canals are largely navigated; the same channels which cause the produce to be raised, serve to carry most cheaply and easily that same produce to market, the double duty thus enhancing the beneficence of the work. A really admirable project for canal navigation in the upper part of the river Godavery, which would have connected the Central Provinces with the Bay of Bengal, was undertaken by the Government and prosecuted to a considerable length, but was afterwards relinquished, as some think unadvisedly and unfortunately. Some authorities observing the advantages of inland water traffic have urged the Government to construct canals for communication, instead of railways. But such proposals are deemed by other authorities to involve extremely difficult questions of hydraulic engineering, and have not generally found favour. For the main lines of communication in India, railways are still preferred.

At one time endeavours were made to introduce important canal projects into India by means of private enterprise conducted by companies. The Madras Irrigation Company was thus formed for the execution of canals on the Tumbadra and Pennar rivers and still exists, though, after performing much excellent work, it has had to contend with many financial difficulties. The canals in Orissa were commenced by a company which afterwards transferred its rights to the Government by whom the operations have been continued.

At the head-works of the canals, and at other suitable places, the engineers have established extensive workshops where technical instruction is afforded to Natives, and sometimes to Europeans and East Indians.

Although many of the existing canals, and some of the projects yet to be undertaken, may yield a good financial return, the hard question with new projects is how to frame them so that they shall yield at least a sufficient income, that is enough to cover the interest payable by the State on the money to be borrowed for the outlay. Few pursuits are more fascinating to the mind than to visit localities where, in the bosom of the hills, lakes can be formed by arresting the torrents in their headlong course, and then to imagine how these stores of water shall confer fertility on arid lands, diffusing life and civilization around. But to these glowing reflections there always succeeds the chilling calculation as to whether these stores of water can "command," that is, be made to reach, sufficient areas of productive soil to make the storing worth the cost in money. Disappointment is frequently felt on the discovery that the projected works, if executed, would not reimburse the State for the interest on the outlay. The question then arises whether the State can afford to incur the cost. This question ought to be borne in mind by those who, with humane intentions, looking on vast volumes of water annually wasted, and on unused sites for storage, thereupon urge the Government to continue undertaking works, without, perhaps, sufficiently weighing the financial incidents.

A summary of the length, in miles and round numbers, of the canals will present some idea of the magnitude of the canal system of British India. This subject is set forth in Buckley's recently published work on the finance of each one of these irrigation works in detail. The total length of the main canals and branches (exclusive of distributories) in the Presidencies of Bengal, Madras and Bombay amounts to 4900 miles. In this the canals of the Cavery or Tanjore system are not given; their length, however, cannot be less than 700 miles. To these are to be added the inundation canals of the Panjab, 1550 miles, and the canals of Sind, 5600 miles. Thus there are 12,750 miles of canals greater and lesser. The total length of the distributing channels is not known; but in northern India alone, it amounts to 8300 miles. The area now irrigated amounts to 1,900,000 acres in Madras and Bombay, 360,000 acres in Behar and Orissa, 1,450,000 acres in the North-western Provinces, 1,350,000 acres in the Panjab and 1,250,000 in Sind; in all 6,310,000 acres; or nearly six and a half millions of acres. The area irrigable by the canals is yet considerably greater than even this large total; so that the existing system is still capable of development. The capital outlay by the State on this canal system may be set down at at 20¼ millions sterling, on which the net returns yield an interest of 6 per cent. These facts shew why the system claims to be the finest of its kind in the world. All this, too, is exclusive of a great number of petty irrigation works in many parts of the country, from Rohilkhand in the north to Tinnevelly in the south, of which the statistics would be tedious.

Apart from the direct receipts from the canals, there are many indirect benefits which accrue in all cases. These benefits are represented by the security afforded to agriculture, the insurance provided for the people against the extremities of drought and famine, the protection of the land revenue, the instruction of the husbandmen by the example of the superior husbandry established, and the introduction of superior products. The value of the canals during the recent famines has been inestimable; without the irrigation, these calamities, great as they were, would have been indefinitely greater. The value of the produce which the canals saved in order to feed a famishing people, equalled the capital outlay on their construction.

CHAPTER XV.

RAILWAYS AND ELECTRIC TELEGRAPHS.

Lord Dalhousie's design for railway system—Line from Calcutta to North-west frontier—From Calcutta to Bombay—From Bombay to Madras—From Lahore to Karachi—Projected extension to Candahar—Line from Bombay to Agra—In Rohilkhand and Oudh—In Behar—In Bengal—In Central India—In Berar and Nagpur—In Southern India—From Goa to southern Deccan—In Burma—Railways of two kinds, Guaranteed and State—Advantages of the Guarantee system—Passenger traffic—Goods traffic—Rolling stock—State railways—Capital furnished by Native States for railways—Broad and narrow gauges—Railways in time of war and of famine—Introduction of electric telegraph—Lines belonging to Guaranteed railway Companies—And to the Government—Telegraphic communication between India and England—Also between India and other countries.

THE railways of India have advanced, are advancing, and will ere long comprise a total length of nine thousand miles; possibly this length may be exceeded by some hundreds of miles in the course of a few years. Such a total mileage is considerable in itself, no doubt, and will be regarded as remarkable in reference to the distance of India from England, whence all the resources for the construction of railways have to be drawn. It is to be remembered that in Europe and America, the works were constructed at home in the midst of resources, close to the very centres of industry, in the native air of the engineers and artificers, in the land of their professional practice, and with every possible advantage of circumstance, climate and labour. Whereas, the works in India were completed at a vast distance from home and from the sources of supply, under many disadvantages of climate, with a scanty labour market and untrained labourers. Again, in India the engineers were landed in a country with circumstances novel to all their professional and practical experience, and began their work often in a malarious climate and occasionally in localities dangerously insalubrious, frequently suffering in health and sometimes losing life. For India, the rails, girders and engines had to be sent round the Cape in sailing ships, or by the Suez Canal and the Red Sea in steamers.

Thirty years have elapsed since the East India Company undertook the construction of railways in their vast territories. Lord Dalhousie was the Governor-General who first laid out a comprehensive scheme whereby the length and breadth of the land might be permeated by railway communication; and this national design will constitute one of his many titles to posthumous fame. The main idea, then formed, has been subsequently enlarged, but its principal features have been preserved.

The scheme was, and is, to connect Calcutta with the North-west frontier by a trunk line 1500 miles in length, having its terminus at that port and capital, and proceeding to upper India through Allahabad, with a short branch to Delhi, then passing through Lahore towards the north-west extremity of the frontier, and ultimately crossing the Indus at Attok and entering Peshawur. This railway was to have a chord line across the eastern end of the Vindhya range near the coal fields, and a loop line along the bank of the Ganges. It was to run up the whole valley of the Ganges; crossing the river Sone once and the Jamna thrice; then it was to cross all the five rivers of the Panjab and lastly the Indus. It was to traverse for the most part a champaign country, consisting of the plains of upper India, or Hindostan, and of the Panjab, till it approached the Jhelum river, when it would enter very rugged ground continuing nearly to the terminus at Peshawur. Although there were no difficulties in respect to the crossing of mountains, the viaducts must be of the very largest character. There is a short branch from Jhelum to the salt mines.

From this main line at Allahabad, another line of about 700 miles was to be taken, surmounting the low hills of Bundelkhand

and thence running down the Nerbadda valley from Jabulpur, passing through a gap in the Sâtpura range into the valley of the Tapti, and descending the precipitous side of the Western Ghat mountains to Bombay, with large viaducts over the Nerbadda and the Tapti, and with a mountainous incline of great difficulty. Thus the two capitals Calcutta and Bombay were to be connected by rail.

Then from Bombay, there was to be a line of about 800 miles, ascending the Western Ghat mountains near Poona, crossing the great plateau of the Deccan, entering the Madras Presidency, and so approaching the Eastern Ghat mountains which it would descend on its way to Madras. It would have a chord line joining in Khandesh the trunk line to Calcutta; also a branch to Hyderabad, the Nizam's capital in the Deccan. There would be viaducts difficult in character though not of great size; but the crossing of the mountains would demand works of magnitude and difficulty. Thus railway communication was to be established between the two Presidencies of Madras and Bombay.

These are the primary lines of railway communication; but besides these, there are several lines of much importance.

From the trunk railway at Lahore, the capital of the Panjab, there runs a line down the valley of the river Ravi, past Multan, crossing the Satlej and entering the valley of the Indus, crossing the Indus at Sakar, and passing along the right bank of that river, surmounting the low range of Laki hills which impinge upon the river bed, and then proceeding to the seaport of Karachi. The country, with the exception of the Laki pass, is flat; but the bridging of the Satlej and of the Indus is very formidable. Thus railway communication is maintained between the sea and the Panjab, and between the mouths of the Ganges and of the Indus; the route also between England and the north-west frontier of India is considerably shortened.

From Sakar, where the line crosses the Indus, a temporary line has been carried to Sibi near the Bolan Pass, and an extension towards Candahar has been projected.

From the harbour of Bombay, a line is carried along the west coast in the province of Gujerat, having branches into the peninsula of Kathiawar, crossing with large viaducts the Tapti and Nerbadda near the mouths of those rivers; then entering the hilly country of Rajputana, but avoiding any difficult passage over mountains, till it reaches the Jamna, which river it crosses near Agra and so joins the trunk line of upper India; this railway carries the cotton of Gujerat to Bombay for exportation. Thus, northern India, already connected by rail with the seaport of Calcutta, will be similarly connected with the seaport of Bombay.

There are cross lines running through the fertile plains of Rohilkhand and Oudh, between the river Ganges and the Himalayan mountains, connecting these territories with the main trunk line of northern India. These lines have viaducts over the Ganges at Cawnpore and at Aligarh; there will also be a viaduct over the same river at Benares.

Similarly, there will be cross lines through the rich territories of north Behar at the foot of the Nepal mountains.

From Calcutta, a line runs through eastern Bengal, and thence through northern Bengal to the foot of the Himalayas at Darjiling, over a level country, but having many bridges, and requiring a viaduct over the broad and shifting river which is a continuation of the Ganges, if such a work shall be found practicable. There is to be a short railway in Assam from the Brahmaputra to the coal mines of Makum.

At a point on the trunk line from Allahabad to Bombay, in Nimar north of the Sâtpura range, a line is conducted up the lofty sides and spurs of the Vindhya range, with works of some magnitude, to the plateau of Malwa to join the railway from Bombay to Agra. From near Nimar, also, there is to be a branch to the capital of the Bhopal State. Again, from Agra there is a branch to Sindhia's city of Gwalior. Thus Central India is connected with the seaport of Bombay and with the inland region of Hindostan.

At another point, on the same trunk line but south of the Sâtpura range, a line has been taken eastwards to Nagpur, and is now being extended further on the east towards Calcutta. This line carries to Bombay, for exportation, the cotton of the provinces of Berar and Nagpur, and will, if ultimately extended, give a straight route from Calcutta to Bombay, instead of the existing route above described which is slightly circuitous.

In the southern peninsula there is a connected series of railways. One trunk line stretches from sea to sea, from Madras on the Coromandel coast to Beypore on the Malabar coast, crossing a gap in the Nilgiri mountains. From one point on this line there runs a branch to Bangalore in Mysore; and from another point there begins a railway to Negapatam on the Coromandel coast. Again from Madras, a line starts southwards, nearing Pondicheri (to which place there is a branch), passing to Tanjore and then from Trichinopoly southwards through Madura and Tinnevelly in the neighbourhood of Cape Comorin. These railways run through a generally level country (except in the neighbourhood of the Nilgiris and Mysore) without any extraordinary difficulty.

From Goa, on the west coast south of Bombay, a railway is projected under the joint auspices of the British and Portuguese Governments, which ascending the Western Ghat mountains, is to pass through Hubli near Dharwar, the mercantile capital of the southern Deccan, and afterwards to join the trunk line between Bombay and Madras. There will ultimately be a branch from Hubli to Sholapur in the Deccan.

A line has been projected to commence from the railway already mentioned in Gujerat, to skirt the Sindh desert, to enter the valley of the Indus near Hyderabad and to join the railway already described as running down the valley of the Indus.

From the seaport of Rangun as a terminus, there is taken a line to Prome, in the mid-valley of the Irawaddy, thus connecting the littoral province of Pegu with the regions of Ava and upper

Burma. A line has also been projected from Rangun to Tonghu in eastern Burma.

There are, or will be, branches in lower Bengal, in southern Behar, in the middle of Hindostan, in parts of the Central Provinces, in the Presidencies of Bombay and Madras, and in some of the Native States of Central India.

The above sketch comprises the existing system of Indian railways; most of them have either been or are being constructed. The total length of the lines, open for traffic, amounts to 8611 miles. This total is being gradually increased year by year; additional lines are proposed, with a total length of 1850 miles.

The railways in India are constructed and managed under two different systems, one that of the Guaranteed Companies, the other that of the State. The capital expended on all the railways up to April 1880 was £123,124,514. Of this sum, £97,327,851 had been expended on Guaranteed lines, £24,403,797 on State lines, and £1,392,866 on lines in Native States. Of the total mileage, 8611 miles, shewn above, 6073 miles belong to Guaranteed Companies, 2363 to the Government, and 175 to Native States.

A Guaranteed railway Company is one to which a certain rate of interest on the capital outlay is guaranteed by the Government; with the proviso that if the profits after defrayal of working expenses shall exceed the rate guaranteed, which has generally been five per cent., such surplus profits shall be divided between the Government and the Company. The Government in the first instance pays the interest on the capital to the shareholders, chiefly English as the funds were raised in England, and the earnings of the railways in India are paid into the State Treasury. Under this system, the Government has considerable powers of control over the amount of capital raised, the selection of the line, the designs of the works, the strength of the establishment, the rates and the fares. It appoints a Government Director, with the power of vote at the

Board of Directors in England, and engineer officers in India to guard its interests. It grants land for the line, the stations and appurtenances, free of charge. In other respects a guaranteed Company is like an ordinary Company; with the concurrence of the Government Director it appoints all the persons employed on the line, it selects on its own judgment the chief officials; and they are all its servants. The railway stock, thus created, has always stood high in the English market, somewhat higher than the securities of the Government itself, by reason of the prospect of surplus profits accruing. After the opening of the lines, the net earnings defrayed only a part of the interest on the outlay, the remainder thus becoming a charge upon the Government. For many years, the guaranteed interest formed a large heading in the State expenditure. The total of the sums thus paid by the Government amounts to nearly 27 millions sterling. This is regarded by many as a reasonable price for the advantages obtained by the country from the railways. Of the several Companies, the principal one has of late been generally defraying the charges for interest and has occasionally divided a surplus profit with the State. Other Companies have sometimes been able to accomplish a similar result; some, again, have not been able to effect this, though it is hoped that they will do so in time. The several Companies are designated thus: the East India, the Eastern Bengal, the Oudh and Rohilkhand, the Sind, Panjab and Delhi, for northern India; the Great India Peninsula, the Bombay, Baroda and Central India, for the central and western parts of the country; the Madras railway, and the South Indian, for the southern portion of the empire.

Notwithstanding the results attained by this system, some authorities have believed that at least equally great results might have been secured by the State operating through its own agency directly, and at a less cost. They see disadvantages in such important public interests being entrusted to private Companies, which, by reason of their dividends being guaranteed up to a profitable rate, have not the same incentives to exertion which ordinarily are present with railway companies. The Government, they say, despite its large powers of control, has not the real check upon extravagance and the actual means of enforcing economy which ought to pertain to the authority upon which the ultimate responsibility devolves. The State, it is alleged, could have borrowed the capital at a cheaper rate than that of the guarantee, and could have managed the lines more efficiently and economically.

On the other hand, the system of guaranteed railways has been followed in India by many consequences of signal value and importance. It secured many years ago a separate financial basis in England for the railways. That basis was independent of the difficulties which beset novel undertakings in distant regions, and was free from the uncertainties attending a large outlay by Government in such a country as India. The constructive operations proceeded steadily and uninterruptedly, without cessation in consequence of other pressing calls, and without any want of funds. During the same period, State works of material improvement were occasionally stopped by reason of military or political contingencies, and were frequently retarded from financial deficits. In the troublous years, when the greater part of the country was convulsed by the war of the mutinies, the railway works were carried on, while almost all public works belonging to the Government, except military buildings, were unavoidably suspended. The guarantee system appealed to other investors besides those who ordinarily invest in Government securities. It thereby developed fresh resources from which funds could be obtained for material improvement, thus relieving the strain upon the credit of the State. It induced the English capitalists, and the moneyed classes generally, to take an interest in the advancement of India and to lend a moral support to its administration. It infused new blood into the profession of civil engineering in India, introducing men of high capacity, and of experience won in the best schools in Europe.

It gave to India the services of ready-made administrators for the working of the railways. The names may be recalled of many men, engineers or administrators, who have become distinguished under this system, Stephenson, Turnbull, James Berkley, W. P. Andrew, French, Mathew, Prestage. Thus new strength and experience were added to the administration of India. The experience, too, was of a kind which the resources of Government, abundant as they were in talent, could not at that time have supplied. The work of the Companies has been most ably seconded by the late Sir James Cosmo Melvill, by General Sir William Baker, R.E., and by Mr. Juland Danvers, gentlemen in the service of Government, and by the consulting engineers in England, Sir John Hawkshaw, the two Rendels and Mr. George Berkley. The abilities and resources of several well-known English contractors have been called forth in the service of India; such men as Brassey, Wythes, Henfrey, Glover, Faviell. In short, the guarantee system afforded several essential advantages which could not otherwise have been procured. Without it, the country would not have obtained the national benefit of railway communication within a reasonable time. It deserves, therefore, the ungrudging acknowledgment of all who have at heart the welfare of the country.

The existing arrangements, however, between the Government and the Companies are for a limited period only, and can be terminated on certain conditions. With most of the Companies there is a considerable portion of this period still unexpired. In the case of one Company, however, the East India, the Government has exercised its power of acquiring the property of the railway, but has leased to the Company the management of the line, which arrangement is a recognition of the merits of the guarantee system.

The Guaranteed Companies, represented by boards of Directors in London and by Agents in India, have generally maintained excellent relations with the Government, and in times of emergency have devoted themselves to fulfilling the behests of the

State with the same degree of zeal as that displayed by public departments. On several great opportunities of famine or war, they and their servants have won the emphatic thanks of the Government. On some State occasions, such as the tour of the Prince of Wales, and the Imperial assemblage at Delhi, the railway officials have vied with the officers of the State in loyalty and activity.

The Companies, though to some extent employing Natives, endeavouring to train them as guards, as locomotive mechanics, even as engine-drivers, and engaging them largely as station masters, do yet employ Europeans for a great part of the work that requires technical training and steadiness of nerve. Consequently the number of European employés, thus introduced into the country, is considerable. For them every possible advantage socially is provided by the Companies, namely churches, clergy, ministers, hospitals, medical attendance, schools for boys and girls, reading-rooms, recreation grounds and gardens. They are encouraged to organize themselves by forming clubs, and associations for various excellent purposes, especially for volunteering. Indeed, the volunteer movement has been very successful among the servants of the Companies, and produces a force equal to three battalions of infantry. At many points of the lines, such as central workshops, changing stations and the like, well-ordered settlements of European employés exist, resembling little colonies. The men being volunteers, can defend themselves and their stations in event of need.

The passenger traffic is that branch of the business which develops itself more speedily, and overcomes competition more entirely than any other. The Natives were supposed to be indifferent regarding time; but they do not manifest any such indifference in this case. On the contrary, they instantly appreciate the ease and speed of this mode of travelling, which they liken to reclining on a couch borne on the wind with the speed of lightning. They flock in multitudes to the stations, waiting for the trains; though habituated to walking for long journeys, they never walk now, when they can afford to travel by rail. The fares, being at the rate of about ¼d. a mile, are so moderate that the poor can afford to travel thus. The great bulk of the passengers are booked for the third class; the carriages of the first and second classes are but little used by the Natives. Although the virtue of a pilgrimage has been heretofore held to consist partly in the labours of the footsore pilgrims, nevertheless pilgrims in tens of thousands crowd the railway stations, to such an extent that pilgrim trains have to be specially arranged. The necessity for men of all sorts and conditions to ride in the same third-class carriage is believed by some to be softening the hard distinctions hitherto maintained between caste and caste. As the trains running daily are not numerous, it has often happened that the crowds of Native passengers have been more than the railway officials could arrange comfortably at the moment. Such instances, however, are rare nowadays, and the multitudes of Native passengers find their way into and out of the trains, with as much ease and order as could reasonably be expected. Special facilities are afforded for the conveyance of Native ladies of all classes; and of Native princes travelling with retinues. On the whole, the railways are popular with the travelling classes of the Natives. The number of passengers in a year amounts to 43 millions at the present time.

The goods traffic, though successful and popular, has, as compared with the passenger traffic, risen with slower degrees to its present position. However embarrassing the multitudes may be, the passengers must be sent on and conveyed somehow; but if the goods come in overwhelming quantities, they will be detained more or less. If such detention becomes lengthened, as it sometimes has become, it affects the repute of the railways in the estimation of the Native merchants. It even tempts some of them to intrigue with the subordinate employés of the railway for obtaining unfair priority in despatch, and thus leads to divers abuses. Notwithstanding these occasional drawbacks, vast quantities of merchandise, amounting to 8 millions of tons in a year, are sent by rail, for which advantage the people are glad to pay 7¼ millions sterling annually. The saving to the country of time and cost, which really represents value, is a set-off against any charges incurred by the public treasury on account of the railways. There have been sometimes doubts whether the rates are sufficiently low; the traffic managers naturally desire remunerative rates; on the other hand, it is urged that the best way of rendering the railways useful to the country is to have the minimum of charge upon the maximum of traffic. The Companies have made reductions, and are quite alive to the necessity of rendering the fares very moderate. Such a disposition is strengthened by the serious facts of the competition from the river boats, plying in tens of thousands on the lower Ganges and the rivers of Bengal, and in thousands on the Indus; and from the seagoing Native craft which sail past the western coast of Gujerat.

However valuable the services of the railways have been in every emergency, whether of war, famine or commercial pressure, and however strenuous are the efforts of the railway officials on these grave occasions, still anxiety arises in consequence of the rolling stock being insufficient, and especially of the engines being inadequate in number. This defect has been partly remedied of late, but as rule a considerable reserve of engines ought to be maintained in India, ready for emergency. There is this reason, among others, that owing to the difference between the Indian and the English gauges, engines cannot be obtained ready-made in the yards of the great builders in England, but have to be made specially on requisition; and the making of them in any considerable number may occupy several months, while the most pressing need is being felt in India.

The several guaranteed Companies and the State possess extensive locomotive workshops at the principal termini of their lines. Though engines cannot be made in India they can be repaired very well; and when sent out from England in pieces they can be "erected," or put together.

The State railways are making considerable progress, but as yet play a part much smaller than that of the Guaranteed railways. Entering the field later, they have been able to profit by the experience which the guaranteed lines afforded. It was hoped that they would shew cheapness in construction and improvement in management. Though they have avoided the extravagance perceptible in some parts of the guaranteed lines, it is doubtful whether, on the whole, their construction has been essentially cheaper, upon a full comparison being made of all the circumstances and of the topography of the country traversed. Though they are well managed, it is also doubtful whether their administration is better than that of the guaranteed lines, except, perhaps, that their fares for goods traffic have a greater tendency to moderation. At all events, the fact of there being two patterns of railway management in the country, one by the Companies, the other by the State, must cause a salutary emulation whereby the public at large is benefited.

It is noteworthy that Native sovereigns are beginning to invest money in railways constructed in their dominions with the aid of the British Government. In this matter the Nizam, Sindhia and Holkar have set an excellent example, and the Begum of Bhopal is adopting a similar policy.

There has been in India, as in some other countries, a battle of the gauges. The guaranteed lines were constructed with an intermediate gauge of 5 ft. 6 in., which is less than the English old broad gauge and more than that of the English standard gauge. This intermediate gauge is now termed the Indian broad gauge. When the State railways were commenced, a proposal was made that they should be constructed on a gauge considerably narrower than the English standard gauge, namely that of the metre, 3 ft. 3 in., which is now termed the Indian narrow gauge. The guaranteed railways' authorities and the majority probably of the mercantile community, some also of the highest official authorities, are opposed to this narrow gauge. It is likely, in their view, to impede traffic by causing breaks of gauge. It diminishes the interchange of rolling stock, engines, carriages, wagons, in the working of through lines, and it is insufficient for the growing traffic in goods especially. It produces inconvenience, without an appreciable saving of expense either in constructing or working the lines. These views are often supported by the military authorities, with the additional argument that the break of gauge in time of war will be injurious to rapidity in the movement of troops.

On the other side, it is urged that economy is important with railways, as with everything else in India. A narrow-gauge railway, being a smaller thing than a broad-gauge railway, must cost less to build and less to work. Even though the expense be not quite so low as might be expected in proportion to size, still it must be less considerably. In many parts of the country the narrow gauge is large enough for the traffic. The break of gauge, though disadvantageous, is not so seriously inconvenient as to prevent the lines from conferring great benefit upon the trade. Notwithstanding such break, troops and material of war can be conveyed promptly. In time of war the difficulty and the delay are not on the railway line, but on the lines of military transport after the terminus of the railway has been passed. It was contemplated in 1871 and 1872, that, for the most part, the lines in the Panjab, and in Sind, that is in the valleys of the Indus and its tributaries, in Rajputana and Central India, should be constructed on the narrow gauge. The project provided a considerable length of railway uniformly on this gauge, connected and interdependent, thus allowing interchange of engines, carriages and wagons. That part of the project which related to the Panjab and the Indus valley was soon afterwards abandoned, the railways in that quarter having been all constructed on the broad gauge. But that portion of the project which related to Rajputana and Central India has been, or is being, carried into execution, and in this quarter there will be a considerable length of narrow-gauge railways. In the southern peninsula, also, there is a continuous series of narrow-gauge lines near Tanjore and Trichinopoly, extending to the neighbourhood of Cape Comorin. Some other separate State lines, and most of the branch lines yet to be undertaken, have been, or are to be, constructed on the narrow gauge. In reference to the importance of keeping down the capital account of the railways, which is really a part of the national debt, economizing the current expenses so that the net earnings shall represent a profitable rate of interest, and husbanding the limited means of the country for the completion of much extension still needed,—it is earnestly hoped that the narrow-gauge railways will be so managed that they shall answer the economical expectations with which they were introduced.

The potent accession, which the railways have brought to the military power of the Government, has been proved on many occasions of late years. The proof has been signal during the recent campaigns in Afghanistan, and will be still more emphatic as emergencies in the future may demand supreme efforts. The military advantage alone might be held to justify any financial sacrifices which may have been incurred for the sake of establishing communication by rail over the wide area of the Indian empire.

Even more remarkable is the advantage acquired in coping with famine, a fell foe whose attacks are of periodical recurrence. If public opinion in England demands that when millions of Indian people are threatened with starvation, the Government shall leave no saving remedy untried which the science of the nineteenth century can devise, then this task cannot possibly be fulfilled without the possession of railways throughout the length and breadth of the land.

The introduction of the electric telegraph into India may be appropriately mentioned in connection with railways. All the railway lines, whether belonging to the guaranteed Companies or to the State, have their electric telegraphs, which besides performing the railway business, despatch many messages for the public.

Separate from these is the Government telegraph, which was introduced into India in 1853, at the recommendation of Lord Dalhousie and carried out mainly through the exertions of Sir William O'Shaughnessy. It has since that time been extended to all parts of the empire and has been carried across valleys, along mountain-sides or over rivers of great breadth, in a manner reflecting the highest credit on the skill of the officers concerned. The cost of the lines amounted in all to 3½ millions sterling, their total length is represented by 19,100 miles, and 1¾ million of messages, public and private, are despatched annually. In times of famine, the telegraph has been rapidly extended into the heart of the distressed tracts, and has been of the utmost assistance to those engaged in the work of relief. In time of war, it follows the armies in the field with much regularity and constitutes a real military resource, and in every sort of emergency it has added much to the power of the Government. It is largely used by the officers of the Government, and greatly facilitates the despatch of affairs in an empire where the postal distances are so great. The European non-official community have used it greatly from the first, especially those engaged in trade. The Natives were somewhat slower in making full use of its advantages, but the Native merchants now avail themselves of it as much as the European. Its use has not, however, yet spread to the middle and humbler classes corresponding to those classes which resort to it in England, probably by reason of the minimum charge of one rupee (two shillings) for a message. If a reduction in the charge shall be found practicable, there will be an increase of messages. The messages are transmitted with satisfactory accuracy; in a manner which is creditable to the management of the department and commands the confidence of the public. For some time the receipts did not cover the expenses; they are now, however, beginning to exceed the expenses and to yield a moderate net income.

There are two lines of telegraphic communication between India and England. Of these, one runs by a submarine cable across the Indian Ocean to Aden, and thence by the Red Sea to Egypt; it belongs to a private Company. The other runs along the coast of Beluchistan to the mouth of the Persian Gulf, then passes up the Gulf by a submarine cable to Bushire, thence by land across Persia to Tehran, where it joins the European system; it belongs to the British Government. With these two lines, the telegraphic communication is safe from interruption. The value of such communication for State purposes is manifest, and the utility to merchants is equally great, most of their important business being transacted by these means. The expense of transmitting messages over a line of such length deters individuals from using it largely; but to those who do employ it for some important personal concern, its usefulness is beyond description. To the general community, in respect of news, it is most convenient; the arrangements for telegraphing public information of importance and interest, are complete. Whatever happens in England, Europe or America, whatever is said by statesmen or written by publicists, is known a few hours afterwards throughout India. The correctness with which the messages are transmitted over several thousands of miles of land and sea, is honourable to the officers and employés of the departments concerned. The accuracy with which cypher messages are transmitted, by this long line through so many countries, is remarkable. The Indian Empire is now in telegraphic communication with China, Australia and South Africa.

CHAPTER XVI.

ROADS AND EMBANKMENTS.

Roadmaking under Native rule—Under British rule—Principal lines of British roads—Their value and character—Their noteworthy features—Bridging and metalling—Pack-bullocks in part superseded—Carts with draught-bullocks substituted—Embankments in Bengal, Behar and Orissa—In the valley of the Indus.

ROADMAKING was from the earliest ages neglected in India to a degree which would hardly be conceivable by any Englishman who had not travelled in the East. The Buddhists and Hindus who hewed spacious chambers out of rock-formations, the later Hindus who dammed up rivers with dykes to form reservoirs for irrigation, the Indian Muhammadans who in structural design and architectural conception have not been excelled by any modern race of men, seem never to have bent their minds to the subject of roads and communications. In some few provinces, highways for warlike bands or for peaceful caravans, were marked out but not constructed. It was often deemed sufficient to indicate the route by minarets at fixed intervals of distance, and by commodious caravanserais for wayfarers at every stage. Here and there, bridges were constructed, solidly massive, indeed, and well founded, but clumsy and unpractical, and affording by their ruins and remains a strange contrast to the other surviving structures of that period. Not only in the rainy or close season were ordinarily-sized rivers impassable (as might be expected), but also their passage even in the fair, or open season, was equal to a day's march. In the champaign districts, strings of carts could, though with difficulty, drag their length along. But in the hilly districts, which comprise so large a part of the area of the country, wheeled traffic was impossible. There the laden-pack animals and other beasts of burden climbed or struggled, as best they might, up or down the steep and rugged tracks. The shortcomings in respect to roadmaking, however, arose not only from ignorance and apathy, but partly also from design. Every Native sovereign and chief dreaded incursions from his neighbours, and regarded the impassability of the country, from wants of roads, as a sort of natural defence. None will be so obtuse respecting the advantages of roadmaking as those who, in their shortsightedness, wish not to make roads. Ofttimes a British officer, when urging on a Native chief the expediency of constructing such and such a line of road, has been told, in diplomatic terms, that roads for guns and for material of war were being advocated under the guise of roads for peaceful traffic and for commerce. Whenever a Native empire like that of the Moguls, or that of the Mahrattas, arose, its energies were too much absorbed in military and political combinations, for attention to be paid to roads and communications.

Similar preoccupations befell the British empire also, after its first consolidation; English officers were too much engrossed in the pacification of their districts to take up what would then have been regarded as so secondary a matter as roadmaking. The East India Company, so keenly sensitive to all that concerned the welfare of the people under its charge, was at first less alive to the need of roadmaking than it afterwards became; it was only abreast, and not in advance of its time. Within the last thirty years of its existence, however, it turned to roadmaking that far-seeing discernment and that comprehensive grasp, which had procured for it victorious success in so many fields of action. Lines of road, partially bridged and macadamized throughout, were undertaken, from Calcutta to Delhi a thousand miles, and prolonged hundreds of miles further as the frontier advanced; from Bombay to Agra, a distance of nine hundred miles; from Madras to Bombay, a distance of eight hundred miles. These represent only some of the principal among the trunk lines which were begun in province after province and in season after season. The lines of road not only traversed the open steppe-like tracts of the country, but also marched right at the mountain ranges, or made straight for some of the most arduous passes. There was no want of ingenuity in avoiding difficulties, but the contour of the country presented obstacles which had unavoidably to be encountered.

These lines rendered to the country the services which the railways are now rendering far more completely. For many years before the introduction of the railways, the line from Bombay to the north and from Bombay to Madras served for the purposes of military communication and of trade. During a whole generation, the trunk road of the North-western Provinces was the main artery of communication between Calcutta and the north-west frontier. In these several trunk lines the most noteworthy points are, the section through the rugged tracts between the rivers Jhelum and Indus, where the roadway sometimes consists of a continuous series of cuttings and embankments; the roadway along the spurs of the Vindhya mountains near Indore; the passage of the Western Ghat mountains by the Thal pass between Khandesh and the coast, which is perhaps the best instance of roadmaking to be found in the empire; the similar passage of the same mountains by the Bhore pass between Bombay and the Deccan; the line through the Eastern Ghat mountains between the Balaghat districts and the Madras coast.

Besides the trunk lines there are many other roads, of remarkable construction, in all parts of the empire; for instance in the Himalayas, the roads from the plains of Rawal Pindi through the hill district of Hazâra, from the military cantonment of Ambala to the sanitarium of Simla; from Simla towards Chini; from the region of northern Bengal to the station of Darjiling and the tea district of Sikhim; from Mirzapur on the Ganges to Jabulpur in Central India and thence across the Sâtpura mountains to Nagpur; the several passes whereby the Western Ghat range is pierced, such as that near Mahableshwar, near Kolhapur, near Karwar, near Kompta, near Cannanore, near Calicat and Beypur; the line from Poona to the southern Deccan; the ascent of the Nilgiri mountains from the plains of Coimbatur to the sanitarium at Utacamand; the passage of the Eastern Ghat mountains between the coast and the districts of Caddapa and Karnul. Many portions of the mountainous ranges of the empire, such as the Western and Eastern Ghats, the Vindhyas and the Sâtpuras, the Aravalis, yet remain to be penetrated by the roadmakers.

In the passes the roads are usually made complete, with bridges, zigzags, parapets and revetments. In the plains they are partly bridged; and many fine bridges have been erected in different parts of the empire. They are often, however, very imperfectly bridged, or not bridged at all. The trunk lines are usually metalled or macadamized; the materials for metalling are abundant in northern, southern and western India, but deficient in eastern India, especially in Bengal, where they have to be supplied by brickmaking. In several provinces there are still many branch roads quite unmetalled, and these prove very heavy and troublesome for traffic.

The difference, caused by these roads, in the modes of communication and in the habits of the people, is always strongly marked. The pack-bullocks driven by strange tribes, resembling gypsies in some respects, but endowed with uncommon hardihood and perseverance, are superseded, and carts with draught-bullocks are substituted. The carts are not of the inefficient and antiquated build previously in vogue, but are of an improved structure and greatly enlarged capacity; the bullocks are of taller, stouter and stronger breeds. In some, perhaps in most seasons, it is the custom to perform the stage between sunset and sunrise; and along the mountain passes the creaking of the cartwheels and the shouts of the cartmen may be heard resounding all night long. The pack-bullocks, having their gipsy-like drivers, will continue to graze in vast numbers on the mountain plateaux, and will not find their occupation gone, until that yet distant time shall arrive when the road system of the empire approaches completion.

Thus, not only has the professional skill of engineers, but also some of the best talent of civil administrators, been directed to roadmaking, which has in the course of a quarter of a century made gigantic strides. Nevertheless, although the empire can no longer be considered to be roadless, as it was once described, and although the complaints regarding a want of roads are much less heard nowadays than they used to be, it is doubtless held in commercial circles that very much, in regard to roadmaking, yet remains to be done. If thousands of miles have been finished, still thousands of miles have to be undertaken, before the empire can be placed on a par in this respect with any advanced country in Europe. Some of the trunk roads are used less now than formerly, by reason of the introduction of railways. But the opening of railway stations often brings fresh roads into existence as tributaries, or "feeders" as they are now called, to the railway. Here, again, the authorities of the railways will doubtless consider that much more yet needs to be done.

The finance of roadmaking generally, in the empire, has been of late years entrusted entirely to the several Local Governments under the system known by the name of Provincial Services. The central Government of India undertakes to provide funds only for a few lines mainly or solely required for military purposes. The several Local Governments receive annually, from the Government of India, certain aggregate grants for provincial services, among which services roadmaking is included. They may apply to roadmaking such portion of these grants as they deem fit, and to these funds they may add the receipts of local rates imposed by law for roads. With the resources at their disposal, they may construct such roads as are practicable, they being answerable to the public for the result, and not being entitled to apply to the Government of India for any additional funds.

Tramways have been introduced into the city of Bombay by American enterprise, and are managed with that skill which Americans everywhere bring to bear on this subject. They are very successful and carry many thousands of passengers daily, European and East Indian as well as Natives. There is a good tramway in Calcutta along the Strand, belonging to the Port Commissioners, but the attempts made to introduce tramways into other parts of the city have not yet succeeded.

It is difficult to give the total length of the roads which are metalled or macadamized throughout and partially bridged, but it is not less than 20,000 miles for the whole empire.

In previous chapters so much stress has been laid upon the need of irrigation and protection from drought, that it might perhaps be supposed that the opposite difficulty, namely that of drainage and protection from floods, hardly exists. In some provinces, however, protective measures against inundation have long engaged the solicitous care of the Government and the people. In Bengal, Behar and Orissa these operations, on the banks of the Ganges and its tributaries, have been repeatedly subjects of legislation. To one of the laws on this subject there is attached an interesting schedule setting forth a statement of embankments under State control, some old, others new, of which the total length amounts to 1170 miles. The river Gandak in Behar presents a remarkable instance of embankments, broad and high, constructed on both sides for a length of 130 miles, on the efficient maintenance of which depends the safety of districts with a population of not less than two millions. In Orissa there are extensive embankments of ancient date on the sides of the Mahanadi, the Brahmini and other rivers. In northern Bengal there are swamps of many square miles in extent, which at some seasons of the year resemble lagoons. In 1875, the Bengal Government estimated the area under swamps, needing drainage and reclamation, at full half a million of acres. In the valley of the Indus near Bahawulpur, in the southern portion of the Panjab, there are extensive embankments on the bank of the great river. Near Sakar in Sindh the embankments extend for 150 miles on one bank and 50 miles on the opposite bank, protecting the whole of Upper Sind from the devastation which the floods of the Indus would otherwise cause. Indeed, the canal system in that region, the land revenue, the towns, and the line of military communication with southern Afghanistan, partly depend for their safety on the stability of these embankments. There is, however, much difficulty in rendering these works secure against the violence of the Indus when in flood. Improvements in construction are being constantly made, and, when fully completed, the Indus embankments will form one of the finest systems of the kind in any country.

CHAPTER XVII.

PRODUCTS, NATURAL, AGRICULTURAL AND INDUSTRIAL.

Comparison of Indian products with those of other countries—Tea—Coffee—Tobacco—Cinchona—Cotton—Indigenous staple—Local manufactures of cotton by steam machinery—Factory legislation—Production and manufactures of jute—The forests—Destruction in past times—Present conservancy—Climatic importance—Preservation of pasturage—Communal forests—Forest laws—The forest department—Conduct of the people in relation to forests—Mineral resources—Coal—Iron—Gold—Precious stones—Industrial products—Still flourishing on the whole—Exhibitions of art and industry—Effect on Native taste—Merits of Native art.

INDIA will, on a comparison of her raw products with those of other nations, be found to exhibit only a second-rate quality in many of those articles, for the production of which she has long been famed. For instance, her raw silks are not equal in excellence to those of China or Italy. Her produce of sugarcane is inferior in richness to that of Jamaica; her spices have less pungency than those of Ceylon, the West Indies, or the islands of the Eastern Archipelago. Her cotton is far surpassed by that of the United States, and her tobacco by that of South America. Though some kinds of her rice, grown in limited quantities, are of unsurpassed fineness, still the quality of her abundant sorts is excelled by that of the Carolina rice. Her maize is below the standard of southern Europe; her wheat, though beginning to be esteemed and exported, cannot rival in quality the wheat of Great Britain or of the United States. Her indigenous vegetables and fruits cannot be compared with those of European countries; nor her dates with those of Mesopotamia; nor her betel-nut with that of Ceylon; nor her figs with those of Asia Minor. Her vines are inferior, not only to those of France and Germany, but even to those of Afghanistan and Persia. Notwithstanding great efforts in the culture of the febrifuge, her Cinchona cannot be made to match that of Peru. Her wool cannot compete with that of Australia or of Thibet. Her horses, even on her own ground, cannot vie with those of Australia, Arabia or Persia; her bovine breeds are outstripped by those of European countries; and her camels by those of Central Asia. Her mineral wealth, though consisting of coal, iron, copper, borax, manganese, gypsum, and many other things, must be placed in a comparatively humble rank.

The merit of India consists in this, that she produces all these things cheaply, abundantly and passably good.

It is remarkable, too, that the parts of India, which raise some articles in a small quantity, produce them better than those parts which raise them in abundance. For instance, Bengal and Burma produce rice very much, the Panjab very little, but that little is by many degrees superior. Many other provinces have sugarcane besides the Panjab, but the Panjab sugarcane is the best, though limited in quantity. Again, Indian corn or maize is grown largely in the plains of India, and only sparsely in the Himalayas, but the Himalayan varieties are the finest.

Still, there are some articles in the production of which India is at the head of all countries, or is not surpassed by any country. Her tea has of late years been so rapidly rising in repute that the people of China will some day be obliged to look to their hitherto unquestioned supremacy in this respect. In quantity the Chinese tea is still surpassingly great; but as to quality, it is to be noted that the Indian tea is used in the English markets chiefly for flavouring Chinese tea, and this may be regarded as a sign of superiority in favour of India. The quality, and the astonishing increase in the quantity, of Indian coffee are fast causing the Arabian coffee, so famous of old, to be superseded. The indigo of Bengal and Behar has been unapproachable as yet, though its position in the markets of the world is threatened by new dyes chemically extracted from other substances. Still, no plant yet discovered in any clime can rival the dark blue dye of the Indian plant in permanence or in colour, and no dye surpasses the scarlet of the Indian lac. The opium-producing poppy of the mid-Gangetic basin, and of the Malwa uplands, is in quality unequalled. The Chinese have, apparently despite the prohibition by their own Government of the culture, grown the poppy over an extensive area, still their variety is nowhere near that of India in quality. Though the cocoa-nut is a most highly esteemed product in many eastern countries, yet nothing beats the cocoa-nut of the Malabar coast of India. This tree is truly said to furnish all a poor man wants, his food, drink, clothing, utensils and the materials for his house. From one end of India to the other, the introduction of the potato has been most successful, and the root bids fair to become an article of large consumption. The mango-tree is among the most useful of the Indian trees; its wood is turned to many purposes; its fruit is an article of sustenance for the poorer classes, and with the highly cultured varieties, ranks high among the fruits of the world. The teak wood of Burma and of Malabar has such a high merit that it is largely used by the British Admiralty. The cedar is regarded everywhere as one of the queens of the forest, but nowhere is it found richer in quantity, or finer in quality, than among the Himalayan mountains. The ebony of Africa and the india-rubber of South America have long been celebrated; but they may be rivalled by those of Eastern Bengal and other parts of India. The *Eucalyptus globulosa,* introduced from Australia, has been naturalized successfully in the Nilgiri mountains. Horns and hides are things in which quantity is the main object, and in this respect India with her countless cattle has a vast resource. Her oil-seeds, flax and hemp occupy a high place; her jute fibre which enters into so many manufactures, has, as yet, no competitor anywhere. Her oranges, naturalized by the Portuguese on her soil, rival those of southern Europe; but her plantains are not equal to those of equatorial regions. Some of her flowering trees, such as the Champa, the Magnolia, the Asoka, the Lagerstræmia, the Bauhinia, the silk-cotton tree, the Kachnar, the Poinsiana, display great beauty. The rhododendrons of the eastern Himalayas are superb, and as tree-shrubs are among the glories of the mountains. The European flowers when cultivated in some parts of India, such as the Nilgiri mountains, under European supervision will soon enter into rivalry with those of Europe itself; the superiority or inferiority is only a question of capital and skill.

From amongst the many products, a few may be selected for brief notice here.

The production of indigo, once so large in Bengal, has become contracted of late years. The cultivation of the plant ceased twenty years ago to be remunerative to the peasants, who consequently refused to continue it. The European planters held the peasantry to the contracts which had been made for producing the plant. The validity of these contracts was disputed and some agrarian troubles, even disturbances, ensued. Concessions were offered, but the terms, which the planters could afford to give, the cultivators could not afford to take. Ultimately the planting concerns succumbed for the most part, and indigo ceased to be an industry of any consequence in Bengal.

Similar circumstances have arisen, or threatened to arise, in Behar, where the plant is largely produced, but the planters have from time to time been able to make concessions which the cultivators have accepted for the present. Thus the industry has been saved from extinction, and continues to flourish; up to the most recent dates additional concessions are being made by the planters. There is hope that the planters may yet preserve to the country this useful product, remembering that it must decline and fall, unless it can be made remunerative to the peasant who is the original producer.

The tea is mainly a product of the southern slopes of the

Himalayas, of Assam or the upper valley of the Brahmaputra, and of the western slopes of the mountains which bound Bengal on the east. Its increase is among the economic events of the time; in thirty years it has risen from nothing up to thirty-four millions of pounds annually, valued at three millions sterling. Many of the earlier European planters struggled towards the goal of this great success through a maze of difficulties, errors, and disappointments. They thus lost much capital, which has been replaced by capital generally yielding good returns. Their more fortunate successors form a regular profession of specially trained and qualified men. The tea-gardens are now scientifically managed, improved processes are adopted in the factories for the preparation of the leaf, and steam machinery is beginning to be used.

The coffee-planting has an earlier origin, and is carried on amidst the beautiful valleys and hills of Curg, the Nilgiris, Wynaad and Travancore. As a business, it has sometimes suffered from the want of professional knowledge, and it is somewhat subject to vicissitudes of season, to the ravages of insects and to specific diseases. Its production within this generation has greatly increased, and amounts on the average to 350,000 cwts. annually, valued at $1\frac{1}{3}$ million sterling. The coffee-planters also have become a highly instructed profession; their plantations are finely situated and present a gay sight when the trees are in blossom.

Tobacco is largely cultivated for local consumption, but is not exported in any appreciable quantity. Many people are sanguine that with scientific treatment it may be placed in competition with American tobacco. With this view some important experiments have been made in northern India, with assistance from the State and apparently with success.

The Cinchona-tree has been for some years assiduously cultivated by the Government both in the Nilgiri hills and in Sikhim. The plantations are extensive and thriving, and include several species of the tree. Chemical experiments have been made in order to extract from the bark a febrifuge which shall be sufficient and yet so cheap as to be purchaseable by the poorest people; considerable quantities of this useful medicine are being produced.

Silk was once among the most prosperous of Indian products, especially in Bengal proper. The mulberry-gardens, with the trees trained as bushes for the worms to feed upon, afford an interesting sight. The price commanded by the Indian silk in foreign markets, and the exportation, depend much on the yield in China and in Italy, and are therefore somewhat precarious. The production is, however, maintained in Bengal and in many other parts of the empire, and excites much attention. A full account of it will be found in Mr. Geoghegan's elaborate report. Great interest is felt by many people in the production of the "Tusser" or wild silk, produced by worms which feed, not on the cultivated mulberry, but on the trees of the forests. The substance thus produced is thought to be well suited to many kinds of European fabrics; machines for it are being devised and hopes are entertained of its becoming a valuable export. Reference may be made with advantage to Mr. Wardle's very useful treatises on the subject.

Cotton received much attention, both from the Government and from the public, for several years after the American civil war. Much salutary influence in this direction was exerted by the Cotton Supply Association formed in England. Special officers were appointed by the Government to guide the efforts of the people in improving the staple. Dr. Forbes in Bombay and Mr. H. Rivett Carnac in Upper India rendered much service in this way. Strenuous exertions were put forth, by improving the indigenous species, and by naturalizing foreign varieties, to produce a fibre which should be as suitable as the American fibre to the English machinery. These proceedings have been attended with partial success; but all parties concerned, whether the State, the trader, or the cultivator, are oppressed with the conviction that India cannot in this respect compete with America, now that the crop of the Southern States is as large as ever, despite the social changes consequent on the civil war. The interest in improving the staple, once so warm, has inevitably become cool, among the Natives at least. For some years after the war, India, though ceasing to export the abnormal quantities which used to be despatched to England during the blockade of the American ports, continued exporting annually quantities much larger than those she had exported before those events. The exportation has of late been decreasing, though it will doubtless remain considerable. Meanwhile the cultivation of the indigenous species is flourishing, and is stimulated by the establishment at Bombay of factories for the manufacture of cotton goods. The demand for raw cotton is brisk in all the marts; special regulations are made by law to stop the frauds and adulterations whereby foreign substances were mixed with the fibre, and the repute of the Indian staple lowered.

The local manufactures of cotton by steam machinery in India have been much noticed of late. Some twenty-five years have elapsed since the first attempt was made at Bombay, in this direction; a great impulse was imparted to the movement when the cotton trade became so inflated after 1861. There are now 53 spinning and weaving mills in India, of which 41 are in the Bombay Presidency and 5 in Calcutta. These mills employ 10,500 looms and 1½ million of spindles. They mostly belong to private companies, though some of them are owned and managed by individuals. Of the capital, a part belongs to Europeans, the greater portion of it is, however, in the hands of Natives. The owners and managers are generally Natives, though Europeans are sometimes employed as foremen. The concerns have suffered all sorts of mishaps from speculation, misapplication of capital and errors in practice, still many of them have been placed on a sound footing, and on the whole they are very creditable to Native enterprise. The workpeople are Natives of both sexes, including adults and children. The goods produced by the mills are good, serviceable, and free from adulteration. To a limited extent they compete successfully with English-made goods, and with the indigenous goods turned out by hand-looms. They cannot, however, at present compete with the better kinds of the English manufactures, though the chance of their competing in future is gradually becoming stronger.

The growth of these and other manufactures at Bombay and at Calcutta, and the large numbers of Native hands employed, have caused the Indian legislature to undertake legislation for restricting the hours of work in the factories, and to enact other humane provisions on the model of the English legislation in these respects. Some moderate restrictions and provisions are required in a hot climate where, for the sake of good wages in hard times, the Native workpeople are apt to over-exert themselves. In justice to the managers it must be said that the management is generally popular with the Native labourers and their families; and that care is bestowed on the women and children in the factories.

There are other fibrous substances such as coir, which is obtained from the husk of the cocoa-nut, which furnishes excellent material for cables, and which is exported in some quantities. Flax can be produced in large quantities; but the production of it is comparatively small, because the linseed plant, from the stem of which the fibre is obtained, is cultivated for the sake of the oil-seed and the oil, rather than for the sake of the fibre. Several good varieties of hemp are grown and afford capital material for cordage; this article, raw and manufactured, is exported in considerable quantities.

Among the most important of the fibrous substances of India is jute, an article which has come into prominence since the war in the Crimea. This staple is grown on the banks of the Brahmaputra and of its branches, in eastern Bengal. It is cultivated partly for consumption in manufactures within India itself, and partly for exportation. The quantity exported, which is sent chiefly to the United Kingdom, amounts annually to nearly 5 millions of cwts., valued at 3 millions sterling. The jute manufactures in India itself are valued at ¾ of a million sterling yearly. They are carried on at Calcutta, where the factories and the tall chimneys remind the spectator of some of the manufacturing centres of Europe. They consist chiefly of bags for corn, rice, seeds and wool, which are sent to the United States, Australia, Egypt, and to England also. They employ many thousands of Natives of both sexes and all ages.

Among natural products, the forests claim a prominent place.

The forests of India were vast according to tradition, and have been considerable even during periods of authentic history. During some few centuries, they have been shrinking in size and importance, until they are at present inconsiderable for so great an empire as India, which possesses so many ranges of mountains and hills. If the hill-sides generally had slopes which could be cultivated, then the forests, as they were gradually cut down and uprooted, would give place to crop-bearing fields. But the hills are steep, the soil, lying upon rocky strata, is thin, and is speedily washed away by the rains descending violently at certain seasons. The forest is destined by nature to bind the soil with roots, and so to support the lesser vegetation on the ground. Consequently, when the hill-side is denuded of trees, the shrubs, plants, and herbage fail to sustain themselves, and barrenness ensues. The unrestrained clearance of the forests has affected the climate unfavourably, and lessened the supply of moisture in a country already subject to aridity. It has caused wood, a necessary article, to become dear and scarce, and compelled the people to use for fuel substances which ought to be used for manure. It has reduced to a low ebb some valuable portions of the national wealth, and cut off beyond recovery some branches of the imperial resources. For many generations, the forests have been felled whenever firewood had to be gathered for the consumption of the villagers, or new lands reclaimed from the hilly slopes, or towns built with styles of architecture in which wood is largely used, more particularly when cantonments for troops had to be formed, or civil edifices constructed. The felling used to be carried on indiscriminately, without any thought of leaving some parts of the forests, or even a few trees here and there, for reproduction in the future. This destructive process was continued under British rule, and became even aggravated under various circumstances. Timber was needed for the roofing of barracks, and the officers of the public works department used to make contracts with capitalists for its supply. These officers were unwilling to interfere with the operations of the contractors who, having no abiding interest in the forests, cleared them to the last logs, without regard for the consequences of such denudation. The forests had been so little explored that the local authorities seldom became aware of the mischief which was being done. When railways began to be constructed, sleepers were not, as they now often are, obtained from northern Europe, but were procured from local forests, through the agency of contractors, who denuded the forests according to the custom which had unfortunately been established in such cases. The Government theoretically deplored the evil so far as they knew its existence; but its real magnitude remained long unknown by reason of the ignorance which prevailed in respect to the sites, value and stock of the forests.

Within the present generation, scientific attention has been awakened, the Government has bestirred itself, and an effective system of forests has been inaugurated. Mischief, practically immense, has been done already, of which some parts are irreparable, or can be repaired only after the lapse of a long time, while others may be remedied within one or two generations. Of the primeval forests there remain several, still intact, enough to constitute a national resource.

In the lower ranges of the Himalayan mountains, in central India, in the valleys of the Vindhya and Aravali ranges, in the northern and western portions of the Deccan, in many districts of the Madras Presidency, the forests have been for the most part so long destroyed that their restoration is hardly to be anticipated.

But in the higher ranges of the Himalayas, in the central tracts of the Panjab, in the Sâtpura range, in that hilly region where the Vindhya and Sâtpura ranges join, in the Eastern and Western Ghat ranges, they are either preserved, or else but partially destroyed, and may still prove very productive. In some parts of the Bengal Presidency, and in many parts of the Presidencies of Madras and Bombay, the remnant of them is still being invaded bit by bit. Many authorities apprehend that the western and southern provinces of India are, owing to the destruction of the forests, threatened with a danger which is feebly checked, and which, if not arrested, may seriously affect the best interests of the country.

The woods and forests of India from the Himalayas to Cape Comorin comprise, as might be expected, trees of European kinds, the cedar, the pine, the fir, the mountain cypress, the juniper, the yew, the oak, the ilex, the elm, the ash, the maple, the plane, the holly, the laurel, the birch, the walnut, the alder. The Asiatic sorts are the acacia, the terminalia, the ebony, the ficus order including the banyan and the india-rubber tree, the mango, the sandal-wood, the cane, the bamboo, the toon, the neem, the blackwood, the sâl; and greatest of all, the teak. To these should be added the palms, including the feathery date-palm, the palmyra with its fan-like leaves, and the betel-nut palm. The lesser products of the forests, such as myrobalams and other articles, are also considerable.

Many believe that the rainfall is copious and seasonable, or otherwise, according as the woods and forests, and the vegetation subsidiary to them, are preserved or destroyed, while others disbelieve this view, which at all events must admit of much qualification. But, after all due abatements have been made, the view is generally held to comprise some truth. The total rainfall of the whole country cannot possibly be affected by the existence of forests. The average quantity of vapour must come from the ocean and must be condensed somewhere; if it be not changed into rain as it passes across the plains, it will pass on to the mountains and be transformed there. This, indeed, is a matter of common experience; moisture-laden clouds float over the Deccan, leaving it arid, and move on to the Sâtpura range, and, being condensed there, fill the torrent-beds with rain-water which rushes into the rivers and returns ultimately to the plain in the form of inundations. Similarly, clouds sweep over the thirsty plains of Hindostan, and, being condensed in the Himalayas, produce floods in the great rivers. The hope is that, if forest tracts were distributed over the plains, there would be cool surfaces to attract the clouds and to arrest them, as it were, on their way. There are many tracts where forests, if preserved, would grow up within a short time. Thus it is anticipated by many that the climate would be improved, and that the early and the late rains would descend more seasonably than at present. It is remembered that, throughout the world, those regions which possess rich vegetation receive abundant rains, while those which are denuded of vegetation are rainless. It is remarked, too, that those regions in India, which ordinarily receive rain but have been parched by a long drought, are plagued afterwards with immoderate rain.

At all events the forests, and their subsidiary vegetation, husband and store by a natural process the exceeding moisture of the rainy season, for the benefit of the country during the dry season. The streams become better filled and more available for the use of the people; the springs are less likely to run dry, the wells less liable to failure. This consideration becomes peculiarly important in those regions where the canals for irrigation are drawn from rivers having their source in mountains which depend on the annual rainfall for moisture. Near the springs, and along the upper courses of these rivers, the vegetation needs especially to be preserved for the sake of the canals.

The economic considerations relating to the forests are manifestly important, as wood is used largely in the construction of the houses and cottages in most parts of the country. In northern India, where trees are few, the earth, indurated by the sun, affords good material, and the earthen walls are durable, but elsewhere the earth does not always possess a like degree of consistency. For these reasons it is essential that the timber markets should be well supplied. Without interposition by the State, the wood and timber would become scarcer and dearer from time to time, as the forests became exhausted. As coal is not available, the people require wood for fuel; if they cannot obtain wood, they will use cowdung-cakes for burning. The practice of consuming for fuel that which ought to be used for manure, in a country, too, where artificial manure is not available, extensively prevails, is most injurious and tends to exhaustion of the soil. The only means of lessening this practice, is by preserving the forests to provide a cheap and plentiful supply of wood for fuel.

Again, some of the woods and timbers, and many articles of spontaneous production in the forests, are exported largely; and under an adequate system of forest conservancy would add to the trade of the country.

Connected with the forests is the supply of grass for the pasturage of cattle. In times of drought the animals perish in great numbers for lack of fodder; in ordinary times they wander as they graze, and tread down much more than they eat. Conservancy of vegetation would save the woods, the brushwood and the grass simultaneously.

Some authorities consider that in the treeless parts of the country, woods and covers might be planted and reared near every village, to be called "communal forests," for the supply of fuel to the villagers, and for ensuring at least a limited area of vegetation, where the growth of grass would be preserved in the hot season for the cattle, which suffer so much at that period from want of fodder. This project is well worthy of a careful trial in many parts of the country.

Thus the policy of preserving the forests rests upon two grounds, first the improvement of the climate and the retention of moisture, secondly the husbanding of the national resources in timber and fuel for the use of the people. This policy, then, is of much consequence to the well-being of the countryand the nation.

The Government of India has enacted a law regulating all matters connected with forest conservancy, and the provisions of this law are being carried into effect by the several Local Governments. The forests are divided into two categories; first, those which are "reserved," being preserved and worked through State agency, in the most complete manner; secondly, those which are "protected," being preserved less thoroughly. The best timber-markets are mainly supplied from the "reserved" forests. Care has been taken to determine what tracts shall be "reserved," or "protected," and to mark off their boundaries. The area thus defined in the several provinces already, or likely to be defined ere long, will prove to be hardly less than eighty thousand square miles for the whole empire. The primary object of the administration is to preserve the forests for the sake of the country. Due attention is also given to the financial out-turn, much income is already secured, the expenditure is over £500,000 annually, but the receipts amount to nearly £700,000, and in time the forest department will have a prosperous revenue.

The superior officers of the department are for the most part British, trained in the forest schools of France and Germany. The Inspector-General of forests with the Government of India is Dr. D. Brandis, whose services to the empire have been conspicuous in organizing a system of forestry, which is sound and scientific, and is yet adapted to the circumstances of the country. Instruction in forestry is afforded to Natives also; forest schools are established for them, and in time they will take a large share in the administrative work.

As might be expected, the system of forest conservancy, though generally accepted by the Natives who dwell near the "reserved" and the "protected" tracts, is sometimes opposed by them. There must always be some danger lest the foresters should, in their just zeal for conservancy, infringe upon the prescriptive rights of the inhabitants. The local civil authorities are vigilant and prompt in asserting or vindicating the rights of the people in this respect, for the recognition of which rights, indeed, ample provision is made by the law. They should, however, be careful to support and encourage the forest officers in the execution of duties which are of the utmost consequence to the welfare of the country. Many of the hill tribes habitually burn patches of valuable forest, in order that the ashes may so fertilise the virgin soil as to render it capable of producing a crop without tillage. Having reaped one harvest, they leave the spot marked by charred stumps of timber trees, and move on to repeat the same ravage elsewhere. This barbarous and wastefully destructive practice is gradually and cautiously checked, by reclaiming these people from agricultural savagery, and by inducing them to plough lands, and raise yearly crops by ordinary husbandry.

According to the latest returns there appear to be 29,600 square miles of demarcated reserve forests, 3500 square miles of protected areas, and 35,000 square miles of unreserved forests; or 68,100 square miles in all. This appears a comparatively small area for so large an empire, especially when it is remembered that of this not more than one half is effectually preserved. Some extensive forest tracts exist, however, in the Madras Presidency, of which a return remains to be rendered. There are, further, 31,000 acres of plantations in various districts.

Among the mineral resources of India there are a few articles deserving notice.

Coal-beds having a considerable yield, though not of the best quality, exist in many parts of India. The largest are those which have been opened out among the hills flanking the western side of Bengal, and with these there is complete railway communication. There are good seams, successfully worked, on the northern side of the Sâtpura range, overlooking the Narbadda valley through which the railway runs. A considerable bed is being worked in the valley of the Wardha river near Nagpur, and to that point a branch railway has been constructed. Some coal-beds have been found in upper Assam; and a short railway is to be made to them from the bank of the Brahmaputra. The Indian coal is largely used by the railways, the steamers and the factories; the total consumption amounts to half a million of tons annually; and the possible output of the colleries is reckoned at a million of tons yearly. The industry affords employment to upwards of 50,000 men, exclusive of their families. Still, some quantities of English coal and coke are imported amounting to 600,000 tons annually. Other coal-beds are known to exist in the Salt range of the Panjab, in the province of Berar, and in the Palamow extremity of the Vindhya range.

Iron is found in most parts of the empire, and is used in many places for small local industries. It is seldom worked on any large scale, by reason of the want of available fuel, among other reasons. In the undulating country on the west of Bengal, some extensive mines are being worked by a private company with a fair measure of success.

India is one of the oldest gold-producing countries in the world, but during recent ages the supply has been small. Of late some auriferous veins have been discovered in the southern portion of the Malabar coast region, especially in the Wynaad hills, and in the Mysore plateau near Bangalore. Companies have been and are being formed for working the ore; concessions of many square miles have been obtained for this purpose; and sanguine hopes have been raised in the minds of many well-informed persons. The matter is undergoing scientific enquiry by professional experts and trials are being made. There are traces of operations in ancient times, whence it is probable that the most readily available supplies have been worked out. The gold which still remains must apparently be "won," by processes of crushing and reducing. Questions, too, will arise regarding water-power and fuel resources. If mining for gold in this quarter should prove successful, the economic result to the Indian empire would be important.

The supply of precious stones in India is but little now as

compared with what it was in former times. There are still, however, diamonds in Bundelkhand south of the Jamna river, rubies in Burma, and pearl fisheries near Tuticorin in the Southern Peninsula. Among Indian products are included the pearl fisheries of Bahrein in the Persian Gulf, of which the produce is chiefly sent to the Bombay market.

The natural and agricultural products having thus been mentioned, the industrial products claim a brief notice.

It seems to be held by many that the ancient manufactures of the Natives have been largely supplanted by British manufactures, or extinguished under the social changes wrought by British rule, and that consequently a depressing influence is exercised on the national wealth and energy; but this opinion has less foundation than is commonly supposed.

The virtual extinction of the industry, represented by the muslins of eastern Bengal, may be cited as an instance. These delicate fabrics can be made cheaper, though not better, elsewhere, and the fastidiously refined classes who were wont to use them have dwindled away. The number of hands employed in this industry was never very great. Some instances might be adduced, where arts, of extreme beauty but of limited application, have perished, by reason of their being confined to small guilds or to a very few families. Revolutions stopped for a moment the demand; the little bands of artists were dispersed; as individuals died, their skill vanished with them. Such circumstances, however lamentable from an æsthetic point of view, have not produced any effect upon the people, as the number of persons concerned is relatively so small.

The armourer's trade, which once reached an excessive growth in an empire where for some centuries warfare was almost universal and incessant, necessarily languished on the establishment of peace under a settled government. Armoury as an industry once employed large numbers of persons, and as an art was carried to a high degree of beauty. But its gradual cessation in the British territories at least, is hardly to be regretted.

On the other hand, many ancient articles once extensively

made, are still produced largely, though perhaps in somewhat diminished quantities. If the purely indigenous industries of the higher sorts in India, as they now are, could be compared with those which existed in the palmy days of the Mogul empire, some decline would doubtless be perceptible. But if the industries of the coarser and commoner sorts were thus compared, expansion rather than contraction would be observed. If the total number of persons engaged in all kinds of industry, other than agriculture, in 1880 could be compared with that of 1680, the time of the emperor Arungzeb, or of 1580, the time of Akber the Great, it is probable that British rule would not suffer by the comparison, but would rather gain. Those who consult the splendidly illustrated work by Dr. Forbes Watson on the textile fabrics of India, the review by Dr. Birdwood of contributions by India to the Paris Exhibition, the recently published book by the same author on the Industrial Arts of India, and Mr. Baden Powell's Handbook on the manufactures and arts of the Panjab, will see that the country still produces, in great quantities and of excellent quality, nearly all the beautiful articles for which it has ever been celebrated. The people at large, even if they have not increased in numbers, must be at least as numerous as ever, and their clothing constitutes a mighty factor in the national industry. It is notorious that British industry has long been striving, as yet with but moderate success, to supersede this indigenous industry, which still for the most part remains in the hands of Indians. On the other hand, the mining or metallurgic industries of India have been fast increasing under British rule. Several new industries have arisen, so well known in connection with cotton, jute, indigo, silk, tea and coffee. The works of material improvement now executed, to an extent not equalled by the architectural or structural efforts of former dynasties, have developed a new series of mechanical industries affording much occupation to the working classes. Thus a detailed survey of the whole field would probably shew that, in respect of economic effect, the arts and industries of India are more important than they ever were, and employ a greater number of hands. It is true that numbers of persons, once otherwise employed, have during the last two generations been thrown back upon agriculture. Such persons, however, will be found for the most part to have come, not from the industrial classes, but rather from the classes formerly engaged in the defence and administration of the country.

On a review of the Indian Museum in the art department at South Kensington, and of the several illustrated works which have been published, it will be apparent that India still has the taste and the faculty necessary for the production of works of industrial art, that her handicraftsmen still have the leisure and the inventive power which signalized them of yore, that her chiefs and upper classes still appreciate and encourage the production of really beautiful things in the utmost variety. The gold and silver plate, the metal work in brass, copper and tin, the damascened work, the trappings and caparisons, the mother-of-pearl of Ahmedabad, the inlaid work of Agra and of Bombay, the work of Vizagapatam, the sandal-wood carving, the carved ivory horn and tortoise-shell, the lac work, the cotton fabrics, the gold and silver lace, the embroidery, the carpets, the pottery, and most of all the enamels, worthily represent the work of these times, in comparison with former ages. The art of enamelling is in the first rank of the handicrafts of the world, and is pursued in India to the highest degree of perfection yet known. It cannot at any previous epoch have been more successful than it is now, and probably it is carried on with a greater variety of device and of method than ever.

When the Native princes and chiefs of the empire attended the Imperial Assemblage at Delhi, the mass of articles of luxury and adornment, then collected, probably equalled anything ever seen in the camps that were marshalled, or the courts that were held, by the Moguls. The presents offered to the Prince of Wales, during his visit to India, by the Natives in order to illustrate the arts and industries of their territories, probably rivalled in taste, beauty and variety any offerings ever laid at the feet of a Mogul emperor.

Although the Indian manufactures may be regarded as comparatively satisfactory in respect of number, variety and quantity produced, they have been passing through a critical period as regards artistic quality. The good principle, upon which fine art exhibitions were instituted in Europe, asserted itself in India. Similar exhibitions were held in many provinces of the Indian empire, and from India were sent extensive contributions to the exhibitions held at Kensington, at Vienna, and at Paris. The British Indian section in the Paris Exhibition of 1878 was specially notable for the effect it produced on the minds of European spectators, by whose means a knowledge of the industrial arts of India was disseminated throughout Europe. The interest of the section was heightened by the consideration that therein were included the presents proffered by the Natives to the Prince of Wales during his visit to India, which were graciously lent by His Royal Highness for the purposes of the Exhibition. This unique collection of presents, illustrating the whole field of Indian art and industry, and so replete with instruction, has been most considerately placed by His Royal Highness's desire temporarily at the disposal of the local authorities at many places in the United Kingdom and the Continent of Europe, for the inspection of all lovers of industrial art, and for the information of the public respecting the progress and condition of India herself.

The proceedings at these exhibitions doubtless drew European attention, in a much greater degree than formerly, to the productions of India, and augmented the demand for them in the markets of the world. The Native mind, too, was enlightened in respect to the practical application of European art. The Natives were stirred with a sense that their works were being noticed in European circles. At the same time, however, another effect of a dubious character was produced, as the Natives began either to imitate European models absolutely, or to engraft, upon their own works, accessories borrowed from European styles. In all cases of such imitation or admixture the result was unsatisfactory, and conduced to the vitiation of the Native taste. As an instance, the recent circumstances of the Cashmir shawl manufacture may be recalled. These shawls were esteemed not only for their matchless colouring (due to the peculiar qualities of the air and water of that wondrous valley of Cashmir) but also for the appropriateness of the peculiar elaboration in the designs. Imitative fabrics were commenced in the Panjab with the aid of skilled workmen from Cashmir, but never equalled the superb originals. The demand becoming brisker in the Parisian markets, French agents came to purchase in India. In course of time the shawls began to be made more and more after European designs, and to lose their characteristic loveliness. Again, the Indian pottery, from Sind and elsewhere, began to be admired, and came into demand. For a moment there was fear lest it should be spoiled by the imitating of European designs; fortunately this error was averted.

It is to be hoped that these and all similar mistakes may be avoided, as the real merits of indigenous Indian art become recognised. This art, formed through the labour of many centuries, and never obscured by the shadow of even the darkest adversities, like a marble monument retaining its beauty despite the stains of time and the rough usage of barbarism, seems now to be appreciated more and more by artistic judges, and to be the subject of æsthetic culture. It has been produced by generations of hereditary artists, who from father to son dedicated thereto their hearts and minds. Its forms, arising from sound and exact ideas originated by nature herself, are worked out with tasteful and fitting detail. Its colouring, sombre yet rich, with blended tints, softened hues and modulated effect, relieved with just enough of chastened and harmonious brightness, is admired by all those who love to see true principles applied to human industry.

CHAPTER XVIII.

COMMERCE, EXTERNAL AND INTERNAL.

Foreign trade of India in former times—The "East-Indiamen" ships—The "Green's" ships—The Peninsular and Oriental Company—The Suez Canal—Direct dealings of India with the Continent of Europe—Africa, Asia and Australia—France—The United States—Italy—The Mauritius—Particulars of trade with United Kingdom—Shipping for the most part British—Coasting trade—Balance of trade—How adjusted—The Home remittances—Value to India of her export trade—Food-supply generally sufficient—Internal trade of India—Registration of it—Land communication—River navigation—Tendency towards equalization of prices.

THE foreign commerce of India has always been surrounded by a strange and marvellous interest, has been the theme of essayists and antiquarians, and has even inspired the verse of poets. In recent times it has attracted the severer scrutiny of economists, and has been regarded by some inquirers with misgivings. It forms one of those beacon-lights to which all the believers in the progress of the country triumphantly point. It binds England to her eastern dependency with ties of mutual interest, which are important apart from the higher considerations of policy.

The "East-Indiamen" ships that once bore this commerce have passed into that domain of history, which comprises the maritime annals of Britain. They were succeeded by a class of sailing vessels, rounding the Cape of Good Hope and carrying passengers as well as freight, of which ships many were called after the surnames of the ship-building firms to whom they belonged. The name of a "Green's ship" sounds to Anglo-Indian ears as a synonym for speed under canvas, and for skilful seamanship in tempests. These ships, too, were once freighted with the despatches narrating the momentous events in the East. For those who are habituated to the regularity of postal communication in the present day, it is difficult to realise the anxiety with which the arrival of these vessels used to be awaited in India. The importance of the sailing ships was much diminished by the establishment of the Peninsular and Oriental Company, which carried by the overland route through Egypt all the mails and the treasure, most of the passengers, and some of the most portable and valuable articles of trade. Still, however, the mass of the trade, consisting of cheap and bulky articles, continued to be carried by the sailing vessels round the Cape. Their importance then received another and a heavier blow from the opening of the Suez Canal to maritime traffic.

Before the Suez Canal had been actually tried, it was known that the Red Sea could be navigated by steamships only and not by sailing ships. It was supposed that the freight charges on steamships would be so much dearer than those on sailing ships, that steam-navigation in the Red Sea would be virtually excluded from competition with the sailing ships round the Cape, for the bulky articles composing the greater part of the trade. This supposition was certainly justified by all antecedent experience of the relative character of the two kinds of ships. But since the Canal has been tried, the steamers are becoming more and more able to compete with sailing ships in respect to freight charges, and draw to themselves increasing cargoes of cheap and heavy goods. The sailing ships still ply round the Cape, though with diminished freights, but time is against them, as an insuperable difficulty. The electric telegraph between England and India has affected mercantile transactions in many respects. In a few minutes intelligence is flashed across the intervening oceans and continents, deciding the profit or the loss on critical transactions. Under such urgency, becoming yearly more frequent, the merchants employ even at some sacrifice the steamers which can carry the produce to England up the Red Sea in four weeks, instead of sailing-ships which can carry it round the Cape in four months. Consequently there lie along the quays of the river Hûghli at Calcutta, or in the broad waters of the Bombay harbour, fleets of steamers of great length and of narrow beam, arriving from, or departing for, the Suez Canal. The traveller nowadays wonders at the lines of steamers passing to and fro, by the once dreaded, and still anxious, navigation of the Red Sea. But the exigencies of the navigation in the Suez Canal and in the Red Sea, and the necessity of cheap construction, of speed and of economy in fuel, have caused a new style of ship-building to be adopted for the steamers, which is regarded with some doubt by many seafaring men. The Suez Canal has realised already a success equalling the most sanguine anticipations of its designer, and is destined to achieve still further triumphs. A chorus of satisfaction rose from all India when Ferdinand de Lesseps was decorated by the British Sovereign with the insignia of the Star of India.

The statistics of the external commerce are published in the greatest detail annually by the Government of India, together with a general review of the principal headings by Mr. O'Conor.

In round numbers, on an average of recent years and with due allowance for fluctuations, the foreign trade of India may be valued at 110 million pounds sterling yearly. Out of this amount, 60 millions represent exports, and 36 millions imports, of merchandise; while 3½ millions represent exports, and 10½ millions imports, of treasure. This sum total would be regarded as very important in any country of the world except Great Britain, and is even in Great Britain deemed considerable. Towards this water-mark, as it were, the tide of trade has been mounting for many years, the rise being satisfactorily perceptible decade after decade. In 1860 James Wilson, the then Finance Minister and one of the most scientific economists that ever landed in India, declared the progress of the trade to be among the most conclusive proofs of the prosperity of the country under British rule, and among the most hopeful omens for the future. The trade continued to rise for several years till it received, first a sudden development, and then an equally sudden check, from the events of the American civil war. Afterwards it seemed to oscillate between amounts somewhat above and amounts somewhat below, one hundred millions sterling. It did not sensibly retrograde by reason of the famine of 1874 in Bengal. It was rising favourably (mainly by reason of a quickened demand in Europe for Indian produce) just before the outbreak of the famine of 1877 in Madras and Bombay, when it reached the sum of 124 millions, the highest point ever gained. It then suffered depression, when this famine lasted into 1878, and extended to parts of northern India. This depression became aggravated during 1879, in sympathy with British trade all over the world. It has risen, again, to 120 millions for the last official year, and is still rising. Symptoms of improvement are now visible; their continuance or disappearance must depend on the propitiousness or otherwise of the seasons in India after such grave vicissitudes, and on the revival or stagnation of trade in Great Britain.

Formerly, the trade of India with foreign countries used for the most part to pass through England. Receiving all these commodities in the first instance, England used to retain what she required for herself, and distribute the remainder among her neighbours according to their needs. But of late India has begun to send, direct to the ports of the Continent of Europe, the commodities required by European countries. The commercial intercourse is growing fast between Calcutta and Bombay on the one hand, and Marseilles, Genoa, Venice, Trieste, Havre and Hamburg, on the other hand. India, also, is trading more and more with America, especially with California; and San Francisco is becoming a familiar name to the dwellers in Calcutta. The trade with China has long been, and still is, considerable, though limited in its scope, consisting of opium and cotton goods from India, and silver from China, leaving a large trade balance in favour of India. The transactions with the Australian colonies are growing apace, partly by reason of the demand for Australian horses, and will further increase if the Indian people are sufficiently enterprising to send the most attractive of their wares to exhibitions at Sydney and Melbourne. The suppression of piracy by the Indian Government has caused much extension of the trade along the coasts of the Siamese Peninsula and of the neighbouring islands; and especially on the East Coast of Africa, in the sea of Oman, and in the Persian Gulf. Much commerce, centred at Baghdad, which once passed by Aleppo to the Mediterranean, now passes down the Tigris to the Persian Gulf and to Aden.

The most considerable dealings of India with any foreign country are those which she has with France, and their value has averaged as much as five millions sterling annually. She sends to France oil-seed, cotton, indigo, raw silk and shawls, which constitute the greater part of the trade; and receives in return a small quantity of apparel, silk goods and wines.

The United States are beginning to have a considerable intercourse with India, an intercourse probably destined to attain vast growth in the future. Besides the jute, both raw and manufactured, as already mentioned, India sends to the United States linseed, saltpetre, hides and skins, receiving in return large quantities of kerosine oil and some cotton goods. The importation of cotton goods from America is a noteworthy circumstance.

The trade with Italy has not as yet grown to the extent anticipated on the opening of the Suez Canal, still India exports to Italian ports more than one million and a half sterling worth of cotton, oil-seeds, raw silk and hides, importing small quantities of wines, silk goods, Neapolitan corals and glass beads.

While receiving some moderate quantities of sugar from the Mauritius, in some years, India has sent as much as three-quarters of a million sterling worth of rice annually to that colony.

In these and in other various ways, nearly 40 per cent. of the external trade of India is with foreign countries, an important fact shewing among other proofs the extent of her direct relations with all quarters of the world, and the means she possesses of adjusting the balance of her trade accounts. The proportion as shewn by this percentage is likely to increase, as ocean communication by steam becomes more fully opened.

The remaining 60 per cent. of the trade of India, in merchandise, is with the United Kingdom. The export division of this trade shews a long list of articles, indicating the productive power of the Indian people, despite their comparative poverty. The catalogue comprises cotton, jute, rice, wheat, tea, coffee, sugar, oil-seeds, spices, indigo, lac dye, silk, wool, hides and skins, and other things, worth on the whole 28 millions sterling annually. The imports include cotton manufactures, woollen and silk goods, salt, coal, hardware, metals, machinery, railway plant and rolling stock, and a great variety of manufactures, in all worth, on the average, 30 millions sterling per annum. Of all nations, India has long been among the best, and is now perhaps the very best, customer for the manufactures of Great Britain.

The shipping which carries this sea-borne trade consists, on the average, of 12,500 vessels, with a total tonnage of 5½ millions of tons; steamers and sailing vessels included. Of this number one-sixth consists of steamers, which include upwards of 2000 vessels, with a tonnage of 2¼ millions of tons, nearly one-half of the whole, indicating the progress made in the employment of steam power. Of the steamers, two-thirds come and go by the Suez Canal, and the remainder by the Cape of Good Hope and by other routes.

Of the total shipping, sail and steam, about 12 per cent. is foreign, the remainder being British; in other words, 88 per cent. of the shipping is British. The foreign shipping numbers, on the average, 1300 vessels, with a total tonnage of three-quarters of a million of tons, of which, however, many are Arab. As compared with the several thousands of British ships with a tonnage of several millions of tons, the number of the ships belonging to the mercantile marine of Europe and America, and engaged in this trade, will appear very small. For instance, there are only 244 French vessels, 99 German,

134 Italian, 29 Austrian, 36 Norwegian, 15 Swedish, 20 Russian, and 122 American.

There are also about 4000 vessels which ply between port and port, on the east and west coasts of the country; they are entirely of indigenous construction and are called country craft.

For many years a remarkable characteristic of the external trade has been this, that India sells much more, by many millions sterling worth, to England and to foreign nations, than she buys from them. In other words, her exports are valued at a far higher sum than her imports; and of the imports, again, some part consists of machinery and material belonging to the Government. Thus during recent years, that is since 1868, the value of the exports has exceeded that of the imports by 16 millions sterling per annum on the average. This phenomenon has frequently caused men to wonder how the account of the national trade can properly be adjusted. It has rendered economists apprehensive lest this condition of things should prove inconsistent with the permanent safety of the Indian empire; the country being drained yearly of so much of its produce and receiving so very unequal an amount of produce in return. The account is adjusted largely by the amount which India has to remit to England on the Government account for the "home charges;" and by the sums remitted to England by individuals, whether in the public service or in private employ, or by corporations, banks and others, as their savings or their profits. In other words, England owes India a large amount, the balance on the trade in merchandise. On the other hand, India has to transmit to England, or owes to England, large sums on the account of the State or of private concerns. Moreover, India has, as has just been shewn, many balances or debts, due to her from China and other nations, all which she can, if desired, transfer to England to be used in the general adjustment of trade accounts. In various ways, then, there are abundant means of settling these large trade balances.

India remits a large sum annually for "home charges," at present amounting to nearly 17 millions sterling, the people have to pay the land revenue in cash, and export much produce with a small return of merchandise imported. These facts seem to cause alarm to some economists, and to suggest particularly the thought that India is thus virtually forced to send away her produce. It would, indeed, be more natural and satisfactory if India were to import larger quantities of British manufactures in return for the produce she exports. The magnitude of the remittance for "home charges" has a serious import; it is extraordinary, perhaps even unique, in the annals of the relations between one country and another. It is a pressing matter of policy to reduce, if possible, the amount of the home remittances, or at least to prevent their increasing. For all that, the exportation of Indian produce is a pure source of satisfaction. The people are glad to dispose thus of their property for a valuable consideration; they must be the richer for so doing. If they receive other products in return, well, their artificial wants multiply; if they receive treasure in part payment, the money is doubtless very acceptable to them. If they have a large debt to discharge annually to England, their surplus exportable produce furnishes a resource for this purpose. Whether they had to make a large remittance for "home-charges" or not, and whether they had to pay land revenue in cash or in kind, they would still export as much produce as they could spare, or as much as foreign nations could be induced to take for valuable consideration. As they do not at present require an equivalent in kind in the shape of British merchandise, there might be room for speculation as to how the account would be adjusted if there were no remittances for "home charges" or on other accounts. Some means would doubtless be found, in the settlement of the concerns of the trade between the various nations. At all events, the exportation would be continued and would be one of those satisfactory proofs of the wealth and industry of the people which can be opposed to several unsatisfactory conditions that are admitted to exist.

It may be thought by some that the exportation of so much edible grain, rice, wheat and some other articles, must reduce to a dangerously low ebb the stores of food in an empire so much exposed to famine. It seems clear, however, that the country can dispense with the quantities exported. For, during times of partial scarcity, there always are abundant stores somewhere in the country, though at a distance from the scene of suffering. Even in 1874, when the Government had to import food into distressed districts, the supplies came, not from foreign regions, but from British Burma, which is an integral part of the empire. At that time, too, and during most of the time while the famine of 1877 and 1878 lasted, the exportation of food-grain from the country proceeded briskly.

In further explanation of the balance of trade, the following passage may be quoted from the recent report by the Indian Famine Commission.

"The period from 1854 to 1869 was the time when the capital for the guaranteed railways was being raised, . . . and there was hardly any surplus of exports at this time. In 1869, the construction of guaranteed railways was coming to a close and the system of construction by the State was beginning, and from that time India instead of drawing large sums of capital from England for investment had to pay many millions a year as interest. The great rise in the export trade dates from that time and for the last ten years the excess of exports has averaged about 16 millions sterling (annually). . . . So far as the excess of exports is due to the investment of English capital in India, it is difficult to conceive conditions under which the remittance of interest on foreign capital, judiciously applied, could be less onerous to the country which pays it, for the investment must have led to the outlay of a larger sum than the interest sent away, and the balance of what is thus produced remains in the country. Thus in the case of the guaranteed railways, 100 millions of capital have been raised and spent in India, and 5 millions a year have to be paid in England as interest on that capital; the railways pay these 5 millions by earning a gross income of 10 millions, 5 of which are spent in wages and afford occupation. The people who voluntarily pay the 10 millions for the use of the railways are themselves largely benefited by them."

Besides the external commerce, there is a vast inland or internal trade between the various divisions of the Indian empire. During recent years, many judicious steps have been taken by the several Local Governments to prepare commercial statistics, and to register the trade passing not only across their outer borders, but also between the different territories comprised within their respective jurisdictions.

The interchange of products between the distant provinces of the empire, also the flux and reflux of treasure, have been greatly promoted by British rule and are nowadays much larger than in former times. Communications by road, river, rail, and canal have been improved materially and rendered secure, and the people avail themselves of these facilities abundantly. Many millions sterling worth of products, natural, agricultural and artificial, thus change hands month by month. If a computation could be made of the value of this inter-provincial trade throughout the empire, the sum total would be enormous for the year. The stations for registration of the trade on the sides of roads or on the banks of navigable rivers, would shew tens of thousands of laden carts running backwards and forwards, and even a greater number of boats plying up and down stream. Those which are set on suitable points of the navigable canals would note thousands of boats; those which are established at the gates of towns and cities would supply evidences of trade yielding large octroi revenues. Those which exist on the margin of the great harbours would return a surprising number of country craft, working in the estuaries, creeks, arms of the sea, between the inland provinces and the shore. In the suburbs of the cities throughout the empire, the ever-flowing stream of trade, great and small, imparts to the observer an impression of national vitality bursting forth in every quarter from the humblest to the highest. A potent stimulus has been afforded by the railways; and their goods traffic, though partly maintained by the external, depends partly on the internal, trade. The interchange of the fabrics between the industrial centres, situated at long distances from each other in so large an empire, is greatly promoted. In times of scarcity, the movement of food grain is to be measured by millions of tons. It is to be expected that many of the roads will be occupied by the traffic to and from the railway stations; many trunk roads, however, are crowded at some seasons with traffic which never finds its way to the railroad at all.

Despite the development of land carriage everywhere, the river navigation continues to flourish. The navigation of the upper Ganges and of the Jamna has declined, but that decrease is owing partly to the water of these rivers being diverted to irrigation. It remains to be seen whether the water traffic, which has heretofore been so considerable on the Indus, will be really affected by the railway running along its bank. The navigation of the Brahmaputra and its affluents, of the lower Ganges and its many branches, is quite magnificent, and offers probably one of the finest spectacles of its kind to be seen in the world. The statistics of the boats are difficult to collate and may not yet have been completely collated. Not only every trader and landholder keeps many vessels, but every cultivator and peasant has his boats and almost every labourer his canoe; thus the boats may be reckoned by hundreds of thousands. At several points on the great rivers, the vessels congregate for several months consecutively and form floating cities and marts, where many thousands temporarily dwell, where much barter of produce takes place, where monetary transactions are arranged and banking business done; the concerns being conducted afloat. Often in the daytime the horizon is whitened by the swelling sails of the numerous flotillas. At eventide in sequestered creeks and coves, sheltered by umbrageous groves and feathery bamboos from the blasts and squalls which sweep over the expanses of the broad rivers, there lie moored under the banks many rows of these vessels with their forests of little masts. These craft have various builds, forms and styles adapted to the characters of the various rivers. There are many changing stations, where the lesser boats from the upper basins and valleys tranship their freights to the larger boats able to brave the broad estuaries which ofttimes surge and heave with waves like the sea. The many building-yards, at divers points on the banks of the rivers, where these vessels are built, will be found full of activity and bustle and belong entirely to Natives. The quantities of timber required for boat-building are so vast, that the maintenance of an unfailing supply from the forests of the country is becoming a matter of anxiety to the State forest department. The amount of Native capital engaged in the building of the boats, and in the traffic which they carry, must be very considerable even if judged by the standard of advanced nations.

Among the effects of the development of internal trade is the tendency towards equalization in prices. In former times it used to be proverbially said that in one quarter the food grain might decay and perish, while there was want or hunger in another quarter. Even in quite recent times there has been a glut of grain with very low prices in some districts, while in other districts, not very distant, scarcity and very high prices prevailed. The possibility of such a state of affairs has now for the most part disappeared; though perhaps a few instances of the sort may exist here and there. Despite this levelling and equalizing tendency, however, there is still a considerable difference in prices in various parts of the empire, which though less perceptible now than formerly, will probably last for some time to come. In northern India grain used to be superabundant and extremely cheap, so much so that land-holders experienced difficulty in realising money for their produce in order to pay their land revenue in cash. Comparative cheapness still reigns there, except at times of exceptional drought. In eastern and southern India moderate prices have generally prevailed, save during times of famine; but in western India dearness has been for many years prevalent generally, intensified in times of famine, and seldom relaxed materially even when plenty smile around.

CHAPTER XIX.

PUBLIC HEALTH AND SANITATION.

Organization of Sanitary Department—Vital statistics—Popular instruction in hygiene—Purification of water supply—Water-works of principal cities —Conservancy in towns—Sanitary engineering—Utilization of sewage—Lodging-houses in towns—Dwellings in villages—Examination of food—Small-pox—Vaccination—Contagious diseases—Hospitals and dispensaries.

THE importance of sanitation has always been recognised by the British Government in India, and efforts have from time to time been made in this direction. The diseases, in some degree preventible, to which the Natives are subject, have been mentioned in the chapter on the material progress of the people. The medical measures are not only curative but preventive also. The sanitary proceedings were, fifteen years ago, brought under the concentrated supervision of a Sanitary Department, which was then formally constituted as an integral part of the civil administration. A Sanitary Commissioner has been appointed to serve as the professional adviser of each of the several Local Governments; under him are several sanitary assistants, all medical men; under them again are sub-assistants of lesser grades. Inasmuch as there are several such Local Governments in the empire, a considerable staff of sanitary officers has thus been organized. There is a Sanitary Commissioner of a still higher grade, attached to the Government of India, who acts as professional adviser to the supreme authority. Annual sanitary reports are prepared by the several Local Governments, are reviewed in the first instance by the Government of India, and are ultimately examined by a Commission of experts in England. This commencement of a sanitary system is a foundation on which a philanthropic structure may be erected. It is a plant which, though but a sapling now, will grow and bear fruit hereafter.

The measures adopted by the Indian Sanitary Department, relating to the troops and to the military stations, will be described in the chapter referring to the Army. Those relating to the civil stations, the towns or the country, will be mentioned now.

The primary step has been the preparation of vital statistics, that is, returns of the numbers of persons born in every place throughout the empire, and of those deceased, together with a note of the diseases from which they died. This registration, which constitutes a basis of fact for the devising of improvements, has been unavoidably entrusted to men having only an imperfect education, and destitute of special training. It has extended over a vast area, and among a people slow to appreciate the uses of such information. Consequently the returns, though gradually improving, are defective indeed, but still supply something which is better than an utter blank of knowledge. In the larger towns, and in selected rural localities, the returns, being prepared by trained men under special supervision, are much more trustworthy, and afford data for checking the registration in the country generally.

Short treatises in the vernacular languages are prepared under the title of hygiene primers. Under some of the Local Governments, sanitary codes compiled in simple and practical terms, such as all men can understand, advising them what to do and warning them what to avoid, are being circulated among the villages. In so vast a country, it will be impossible for any government, however highly organized, to ensure anything approaching to general sanitation, until the people, now so ignorant and apathetic regarding this subject, shall have become more intelligent in respect to curative or preventive measures. Meanwhile, the Government is dealing with those evils which are more easily remediable and those requirements which are more immediately pressing.

In the first place, attention has been effectively turned to the purification of the water supply at the capital cities, at the larger civil stations which include bazaars of an urban character, and at most of the towns in the interior of the country, a matter which vitally affects the public health, and the neglect of which is the cause probably of more sickness than all other causes put together. The water-works of the three Presidency cities, Calcutta, Madras and Bombay, though still needing enlargement, according to the changes in circumstance and the growth of population, may yet take rank with similar works in the great cities of the world. They afford such an average supply per head of the people as would be esteemed tolerable by sanitary authorities, though perhaps not abundant for all personal and domestic uses. For Calcutta, the water is pumped with engines from the river Hûghli into filtering beds and thence conducted by pipes over a length of fourteen miles to the distributing machinery in the city. At Bombay, the water is stored in two great artificial lakes, in the midst of low wooded hills, with massive dykes, and is conducted to the city by pipes extending over twenty miles of distance before it reaches the distributing channels. Similarly, the water supply of the Madras city is drawn from a lake formed in a low natural basin with a dyke of remarkable length, breadth and solidity. Works of the same kind, but less in degree, have been executed at most of the civil stations and of the towns throughout the empire. At all these towns, municipalities have been established, and one of the most obligatory tasks of every municipality is acknowledged to be the supply of water. The provision of such supply is the measure to which the people are most ready to give their support. Several millions sterling have from first to last been expended on these works in the whole empire, and additions to the list of them are being constantly made. While in some parts of the country the villagers drink from streams pure and uncontaminated, in other parts they drink from wells and tanks contaminated to a degree which by authorities in Europe would be deemed incredible. Thus there remain impurities in the water, both for drinking and for washing, which are evils of themselves sufficient to account for much disease, and which the people apparently do not care to remedy.

The same account, *mutatis mutandis*, may be given of conservancy, including the management of sewage and town drainage, and all arrangements connected therewith. The works at Calcutta, Madras and Bombay, are on a scale befitting capital cities; there are similar works of a lesser degree at all the cities, the civil stations and the towns in the interior of the country; every municipality holds itself chargeable with the duty of dealing with the subject. Several millions sterling have been expended for this purpose, after designs furnished by scientific experience. Still, most of the villages and even the environs of many of the towns, remain in an unsanitary condition. European conservancy, as applied to India, has not, as yet, won fully the confidence of the Natives. They are inclined to doubt the value of the scientific or professional remedies, some of which they think produce fresh evils as great as or greater than the evils, the removal of which has been effected or at least attempted. Doubtless, there is fear lest, from error in design or from imperfection in workmanship, the sewage pipes and the drains should prove, like edged tools, dangerous to those who use them.

Here, then, is much scope for sanitary engineering, a branch of science which is comparatively young even in Great Britain, and in India has hardly passed its infancy.

For these improvements, water supply, conservancy, and other useful works, both in the capital cities and in lesser towns, the State has advanced and still advances, large sums of money. It is considered, as a rule, better that the municipalities should borrow from the State, rather than in the market, because the State can afford to lend at cheaper rates of interest. For facilitating these arrangements a general law for the empire, besides several special laws for some of the capital cities separately, have been passed. Most of the municipal improvements have been executed from funds thus obtained. In some cases, however, municipalities have been allowed to borrow in the open market when the rates of interest appeared favourable.

The utilisation of sewage might, throughout the empire, be made the means of improving the health of the people and of fertilizing the soil, though this is done but little in the interior of the country. At several of the capital cities, however, and in other towns of importance, the municipalities have disposed of sewage to neighbouring landholders, and this example is in some provinces being followed to some extent in whole tracts or groups of villages.

The examination of dwellings in the towns is seldom or never seriously attempted; the inhabitants are hardly prepared for it as yet. Nevertheless, the condition of many dwellings, especially the large Native lodging-houses, in some of the greatest cities cannot be much longer tolerated by public opinion. The want of ventilation is among the primary defects of the urban dwelling-houses; and if the owners will not introduce reform spontaneously, they will perhaps some day be obliged by regulation to do so. In the villages generally, the cottages are fairly well ventilated, better, perhaps, than those in European countries. But the practice which the villagers have of penning their cattle in the same houses with themselves, or in the narrow courtyards where they and their families eat and sleep, is very deleterious.

Under these circumstances there need not be any surprise when the analyses, made by sanitary authorities of the air of many dwellings in towns and cities, present remarkable degrees of impurity. It is most fortunate that the greatest cities in India are either on the sea or within reach of it; and that the sea-breezes penetrate so far inland among the towns and villages. In the rural tracts, the people live very much out-of-doors among the fields, where the crops are growing at most seasons in the year, and where, consequently, the air is fresh and life-giving.

Although adulteration has not caused any particular scandal in India, the examination of food is nevertheless recognised to be important. In times of scarcity, much mouldy or fermented grain is brought to market, and many of the lower castes are in the habit of eating diseased meat. These people are prevented, by the ancient prejudice, from killing cows or bullocks for consumption, but they may eat the meat of the animals when death has come from natural causes; and this is largely done in some places. Fish-curing is much practised in the coast districts, which are generally very populous; much of the fish nominally cured, has really passed into a certain stage of decomposition. Some of the milk consumed in the cities has poisonous germs in it, and to this origin some striking instances of illness have some times been traced. Inspection of all these matters is proceeding satisfactorily in the principal markets throughout the empire.

Small-pox is universally prevalent, carrying off tens of thousands of victims, children especially, in almost every province year after year and injuring or disfiguring others for life. The Government has for many years made persistent efforts to arrest the disease by means of vaccination, with remarkable success in some districts, like that of Kumaon in the Himalayas, but generally with indifferent success, and often without any perceptible result. The practice of vaccination not being in vogue, inoculation used to be largely adopted by the Natives in many districts, but has now been prohibited, though not always prevented actually. The State everywhere undertakes or encourages vaccination. Hundreds of Native vaccinators are employed; and returns are rendered of large numbers of persons said to be successfully vaccinated. Nevertheless, small-pox appears again and again with terrible manifestations before the people, and causes them to disbelieve the efficacy of vaccination. In this disbelief, they will not seriously co-operate with the State in rendering vaccination universal. Without real co-operation on their part, it is impossible to carry out such a measure. Wherever circumstances have enabled the authorities to vaccinate the whole population, the disease is prevented, and the people believe in the preventive. But as circumstances seldom admit of this, the vaccination is unavoidably desultory, its results are casual and incomplete, its extension is not promoted, or is even indirectly resisted, by the people. In some of the principal cities and in other places the vaccination is legally compulsory and is really enforced with the usual benefit; in other places the power to enforce it is vested in authorities who feel some natural hesitation in exercising it against the will of the people. The desideratum is to render the preventive measures strict, absolute and universal in limited areas of country, so that the people may see that the consequence of vaccination is the stoppage of small-pox. Once they are convinced of that, they will be foremost in supporting these measures, and the effect of their example will spread to the surrounding districts.

The special diseases known as "contagious" exist lamentably in most of the great military and civil stations throughout the empire and in nearly all of the great cities. For the sake of the troops, especially the European, the Government has passed laws, and taken steps for at least checking these fell diseases. Lock hospitals have been maintained and are generally filled with patients. In a few places these proceedings have resulted in prevention, but in most places the imperfection in their result, or their utter want of success, prove the difficulties which practically intervene. In the cities which are beyond the limits and the immediate vicinity of the stations, there is an equal need of prevention, and laws have been passed empowering the authorities to introduce preventive measures. The Government has, however, hesitated to take practical steps; in various ways there is indirect opposition from some quarters; and there is sometimes a feebleness of conviction among the authorities. For the most part, however, the officials and the best men among the Natives are alive to the nature of the evil; and it is to be hoped that, sooner or later, public opinion will aid the Government in ensuring success to measures for which the legislature has made ample provision. Such success, if attained, would prevent much misery, which not only affects individuals, but is transmitted from generation to generation.

The measures above described, relate chiefly to what is termed preventive medicine. The Government also does much in the way of curative medicine, or medical relief, by establishing, or encouraging the establishment of, hospitals and dispensaries. At the Presidency towns the hospitals attached to the several medical colleges are fine institutions worthy of capital cities. One of them, the hospital for Bombay, was founded by Sir Jamsetji Jijhibhoy, one of the most munificent and philanthropic of her citizens. Similar hospitals have been established by private bounty at other central towns and stations, such as the hospital at Poona, which bears the name of Sassoon, its distinguished benefactor. Many other native gentlemen, such as Sir Cowasji Jehangir, Mr. Byramji Jijhibhoy, Mr. Jaganâth Shankarset, have been honourably distinguished by their benefactions to medical institutions, including hospitals and dispensaries. In every province of the empire, Native gentlemen have come forward with liberal contributions. Assistance is obtained from local and municipal funds, and from public subscriptions in which Europeans as well as Natives bear a part. The Government affords aid, always on the condition of private resources being collected. Accordingly, these institutions are found at the principal places in the interior of every district in all the provinces. Additions are made year by year to their number, of which the total now amounts to upwards of eleven hundred for the whole empire. At each of them there are competent Native practitioners; the chief of them are under the immediate care of European medical officers; and all of them are periodically inspected by European medical authorities. They vary in size; at all of them there is suitable accommodation for indoor patients, both male and female; surgical operations are performed, and medicines are dispensed daily and gratuitously to outdoor patients. At some of the larger institutions, reasonable charges are made upon patients who are able to pay; but for the mass of Native recipients, indoor and outdoor, the relief is gratuitous and charitable. It is difficult to present an exact statement of the numbers of these patients, because the same persons may appear in the returns several times within any given period. During the year some millions of persons in the whole empire attend at the dispensaries to obtain advice and medicine; hundreds of thousands are received and nursed as indoor patients; tens of thousands undergo surgical operations, many of which are of a critical nature. Public confidence in European medicine is increasing; the fame of the surgical skill displayed by the British surgeons and by the Native surgeons trained under the European system, spreads far and wide.

The measures adopted for training and instructing Natives as medical men, and as medical practitioners, have been described in the previous chapter on education.

Notwithstanding all these measures of curative and preventive medicine, the average death-rate among the Natives is unfortunately high, being not less than 3½ per cent. At some times and in some places, the rate is in excess of this. According to the experience of happier climes the rate ought not to exceed 2½ per cent.; in salubrious districts it is only 2 per cent., or even less. Hence will be seen the vast field which exists for the beneficent operations of medicine and sanitation, a field which is, as yet, very imperfectly occupied by the State and the public in co-operation, but of which the occupation is gradually advancing.

CHAPTER XX.

FAMINE.

Famine under Native rule—Under British rule—In Behar and Bengal in 1874—In Madras, Bombay and elsewhere in 1877—Public charity in England—In India—Mortality—Advantages of railways—Calamity in 1874 compared with that of 1877 and 1878—Precautions for preventing mortality—Sanitary department—Distressed people to be prevented from wandering—Relief works—Village inspection—Relief houses—People not demoralized nor pauperized by relief operations—Good conduct of the peasant proprietors—Prospects of material improvement—Supply of food by private enterprise.

DURING the five years, which passed between 1873 and 1879, India has from one end to the other been visited by famine and pestilence, the like of which has not been seen for several generations. Inasmuch as the saddest experience has shewn that sometimes these calamities come in quick succession, or run in cycles of years, no man can certify that the country has even yet emerged from the dark depths of misfortune. Apart from the historic famines of India, the famines of the nineteenth century have been partial in extent, though intense within limited areas. Under Native rule, when famine occurred, there was no want of commiseration on the part of the rulers. Almshouses were opened, the most pitiable creatures were fed, charity in many ways was dispensed and some attempts were made to employ labourers thrown out of work. These measures, however well-meant, were casual and desultory; the arm of the State was paralysed, and the visitation was regarded as lying beyond the range of human action. Thus, no systematic or effective efforts were made to prevent mortality, to provide work and wages for the able-bodied temporarily destitute of employment, and to afford sustenance to those who were too feeble to work.

Now, under British rule, the obligation of the State to do all of these things, to the utmost of its power, is acknowledged. The Government has upon every occasion during this century put forth signal efforts for alleviation, and has thereby done much good to the suffering people. Its success, however, was seldom commensurate with the energies exerted, or with the expenditure incurred. The excitement which sprung up, when during 1865 and 1866 the measures adopted respecting the Orissa famine were thought too tardy, proves the sense of responsibility abiding in the public mind.

When, ten years later, a still worse famine threatened in Bengal and Behar, this sense was quickened, partly by reason of the manner in which the people of England grasped the peril to which their Indian fellow-subjects were exposed. The English Press spared no pains to describe the emergency, and some of the leading journals of London were represented by correspondents specially despatched to the scene of trouble. The Government itself was, as it ought to be, firm in its own conviction of what was, and what was not, necessary, and, relying on its own conscience, was quite prepared to resist any demands for excessive measures being undertaken. Nevertheless, the force of opinion in England imparted strength to opinion in India, and caused the remedial efforts to be maintained at a high degree of tension. A very heavy expenditure was incurred, upwards of six millions sterling net, after deducting recoveries and the like from the gross expenditure. A corresponding large number of persons were fed or otherwise assisted and relieved, and in general terms it may be said that no lives were lost. The drought, however severe, was of comparatively short duration; the succeeding season was propitious and plenty returned.

During the two years 1875 and 1876, the country had respite, but in 1877 the calamity began to reappear, this time in the Presidencies of Madras and Bombay, and in the kingdom of Mysore. The Government girded itself yet again more to contend with this enemy for the sake of the lives of the people. When the following season shewed no abatement, but, on the contrary, a continuance of the famine in a still more aggravated form, the sympathy of England lent the utmost moral support to the efforts of those engaged on the spot in remedial operations.

The heartiness of that sympathy was evinced by the munificent subscriptions, raised partly through the agency of the Lord Mayor of London, partly also through many charitable agencies throughout the United Kingdom, and amounting, on the two occasions, taken together for 1874 and 1878, to nearly one million sterling. Great as was the material assistance afforded by these subscriptions, the moral effect upon the grateful loyalty of the Indian people was greater still. Public charity of a like kind was evoked in India itself, both on the part of Europeans and of Natives, and the full extent of this charity cannot be approximately represented by any statistics. The Government performed its part by undertaking an extraordinary variety of useful works, by employing several millions of persons, by feeding with gratuitous charity several millions more, and by incurring an expenditure which, from 1874 to 1879, has been reckoned at the grand total of sixteen millions sterling.

Nevertheless, there has been much mortality, in southern India especially, and if the diminution of the birth-rate be taken together with the augmentation of the death-rate, the total population will probably be found to have lessened by several millions, during the cycle of calamities. If the general belief in the normal rate of increase of the population be correct, and if that ratio shall have been at all maintained during the period in those provinces which for a time escaped the visitation, the net diminution of the population may be thereby affected, as there will be some increase to be set against the decrease. Conjectures need not be hazarded now, as the result of a future census is awaited. Of those who perished, many were destroyed by causes other than starvation; still the fact remains that, despite all measures of relief, many succumbed to famine alone. And in the face of the unstinted generosity of the Government, the boundless devotion of its officers, the administrative skill employed, and the heavy expenditure borne, this fact may cause the most confident to hesitate, and the most sanguine to despair.

As compared with Native rule, too, the British Government had, from 1874 to 1879, in the possession of railways an advantage unprecedented in the history of Indian famines. The railways carried food supplies measured by millions of tons, over distances of many hundreds of miles, at rates much cheaper than those of the old land carriage, and at a season when deep mud and swollen rivers would have impeded traffic of that sort. Irrespective of railways, transport by sea would have accomplished much; still, without railways, the grain markets in the distressed districts would not have been so well supplied as they were. If they had not been so supplied, the difficulties of this terrible time would have been indefinitely aggravated. Those who were responsible for the relief operations in that famine felt devoutly thankful that the railway system had been so far completed before the calamity occurred.

The precedent of 1874 in Bengal and Behar will doubtless be regarded by some authorities as proving that, under certain conditions, life can be saved, mortality averted, and success attained without any drawback or abatement. On that occasion, however, the calamity, though very severe while it lasted, was of comparatively short duration. It was not accompanied or followed by sickness and pestilence; on the contrary, its concomitant circumstances were favourable. The territory and the population were so situated as to readily come under supervision and inspection. These favouring or mitigating circumstances, were in marked contrast with the adverse circumstances attending the next famine in 1877 and 1878. The expenditure in 1874 was very heavy; on this account it has been criticised, and sometimes condemned as having been lavish. The relief was liberally afforded; it also has been censured as excessive. On the other hand, it is to be urged that the people shewed no symptoms of being pauperized or demoralized, that they would not have sought for or taken relief unless they had needed it, and that as soon as the succeeding rains began to fall, no time was lost in sending them back to their homes and their fields, whither, indeed, they willingly went. Much of the expenditure arose from the necessity, peculiar to this case, of importing grain on account of Government. The threatened tracts were beyond the reach of the grain trade, according to the currents in which it ran at that time. It so happened that the trade was not supplying the markets, the depletion of which signified starvation to millions, and Government was obliged to undertake the importation. This importation, if necessary for the first year, might be equally necessary for the second year, as experience shewed that these calamities often last for two years; therefore a reserve supply had to be stored. It came to pass, however, that the second year proved propitious, so the reserve remain unused, causing loss to the State. Still, if the formation of the reserve was justifiable, the fact of its not having to be called into play would fail to prove it to have been inexpedient. These several circumstances account for nearly half the expenditure; they were peculiar, and are not likely to occur elsewhere. They would not recur, even if famine were to return to that very territory, because of the improvements in communication which have since been introduced. If, then, this abatement be made, the remainder of the expenditure will not appear excessive. It was indeed heavy as regards the State, and liberal as respects the people. The absence of mortality is admitted on all sides, and the result was regarded with lively satisfaction by the chief organs of Native opinion at the time, which were thoroughly acquainted with the distress, the danger, the relief operations, and the expenditure. The Native chiefs, the landlords of Behar, and the British Indian Association of Calcutta, the wealthiest, the most highly educated and the most independently outspoken body of Native gentlemen in the country, who were all versed in the circumstances, publicly tendered the warmest expression of gratitude on the part of themselves and of their countrymen to the Government after the conclusion of the operations.

But in the famine of 1877 and 1878, the concomitant circumstances were unfavourable, and intensified the main stroke of the calamity. The first year of famine was preceded by a poor or indifferent year and was followed by a second year of drought, causing a prolongation of famine, which is an evil increasing with a progressive ratio every six months that it lasts. *Pari passu* with the famine, cholera advanced as a dread ally in destruction, and small-pox decimated the children. When the prolongation of the famine at length began to yield to rain, the rainfall became excessive, sometimes drowning the new crops, and always afflicting the people with chills, damps and febrile affections. Then the work of death was resumed, this time by malarious fever. In the Deccan a further evil was heaped on the pile of misfortune by the appearance of rats in myriads, which would seem fabulous were it not for the sad evidence afforded by broad areas of harvest-bearing country being laid waste. This final trouble has depressed some districts to a depth from which they will not soon rise. The concatenation of calamities is to be remembered, when the mortality is computed.

When after such events a decrease of population is found to have occurred, it is not to be inferred that the numbers of the decrease represent so many people perished of hunger. Nor is the decrease caused by death alone; it is partly brought about by the diminution in the number of births, the families being scattered, and by the loss of infants at their birth.

In the Presidencies of Madras and Bombay, the suffering people were not, as in Behar, situated in a comparatively concentrated area admitting of supervision; but were interspersed among hills, valleys and areas, partly uncultivated and uninhabited. Consequently, supervision was much more difficult. It became very hard to prevent the people from wandering hither and thither, seeking work and subsistence, but finding none, till their latter state became even worse than their former. In western and southern India the habit of giving and receiving alms prevailed much more than in Bengal and Behar. In consequence, multitudes betook themselves to the capital city of Madras, and to the sacred places which abound in that part of the country, and of these people many reached their destination in a state past relieving even by the most humane efforts.

The system pursued was in principle the same in Madras and Bombay, as in Bengal and Behar. The ideas regarding relief works, labour and wages, charitable and gratuitous relief, kitchens and hospitals, village inspection for searching out misery, were of the same type. There was an equal desire to save life to the utmost of the power and ability of the Government and its officers. Whatever variations existed in practice, arose from diversity of circumstances in provinces widely apart. The only important difference in practice consisted in this, that in southern India there was not quite the same proportion of European supervision as in some other parts of the empire.

In operations for the relief of famine, the importance of ensuring adequate supervision, either by European officers, or by Native officials of status and capacity, cannot be too strongly impressed on the authorities. In default of such supervision, not only will the public funds be wasted or embezzled, but also the mortality will be aggravated. The relief labourers will be cheated of their wages; the recipients of gratuitous relief will be stinted in their doles and pittances; many deserving persons will be turned away; and the returns of the persons on relief will be falsified. Such evils have sometimes occurred; they have generally been prevented; but there is always danger of their occurring. The only means of prevention is the provision, at any cost, of a trustworthy agency for supervision.

The recent misfortunes of India, consisting of a severe mortality notwithstanding large expenditure, and despite the exertions of officers second to none in humane zeal, in benevolent persistency and in unflagging diligence, ought not to cause British officers to despair of saving life in event of even a protracted famine. If the expenditure had not been incurred, and the exertions not been put forth, the mortality might have been double of even what it was, and whole tracts would have been depopulated for perhaps several years. Whereas, the cultivation has been for the most part maintained and with it the revenue has been preserved. Beyond all material considerations of advantage to the State, the lasting gratitude of the people has been earned, and the moral effect throughout the empire has been great.

The instance of Behar, and other instances, shew that if the collateral circumstances are favourable, mortality may be absolutely prevented. But such prevention cannot with any certainty be anticipated, as many untoward mishaps may occur to mar the best laid schemes. The Government must look the difficulty full in the face, and must nerve and brace itself with that determination to succeed which is the surest forerunner of success. The recurrence of famine at intervals of time is to be expected, and the national voice declares that no reasonable cost shall be spared to save life. The prospect of famine thus augments the financial liabilities of the empire, and the public must be prepared for accretion from time to time to the national debt on this account.

From the body of experience which has now been collated; the requisite precautions are well known.

In the first place, the sanitary agency existing throughout the empire should be strengthened and developed, so that there may be skilled observers at hand to interpret to the authorities the symptoms which indicate physical depression of the people. When the character of the scarcity is pronounced and its signs are emphatic, then the authorities are promptly on the alert and decisive remedies are applied. The danger is really greater when the scarcity threatens for a while, and is warded off temporarily by a brief spell of better weather. The officers begin to act then pause; the people are half-suffering and yet half-relieved, though on the whole failing in physical condition. At length the scarcity throws off all pretence of relenting, and comes on with merciless rigour. It is under circumstances such as these, that some of the worst disasters have occurred. A trained sanitary agency, already well acquainted with the physical state of the population, would then be specially valuable to the district authorities, and would enable them to become both forewarned and forearmed.

The next step is to keep the endangered people well in hand; to let those depart who can emigrate with a reasonable chance of success, and who are not likely to return in a state of emaciation; to prevent those who are to stay (and they will be the great majority) from wandering about in quest of food or work; to stop the multitudes from swaying hither and thither in panic and agitation. If these aimless wanderings once begin, mortality will surely ensue. In Behar and Bengal in 1874, it was generally, though not always, prevented; and circumstances favoured its prevention. In Bombay and especially in Madras during 1877 and 1878, it was not, perhaps could not be, prevented. Circumstances hindered its prevention; and much mortality was attributable to it alone.

The relief works, for the employment of distressed people, should be of various kinds, some for the able-bodied, at a moderate distance from their homes, to be supervised by engineering and professional agency; some, near their homes, for the feebler persons, who cannot do much work, yet ought not to be fed without working at least a little.

Then as the scarcity grows worse and the famine positively declares itself, there must be a thorough inspection of all the poorer people in every village, daily or weekly according to circumstances, and those who are found to be either depressed or tending towards depression, must be relieved in such manner as may be expedient. This village-inspection is a cardinal point in an effective system of relief; without it, mortality will not be prevented. It cannot be improvised when the crisis is coming on apace, but must be organized beforehand, and the machinery must be ready in anticipation before it is actually brought into play. For this purpose, the territory must be subdivided into circles and the villages arranged into groups. Over every circle or group there must be placed competent Native officials, and a certain number of circles should be under the supervision of an European officer, or at least of a Native official of trustworthy aptitude. In every village the headman should be required to render assistance; the ancient communal or parochial system of the country is peculiarly suitable for work of this nature. The difficulty will be, not to reject undeserving applicants for relief, but to search out deserving persons who, from timidity or listlessness, will languish at home, will fall where they stand and perish where they fall. Indeed much of the mortality is attributable to this dilatoriness.

Relief houses and hospitals must be established in suitable localities near to the local centres of the scarcity, where sufferers may be received, and whither they may be sent by conveyances when found unable to move. Great care must be taken in rendering these temporary institutions popular, otherwise the poor people will be unwilling to resort thither, will hide themselves to avoid being sent there, and after their reception will even escape thence. They often evinced extreme unwillingness to be thus relieved; and thus arose another cause of mortality. Consequently, it becomes desirable to relieve many of the worst cases in their own houses through the agency of the village headmen, a practice which requires close supervision, otherwise a door would be opened to peculation. These village headmen were not thought in 1877 and 1878 to have done as much as they might, in assisting the State to tend and care for their suffering fellow-villagers. But the duty is one clearly pertaining to these men, and its performance can be enforced, with due vigilance and resolution on the part of the district authorities.

At such a time the work in its various departments becomes very extensive, and much depends on the personal capacity of the European officer at the head of the district. It is the special duty of the Local Government to ensure that the head of every district is a man of the needful ability, that over every group of distressed districts there is a superior officer in command, and that full instructions are circulated among all concerned.

It might be apprehended, perhaps, that a system such as that above sketched, however indispensable to prevent mortality, would inevitably tend to demoralise and pauperise the people and would teach them unduly to lean upon the State in emergencies of this character. Such apprehensions have not been verified by the result. The people never seemed to expect that the State would or could do as much for them as has actually been done. They were unwilling, if they could possibly help it, to come upon relief, preferring to run an excessive risk in searching after sustenance for themselves. Often they were willing to languish at home, rather than ask for public alms. When relieved, they were prompt to return to their ordinary employments on the first promise of reviving prosperity. Whenever rains descended to moisten the earth, the men were off to their fields with hardly an hour's delay. On the whole, the conduct of the Natives, during these crucially trying times, has raised the estimate of their national character and has redounded to their good repute. Indeed, their spirit of self-help, their persevering resistance to the pressure and pinch of want, their patience in life and death, have won the admiration of the most competent witnesses.

The peasant proprietors on all occasions, and in all provinces, have evinced considerable power of self-support and a creditable sense of their obligation to discharge their fiscal liabilities to the State. Very few, perhaps none, of them succumbed to the famine; none of the better classes among them applied for relief in any shape. Some of the humbler classes of them, indeed, received relief, that is, laboured on relief works, but many of them were men who ordinarily went out to work at times when they were not busy in the fields. All these circumstances indicate much improvement since the famines of the past generation, when some of the peasant proprietors swelled the number of those who perished. Certainly the manner in which the area of cultivation was saved by them from diminution proves great industrial power. There was no loss of land revenue in 1874, but in 1877 and 1878 there was considerable loss; however, even then, very much of the revenue was collected, and the collections indicate the existence of resources accumulated during prosperous times. The Government was believed by some to have collected the land revenue with undue severity. If such cases occurred they must have been rare; for it was contrary to the intention of the Government that any undue pressure should be exerted. In Madras, where the famine was worst, the Government certainly shewed all the leniency and considerateness that could be expected. The broad fact is that the mass of the peasant proprietors stood their ground, prevented their lands from falling out of cultivation, and paid a fair portion of their land revenue. It is important that all those peasant proprietors, whom the famine does not reach, should pay their revenue at a time when the State needs all its resources to save those whom the famine does reach. On the other hand, it would be most inexpedient to press unduly for revenue on those who could not pay without impoverishing themselves. These principles are thoroughly understood by the several Local Governments and their officers.

Some good may be educed out of evil if the impulse, which these several famines at first imparted to the progress of material improvement, shall be sustained. The northern Bengal railway, the Behar branch railways, the projects for minor irrigation works in northern Behar, and several irrigation works in the Deccan, are in part owing to the famines. The apprehension of scarcity has promoted the cause of irrigation throughout the empire.

The Government is not likely to be again under the necessity of importing grain to supply the markets during scarcity. The grain trade throughout the interior of the empire was most active during 1877 and 1878, the local resources were vast and the stores of grain accumulated were evidently considerable. The food supplies were despatched by private enterprise with regularity and promptitude to the principal marts of the distressed districts from the provinces where the harvests had been plentiful, by the railways, by the coasting vessels, or by the craft plying in the rivers; and from those marts the local traders again sent the supplies in country carts to the villages.

In 1878, the Indian Famine Commission was appointed by the Government to collect all information which may assist future administrators in the task of limiting the range, or mitigating the intensity, of famines. This Commission consisted of General Richard Strachey as President, of Mr. James Caird, Mr. H. S. Cunningham, and other official gentlemen, European and Native, acquainted with the different parts of the empire, as members, and Mr. C. A. Elliot as Secretary. The eminent names, at the head of the Commission, afford guarantees to the State and to the public regarding the thoroughness of its enquiries and the soundness of its conclusions. After visiting all the districts which had suffered, taking much oral evidence, and collecting masses of information, the Commission has issued an elaborate report, which is not only a repertory of all circumstances and suggestions relating to famines, but is also an admirable summary of economic facts concerning the Indian empire.

CHAPTER XXI.

LEARNED RESEARCH.

Spirit of research has long existed and still exists—Learned works in the past—In the present—Books written to explain Oriental ideas to European readers—Works of historic fiction—Civil and political history—Biographies—Military history—Ethnological works—Books of travel in countries beyond the Indus—Asiatic Society of Bengal at Calcutta—Bombay branch of Royal Asiatic Society—Antiquarian remains—Archæological Survey—Preservation of ancient ruins and monuments.

THE pursuit of Oriental learning imparts grace and dignity to the conduct and policy of England in the East, endears India to the Englishmen whose lot it has been to live and labour there, and engages on behalf of India the sympathy of cultivated minds not only in the United Kingdom but, on the Continent of Europe. The spirit of research regarding Indian antiquities, which animates in the present so many talented Europeans, British and Continental, animated their predecessors also. It may be traced back to the former generation, and even to the earlier days of British rule. It prevailed in the time when Warren Hastings first gave official encouragement to Oriental learning, when William Jones founded the Asiatic Society in Bengal and James Mackintosh a similar association in Bombay, when Colebrooke and Horace Hayman Wilson began to search out the riches of Sanskrit literature. It was felt when Anquetil du Perron investigated the doctrines of Zoroaster as brought by the Parsis to India, when Reinaud drew the notice of Indian students to Albirûnî and other Arabian authors, when Bryan Hodgson discovered a mass of independent Buddhist writings in Nepal, when Burnouf threw critical light on the history of Buddhism, when Stevenson investigated the origin of the Jain religion. It moved William Hay Macnaghten to epitomise the Hindu and Muhammadan codes for northern India, and Strange to analyse the Hindu law in the southern peninsula. It spread far and wide when James Prinsep entered upon the field of archæology, deciphered inscriptions that had defied all previous attempts at interpretation, and, in conjunction with Turner of Ceylon fame, elucidated the spread of the Pali language. The works of these great men departed, and many other labourers in the same field who might be mentioned, attest the attractions which India has always held forth to the European intellect. Their efforts evince the recognition by the ruling race of the necessity of erudition for the due discharge of the responsibilities which conquest brings in its train. Nor did this zeal for learning endure only while the novelty and strangeness of Indian affairs lasted. It still endures as bright as ever, and, encouraged by the achievements of the past, it strives to sustain the onward flight and even to soar higher. Men still feel as keen a desire, as heretofore, to gather together the countless fragments of historic evidence, to exhume the buried remnants of the past, to unlock the oriental treasures still lying in obscurity, and to display them all to European view.

Within the present generation, many men, either recently deceased or still living, have emulated their predecessors in learned research. In illustration of this subject, honourable mention must be made of John Muir's translation of, and commentary on Sanskrit texts; Max Müller's analysis of Oriental religions, and numerous dependent works on Sanskrit literature; the contributions by Goldstücker and Bühler to Sanskrit learning; Monier Williams' various Sanskrit publications; John Wilson's elaborate account of the castes among the Hindus; Burnell's palæography of southern India; Alexander Duff's graphic description of the religious practices in Bengal. Eminent examples are also to be found in Edward Thomas's numismatic and archæological researches; Alexander Cunningham's memoir on the Buddhist topes at Bhilsa, and his more recent work entitled 'Corpus inscriptionum Indicarum;' Barthélemy St. Hilaire's religion of Buddha; Martin Haug's researches in the religion of the Parsis; Trump's translation of the sacred books of the Sikhs; Jacobi's inquiries into the tenets of the Jains. Again, signal instances are to be observed in Sprenger's 'Life of Muhammad' in German, prepared after close study of the original Arabian authorities; William Muir's 'Life of Muhammad' in English, derived from Arabic sources; Baillie's treatises on Muhammadan law; Elliot's Muhammadan historians; Blochmann's translation of the first part of the institutes of Akber the Great. These, and many other works which might be mentioned, sustain fully the reputation of the present age. Conspicuous to the eye of all readers are Fergusson's beautifully illustrated and most interesting works on Indian architecture, on the rock-cut temples and on the tree and serpent worship. To this distinguished list must be added the work in English by a Native of Bengal, namely the antiquities of Orissa, by Rajendra Lal Mitra; and in Urdu by a Native of Hindostan, namely the monumental remains of Delhi, by Syed Ahmed.

Elaborate histories and reviews have been published of the current literature in the several languages of India, which is richer and more varied than would at first sight be supposed. Such are the periodical reviews by Garcin de Tassy, and by Jules Mohl, also the more original work by Weber. The people of India owe much to these distinguished foreigners for thus awakening the interest of the intellectual world in Europe.

There are also many books written nowadays for the purpose of presenting eastern ideas and thoughts in a form readily intelligible to the English reader, such as Monier Williams' extracts from the best and wisest dicta of Hindu sages; Talboys Wheeler's representations in an abstract shape of the classical epic poems of the Hindus; Mrs. Manning's ancient and mediæval India; Griffith's renderings in verse of classic Hindu poetry; Kinloch Forbes' annals of ancient Gujerat; Theodore Hope's illustrated work on the architecture and antiquities of western India; Rhys Davids' description of Buddhism; Hunter's works on rural Bengal, on Orissa and on the Indian Musulmans. To these may be added Arnold's poems on Buddha the saint and reformer, entitled 'The Light of Asia.'

History has always formed an important part of Anglo-Indian literature. Erskine's account of the Central Asian conquerors of India; Tod's life-like description of the Rajputs, drawing the sympathies of all men towards that gallant race; Brigg's translation of Ferishta; Mountstuart Elphinstone's description of ancient India and history of the Muhammadan dynasties; Orme's narrative of the military and political transactions in southern and western India, written when the data were fresh and many of the actors surviving; Grant Duff's excellent history of the Mahrattas, prepared when persons versed in the transactions were present to interpret the records; and Malcolm's Central India; are standard works which do not lose their interest from lapse of time. Additions to the chronicles of India have been made by Henry Yule's analysis of Marco Polo's travels, and by his work entitled 'The Journey to Cathay.' The history of the Muhammadans has been in part continued by Keene's 'Decline and Fall of the Mogul Empire.'

The threads of the political and military history of modern India, as left by the standard works of Mill and Thornton, have not yet been fully taken up. The two matchless essays by Macaulay on Clive and Warren Hastings still afford delight to every reader, European or Native. Kaye's history of the first Afghan war, and his unfinished narrative of the war of the mutinies, are worthy records of those events. Malleson has now fully completed his graphic narrative of the war of the mutinies. He has, in former works, depicted the struggles between the English and French by sea and by land for the mastery of India, and has accorded due admiration to the gallant antagonists of his countrymen. Durand's posthumous and unfinished work on the first Afghan war is full of interest. Special portions of the military annals have been embraced by such works as Broome's history of the Bengal Army, Leach's history of the Indian Navy, and Laurie's history of the Burmese wars.

The recent civil and administrative history of India, as contradistinguished from the military and political, remains to be written, in full detail, beginning from the time of Lord William Bentinck, which was an epoch of moral and social reform. For this, however, the ground has been prepared by Marshman's history, Campbell's modern India, Cust's various essays, Chesney's Indian polity, Kaye's account of the measures of improvement under the East Indian Company, Charles Raikes' graphic notes on the rural affairs of the North-western Provinces and on the Sepoy revolt. The quarterly periodical, entitled the 'Calcutta Review,' has been sustained for the last thirty-five years as a record of Anglo-Indian thought. Administrative reports are published annually by the Government in India for every province and for each department of the State. An annual review of the moral and material progress of India is prepared by the India Office in London, and presented to Parliament; among these were the able and comprehensive summaries prepared by Clements Markham. Aitchison's text of the treaties between the British Government and the Native States, with introductory notices and index, occupies many volumes.

Biography has lent her aid in laying the foundations of history. Kaye brought out Lives of Anglo-Indian statesmen, Metcalfe, Malcolm, and others. An account of Dalhousie's rule in India has been written by Arnold, but the time has not yet arrived when, according to the directions in the will, the papers can be opened which will vindicate the policy of that great administrator. Hunter's Life of Lord Mayo records a great career prematurely terminated. The memoirs of Bishops Wilson, Cotton and Milman, and the Lives of the great missionaries Alexander Duff and John Wilson, by Dr. George

Smith, throw light upon the moral and religious progress of the time. The Life of Henry Havelock has been written by Marshman. A Life of Outram, by Sir F. Goldsmid, has recently appeared. The Life of Henry Lawrence has been written in part by his attached friend and pupil Herbert Edwardes. When the Life of John Lawrence, now in course of preparation, shall appear, the story of that gifted and illustrious brotherhood will be told.

Historic fiction fills a place in Anglo-Indian literature. The popular works of Meadows Taylor, such as the novel of 'Tara,' portraying the revolt of the Mahrattas against the Moguls; the 'Confessions of a Thug,' throwing a lurid light upon crimes peculiar to India, and other works by the same author; Kaye's novel, entitled 'Long Engagements,' William Arnold's 'Oakfield,' and many works of fiction,—illustrate the India of the past and of the present.

The ethnological and linguistic considerations relating to the aboriginal and other races of India have been elucidated by Beames' able work and by Dalton's illustrated volume.

The books of travel and adventure by the pioneers of the military and political enterprise of Britain, first beyond the Indus, and then beyond the Oxus, would by themselves fill a catalogue of fame. No Englishman can meditate without emotion upon the names of Moorcroft, Burnes, Conolly, Abbott, Pottinger, Wood, Masson; men who were consumed by ardour for geographical discoveries, which should advance the standard of British influence for the good of mankind, and who, amidst their personal distress and physical sufferings, ever thought and felt for their country. These books deserve the attention of the rising generation of Englishmen in the East, as exemplifying the indomitable qualities which have characterised, and will doubtless always characterise, the representatives of their race in India. The same spirit has urged on British officers towards eastern Thibet from the days of Bogle and Manning to the recent time when Edgar explored the frontier of Sikhim. Adventurous travelling still has its charm for many, as is proved by Cooper's journey across China, Shaw's sojourn in Ladakh, Gill's march from China to upper Burma, and other signal instances. Henry Yule has written geographical prefaces to Wood's account of the journey to the Oxus and to Gill's diary of the march in China. He has himself contributed to this section of literature by his graphic work on the mission to Ava.

Statistical, local and topographical information has always been prepared voluminously in India, but has often remained in a disarranged and ill-digested condition, detracting much from its usefulness. Among the first and greatest efforts in this direction was Buchanan Hamilton's elaborate work on northern Bengal, the Mysore province and other parts of the country, which, in reference to the early time when it was written, is a monument of exploring and investigating skill, and is still read by many to their instruction and advantage. These important steps were followed by Thornton's Gazetteer, which long continued to be a standard work of reference. In more recent times there have appeared the full and learned guide-books to western and southern India by E. B. Eastwick. More important still, the Government has organized a Statistical Department and placed at its head, as Director-General, Dr. W. W. Hunter, an officer of eminent qualifications. To this department is entrusted the task of causing a Gazetteer to be prepared giving, for each district throughout the whole empire, all the details that could be required by the most laborious and conscientious officer engaged in the civil admistration. The work for the various provinces is prepared on the spot by officers chosen and appointed thereto by the several Local Governments, on a general plan laid down by the Director General. The manuscripts are then transmitted to Dr. Hunter after being approved by the Local Governments, are edited by him and printed in England. The work has been done in some provinces, but remains to be completed in others. It has been finished for the provinces under the Government of Bengal, and already extends to upwards of twenty volumes. A most useful "Statistical Abstract" is issued yearly from the India Office in London, under the signature of Sir Louis Mallet.

The Asiatic Society of Bengal has been surrounded by the best intellectual associations of British India, from the days of its illustrious founder, Sir William Jones, down to the present time. It enjoyed for many years the services of James Prinsep as Secretary, who not only dived into the depths of antiquarian lore, but served as a focus of energy and zeal for others, and trimmed the lamp of learning for the encouragement of his fellow-workers. No man has left a memory more fragrant among the learned than he. The volumes of the Society's journal, which were edited by him, are placed with respectful regard on the library of every antiquary. The Society has still a large number of members, European and Native, and its journal is rich in knowledge applied to diverse subjects. Similarly the Bombay branch of the Royal Asiatic Society, from the days of its distinguished founder, Sir James Mackintosh, down to the present time, has been the embodiment of much that is highest in the mental efforts of Englishmen in western India. The number of its members, European and Native, is still considerable, and its journal displays learning and talent. But it is not possible that these two Societies, though most highly esteemed and respected, should hold quite the same place which they once held. The comparative proximity of England in these days induces authors to offer to the Royal Asiatic Society in London, and to other English Societies formed for special objects, papers which in other days they would have offered to the Societies in India. Many scientific fields in India are now occupied by the Government, which used to be left to the meritorious, though casual, enterprise of private persons. From these causes the domain of natural and physical science has, for the most part, passed out of the hands of these Societies. Their journals, however, contain scientific articles; and in the realm of antiquarian and learned research they are still potential.

It must be acknowledged that for a long time the Government, oppressed by other cares, omitted to examine the antiquarian remains which lie scattered over the face of the whole empire. The amazing extent of these remains seems to baffle investigation, which discloses more and more rewards to the searchers, as they probe deeper and deeper. The profoundest enquirers apprehend that there may still be many undiscovered vestiges of races and dynasties, of which no other records are to be found. Of late years the Government of India has established an archæological survey, on a scale equal to that of its other great undertakings in the direction of learning and science. This survey will, if prosecuted to its legitimate conclusion, be worthy of the empire. It is in the charge of General Alexander Cunningham, a man of the highest qualification for the work. Already several volumes of its proceedings have been published, embracing, among other things, some of the best Buddhist remains. As an adjunct to this general survey, the Government of Bombay have for several years past been conducting a special survey of the antiquities of western India in charge of Mr. Burgess. This survey has made among other things a complete examination and record, with illustrations, of all the artificial caves and rock-cut temples of the Buddhist period in western India. In conjunction with this survey, Mr. Fleet has rendered great service in respect to Canarese and Sanskrit inscriptions. Mr. Burgess also prepares a periodical, entitled 'The Indian Antiquary,' and replete with the current records of research. In these surveys, the photographer's art, which flourishes in the clear light under eastern skies, is a helpful handmaid, and does artistic work which human hand and eye, however assiduous and untiring, could never have accomplished. The photographic representations of Indian antiquities now form a valuable collection which in former days could not possibly have been procured.

The preservation of ancient monuments is a duty clearly pertaining to the Government in an empire like that of India.

It must be sorrowfully admitted that this duty was neglected, or imperfectly discharged, for many years. Acts of utter vandalism have been perpetrated by persons engaged in public works, and by others, which it would be painful to recount. Stones, valuable to the antiquarian, have often been used as material for modern structures. Such proceedings are prohibited, and, it is to be hoped, are prevented. At the best, however, bricks and stones are constantly pilfered from ancient ruins by the Natives for their own use. The duty of conservation is being recognised by the Government of India, and by the several Local Governments, and it is to be expected that some result will be secured. Separate departments have been constituted in different parts of the country for the purpose; and recently the Government has appointed to this special duty Captain Cole, who is devotedly attached to the pursuit and who inherits a name distinguished in art.

CHAPTER XXII.

PHYSICAL SCIENCE.

Great Trigonometrical Survey—Topographical Survey—Astronomical observatory at Madras—Meteorological observations—Botanical Gardens, and Herbaria—The Geological Survey—Natural History—Imperial museum at Calcutta—Ornithology—Zoological Gardens—Death of Basevi and Stoliczka—Pisciculture—Organization of an agricultural department—Model farms—Popular instruction in agriculture—Veterinary art.

THERE might, perhaps, have been fear lest the Government in India, amidst its many urgent avocations, should find but scant leisure for promoting the advancement of physical science. Nevertheless, it has effected much in several branches of science. and has carried on several scientific operations of magnitude and importance.

The Great Trigonometrical Survey is one of the earliest and the best sustained among the scientific undertakings of the Government. It has served as a basis and a guide for all other surveys in India, and has contributed much to general science. It has covered the country with a network of triangles, greater or lesser. By these operations it has measured a large arc of the meridian, which has supplied important data for determining the dimensions and figure of the earth. It has recently supplemented these operations by pendulum observations, conducted with great care over the whole area between Thibet and the Indian Ocean. It has determined the altitude of most of those peaks of the Himalayas which are covered with perpetual snow, and of all the principal mountains, hills and plateaux in the continent and peninsula of India. The name of one of its Superintendents, Colonel Everest, has been given to Mount Everest, the highest peak discovered in the Himalayas, and the loftiest point as yet known in the world. Its geodetic operations have been extensive, determining by measurement and observation, the figure, curvature, dimensions and areas of the land in many portions of India, and have thus contributed much to the scientific representation of the contour and configuration of the country. Its services to geographical rectification have been invaluable, and it has furnished many of the fundamental data on which large schemes of material improvement have been devised. It constitutes the real backbone of the system of surveying, which has at length made India equal to any country of the world in respect to geographical and topographical information. It has raised up a school of officers highly qualified in this branch of science. The Government has always readily permitted these officers to co-operate in such scientific researches as the observations of the total eclipses of the sun and the transit of Venus, for which India has offered special facilities. It has also participated in the general system of magnetic observations which were simultaneously conducted all over the earth.

The Topographical Survey of India, proceeding on the fundamental data furnished by the Great Trigonometrical Survey, has made the most detailed delineation possible of many of the mountainous regions in the country inclusive of the Himalayas, exhibiting not only every hill-side, mountain top, rivulet, valley and table-land, but also every ravine, torrent-bed and drainage line. With the aid of these maps, many affairs can be considered in the cabinet, for the preliminary treatment of which much labour in the field would ordinarily be required. Lines of march can be determined, territorial boundaries provisionally fixed, material improvements devised, and administrative arrangements effected. When repeatedly tested by these operations, the accuracy of the Topographical Survey has been abundantly verified. Some of the surveys possess an extraordinary interest, such as those of Cashmir, of Ladakh, of Huzara in the Panjab, of the Western Ghat mountains near

Bombay, of Mysore, of the canal region on the East coast, of the tea districts in Assam, of the coffee districts on the Malabar coast. When the height, steepness and ruggedness of the Himalayan mountains, the jealous supiciousness, covert opposition, or overt hostility of many frontier tribes, the extent of the Indian mountainous ranges, the malarious insalubrity of the pent-up valleys and tangled thickets, the varieties of climatic inclemency from ice and snow to burning heat,—are all duly remembered, then will the difficulties of the topographical map-work, as well as its beauty and usefulness, be appreciated.

The situation of Madras being suitable for astronomical observations, especially in respect of the southern hemisphere, an observatory has been long established there. Mr. Pogson, the Government astronomer, is a man of eminence and repute; and the proceedings of his department are esteemed in the scientific world.

The meteorological observatory at Bombay is peculiarly well placed for observing the phenomena of the monsoon, as the masses of rain-cloud burst in torrents every summer. It has been established for many years, and has been ably managed by Mr. Chambers, with various scientific appliances, chemical, magnetic and others. During recent years the Government of India has organized a meteorological department for the whole empire, at the head of which was placed Mr. Blanford, a gentleman of eminent qualifications. An observatory, with several lesser or branch observatories, has been established in each of the several divisions of the empire. The observatory at Calcutta, for Bengal, is under the care of Mr. Elliot, a highly qualified officer. The observations, thus made by the department in all parts of the empire, are collated, and from the central office are issued reports regarding the state of the atmosphere, together with some forecasts of the weather, for public information. These reports have an especial interest during the rainy season, and at times when scarcity is impending.

Botany, as a science, has always flourished in India since the very dawn of the nineteenth century. The several types of floras existing within the limits of the Indian empire are alpine, desert, temperate, tropical, and are allied to the floras of adjacent countries, Afghanistan, Thibet, and the Malayan regions. The Indian flora represents a great, perhaps the greater, part of the vegetable kingdom. The Government of India has contributed numberless specimens to the botanic science of the British empire, and it is in some degree to her Indian, as well as her colonial, possessions that England owes her unrivalled collection of plants, which have so greatly facilitated the study of systematic botany. Among the medical officers of the Government, some have been the fathers of Indian botany. Of these one of the foremost was Dr. Roxburgh, superintendent of the botanic garden at Calcutta. This garden is of great size, having an area of 272 acres. It was, by the labour of many years, well stocked, but suffered severely from the cyclone of 1864, when sad havoc occurred. Its misfortunes were renewed by the cyclone of 1867; but subsequently great efforts have been made to re-stock it, and to improve its grounds.

It possesses a herbarium, which has received the collections made at various times by distinguished botanists, such as Wallich and Griffith, and contributions given by persons in other countries devoted to the cause of botanic science. More particularly is it indebted to Sir Joseph Hooker of Kew, who has presented many valuable specimens, and has been a great benefactor of the institution. Specimens of foreign floras have been obtained for it not only from the Royal Botanic Gardens at Kew, but also from the botanic gardens at Kandy, Batavia, Melbourne, Adelaide, St. Petersburg, Munich, Palermo, Chicago. It has suffered from the premature and lamented death of its curator, Dr. Kurz, but exertions are still made to maintain its progressive development. The botanic garden at Seharunpore, near the Ganges canal in northern India, was, through the scientific exertions of Royle and Falconer, established and richly stocked; with it also is associated the name of Dr. Jamieson, who was among the first to render the culture of tea successful in northern India. There is a botanic garden at Utakamand in the Nilgiri mountains, a region highly suited for the growth and culture of tropical plants, and of other plants also, by reason of its altitude. At Bangalore, on the elevated and adjacent plateau of the Mysore province, there is an excellent botanic garden. The Bombay Presidency has not as yet any botanic garden worthy of the name. The heavy and continuous rains for four months during the monsoon season are unfavourable to the formation of such a garden. Steps have been taken to found a botanic garden near Poona, which is a suitable locality, with what degree of success remains to be seen. Of the many botanic books, treatises, and journals on Indian botany, there may be selected for mention Sir Joseph Hooker's most interesting travels in Sikhim; Dr. D. Brandis' 'Forest Flora of Northern India,' written with a special view to the work of the forest department, but replete with general instruction, scientifically arranged; Dr. Balfour's work on Indian trees, and Cyclopedia of southern Asia; and Captain Drury's account of the useful plants of India. 'The Flora of British India' is in progress, and is being issued with the eminent authority of Sir Joseph Hooker.

The Geological Survey is, next after the Trigonometrical Survey, the largest scientific operation yet undertaken by the Government of India. It has been in progress for about twenty-five years, and with its past proceedings the name of the late Dr. Oldham has been honourably connected. It contains many highly qualified officers, who bear much fatigue and sickness from travelling in many of those insalubrious localities where geological investigation can best be made, but who are sustained in alacrity and zeal by the love they feel for their scientific work, and by the countless novelties which are presented during a sojourn among the wilds of the country. The wonderful attractiveness of these long marches, despite the wasting fever, the heat, the damp, the chill, which are inseparable from them, is illustrated by the recently published book by V. Ball, entitled 'Jungle Life in India.' The details of the geology of the empire, so far as they are yet known, are given in the manual of Indian geology by Medlicott and Blanford. The Geological Survey has now touched most of those points or lines in the empire that claimed priority of consideration, such as some of the formations in the mountainous ranges of the Himalayas, the Vindhyas, the Aravalis, the Sâtpuras, the Western Ghats, including the Nilgiris, and the Eastern Ghats. It has surveyed most of the coal-bearing strata which have as yet been discovered, such as those of the hilly tracts of western Bengal, through which the chord line of the railway runs; the Mopani mines on the northern slope of the Sâtpuras near the line of railway in the Nerbadda Valley; the field near the Wardha river, to which a branch railway has been made; the tracts of western Bengal which produce the iron-ore. It has, among many other operations, examined some of the limestone and sandstone formations in various parts of the empire; much of the trap regions of western and central India, many, also, of the metamorphic series. It will, in due course of time, embrace the whole empire. Much, however, remains to be surveyed in so extensive and varied an area as that of India. The geological department has furnished, with specimens of every sort, a large compartment of the imperial museum at Calcutta. Its records constitute a valuable repertory of scientific information. It issues, also, an illustrated periodical, describing the palæontological remains discovered in India, and entitled the 'Palæontologia Indica.'

Attention has been bestowed by the State upon Natural History. The collection of specimens, belonging to the Bengal Asiatic Society, has been transferred to the imperial museum at Calcutta; and among the gentlemen in charge of the museum there are professional naturalists. Sir Joseph Fayrer's illustrated works on the snakes of India will repay attentive study.

In entomology, collections have been made, such as the collection of coleoptera by the late W. Atkinson. The ornithological department of the museum is excellently arranged, and is enriched with the collections made by many persons in the service of Government and by private gentlemen. Dr. Jerdon's book on the birds of India will long continue to be a standard work for reference, as it embodied all or nearly all the knowledge available in his day. Subsequently much has been done for Indian ornithology by a number of gentlemen who are fond of this scientific branch, and have opportunities for pursuing it. At the head of them is an eminent member of the public service, Mr. A. C. Hume, under whose management the periodical entitled 'Stray Feathers,' has been issued.

Some impulse has been imparted to the practical study of Natural History among the Natives, by the establishment of the Zoological Gardens at Calcutta, which was opened under the gracious auspices of the Prince of Wales shortly after New Year's Day in 1876. Having been well stocked with animals, they have become very popular, and are thronged with Native visitors. There is a nucleus of a similar institution in the Victoria Gardens at Bombay, but it has not yet been fully developed, the climatic conditions being not so favourable as those of Calcutta.

Among the martyrs of science in India there should be mentioned Basevi, of the Great Trigonometrical Survey, and Stoliczka, of the Geological Survey, both of whom perished among the inhospitable mountains which separate Cashmir from Yarkand.

Attention was at one time given to pisciculture, under the care of Dr. Day, in consideration of the wastage of the fish-supply of the rivers, which constitutes an important article of food to many classes of the people; but no result worthy of note ensued.

Agricultural science is second to no science in practical importance to India, and indeed may be deemed practically more important than any other, by reason of the overwhelming magnitude of agriculture as an industry. Nevertheless, the Government has as yet done but little on this behalf; nor has it shewn any vivid comprehension of the manner and the means whereby the science may be cultivated by those in power, and thence diffused among the people. In 1872 a department of Revenue, Agriculture and Commerce was established in the Government of India, under the supervision of Mr. A. O. Hume, an officer of great practical ability, in order that the attention of the supreme authority might be better concentrated on these economic objects. But this department was nothing more than a branch of the Secretariat of the Government, and its primary object was avowedly revenue. It has been recently abolished for the sake of economizing establishments, and its work has been transferred to the other branches of the Secretariat. Lord Mayo, when Governor-General, desired to found a department which should be devoted solely to agricultural science; and the scheme is quite practicable. Care would have to be taken that whatever experiments are made, or whatever directions are urged on the attention of the people, should be arranged through the several Local Governments, and that they should have the executive management of the operations. Otherwise, if any attempt were made to manage these matters through some central authority under the direct command of the Government of India, irrespective of the Local Governments, there would be clashing of authority, the people would be bewildered, and no real result would be obtained for science. But if this were judiciously arranged, nothing would be easier than for each Local Government to appoint a gentleman, professionally trained in scientific agriculture, to be its adviser respecting the introduction and diffusion of agricultural science. There would be several such gentlemen in the empire, as there are several Local Governments, and under them a scientific staff of Europeans and Natives would gradually grow up. The Government of India would also appoint a gentleman, of high status in the profession, to be its adviser, and to assist it in giving general instructions to the several Local Governments. Some years ago, the Government of the North-western Provinces appointed a special director of agriculture, and doubtless much benefit has arisen from this arrangement. Time must be allowed before any appreciable result could be expected from the proceedings of the agricultural department for the empire at large. With such a staff of scientific men working in all the provinces, a body of practical knowledge would be accumulated, and based upon the application of proved principles to the existing circumstances of the country.

Thus, whatever experiments were made, would be scientifically conducted, and would be really instructive. Whereas, many of the experiments heretofore made in model farms, if scientifically commenced, have often failed to be brought to a scientific issue; and have probably retarded rather than promoted agricultural science. Simultaneously with these operations, agricultural instruction would form a branch of the national education; there would be separate schools of agriculture, or agricultural classes in existing rural schools, and agricultural colleges for the more advanced Native students, as explained in the previous chapter regarding education. Year by year there would be more and more Natives in some degree qualified by education to appreciate scientific information and to afford assistance in conducting experiments. The agriculture of an empire, carried on with a knowledge, empirical indeed, yet derived from the practice of many centuries, cannot be quickly altered, but may be gradually improved. In several respects the Indian peasant is fairly well accomplished, such as discriminating the qualities of soils, discerning the times for sowing, weeding and keeping the crops clean, avoiding hedge-rows and making the most of every foot of ground. But in ploughing and other parts of husbandry he is deficient. Though some fields are well manured, still the want of manure in many of the fields is one of the most serious of existing faults in the condition of the country. The dung of cattle is, in many districts, diverted from its proper uses as manure, and is used for fuel. The bones of dead cattle, instead of being utilised for manure, are for the most part wasted. Sewage instead of being utilised for the good of the fields is but too often allowed to stagnate for the injury of man. These circumstances lead to the apprehension that there must be some slow exhaustion of the soil going on. The best means of arresting such deterioration will be found in the diffusion of agricultural knowledge.

Connected with this subject, there is the veterinary art, in no country more important than India, where the cattle form a part of the capital of the largest class in the country. It has been already seen in the previous chapter, relating to material progress, that the cattle are still very numerous, though decimated by the recent famines. Even in ordinary times, destructive murrains and cattle plagues are of too frequent occurrence, some of which arise from preventible causes. If scientific agriculture were to take root in the country, veterinary schools and colleges would arise, where Natives might be instructed in all that relates to the welfare and preservation of the cattle.

CHAPTER XXIII.

WILD ANIMALS AND SPORTS.

Advantages from sport—Big game in champaign country and in mountains—Season for sport—Spearing the wild boar—Tiger-shooting—The "man-eater"—The panther—Dangerous when he becomes a man-eater—Wounds from carnivorous animals—The hunting Cheeta—The bear—The elephant—The bison—The rhinoceros—The alligator—The Himalayan ibex and *Ovis Ammon*—Anglo-Indian literature relating to wild sports.

ALTHOUGH the subject of savage animals and wild sports may seem at first sight to be wanting in seriousness, still an Englishman's knowledge of India would be meagre, jejune, lifeless, unless he knew something of the *feræ naturæ*, which are the denizens of the forests still remaining after the invasion of the plough and the axe, and which are being driven from the plains to their last strongholds in the everlasting hills. If a man be an accomplished and fortunate sportsman, he probably receives more of exciting pleasure from the country than any other person. Though he may not bend himself to acquire knowledge, yet his sporting pursuits bring him into the way of all sorts of useful information regarding the land and its inhabitants, which he easily and naturally gains and which he could hardly gain by any other means. If he be a careworn administrator, it is a great advantage to him in his profession to be an adept, in the saddle, or with the gun. He is thereby all the more able to retain that buoyant spirit and that springy disposition, which are essential for combating the depression and enervation of a career in the tropics. Even if he be but an erring marksman, and an unsuccessful hunter, still he must be acquainted with the lairs, haunts, tracks and habits of the beasts of the jungle, he must be fond of the sequestered nooks where they crouch and the hidden pathways where they prowl, if he would see aright the realities of India.

> "Ego vitam agam sub altis Phrygiæ columinibus
> Ubi cerva sylvicultrix, ubi aper nemorivagus."

The matter, too, has its saddening, as well as its pleasurable aspect, because many thousands of Natives yearly fall victims to the ravages of wild beasts and to the bites of venomous reptiles, despite the efforts of the authorities to encourage the destruction of these animals. The loss of cattle also, from the same causes, is considerable.

It is notoriously a subject of complaint among sportsmen that the spread of cultivation and habitation has driven the big game away from the vicinity of stations and from easily accessible localities. The ravages of wild beasts have induced the Government to offer rewards for destruction, and thus many a Native for the sake of lucre kills animals at the moment, which might ultimately have been pursued by gentlemen for love of the chase. Still, the animals find fastnesses in the numerous mountain ranges which ramify throughout the empire, and in the stupendous Himalayan range which shuts out India from Central Asia. There they await the onslaught of the hunter; and thence sometimes they daringly issue forth to court the combat with civilized man.

In the rainy season of summer the animals roam so far afield and so constantly shift their abodes, the woods and the brushwood become so thick in foliage and so tangled in growth, the tracks are so impervious, and the mist or the downpour is so depressing, that the hunter must rest in enforced idleness, and hang up his horn, spear and rifle. In the autumn, the malarious exhalations warn the most hardy and adventurous to beware of entering forests where in a single night a life-long malady may be contracted. In the winter when the atmosphere is cleared of autumnal taint, the sporting season begins, and improves every month as the hot weather approaches. It is at its zenith during the heat, when the animals must perforce lie up, and must resort to certain known springs or pools for slaking their thirst. Then it is that they are caught in a dilemma which cannot be evaded by night or by day. Many a moonlit watcher on a summer night, perched up among the branches of trees, has been rewarded by seeing his game fall to the rifle-shot.

One of the few wild sports which can be enjoyed near at home, in the midst of the inhabited country, is that of hunting on horseback the wild boar, and piercing him with a spear, without any assistance from hounds. This sport is followed in almost every part of the empire. Herein are required the highest proficiency of the horseman as well as the spearsman, and fleetness together with unfailing obedience to the rider's hand on the part of the horse. The high average of accidents to both man and horse, attest the arduous character of this chase, if hotly pressed against a boar that is worthy of the steel. Thus, hog-hunting, if pursued in the highest form and style, is truly the queen of Indian sports. The best kind of boar is one that, having fed highly on the most nutritious of the husbandman's crops, has great speed for a moderate distance, a short temper and a desperate courage. He is not formidable, as he bursts from his reedy cover, and hies away at a galloping pace, if the hunters can catch him up and pierce him as he runs. But if, on breath failing him, he suddenly stops, squats for an instant facing his pursuers, and charges with a grunt of fury, then the critical moment is arrived. If the hunter receives him on the spear-point, well. The infuriated brute will press on towards his foe, although every struggle drives the weapon deeper into his own vitals. But if the spear misses, then the horse, at least, is in danger of being lost. One turn of the protruding tusk as the boar rushes past, severs bone, sinew and artery, as with a knife; many a gallant steed has thus bitten the dust. The boar's repute for fearlessness is such, that the Natives have a proverb to the effect that if a tiger and a bear happen to be standing by the river side, he will step down between them, in order to drink his fill.

Tiger-shooting is sometimes attempted on foot, and then

demands special skill and wariness. It is more commonly undertaken either from a perch constructed amidst the branches of trees, or from the back of a trained elephant. It is comparatively safe, if the elephant is staunch and steady, as he generally is, because in his sagacity he relies on the rifle of his rider arresting the tiger as it springs with a terrific bound. If the elephant, from want of confidence in his master's rifle, or from any other cause, becomes terrified and unsteady, he will rush, regardless of his rider, among the outstretching branches of the trees, whereby a new danger is added. The feline nature of the tiger makes him an arrant coward, until the last hope of escape is closed, but when desperation possesses him, he will leap upon his pursuers in a manner quite magnificent.

The tiger is found under various conditions of abode and habit. His normal state is when he dwells in the heart of the forest and lives upon deer and such-like prey. Often, however, he lurks in the edge of the woods, near cultivated ground, or close to pasturage frequented by the herds, and then he stealthily seizes the cattle. If not shot down or hunted out, he and his progeny would cause so much annoyance to the villagers as to drive them from their homesteads. Sometimes in north-eastern Bengal, at certain seasons he quits his Himalayan abode, swims the broad rivers, and under cover of night traverses the open plain, till he reaches the patches of tall reeds and grasses near the banks of the Brahmaputra. From that refuge, he darts forth to decimate the cattle of the neighbouring villages. Thus arises the sportsman's opportunity, the cover, dense but limited in space, is surrounded, and the tiger, feeling himself environed by his doom, gives battle straightway.

The real danger in tiger-shooting is when the beast, being by wounds incapacitated from further retreat, lies down despairingly in some position from which he cannot be dislodged, and when the sportsman, eager to possess his game, is tempted to venture into too close quarters. The energy of the dying tiger flickers up suddenly; and even when he is seemingly near his last gasp, his waning life flares up with dread power to maim and maul the foe who comes within reach of his teeth or claws. Some of the saddest accidents in the records of sport have happened in this way.

Sometimes the tiger, having successfully preyed on the village cattle, begins to attack the villagers themselves, and then he is called by the awe-inspiring name of "the man-eater." He betakes himself to this dread pursuit, either because from infirmity he can no longer catch the nimble denizens of the forest, or because he happens to have perceived that man is easier to be killed than any other creature capable of affording food. Then all the stealthy and cunning instincts of his nature are intensified. He seems to feel that man, if warned or alive to danger, has some peculiar power of resistance, so he steals along, silent as the grave, towards his victim. The unsuspicious person walking quietly along, feels suddenly a paw laid like a hammer on his head or shoulder, like a bolt from fate; and in an instant all is over. A "man-eater," if unchecked, would soon cause the depopulation of villages, as the survivors fly their homes in terror. But a report of this apparition is immediately made to the authorities, and the scourge is soon removed.

The animal called locally the panther by Europeans, is a sort of leopard, grey in hue with beautiful spots, slight in frame, but with great motive power in the limbs, with retractile claws, and sharp teeth. If not attacked, he is generally harmless to man. But if hunted and driven to any extremity, he shews a terrible sagacity, different from that of other animals. He charges, not wildly, but with a definite aim which seldom misses its object of closing with his human foe. If perchance he fails, he instantly repairs the mistake, and repeats the assault with greater precision. If the foe be perched in a tree, he will climb up with amazing agility to seek his revenge. Having overthrown one of his assailants, and inflicted desperate wounds, he will pause to turn and charge another of those who have provoked him. Sometimes having rid himself of the sportsman, he will dash off to wreak his fury on passers-by who have not been concerned in the hunt. When in this mood, he is the most formidable beast that stalks the earth. He very rarely betakes himself to man-eating; when he does, every effort must be exerted to compass his destruction, for the sake of the neighbourhood against which he would bring his dire sagacity to bear. Even he, however, is not proof against human ingenuity in trapping. The authentic traditions of a panther in the hills between Jabalpur and Nagpur used to be told with bated breath by the witnesses. He killed men from sheer vice as well from desire for food, and his range of destruction during a single night would be wide. At even-tide a Native family would be gathered for supper in front of their cottage door. In the twinkling of an eye, a horrid form flashes before them, and one of their number is hurried away. The survivors, terror-stricken, follow, and find him a short distance off, dead, with a gaping wound in his throat from which the blood has been hastily sucked. At midnight in another village some miles off, a couple are fast asleep in the cool night-air outside their homestead. Suddenly a death-shriek arises, one is taken, the other left. The neighbours, aroused by the cries, search and find, close by, the corpse, from which a few shreds of flesh have been torn. Towards dawn in a field, again some miles off, peasants are sleepily tending their crops, one of them instantaneously disappears from their midst, before the others can realise the visitation. Once more there is the same finding of the body, with a wound of which the nature discloses the identity of the destroyer. The terror can be imagined which such occurrences, at various hours of the same night in places at some distance from each other, spread among the people to whom the panther seemed to be ubiquitous. For some time his activity enabled him to elude capture; at length he was mobbed and slain.

Besides other reasons, there is a particular reason why the sportsman should, if possible, avoid wounds from carnivorous beasts, which is this, that their claws and teeth are often tainted by the putrefaction of animal substances, and thus communicate a fearful and incurable poison to the blood of the sufferer. Sometimes even a scratch, apparently innocuous at first, becomes inflamed and sloughs with gangrene, causing a slow but most distressful death. Some known instances of this nature are too shocking to relate.

The "Cheeta," a sort of hunting leopard, is kept by Native princes and chiefs for sport; he has the jaw and teeth of a panther, but his claws are not retractile and are less harmful; his agility for a few seconds, perhaps for a minute or so, is astonishing, but his staying power is slight. He is trained to rush at and seize the black buck, in this wise. He is placed, blindfold with a hood, inside a small Native chariot or cart, drawn by bullocks and surrounded by people, to the sight of whom the deer are accustomed as they graze on the green crops. The unsuspecting herd, led by the buck, allow the cart to approach to within a short distance of fifty to a hundred yards. At the right moment, the hood is withdrawn from the Cheeta's eyes, and the buck is disclosed to his gaze. The speed can be imagined with which the buck starts off in his agony of fear. With a few flying bounds the Cheeta is on him, with teeth fleshed in some vital part. If, however, the buck can make good his flight for a hundred yards or so, he is saved, for the Cheeta having expended his activity in a few bounds, abandons the pursuit.

The bear, of many species or varieties, is found in all parts of India; he is often a timid and stupid creature. If, on rushing out of a cave, or otherwise suddenly coming in contact with an assailant, he should fight with his natural weapons, then his hug, scratch and bite are tremendous. When wounded, also, he may make a charge which, if brought home, will prove fatal to the sportsman. It was in this manner that, by a deplorable and lamented mishap, Lord Henry St. Maur was killed by the bear which he had mortally wounded. In the

Himalayas the bear will sometimes evince surprising strength and courage, and will rush up to the muzzle of the sportsman's gun; even the barrel of a gun may be bent and indented by a bear maddened with wounds and excited in the fray. Sometimes a bear, without any hostile intent, will hang about the forest pathways during twilight or after dark. Then the sportsman or the passer-by, going home at nightfall, must beware lest unconsciously he should walk right up against the beast, which will by instinct strike at the human face, and with one sweep of its claws will mar every feature. If he meets a she-bear with her young, he may attack if he is sure of his means and his opportunity, otherwise he will bear in mind her extraordinary vigour and ferocity if she fears being robbed of her whelps.

The elephant is caught in several parts of the empire by the British Government, and by some of the Native sovereigns, for purposes of war and of State shows. The best hunting-grounds are in the hill country of Eastern Bengal, the Nepal territories and the southern portion of the Nilgiri mountains. The depôts, where the captured elephants are kept, have the local name of Khedda. The sportsman also has his opportunities; but the sport generally requires an organization beyond the means of an individual. The gregarious habits of the elephant are well worthy of attentive notice. His daintiest food consists of the wild plantain and the tender shoots of the young bamboo. He resorts periodically to saline deposits, for which he has a strong craving and which are called locally "salt-licks." Sometimes he is captured by the well-known device of alluring him with decoy elephants, and by taking that opportunity to fasten and secure him. Sometimes he is skilfully enclosed between fences, wide apart at first, but gradually narrowing to an apex like the letter V, and he is driven towards that apex by the beaters. The struggle can be imagined which he makes against the stout barriers of the V, when his danger is fully realised by him. If at some earlier time in the day he takes alarm, and makes good his escape, the ease with which his huge, ungainly and apparently unwieldy limbs ascend and descend the steepest hill-sides, and the force with which he crashes through the opposing thickets, astonish beholders. For some days after his capture, the grief, rage and chagrin, indicated by his movements and demeanour, afford a sorry spectacle. He soon, however, becomes reconciled to his lot, and seems to find his happiness in the ways of civilized servitude. He breeds but seldom while in captivity, but his longevity renders him a valued member of an establishment. A young elephant of tender age is petted by Natives as among the choicest of animals. But if a tame elephant happens to become loosed in any locality suited to his natural habits, he reverts to his wild life, and then his recapture is difficult for mankind, with whose devices he has had acquaintance. In some places, herds of wild elephants are known to have been descendants of domesticated elephants escaped from slavery.

The bison is found in most of the hill-ranges of India, and affords sport which is interesting without being specially difficult. The critical moment is when, with lowered head, he rushes like a whirlwind at his enemy.

The rhinoceros is found principally in the forests skirting the base of the eastern Himalayas. He is sometimes shot, at other times he is captured young, and reserved by Native princes for their wild-beast shows.

The alligator is seldom pursued for sport, though marksmen often delight in shooting him while he lies on the edge of the waters, as he is a monster hated by all men. There are two species; one the "sharp-nosed," which preys on fish, and is harmless. The other is the "snub-nosed," which subsists upon carrion and will seize human beings when opportunity may offer, and which is the alligator of such ill-omened fame. Being amphibious, he lives often in the large tanks which are so common in the country. When moving timidly at dawn or by twilight from one tank to another, he is awkward and discomposed, having but slight power of movement on land. His limbs are small and his potent tail is of little use out of the water. He reposes chiefly in the depths of the pools of rivers, but he loves to emerge and bask on the sandy bed or rocky surfaces near the banks under the broiling sun. As he lies in utter stillness, he seems at a short distance to be a grey weather-beaten log of wood. In this manner he will often remain at a short distance from the water's edge, a few yards perhaps. If any person, passing by or going to the water's edge to drink and bathe, mistaking the alligator for a log, or not noticing him at all, should come between the monster and the water, then all is over in a moment. The alligator, propelled by his powerful tail, makes a sudden rush, and plunges into the water with his victim in his jaws. If the stranger, however, passes on the outer, or the land side, of the alligator, he is probably safe; the monster, seeing a man approach, will betake himself to his proper element. It is the presence of the alligator that renders bathing in many of the most picturesque rivers so unsafe. European soldiers and others are sometimes thus carried away while swimming. Occasionally the alligator will lie in wait in the water for creatures approaching the margin, in order to seize them. The Natives say that he can, with his terribly armed jaw and with the leverage of his tail, seize, and drag into the water, even a tiger when bending forward to drink on the river's edge. Such a thing is quite possible, and the resistance of a tiger, once caught in this iron grip, would be ineffectual. A sad tale was told thus in eastern Bengal. Some women were bathing in the Brahmaputra; suddenly a gaping mouth, with long rows of teeth, emerged from the water, and seized one of the women by the waist. For a moment the monster rose half out of the water, brandished his victim aloft, and then disappeared with her under water to be seen no more.

The hunting of the ibex and the *Ovis Ammon*, the mountain goat and the wild sheep of the Himalayas, demands not only the highest skill of the marksman, but also the nerve, patience, and endurance of the mountaineer. The game is rarely to be descried and most difficult of approach, and at the best, the practised and proficient sportsman will find only few rewards. But he will live, move, and have his being amidst the "mountain gloom and mountain glory," and he will commune with nature in her sublimest moods.

Anglo-Indian literature abounds in stirring narratives of sport and travel, such as Shakspeare's wild sports in the East, the old Forest Ranger, the Wild sports of the Deccan, Colonel Markham's sporting tour in the Himalayas. Among books recently published, the wonderful interest surrounding the life of those who seek their diversion in the forest, is charmingly illustrated by Forsyth's work on the forests of Central India, by Lockwood's 'Natural History, sport and travel,' and by Sanderson's 'Thirteen Years among the wild beasts of India.'

CHAPTER XXIV.

NAVY AND MARINE.

Early naval enterprises — Piracy — The Indian Navy — Naval arrangement between the Government of India and the Admiralty in London — The Persian Gulf—Defence of Indian harbours and coasts—Steam Navigation Companies—The Indian Marine—Marine Surveys—Tidal observations—Shipwrecks—Native passenger ships—Port of Calcutta—Cyclones in the Bay of Bengal—Pilots on the Hûghli—Madras pier—Dockyards at Calcutta and Bombay—Wet dock and foreshore at Bombay—Karachi harbour—Examination of lesser harbours—Lighthouses.

THE ultimate position of the English in India was in part won after arduous naval contests with the French, in which the navies of both Powers equally distinguished themselves. With the Native Powers the struggle was for the most on land, and but seldom on the sea. The earlier Hindus and the Muhammadans did not affect maritime warfare. The Mahrattas, however, having the seat of their power on a long range of mountains, whence they looked down upon the littoral districts at their feet and the ocean with its shores studded with rich seaports, aspired from the first to establish a power, which, though not to be dignified with the epithet of naval, was essentially maritime. The numerous country craft of the Malabar coasts were manned by Native mariners of hardihood and courage. Upon these vessels Sivaji, the Mahratta king, mounted his guns. With the fleets, thus composed, of small war-ships, he used to swoop upon the defenceless coasts, and effect some of his most startling conquests. These proceedings greatly stimulated piracy, always rife in the Indian Ocean, and inured the seafaring men to fighting on their own element. When the English, then, appeared on the scene, to claim ascendency first and then supremacy, they found enemies on the sea as well as on the land. Besides English-built ships of war, many country vessels with suitable armament were employed to reduce Mahratta enemies or to punish pirates.

For many years a separate Navy, bearing the now time-honoured title of the Indian Navy, was maintained by the East India Company for the control of maritime affairs in Indian waters, with its headquarters in the Bombay harbour. According to the naval needs of the time, it was effective as a fighting machine. Besides warlike operations, it rendered service to the country in many fields of action, and it acted as the armed and disciplined police of the Indian seas. It was the agency for the suppression of piracy, and for the hunting of the pirates into their lairs on land. Its officers examined all the coasts of India itself and of all neighbouring country whither Indian ships resort. They laid the foundation of the marine surveys, provided charts of the harbours, took soundings of the channels. and explored navigable rivers or estuaries for long distances inland. Thus the flag which they hoisted was the symbol of much gallant and honourable service.

But while the officers and men were maintained in full vigour and efficiency, the ships, which had been good in their day, were becoming obsolete, by reason of the changes in naval architecture and armament. If new vessels were to be procured from time to time, according to the changeful types of ship-building, also with officers and men versed in the newest forms of nautical instruction, it was preferable that both ships and crews should come direct from the Royal Navy. It was therefore determined to abolish the Indian navy, as a naval force. A marine, indeed, was permanently required to perform many duties, subsidiary to war but not actually warlike. But it was not expedient to retain the officers and men for a marine which they would regard as an inferior service; so they were paid off and admitted to pension, with due recognition of the services long rendered to the country by themselves and their predecessors. Some among them, who were chosen on account of general aptitude, consented to remain in the marine, which was provisionally maintained in order to carry on the public service. A large financial saving was immediately obtained by these measures.

An arrangement was then made whereby a certain sum should be paid annually by the Indian Government to the Admiralty in London, whence a certain number of ships of war was to be furnished for the protection of British interests in Indian waters. To the ships thus supplied were added some others for the service required on the East Coast of Africa; and all were placed under one Admiral, whose naval jurisdiction extended to Aden and the Red Sea, to the Persian Gulf, to Zanzibar and Madagascar, to Bombay and Karachi, to Ceylon and the Straits of Malacca, to the Bay of Bengal, to the ports of Calcutta and Rangun. This arrangement operates efficiently, and the relations between the Indian Government and the English Admiralty are satisfactory; though here, as elsewhere, there are complaints of the ships of war not being in sufficient strength for the protection of so many scattered interests. Many authorities think that there ought to be more of naval demonstration than there actually is, at the very important harbours of Bombay and Aden.

The extreme heat in the Persian Gulf during many months in the year, and the consequent sufferings of the crews of the ships of war unavoidably stationed there to preserve order, have induced some authorities to consider whether some of the ships serving in those waters might not be manned by Native Indian crews, drawn from the seamen called "Lascars," who abound on several of the coasts of India. The lascars navigate the country craft which ply in the Bay of Bengal and the Indian Ocean. They are skilful, hardy and competent men; they are largely employed in the steamships of the European Companies which carry the mails, and in many other steamships; and they could doubtless be trained to the duties on board ships of war. Their officers would be English, and a ship of war thus manned would stand in the same relation towards the ships having European crews, as that in which a regiment in the Native army stands towards the English forces. The demand for the lascars having increased so much of late, these men are more difficult to obtain now than formerly, and their wages have risen.

The defence of the coasts and harbours of India, against attack from the sea, has frequently occupied the thoughts of the Indian Government. Fortunately Calcutta, with its great port crowded with shipping, possesses natural defences of an extraordinary character. It is built far inland on the banks of a river which is navigable for ships of the greatest draught if they are well piloted, but which, with its tortuous channels and shifting quicksands, will speedily engulph any ship which is not so piloted. The pilotage is entirely in the hands of the British Government; and it were needless to anticipate the fate that under these circumstances would overtake a hostile squadron. Rangun, the capital of British Burma, is also built inland on the banks of the Irawaddy, but is much more accessible, and has a port with much shipping at certain seasons; its position is not free from anxiety, although precautions have been taken. A similar remark is applicable to Madras, which has, however, only an open roadstead, and no real port at all. On the western coast, the harbour of Karwar is assailable from the sea, but, though the prosperity of the place has been rising, no important interests are as yet centred there. The important harbour of Karachi is also liable to naval attack, but it has been placed, provisionally and temporarily at least, in a state of defence; and could at comparatively slight cost and in a short time be rendered adequately defensible. For the vitally important positions of Aden and Bombay, schemes of fortification have been elaborately prepared, but not carried into execution, partly by reason of the costliness, and partly on account of doubts whether such fortifications constitute the best means of defence. At Aden some batteries have been erected, but more are yet needed; it is felt, however, that, in event of war, some naval force must be maintained there. At Bombay, also, batteries have been erected at several points, though some additions to them are yet needed. Two efficient iron-clad turret-ships are stationed there permanently for harbour defence; these are fully armed, though not as yet properly manned. The establishment, suitable for them under the circumstances, is under consideration, and crews could be sent out for them from England at the shortest notice. The Bombay harbour, in addition to the large expanse where the shipping lies, possesses a considerable area of water in the rear, and under the cover of, the island of Elephanta, whither, in event of danger, the mercantile shipping might be sent to a secure and sheltered anchorage, which circumstance constitutes a great advantage. Besides these principal situations, there are long lines of coast in India dotted here and there with rich little seaports offering temptation to a naval enemy, for the protection of which reliance must be placed upon the Royal Navy.

There is a flotilla of transport vessels, plying between England and Bombay through the Suez Canal, for the conveyance of European troops backwards and forwards. These are commanded by officers of the Royal Navy; they are truly magnificent vesssels, the very finest of their kind; and each of them can carry from a thousand to thirteen hundred men besides her crew.

The steam fleets, numbering many vessels, of the two Navigation Companies, the "Peninsular and Oriental" and the "British India," are under contract with the Government for conveyance of the mails. They constitute an integral part of the maritime resources of India, because, according to the agreement, their vessels are to be placed at the disposal of Government, for any emergency, military or other. Their value has been satisfactorily tested on urgent occasions, such as the transport of vast supplies of food-grain from Burma to Bengal during the famine of 1874, and the despatch of a force from Bombay to Malta in 1878.

For some time after the abolition of the Indian Navy, the marine service of the empire, consisting chiefly of the transport of troops between Bombay, Aden and Karachi, and between Calcutta, Madras, Burma and the Andamans, was carried on passably well, though it remained in a somewhat uncertain condition, with a tendency towards deterioration. It has, however, during recent years been reorganized into a regular service, with the advice and assistance of Admiral Bythesea of the Royal Navy, and will soon shew much improvement.

The marine survey of the coasts and harbours, great and small, throughout the empire, has been vigorously undertaken. This is much needed, even where old surveys exist, by reason of the shifting character of the ground. Doubts often prevail about the depth of the navigable channel, which uncertainty causes accidents to occur.

Tidal observations have been made by scientific officers. In order to obtain a more exact knowledge of the tides of the Indian seas, which have certain important peculiarities, registers have been established at several places on the coast, with self-acting gauges, whereby data will be gradually secured which will enable the officers to calculate the tides of all the chief ports, with a precision hardly yet obtained in any other part of the globe.

Shipwrecks and other mishaps at sea are of too frequent occurrence in most parts of the world. In Indian waters they unhappily are as common as anywhere, are generally very distressful in their character, and sometimes are found to reflect discredit on those concerned in them. Due provision is made by law for enquiry into all such occurrences, and the investigations are promptly and strictly enforced by the authorities.

There are regulations sanctioned by law for sanitation, order, and security on board the ships which carry Native passengers backwards and forwards across the seas, pilgrims, emigrants and others. Much protection is hereby afforded to these people, who would otherwise be exposed to many perils or distresses.

At Calcutta, as the port consists of a broad navigable river, there is necessarily a difficulty regarding space, which difficulty is overcome by the ships being moored close together with chain moorings of great strength, alongside the quays and jetties. In these moorings the primary object is adequacy of strength to resist the cyclones, with which that region is periodically threatened, and which are sometimes lamentably destructive. That the resisting power of the moorings is considerable may be believed, but whether it would bear the supreme strain of a violent tornado, is more than any one can say. If the ships do break away from their anchorage in a confined harbour like that of Calcutta, the consequences are lamentable. The new quays, the several jetties thrown out from the bank into the deep channel of the river, the warehouses and the new strand road have been constructed in a manner which, though unambitious, is efficient and economical. The financial result of these works is favourable; the outlay being moderate and the returns considerable. The pontoon bridge across the Hûghli at Calcutta is one of the finest structures of its kind ever erected, and secures almost uninterrupted communication across the river, between the capital on the one bank and its great surburb of Howra on the other bank, at a comparatively cheap cost. If the ships were to be torn from their moorings by a cyclone and driven at a considerable speed against the pontoons, the structure must give way and add to the general ruin. Such an occurrence would, however, prove fatal to any structure that might be raised, even of the most solid masonry.

After comparative immunity for many years, Calcutta was the scene of a terrific and destructive cyclone in 1864, and again in 1867. The town and neighbourhood of Masulipatam, on the eastern coast, was visited by an hurricane of this kind, and in the dead of night the inhabitants and their dwellings were submerged by the sea driven from the force of wind beyond its natural bounds. The most awful visitation was that which befell, in 1876, the delta districts of south-eastern Bengal, where the Brahmaputra and the Megna rivers unite their broad waters before mingling them with the ocean. At midnight a furious wind drove the sea-water into the estuary, thus banking up the river-water for many miles, and so causing many thickly-peopled tracts to be partially submerged. The wind, then circling round, after the manner of cyclones, brought its force to bear on the accumulated mass of river-water, driving it seawards. Thus there was a tremendous refluence of the flood, completing the submergence of the entire neighbourhood, and drowning hundreds of populous villages under many feet of water. More than one hundred thousand persons were drowned in the darkness of that night. The morning broke upon districts where the retiring and subsiding waters disclosed death, ruin and devastation.

The Pilot Service has always been carefully organized on the Hûghli river, where ships of the deepest draught have to be guided carefully through upwards of a hundred miles of a river-course, having tortuous and changeful channels, and abounding in treacherous sands, upon which if a vessel impinges, or even touches, she will be endangered or lost. The Service has its headquarters at Calcutta; it consists entirely of Europeans who devote their lives to studying the navigable channels, which vary from season to season, and of which they must possess the most exact knowledge. Improvements and modifications in its organization have been made according to the circumstances of the time, and the pilots are, as a rule, very able and competent men.

The position of the Madras port does not afford much room for harbour works. An important pier has, however, been constructed, with the advice and assistance of Mr. Parkes, the harbour engineer, and may be still further enlarged.

At Calcutta and Bombay there are dockyards belonging to the State, not indeed sufficient for any considerable naval purposes, but adapted to execute some work for ships of war, to repair vessels of the Indian Marine, and to perform many services for the mercantile shipping. At both these great ports there are several private dockyards.

At Bombay, a wet dock has been constructed to accommodate

thirty vessels of 21 feet draught, having an area of 30 acres, with stone revetted sides, with locks and gates of the best and strongest description, and with powerful hydraulic cranes. Adjoining this are quays, landing-places, warehouses and every sort of accommodation for vast quantities of merchandise. The cost of the dock has amounted to ¾ million sterling; the outlay for the subsidiary works being in addition to this. The dock itself is excellent both in design and execution, and with it the name of the engineer-in-chief, Thomas Ormiston, will be always associated. The foundation stone was laid by the Prince of Wales in November 1875, and in honour of that auspicious event was called "The Prince's dock." There were other private docks and interests, adjoining the Prince's dock. These have been purchased on behalf of the public, and the whole foreshore of the harbour has been placed under a trust consisting of Port Commissioners, appointed or elected in conformity with an Act of the legislature. The capital outlay amounts to 4¼ millions sterling on the extensive property thus created, which consists partly of lands laboriously reclaimed from the sea in the harbour, to the advantage of sanitation as well as of commerce. The interest on this outlay, which is guaranteed by the State, will be defrayed from the dues levied on the trade, and from the rents for the extensive accommodation provided ashore. These arrangements will, it is hoped, be found worthy of a seaport which, in respect of size, convenience and geographical situation, is one of the finest in the world.

The Karachi harbour possesses a commanding situation geographically, and must always be of much importance. If it had only something of the expansiveness of Bombay, where ships can ride and swing, it would soon rise to a high rank among harbours. Many improvements have been devised with the advice of Mr. Parkes, the harbour engineer. Unfortunately the deep-water portion of the harbour is limited, there is something of a bar at the mouth, and incessant dredging is necessary. A breakwater has been constructed; improved dredging machinery has been provided; a commodious pier has been undertaken; and an efficient staff of harbour engineers is maintained.

Port dues are levied at all the ports, and though complaints are still made occasionally by those concerned, still efforts are made to keep these dues as low as may be consistent with the demands of the service of the ports.

A general examination, by the orders of the Government of India, of the harbours, has been carried on by Mr. Walker, the harbour engineer. A further examination in detail has been made of the lesser harbours, of which many are little more than open roadsteads. The harbours of Karwar and of Goa or Marmagaon, however, are sheltered by headlands, and may be termed real harbours for a limited number of ships with deep draught. On the west coast, south of Bombay, there are several small harbours properly sheltered with tolerable accommodation for a very few large vessels. By marine surveys, by lighting and other local arrangements, the Government is endeavouring to make the most of these natural advantages. The Karwar harbour promised to become very important, if the railway had been made from thence to the southern Deccan. Its importance will, however, be transferred to Marmagaon, now that, with the co-operation of the British and Portuguese Governments, the railway from the coast to the southern Deccan is to start from Goa.

Much progress has been made in lighting the principal points in the coasts, for the assistance of mariners at night. Excellent lighthouses are provided at Bombay, Aden, Karachi, Madras, the Sandheads at the mouth of the Hûghli, and on the salient points of the Burmese coast. Lesser lights have been established at numerous points on both the eastern and western shores. A lighthouse is still grievously needed at Cape Guardafui on the extreme north-east promontory of the African coast, near the island of Socotra, south of Aden. In the vicinity of this fatal headland, several ships are wrecked yearly, some of which might be saved if a light were established there.

CHAPTER XXV.

THE ARMY.

Constitution of the armies in India—The European soldier—Marked improvement of his condition—Short service system—Former local European army—Strength of European garrison in India—The Volunteer movement —The Native army—Basis of its fidelity—Three Native armies, according to the three Presidencies—Castes and tribes among the Native soldiery—Families of Native soldiery in their quarters—Physique and conduct of the Native army—Enlistment of the Native soldier—His pay and allowances—Recent difficulty in obtaining recruits—Officering of the Native army—Native officers—Regular and irregular systems—European officers—The staff corps—The Native cavalry—The ordnance department—The commissariat—The transport service—Audit and account—Established strength of military forces.

THOUGH the army of India, as a combined military force, can, for war, be worked as one engine, or wielded as one force under the orders of the Government of India, yet there still are, technically and departmentally, three armies, namely, the Bengal army, directly under the Viceroy and Governor-General in Council, the Madras army under the Government of Madras, and the Bombay army under the Government of Bombay. The Governments of Madras and Bombay and their respective armies are subordinate to the Government of India. The Native portion of each of these armies is kept quite separate, and much importance is attached to this separation. The European portion consists of certain Regiments of the British army, which are attached temporarily to the establishment of each of the Indian armies and are periodically relieved. The European batteries and regiments are interchangeable from the establishment of one army to that of another.

As the European soldier in India is the mainstay of the State, his condition has always been an important matter, engaging the solicitude of the Government. The magnitude of the subject has fully doubled since the augmentation of the European forces consequent on the war of the mutinies in 1857.

A survey of the present condition of the European soldier in India will afford grounds of satisfaction and thankfulness to those who are able to take a retrospect of his former condition. Within the memory of living men, his barracks were wanting in spaciousness and in ventilation, and his surroundings were at most stations insanitary. His married quarters were utterly unlike English homes. He was usually unlettered, his reasonable amusements were few, his temptations to vice many, and his habits but too often tended to intemperance. He worked out his time of Indian service in the hottest plains without respite in the cooler hills, and if sent by medical advice to a sanitarium, he was subjected to the hardships of a toilsome journey.

Nowadays, his lofty and commodious barracks are, with the exception of those at a very few stations, constructed so as to afford abundance of air inside and to receive complete ventilation from the outside, so as to admit the cheerfulness of light and yet at will to be shaded from the sun's glare. The appliances for bathing and for healthy recreation are complete. Workshops and garden-plots are provided for those men whose tastes are mechanical or horticultural. Industrial pursuits are encouraged and exhibitions are held for the display of soldiers' workmanship. Brightly lighted buildings are provided for libraries, for reading-rooms, and for playing games of skill, in order to draw men away from taverns and other places of low amusement, and to enable them to spend the long evenings reasonably and happily. These reading-rooms are crowded during the leisure hours. The schools both for adults and for children are superintended by certificated teachers. The improved education of the men is evinced by the little pictures, the prints, the photographs and the small bookshelves which they hang round their cots in the barracks. The quarters for the families of the married soldiers represent all the cleanliness, homeliness and comfort of the best English cottages. The drainage around all the barracks is much developed. At some of the stations there are parks and spacious pleasure gardens close at hand, to which the men and their families may resort. Sanitaria, in exhilarating and invigorating altitudes, are provided at easy distances, to which the sick soldiers may be quickly and comfortably conveyed. Barracks are built at selected places in the Himalayas, in the Nilgiri mountains and on plateaux enjoying a favourable climate, to which every European regiment may be sent in its turn for serving a portion of the time to be spent by it in India. Large numbers of the men deposit money in the regimental savings-banks in India, or remit it to their families in the United Kingdom. The sum of the deposits in India amounts to £180,000, and of the annual remittances to £142,000.

The welfare of the orphans of European soldiers is provided for in the Lawrence Asylums at Kusowli, Utakamand and Abu, named after their munificent founder, Henry Lawrence, and partly supported by the State.

The defects of the former barracks were, want of plinth elevation in ground, whence malaria was much exhaled during certain seasons of the year; imperfect ventilation and insufficient allowance of air in cubic feet per head; ill-arranged drainage in the immediate vicinity of the buildings. An improved design of barracks was introduced in the time of Sir Charles Napier before the war of the mutinies. After that war, the augmentation of the European forces brought the question of barrack accommodation into fresh prominence. The matter was taken up earnestly by Lord Lawrence when Governor-General, the Commander-in-Chief being Lord Strathnairn, and then Lord Sandhurst, and designs for barracks of the best possible kind were approved. The buildings were to be double-storied, in order that the men might have the benefit of sleeping upstairs out of the reach of exhalations during the close season and in a cooler atmosphere during the hot; whereas all the old barracks were single-storied. A further impulse to the work was given by Lord Napier of Magdala when Commander-in-Chief. Many of the barracks at different stations in all parts of the empire have been constructed on these improved designs. Neither pains nor expense have been spared by the Government to make the buildings everything that could be desired. As structures, they are probably equalled by few barracks in any country in the world, and not surpassed anywhere. They afford testimony to the care bestowed by the Government on the welfare of its European soldiers, and they must doubtless conduce to the health of the troops. They are expensive unavoidably; it costs not less than £150,000 to thus house and accommodate a battalion. The expense, however, will hardly be grudged if the welfare of the European soldier is thereby secured. The buildings are deemed spacious and commodious by competent judges; though many authorities still doubt the necessity of having them double-storied, in some stations at least; and hopes have been expressed to the effect that some economy may be introduced into future buildings of this description.

Besides the several sanitaria in the Himalayas, the Nilgiris and other hills, for those sick soldiers who may be restored to health by a brief sojourn in a cool climate without being sent back to England, there are some places in the Himalayas where whole battalions are stationed so as to have the benefit of the mountain air; such places are Sabathu, Dagshai near Simla, Chakrata near Massuri, Ranikhet in Kumaon, and Marri near Hazara in the Panjab. Similar accommodation has to some extent been provided near Utakamand in the Nilgiris. However excellent this plan may be in itself, it ought not to be carried too far, because the presence of most of the troops is required in the plains and close to the great centres of Native life, where a spark may produce a flame, politically, which if not stamped out forcefully at once, may blaze up into a conflagration. It was the want on the spot of the European troops, who were only a few marches off, that gave the mutinies of the Native troops in 1857 a chance of spreading so rapidly. But this consideration, like so many other military considerations, is greatly affected by the completion of railway communication.

There is in India the same sort of average of military crime as in other countries. The highest Indian military authorities ascribe to drink much of the crime which exists. If the soldiers only abstained from drinking, they would be comparatively free from crime and from military offences. During the last generation drunkenness was notoriously common; of late years it has been happily diminished. Malt liquor has been largely substituted for spirits, the facilities for obtaining country-made spirits have been curtailed. The old-fashioned rules have been modified whereby spirits were served out in a manner which according to the light of former days was deemed beneficial, but which really offered temptations to insobriety. Still, the efforts of the authorities to place distilleries and liquor shops beyond the reach of the soldiers are often unsuccessful, and the subject causes constant anxiety. Meanwhile, associations for temperance, or total abstinence, are formed among the soldiery, and have several thousand members. Doubtless sobriety will increase *pari passu* with the improvements in the education and in the moral status of the men.

Much discrimination is exercised by the medical authorities in invaliding and sending home to England all soldiers who have become physically unfitted for efficient service in the Indian climate. When these men have been eliminated, the health of the soldiery may be pronounced good on the whole, and at some stations very satisfactory. There is, however, one grave drawback, namely, that of contagious disease. The legislature has accorded ample powers, and the local authorities have put forth persistent efforts, for the prevention of this plague. The examination of infected persons has been carried out, and lock hospitals for their cure have been established everywhere. At Calcutta especially, and at some other places, much success has been achieved. But at most stations the success has been only partial, and at many stations miserably imperfect. It is melancholy to reflect that out of the total European force some thousands are on any given day to be found temporarily disabled from this disease which is preventible, and therefore ought not to exist. Many thousands more, during the course of their Indian service, suffer sooner or later from this complaint, which must more or less impair or even undermine their constitutions. The local authorities are constantly attending to this painful subject, and if they shall prove successful, they will achieve a result than which no greater boon could be conferred on the European soldiers in India. If the Government shall continue seriously to address itself to the task of prevention, full success must follow. But there are many elements of opposition in cases of this sort, both direct and indirect, and for the overcoming of these, firmness and resolution as well as patience and considerateness are requisite.

The consequences of the "short service" system, in introducing men of immature strength and physique into the ranks, are beginning to be felt in India. Still, the regiments which arrive from England are, with some exceptions, composed of fine material. Complaints are, however, made of the difficulty in obtaining experienced non-commissioned officers. And the objection to sending so many time-expired men back to England, just when they are becoming useful in India, is clearly perceived.

There was once a considerable force of European cavalry, artillery and infantry belonging to the East India Company, which was, in 1859, amalgamated with the Royal Army. This system had some advantage, as drawing upon additional recruiting grounds in England. The transactions arising out of the amalgamation led to questions between the Government and the men, which were followed by some strange events whereof the full history has not yet been written. The men considered themselves aggrieved by the terms of the amalgamation; they were technically in the wrong, but there were circumstances which might make them think that they were in the right. They then committed acts of dangerous insubordination in different parts of the country. There was, for a time, some peril to the empire, which was averted by the firmness, wisdom and considerateness of the Government at that time. The warnings of this experience are doubtless remembered whenever the idea of restoring a local European army is resuscitated.

The cost of the European army becomes heavier than ever, owing to improved pay, armament, equipment, professional instruction and other measures for improving the condition of the soldier. Consequently many authorities are induced to reflect whether the present European garrison of the country, 66,000 officers and men, can be safely lessened. But the conclusion almost universally arrived at is—that it cannot. The force is judiciously disposed so as to hold all the strategic points, to dominate all the important stations and to command all the main lines of communication; there is reasonable hope of its proving sufficient as a garrison in ordinary times; but more than this cannot prudently be said.

Volunteering in India is restricted to Europeans and East Indians; among them it flourishes as a permanent institution. There are corps of volunteers at the three Presidency cities, and in most of the principal towns and stations in the interior of the empire. The men in the service of the several railway companies form themselves into volunteer corps. The rules, conditions and privileges of volunteering are prescribed by the Government of India after the model of those in the Volunteer army of the United Kingdom. The corps are inspected periodically by military authority, rifle-shooting is much encouraged, associations for this purpose are formed, and a fair degree of soldierly efficiency is attained. The detached corps in the interior of the country are often weak numerically, but the total strength of the volunteers in India may be computed at five battalions, and this constitutes some addition to the European garrison of the country. The value of the volunteer movement is to be estimated not only by the numbers it may produce in time of peace, but by the moral effect it has upon the European civil community in India, teaching them to be self-reliant in respect of armed defence, and imparting to them that confident bearing which arises from discipline and training, and which tends to overawe the evil-disposed when troubles threaten. Should they be at any moment called upon, the volunteers are able to occupy many of the points where British interests are centred, and to defend the places where they reside. If they had been enrolled before the disturbances of 1857 they would have been of the utmost use in the capital cities at that time. In the event of a general disturbance arising, their present numbers would increase, their spirit would rise high, and they would render much service to their country.

Next after the European army, the Native army is a main stay of the State, because British soldiers are necessarily few and costly. The obligation of maintaining a force of 66,000 British soldiers, in so distant a country as India, causes a severe drain on the warlike resources of the United Kingdom, and would indeed tax heavily the means of any military power in the world. It would be difficult to provide the men for any large augmentation of the European garrison in India; and even if the men were found, the country could not bear the expense of maintaining them. The importance of the European soldier is equalled only by his costliness. Not only in his maintenance, ordinarily three times, perhaps even four times, as expensive as that of the Native soldier; but his lodging and accommodation in an eastern or tropical climate demand a vast expense. His transport, also, to and from India by sea, though easy for the maritime power of England, involves a large outlay chargeable to India. On the other hand, the Native soldier is maintained in comparative cheapness. From his pay he provides himself with food; and no rations for him have ordinarily to be supplied by the State. More especially he needs no expensive barracks; a small allowance is made to him to help in defraying the cost of his hut. Native soldiers, or Sepoys, have been easily procurable in any number that might be required. The recent difficulty in obtaining recruits will prove to be transient. However thrifty the Government may be respecting the number of its Native soldiers, still that number must be considerable. There are only 130,000 Native soldiers belonging to British India, and of them some are stationed in the Native States. These, together with the European soldiers, make up a force of 196,000, officers and men, which may be regarded as a moderate strength for an area and a population so great.

The fact of the garrison not exceeding 196,000 men is eminently creditable to the peaceful and loyal character of the people at large. Nevertheless, the Natives are not wholly docile, but comprise some turbulent, even warlike, elements. The country must be garrisoned in a competent manner and the dominant points in it must be held. Small insurrections here and there from time to time are to be apprehended even during peace, and during political or military disturbance are sure to spring up in divers directions. Indeed, whenever anything occurs to shake the wonderful fabric of physical and moral power combined, which constitutes British dominion, and such things do occur sometimes, then disturbers arise in multitudes, none can say whence or in what manner, like insects on a hot day, or like the fabled warriors from the ground sown with dragons' teeth. At such a moment everything depends on the military potency of the Government to withstand or resist the gathering and thickening troubles. If the Government can then stand erect and masterful, it restrains the elements of mischief as a mighty dyke holds back the torrents rushing to form a united volume of flood. If it cannot so stand, then a cataclysm ensues, as when the surging waters overtop the dykes and sweep in an uncontrollable inundation over the land. Such an apprehension is not fanciful, but is derived from positive experience, which proves that such events have happened, and indicates how they might happen again. Now, although the European soldiery form the vertebra of the body politic and also supply the nervous force, still they are not and cannot be sufficiently numerous to perform all the functions of the system, and to do all the work of the limbs. If such duty were imposed upon them, their energies would be frittered away in operations which could be carried out as well, or even better, by Native agency. The Native soldiery being in the land of their birth, can render service under climatic conditions which would cause great mortality among the European soldiery, if encountered by them.

Therefore a considerable Native army must ever be employed as an indispensable condition for the preservation of British rule. For financial reasons it is essential to reduce the military forces to a minimum, down indeed to the very verge of safety. But if from economic though misguided zeal that limit were to be overpassed, then there would be risk of the whole edifice toppling over, or tottering to its fall.

On the other hand, there has been an equally great danger in maintaining too large a Native army. It was the overgrowth of this army which in part caused the mutinies of 1857 and the war which ensued. There were, doubtless, concomitant causes; the soldiery had some grievances which were real though exaggerated by imagination. The men had been drawn too largely from the Brahmins of Northern India, a class somewhat disposed to fan any flame of excitement. Various political circumstances had rendered many people eager to snatch any opportunity of striking at British domination. Still, one cause was this, that the soldiery had acquired a sense of power, a consciousness that they held the scales to determine whether British authority should be vindicated, or for a time be humbled. They held wholly or partly many of the treasuries, fortresses and arsenals. At many of the principal stations they had a clear superiority of physical force over any Europeans that could be brought into action. They could at will seize the treasure amassed under their eyes, and much also of the *matériel* of war. Swayed by all these temptations, the ring-leaders gave the rein to the ambition, the fanaticism, the national sentiments, which are still unextinguished in the Native breast. The men followed in that wild, unthinking and excited way, which is common to Orientals. In short, the war of the mutinies occurred largely, though not entirely, because the Native army was too strong relatively to the European forces in the country. Here, then, was the lesson to be taken to heart by the British Government. If the Native army is ever raised to a strength overmastering the European forces in the country, then no perfection of military system, no possible management, however equitable and considerate, will secure its fidelity. It will turn and rend its masters, who will find that in organizing it at excessive strength they have only created a Frankenstein for themselves. Let the due proportion between the European and Native forces be preserved. Let the Native soldiery see that the European soldiery have the superiority at the principal treasuries, arsenals, fortresses, military positions and strategic points. Then the Native army, if well treated, organized and managed, will be faithful and trustworthy up to a certain point, and will prove an excellent instrument in British hands for doing essential work which could not be done otherwise.

There is, however, a point at which, even under these conditions, the Native army cannot be trusted. The loyalty and fidelity of the Native soldiery are of a type different from that presented by the same qualities in the European soldiery. With the Native soldiery these qualities mean attachment to a good and kind master, an anxiety to serve him well, because he can reward and punish, a belief in his capacity to maintain the system under which pay and promotion are guaranteed during the active time of life, and pension during the declining years. There is a thought that while they are under his standards, far away from their crops and cottages, he keeps their relatives in safety, and their homesteads in peace. There is also a remembrance of his victories and successes in the past, with a trust that the same fortune will prove constant to him in the future. All this is implied, indeed, but, as a rule, nothing more. There are not included the patriotism, the pride of race, the feeling of nationality, and the personal attachment between the State and its defenders, which, in addition to the sentiments above described, animate the European soldiery. Consequently, if the British Government should ever seem to stagger under the shock of any kind of adversity, the fidelity of the Native army must necessarily be dubious. That army cannot possibly have the same motives as the English troops for fighting to the bitter end, and standing faithful to the utter extremity. The faith of the Native soldier in the star of British fortune is too strong and clear to be easily dimmed. But if that faith were to become weakened or obscured, some catastrophe would ensue. Here, then, is one cogent reason, among many others, why the British Government must preserve its weight and influence intact.

Profiting by experience, the British Government has arranged with exactitude the due proportion between the European and the Native armies. Since 1857 the strength of the Europeans has been raised and of the Natives diminished; so that the Natives are now not more than two to one of the Europeans. In other words, out of the total force, one-third is European and two-thirds are Native. Moreover, the forts and arsenals, the chief strategic points, and some of the principal treasuries, are held partly or wholly by Europeans. At every large military station in the empire there are enough Europeans to hold their own, even in the event of a mutiny. On the other hand, there is no semblance of distrust towards the Native troops, who take a share in guarding and garrisoning the country, having many honourable and important duties confided to them. No actual guarantee can be given as against mutiny or any other calamity;

but many effective precautions have been adopted. It would not be expedient to employ more than two Natives to one European soldier; but it would not in the opinion of many authorities be practicable to carry on the public service with less. The question whether any numerical reduction in the Native army could be prudently made, has been recently much discussed. Some eminent authorities apparently consider that a moderate reduction is possible. But any reduction would be seriously deprecated by many whose views on military and political subjects command attention.

Another arrangement, relating to the efficiency as well as the fidelity of the Native troops, is their division into three armies, namely those of the Presidencies of Bengal, Madras and Bombay respectively. The soldiers of the three armies belong to various religions, and are dissimilar in caste, in tribal associations, and in language. Though they may all know the Urdu or Hindostani tongue enough for practical purposes, as a lingua franca, yet their several vernacular languages are quite different. As their homes are in most cases hundreds of miles, and in some cases thousands of miles apart, the differences between them amount to varieties in nationality. Each army is under its own Commander-in-Chief, and has distinct headquarters, organization, and traditions of its own; so that the three form definite entities. Each army ordinarily serves in its own Presidency or division of the empire, and in territories comparatively near the homes of the men. It is, however, liable to serve, and parts of it are frequently serving, in other parts of the country, and in other Presidencies. This arrangement, while in nowise affecting the uses of the army for imperial purposes, does tend to prevent combination for any evil ends. It did to some extent check in 1857 the course of the mutinies, when they were spreading like wildfire in the prairies. Undue reliance must not, however, be placed upon it, as being alone adequate to prevent unlawful coalition. It opens every recruiting-ground in the country, and enables the State to draw men from every tribe. It also renders the military service popular, and avoids the discontent which would arise if men had permanently to serve in districts remote from their homes. Men from northern India will indeed accept service in the Bombay Presidency and in the Deccan. Native soldiers from all parts of India will willingly go, for a short tour of service or for a campaign, to any portion of the globe. But a battalion of Panjabis would be miserable if permanently quartered in southern India, or a battalion of Madrassis in the Panjab, or a battalion of Bombay Mahrattas in Bengal proper.

The Commander-in-Chief of each of the three Native armies appoints the officers, European and Native; and upon his supervision the tone and discipline of the service largely depend. It is essential to keep intact the status and dignity of his high office.

Each army is composed of various castes, inhabiting territories some distance apart. Though the flower of the Bengal army is derived from the Panjab, of the Bombay army from the western coast, of the Madras army from the eastern coast, still many other tribes are intermingled in every regiment. This arrangement is a precaution against evil combination. Overmuch dependence must not be placed upon it as a safeguard, inasmuch as community of discontent, from any cause, may produce universality of disaffection among classes otherwise diverse. Still, neglect of this precaution would add to the chances of mischief. One of the collateral causes of the mutiny in 1857 was the fact that in the Bengal army too large a proportion consisted of Brahmins from Oudh, belonging to a Hindu caste, which was more likely than any other to become susceptible of headstrong impulse, and which dwelt in a province where recent political events had inevitably provoked hostile intrigues. The Brahmin soldiery having mutinied in a mass, the authorities ceased to enlist men in Oudh or in Hindostan, but they were nearly falling into an opposite extreme almost equally dangerous, for they enlisted too large a proportion from the

Panjab, a province which furnished so many gallant and faithful soldiers during the crisis of the mutiny. But the Panjabis, though admirable servants of a power which was seen to be really the master over them, and though differing in temper from the men of Hindostan and of Oudh whom they despised, were still imbued with many sentiments of race, of birthplace, of nationality, and even of sectarian religion. They would soon have begun to think whether they were not the restorers and upholders of British authority, and whether in that case they might not advantageously assert their own position. There was really more peril on this score in 1858 and 1859 than was perhaps realised at the moment. It was averted chiefly by the prudent conduct of the Local Government of the Panjab. The risk was subsequently obviated by a judicious intermixture of other tribes; and the only use of recalling the circumstance now, is to shew how many pitfalls lie in the path of British administrators in the East.

There are many castes and tribes in the empire which furnish fighting men of good quality. The races capable of supplying the best soldiers are the Sikhs of the Panjab, the Gorkhas from the valleys near Nepal, the Muhammadan Pathans of the north-west frontier, the Jats of the country round Delhi and Agra, the Mahrattas of the Western Ghat mountains, and the Rajputs of various provinces. In former days the Telugus of the eastern coast would have been added to this list, but they are less prominent in the present time. The name of the Brahmins of Oudh will readily suggest itself, but, since the events of 1857, they have forfeited the place they once held in military estimation. The best cavalry troopers, ready-made horsemen, used to the saddle from their youth, are obtained from the Muhammadan tribes in the country between Delhi and the Satlej. Good horsemen are also to be procured from among the Sikhs and the Mahrattas.

A further matter which concerns the fidelity and efficiency of Native troops, is the practice which partially prevails whereby the men are permitted to have their families, wives, children and other relatives, with them in their huts in the ordinary cantonments. This is in vogue, almost universally in the Madras army, to a considerable extent in the Bombay army, and but little, indeed hardly at all, in the Bengal army. It causes the military stations to be filled with non-combatants, encumbers the line of march from one cantonment to another in time of peace, and causes some trouble when the families are left behind in consequence of the troops proceeding on war service. But it does tend, on the other hand, to render the men steady and quiet, indisposed to embark on any mischievous course, and disinclined to revolt against authority. The Madras officers probably lay great stress on this practice, as having helped to save the men from catching the infection of the mutiny in 1857. Positive trust ought not, however, to be reposed upon this as a preservative, for experience has shewn that in some instances the men were but too near being led into mischief, notwithstanding the presence of their families.

In physique the troops of the Bengal army are fine men, of good stature and martial bearing, not so broad, thickset and solid as British troops, but they have a height, in inches, not inferior to any troops anywhere. They are better suited than other Native troops for work in which sheer weight and strength are needed, and in which the rigours of cold have to be endured. The Bombay soldiers are shorter and smaller, though hardy and active men, bred for the most part in the hills, and full of staying power in rough marching. The Madras soldiers are slighter still, but steady little men, with light frames and much endurance; they are accustomed, however, to more nutritious food than their comrades in the other armies.

In discipline, training and conduct, the men of all three armies are much the same. Their behaviour in quarters is uniformly excellent everywhere; their demeanour is most orderly; sobriety generally prevails; drunkenness and insubordination are rare; military offences are slight and few. It is to be borne in mind that the Bengal army is drawn from the most martial and the physically strongest tribes in the empire, and constitutes more than one-half of the total Native forces. Still it is important not to let the other two armies feel any sense of inferiority, or the Bengal army regard itself as occupying a superior position and as indispensable to the State; but to apportion the responsibilities of service, and the opportunities of distinction, to each army, according to its size and capacity, and so far as circumstances may permit.

In some cardinal respects the Native army differs from the armies of European powers. There is nothing in the shape of conscription; the enlistment is voluntary, and heretofore the service has been sought for as a valued profession. There has hitherto been no such thing as short service; on the contrary, the enlistment is for a long period. The man generally regards the service as a lifelong provision, which is to afford him pay throughout the best years of his life and pension afterwards. Dismissal from the service is usually dreaded as a punishment, and as the forfeiture of much that is valuable; the certainty that such dismissal will not be ordered without enquiry or trial, is respected as a safeguard. Some Native soldiers have, indeed, at all times been found to take their discharge voluntarily, but until recent years such withdrawal has not been common. In these respects the relation between the British Government and the Native soldiery has been peculiarly happy. The furlough regulations also add to the comfort and contentment of the troops, whereby the men are permitted periodically to revisit their homes and their families, if the families are not with them in cantonments. In the early days of British rule military service was very popular, and indeed much prized. Lands had everywhere fallen out of cultivation, owing to war or devastation, and agricultural labour was little in demand. Revolutions had thrown out of employ numbers of men unaccustomed to industrial pursuits, or disused from such pursuits by martial avocations. The labour markets were depressed, trade was stagnant, wages were low. The Government fixed the pay of the Native soldier at what was then thought a liberal, perhaps a handsome, rate, as a wage better than that which the soldier class could otherwise obtain.

This military wage has, however, during the lapse of time become less and less favourable as compared with the wages of civil life, since all available hands have, during a peace of more than two generations, been drawn off to the reviving or expanding cultivation, the brisk labour markets, the rising industries, the growing trade. From time to time slight improvements have been made in the wage, additional allowances and advantages have been conceded, so that the State might still command a part at least of the flower of the population for its armies. Again, the value of the wage to the recipient must largely depend on the price of food-grains. In all parts of the country the price becomes exceptionally dear during the periodically recurring drought, and in many parts of the country within the last fifteen years a dearness has set in which threatens to be permanent. Therefore the Government, assuming the military wage to be regulated in some degree by its relation to the prices of food, allows compensation to the soldiery whenever that price is dearer than certain declared rates; though no reduction whatever is ever made if the cost of the Native soldier's ration falls below the normal rate. In time of drought or scarcity, the amount thus allowed to the soldiery is considerable. Nevertheless, the conviction is gaining ground that the advantages of the military service are becoming less and less attractive to the petty yeomanry and to the better class of labourers. Recruits have of late been offering themselves in less abundance; whereas formerly there used to be some considerable competition, and young men used to remain in attendance on the regiments, waiting for vacancies. Within the last year or so there has been an actual difficulty in obtaining recruits in sufficient numbers for the large requirements of the army during the recent campaign, a phenomenon observed for the first time in British India. The difficulty may partly arise from the prospects of extraordinary hardships during the snows and frosts of the winter among the northern mountains, and may, it is to be hoped, be mitigated or disappear hereafter.

During recent years, also, the number of those Native soldiers who voluntarily take their discharge is worthy of note. Such men are often in the prime of life, and there is doubt as to what becomes of them after they leave the army; they mostly return to civil occupations, some perhaps continue their military life in the service of the Native States.

Another peculiarity in the Native army is this, that the Native commissioned officers have grades corresponding, though under Oriental names, as nearly as possible with the European grades, receive pay quite equal relatively in Native society to the pay of English officers, and yet rise entirely, or almost entirely, from the ranks, partly by selection, but chiefly by seniority. According to the old arrangement, there was in each regular regiment, besides the Native commissioned officers, a complete set of European officers. Thus if the Native officers were not of a superior stamp, still there were European officers to enforce strictness and precision in the training, and to lead the way in action. In the Panjab and elsewhere irregular regiments, in contradistinction to the regular regiments above mentioned, were formed from martial races, with a complement of Native officers of chosen merit; and with a very limited number of European officers, also of selected ability. When tried on service or in action, the irregular regiments did at least as well as the regular regiments; it was thought sometimes that they did even better. Certainly, abler Native troops have never been seen in the empire than some of these irregular regiments. The regular system was subsequently held to be open to objection, as providing a duplicate set of commissioned officers, failing to raise the Native officers morally, depriving them of the sense of responsibilities which were really devolved on the European officers, affording inadequate employment to the European officers whose work was shared with the Native officers, and causing unnecessary expense to the State. The European officers were reduced to a number sufficient, as it was believed, to lead the regiment in action, leaving more of the ordinary regimental duty than heretofore to be performed by the Native officers, in the expectation that in the appointment of Native officers selection would be exercised more than formerly. The three Native armies are now organized on this principle, which is approved more in the Bengal Presidency than in Bombay, while it is disapproved by many in Madras. The change has given birth to much controversy everywhere, which is not yet concluded. Despite many differences and shades of opinion, it will probably be conceded at least that, so far as can be judged from appearance and from movements or manœuvres on parade, the troops appear to as much advantage under the new system as under the old; while many will affirm that the Bengal troops are better than they ever were. On active service, too, the Bengal troops will be probably held to have generally done well, with some exceptions, which occur under the new system, as they occurred under the old. Apprehensions are felt by many authorities regarding the effects of the new system with the Madras and Bombay armies in actual action. It seems, however, to be considered by the majority of military authorities in the empire that there is danger lest the complement of European officers should be too small to lead the regiment in action, and to replace casualties among the leaders who are but too likely to fall while leading; that a sufficient number of such European officers must be allowed, which should be not less than nine (combatant) to a regiment, and that it is practically difficult to get able Native officers either from the ranks or from the upper classes of Native society direct.

It is held by some high authorities that more attention should be given than heretofore to the selecting of really competent men to be Native commissioned officers, and to opening a field to them for honourable distinction. As yet the British system has not been quite successful in developing military talent among the Native officers as a whole, although many excellent men individually have been produced.

A change has also been made in the manner of appointing European officers to the Native army. Formerly officers were appointed to this army direct from England and they rose in the service partly by merit, but largely by seniority. Nowadays every officer first belongs to the British army, and serves with a British regiment, in order that he may have the best kind of military training. Then, if so minded, he may within a certain limited time volunteer for one or other of the Indian staff corps, namely the three staff corps of Bengal, Madras and Bombay respectively. After passing the prescribed examination tests for entrance and promotion, he is admitted to the staff corps, which comprises all sorts of military employment, with Native regiments or on the Army garrison and administrative staff, and some sorts of political, civil employments. Thus a European officer, in the Indian Staff Corps, is in some sense one who has obtained his position by special preparation and qualification, has passed certain examinations, and is receiving somewhat more emolument than he could receive with a British regiment. The Commanding officers of the Native regiments are being generally selected for command rather than rising to it by seniority. On the whole, it will generally be admitted that the status and acquirements of the European officers of the Native army have been raised during recent years.

The three staff corps, above mentioned, supply the European officers not only for the Native army, but also for that share in the general staff of the forces which is allotted to the Indian service, while the other share pertains to the English service, and for many branches of military administration. They also contribute many officers to the political or diplomatic service and some to various branches of civil employ. The constitution of these staff corps has been condemned by many as producing an undue proportion of field officers whose promotion is regulated by time, and whose rank thus becomes too high for the regimental duties they have to perform.

The foregoing description, which has related primarily to the Native infantry, is generally applicable to the Native cavalry, where also the change from the old to the new system has taken place. This change has involved a complete alteration of the system of supplying the horses. By the old or regular system, the horses were furnished by the Government as they are to European regiments. But there were always some irregular regiments where the horses belonged to the men; the pay being fixed so as to enable the horsemen to combine among themselves and to form funds for providing the horses. Some of the Native officers were allowed to bring their own men and their own horses, and thus to become influential and enjoy a certain status. Some of the regiments thus constituted have done excellent service in war, and have produced really able Native officers. All regiments, except those of the Madras Presidency, are now horsed on this principle. The large studs for horse-breeding which the Government used to maintain in northern India have been for the most part abandoned. Many Indian-bred horses are still obtained in the market for military purposes, and the Government imports stallions to assist the Native breeders in improving their stock. The Bengal cavalry is mounted chiefly with horses purchased at the horse-shows and fairs in northern India. The remounts for the Native cavalry of Madras and Bombay are largely obtained from the Persian Gulf through the Bombay market. Many of the horses of larger build, required for the purchases by the Government, are obtained from Australia through the markets of Calcutta and Madras. On the whole, a large portion of the horses in the armies of India are of Australian and Persian breeds; the Arabian horses being ridden by the officers only, and being much more scarce nowadays than formerly. The indigenous breeds of horses, renowned of old within India itself at least, have greatly declined within the last two generations throughout the empire; some of them, once famed, have almost died out; some remain and are fostered indirectly by the State, which does what little it can to preserve this local resource. But most of the horses, now seen both in military and civil employment, are of foreign extraction. A few of the old studs in northern India are, however, still maintained by the Government, under a superintendent of horse-breeding operations, and give a fair promise of success.

The Native artillery, once important in India before the war of the mutinies in 1857, was abolished after those events, with the exception of batteries on the north-western frontier, and some mountain batteries, where the guns are carried by mules, which are still manned by Native artillerymen. The artillery in India is now an integral portion of the Royal Artillery of the British service.

The question of forming a reserve for the Native army, after the English model, has been carefully considered. The scheme would probably be found quite practicable under certain conditions, that is to say, Native soldiers would enlist, to serve under the colours on full pay for a limited number of years and thereafter return to their homes on reduced pay, with a liability to be recalled to the standards whenever wanted. But they would expect the reduced pay to be ultimately converted to pension, that is, to be continued, perhaps with some reduction, without the liability of being called out when the time for such pension should arrive. There would, on the other hand, be some objections to such a scheme, inasmuch as many men, trained to the use of arms, would be living in villages remote from supervision. The scheme does not seem likely to be taken up at present, unless it be found possible to spare a considerable number of Native soldiers now serving with the colours. But, as just seen, there is, for the moment, rather a want of men to make up the proper complement. If the scheme were adopted in order to provide an additional military resource, besides the

Native forces now embodied, it would be open to objection on the score of expense.

The departments in India for the supply, equipment and armament of the forces, are maintained in a state of complete efficiency. Even on the gravest and most sudden emergencies there has never been any deficiency in these important respects.

The Ordnance department, though still very important, is not quite so essential as it once was to the safety of the empire. In former days, before the opening of the overland route, when the transmission of *matériel* from England to India occupied several months, the Indian empire would have been in danger if any gust or storm of events found it unsupplied. Consequently, the East India Company maintained in the country the resources on which the efficiency of its forces depended. Almost everything necessary for arming the troops was made on the spot. The guns, gun-carriages, harness, accoutrements, small-arms, ammunition and powder, were manufactured locally. The foundries for casting guns in iron, brass and bronze were on an extensive scale; the powder-factories were considerable, the arsenals were placed in central and commanding positions, the magazines were established at convenient places in all parts of the country. These local resources proved invaluable during the war of the mutinies, when the mutinous Native artillery carried so many guns away with them, and when the losses of small-arms from the same cause were greater still. Had the Government not possessed the means on the spot of repairing this grave damage, its position, already so serious, would have been still further imperilled. The necessity for these precautions was diminished by successive steps in improvement of communications, first by the opening of the overland route, then the introduction of the electric telegraph, then by the completion of the Suez Canal. With the application of science to the manufacture of warlike stores, it was found that some things made in India could be obtained better from England, and could, with the aid of the telegraph and the Suez

Canal steamers, be despatched to arrive in India within a very short time. The precision and elaboration required by modern processes were also beyond the means of the Indian factories. Hence the guns and the small-arms, of the Snider, Enfield and Martini-Henry patterns, are now made in England; and the Indian foundries have been closed. In India, however, there are still made the gun-carriages, the harness, the accoutrements, the small-arms' ammunition and the gunpowder; thus the factories are busy and resourceful as ever. The harness-making has a special interest; the work is durable and well-turned-out, at a large saving of cost as compared with English-made harness, by reason of the quality of the indigenous leather and the cheapness of Native skilled labour. It is carried on at Cawnpore, in the mid-valley of the Ganges. The arsenals and magazines are kept fully stored; and the Ordnance department is managed by officers of scientific training in their profession. Among the principal arsenals, there may be mentioned those of Fort William, at Calcutta, for Bengal; Allahabad and Agra for the North-western Provinces; Ferozepur, on the Satlej, for the Panjab; Bombay for western India; Secunderabad, near Hyderabad, in the Deccan, and Fort St. George at Madras, for southern India.

The clothing for the whole army, European and Native, has always been, and continues to be, made upon the spot, with material imported from England; the Native skilled labour proving both cheap and efficient.

The Commissariat department consists entirely of military men, it has no civilian element, its officers are commissioned officers of the army. In ordinary times its principal duty consists in providing the European soldiers with supplies, as the Native troops do not receive rations from the State. In time of war, however, it often has to supply the Native troops and the camp-followers also. For instance, during the recent Afghan war if there were 60,000 combatants in the field there must have been more than an equal number of non-combatants, so the Commissariat had to provide supplies at that time for at least 150,000 men. On the whole, the Indian Commissariat has always been very successful in this part of its duties. The supplies are good in time of peace, and never fail in the field when the troops are on active service. There has been a tendency to impose other duties on the Commissariat, more especially the department has been burdened with the transport for the army in time of war. If ever it has been open to blame, the real cause was this, that the department was required to attend to too many things simultaneously. In its proper work of supply, its officers are careful to ensure that the soldiers receive good rations, and that the State shall be protected from fraud on the part of contractors and others.

During the recent Afghan war, the difficulties regarding transport have been serious, and have been overcome only by a most liberal expenditure on the part of the State, added to the devoted exertions of its officers. The supply of baggage-camels has become exhausted; within India itself the mortality among these animals has been very great, and may appear at first sight to be inexplicable. Probably not less than 40,000 of them have died in military service between 1878 and 1880. But the camel, though famed for hardihood and endurance under some circumstances, proves under other circumstances to have a delicate constitution, which succumbs and perishes suddenly. With commercial caravans in Central Asia, where he is thoroughly cared for, all arrangements being subordinated to his welfare, and the movements being leisurely, with ample opportunities for feeding, he is most useful, and well deserves his name "the ship of the desert." But on a military line of march where the movements are urgent, and where many things have to be considered, he often fails to receive the care which is necessary to his existence; and without warning often stretches himself out on the sands to die. The long passes leading from India to Afghanistan afford no sustenance for man or beast, during many marches. To lay in supplies for the soldiers and camp-followers, and to carry the *matériel* of war, was a task which often taxed the resources of the authorities to the utmost. To supply or to carry forage for the transport animals was a task which sometimes proved to be beyond the power of the responsible officers. Besides cold and fatigue, there was often insufficiency of fodder to account for mortality among the animals. The same causes have operated during former wars and expeditions in the countries west of the Indus. In the first Afghan war the loss of camels was severe, as recorded in the military annals. The records of the Muhammadan invasions of India shew that then also the conquerors were embarrassed by mortality among their baggage-camels. When, however, the circumstances allow the military commanders to make the necessary provision for the well-being of the camels, these animals prove as valuable in war as they are in peace. In this respect it is important in the beginning of a war to inculcate on all concerned those practical lessons which, if overlooked at first, are learnt at last by painful experience, and after heavy cost of animal life and of money. Besides camels, there are other animals useful for military transport. Pack-bullocks and draught-bullocks are obtainable in many thousands from all parts of India, indeed in numbers practically unlimited. Recent experience has shewn that, in the mountainous regions trans-Indus, roads practicable for the light Indian carts can be rapidly made by the labour of the Native soldiery and the camp-followers. Pack-ponies are procurable in numbers considerable, though limited. Mules are not to be had in large numbers, but the few which are procured prove valuable. For the Transport department the desideratum is to train during peace a body of officers, commissioned and non-commissioned, who shall be versed in all that relates to the management of animals in military service. Such knowledge of itself constitutes a sort of profession, and can be thoroughly acquired only by those who devote themselves to it for many years, yet it is of great importance at the outbreak of war. On such occasions, loss and embarrassment ensue from the want of officers, of various grades, thus qualified. Such qualifications will not be fully possessed by the Commissariat department, unless its organization shall be altered. It were better to organize separately a Transport department in ordinary times, which could be rapidly enlarged on emergency arising.

Circumstances, relating to the estimates of the cost of the recent Afghan war, seem to have given rise to doubt regarding the completeness and sufficiency of the system of military accounts. The system, however, if well worked, ought to prove sufficient, inasmuch as it has been carefully and elaborately devised. It was begun under James Wilson, continued under Samuel Laing and Sir Charles Trevelyan, as finance ministers; Sir George Balfour was its president, and it was managed for some time by Sir George Kellner. Its organization was carefully considered by Mr. Foster of the English Treasury, who was specially deputed to India for the purpose. The several names above mentioned are eminent in finance generally, including that branch of it which relates to account keeping. The system of audit has been fully arranged in all its parts, for the whole empire as divided into the three Presidencies of Bengal, Madras and Bombay, and for each of the three armies which, as already explained, make up the Indian forces. In each Presidency the pay and allowances of the establishments are audited by the Pay Examiners of the respective Presidencies. The accounts of each of the administrative departments attached to the army of the Presidency, as relating to the commissariat, the ordnance, the medical services, the clothing and the like, are audited by departmental Examiners. The audit of all kinds is supervised by a Controller of military accounts for the army in each Presidency. Thus there are three Controllers with their respective staffs of Examiners for the whole empire, all working on a uniform system and method, and under the general supervision of a Military Accountant-General immediately under the Government of India. The accounts, as finally audited by the Military Accountant-General, are embodied in the finance accounts of the empire by the Controller and Auditor-General acting under the Financial branch of the Government. The keeping and auditing of the military accounts are thus managed upon a plan, which ensures local supervision in all the scattered provinces of a widely extended empire, and which is yet so far centralized as to admit of an effective control by the Government of India, through the high officers at its headquarters. For the determination of the expenditure to be incurred for military purposes, a budget in the most detailed form is prepared yearly, and is passed by the Government of India after the minutest scrutiny. According to the budget thus sanctioned, funds are allotted by the Civil Controller-General of accounts to the Military department. Then, the military accountants and auditors are guided by these allotments, and are answerable for regulating the disbursements thereby. In ordinary times, there is no difficulty in keeping the disbursements within the amounts allotted. In time of war or of military emergency, additional sums have to be allotted and large advances made to military disbursers in the field, and in various parts of India, for the provision of transport and supply, and for the numerous and various charges incidental to extensive field operations. More or less delay occurs in accounting for the appropriation of these large and scattered advances, and in bringing the accounts under the regular audit. Hence it follows that, on these special occasions, the audited expenditure falls far short of the funds actually provided from civil treasuries for the ordinary services of the Military department and for the extraordinary charges of the war. In such circumstances the audited military accounts cease to be a trustworthy guide, and the accounts of the civil treasuries of the country afford the only true measure of the current military expenditure.

This chapter may be concluded with the following statement of the established strength of the European and Native army in British India (exclusively of Native artificers and followers) for the year 1877–8, that is, the year before the recent Afghan war. Some modifications have occurred during the war, but after its termination the forces will revert to their normal strength.

Established Strength of the European and Native Army in British India (exclusive of Native Artificers and followers) for the Year 1877–8.

Corps.	Bengal.			Madras.			Bombay.			Total for India.		
	Officers.	Non-Commissioned Officers and Privates.	Total.	Officers.	Non-Commissioned Officers and Privates.	Total.	Officers.	Non-Commissioned Officers and Privates.	Total.	Officers.	Non-Commissioned Officers and Privates.	Total.
European Army.												
Royal Artillery	337	6,542	6,879	144	2,667	2,811	129	2,420	2,549	610	11,629	12,239
Cavalry	168	2,730	2,898	56	910	966	28	455	483	252	4,095	4,347
Royal Engineers	232	..	232	57	..	57	68	..	68	357	..	357
Infantry	1,056	28,364	29,420	297	7,974	8,271	297	7,974	8,271	1,650	44,312	45,962
Invalid and Veteran Establishment	15	15	30	19	105	124	11	..	11	45	120	165
Staff Corps	589*	..	589	373*	..	373	259*	..	259	1,221	..	1 221
General List, Cavalry	42*	..	42	32*	..	32	13*	..	13	87	..	87
General List, Infantry	121*	..	121	59*	..	59	26*	..	26	206	..	206
Unattached Officers	8	..	8	2	..	2	2	..	2	12	..	12
General Officers unemployed	64	..	64	38	..	38	28	..	28	130	..	130
Total European Army	2,632	37,651	40,283	1,077	11,656	12,733	861	10,849	11,710	4,570	60,156	64,726
Native Army.												
Artillery	13	735	748	..	..	..	5	148	153	18	883	901
Body Guard	2	120	122	5	3	8	1	71	72	8	194	202
Cavalry	211	12,805	13,016	35	1,708	1,743	57	3,530	3,587	303	18,043	18,346
Sappers and Miners	81	1,160	1,241	94	1,367	1,461	45	492	537	220	3,019	3,239
Infantry	508	48,298	48,806	320	30,761	31,081	240	22,056	22,296	1,068	101,115	102,183
Total Native Army	815	63,118	63,933	454	33,839	34,293	348	26,297	26,645	1,617	123,254	124,871
Total of European and Native Army	3,447	100,769	104,216	1,531	45,495	47,026	1,209	37,146	38,355	6,187	183,410	189,597

* Exclusive of Officers employed with Regiments of Native Cavalry and Infantry and Corps of Sappers and Miners, who are included in the strength of those arms.

CHAPTER XXVI.

FOREIGN RELATIONS.

India's neighbours, north, east, and west—Aden—Southern Arabia—Socotra—Muscat—The Persian Gulf—Mesopotamia—The straits of Malacca—The kingdom of Ava—Adjacent provinces of China—Eastern Thibet—Yarkand and Kashgar—North-west frontier of India—Afghanistan—Opinion in India regarding Russia—Kokand, Bokhara and Khiva—Boundaries of Afghan dominions—Russian embassy to Caubul—Position of Badakshan and Balkh—Relations of Persia towards Herat—Russian advance on Merv—Yarkand—Persian province of Khorasan—Importance of Herat—Freedom of Afghanistan from Russian influence—Amir of Caubul—Kyber Pass—Kurrum Valley—The Pishin frontier—Value of Candahar.

THE peninsula and continent of India have been likened to an inverted triangle, of which the apex is Cape Comorin, while the base consists of the Sâtpura and Vindhya mountains which form the lower boundary of northern India; both the sides of the triangle being sea-girt. This circumstance affords to one-half of India a natural defence, like in kind to that afforded to the British Channel to England, in itself a priceless advantage. It also furnishes to British maritime power the inexpugnable basis of the sea. But these advantages, however great they may be, are not all-sufficient. For the other half of India, consisting of the basins of the two mighty rivers Ganges and Indus, the richest and most important half of the two, is environed on most sides by mountains and is mainly an inland country; possessing, however, two outlets and two sections of seaboard, at the mouths of the rivers Ganges and Indus, which constitute inestimable advantages to the mistress of the seas. Still, this long mountainous boundary, consisting indeed of several distinct frontiers, opens up to northern India various relations with her foreign neighbours. Southern

India has happily not any alien neighbours, but northern India has several. India's interests are not, however, confined to her mainland of India proper. She has stretched out her antennæ in one direction to Burma, the basin of the Irawaddy, and the Siamese peninsula; and in another direction to Beluchistan and the shores of the Persian Gulf, which are portions of mid-Asia. Again, she has a connection still intimate with the Straits Settlements, which, though now separated, once formed part of herself, and which command the gates of the Eastern Archipelago and the Chinese Seas, protecting the route of her commerce with China. She has also some interest in Sumatra and Borneo, by reason of her growing trade, and her steam-communication, with Australia. Further, she possesses the vitally important outpost of Aden, which guards the outlet of the Red Sea, and which places her in relation with the north-east corner of Africa and the south-west corner of Arabia. Thus, notwithstanding the extent of her border on the sea, she has many neighbours on the land.

The most important outwork of the Indian empire is certainly Aden, having a natural fortress in its volcanic formations of rock, and commanding a harbour which can be made, with a moderate outlay, defensible against hostile ironclads. Situated on a rocky promontory of the Arabian coast, it is close to the Bab-el-Mandab Strait of the Red Sea. It thus dominates the maritime communication with that inland sea which, since the establishment of the overland Egyptian route and the opening of the Suez Canal, has become one of the most frequented highways in the world, equally valuable in peace and in war. As a military garrison, a naval depot, a position for ships of war, an entrepôt of trade, and a coaling station, it is justly styled the Gibraltar of the East. Though comparatively rainless, it possesses the means of storing water for the troops, and for the civil population of Asiatics which gathers in their wake. Being barren, however, it draws its supplies of food from the neighbouring Arab territories and from the

African coast opposite. This circumstance alone, irrespective of other reasons, must cause relations to spring up between the British at Aden and their neighbours in Arabia and Africa. A series of political transactions in Arabia has drawn these relations closer and closer, till the British Resident at Aden has become the arbiter among the Arab tribes throughout an extensive tract of country. In the jurisdiction of Aden there is the little barren island of Perim, just inside the Bab-el-Mandab Strait, and in the veritable doorway of the Red Sea, a position which in time of war might become extremely important. Farther up the Red Sea, on its eastern or Arabian coast, a consulate, partly subordinate to Aden, has been established at Jedda, which is near to the holiest places of Islam at Mecca and Medina, and to which the Muhammadan pilgrims from India, and from other countries, resort in great numbers. These pilgrims land there, sometimes from Indian country craft and sometimes from British ships, in all which vessels sanitary regulations prevail, expressly framed for the comfort and safety of Native passengers.

Opposite Aden is the large island of Socotra which, situated near the north-east corner of the African coast, has an important position. It is now, according to recent political arrangements, virtually under British control. The tribes on the neighbouring African coast, called the Somalis, are not under British supervision politically, but the relations of the Resident at Aden with them are of a close and cordial nature. The sovereignty of Egypt along the African coast from Suez to Cape Guardafui has been recognised by the British Government for some years past as indisputable.

The British control of the Arabian coast is further secured by the treaties with the Imam of Muscat, who rules the shores of the bay of Oman. Near that, again, the northern shore of the Indian Ocean, belonging partly to Beluchistan and partly to Persia, is traversed by a section of the Indo-European telegraph which, running through Persia, connects Europe with Asia.

This section of the telegraphic line is guarded at several points by detachments of Native troops of the British Government.

The Persian Gulf has become practically in many respects a British lake. It is controlled by the British Resident at Bushire, who specially protects its principal industry, namely the pearl fisheries of Bahrein near the Arabian shore, and adopts constant precautions to prevent piracy from again rearing its head in these waters. The coaling depot, the electric telegraph station, the military detachment at or near the island of Kishim inside the entrance of the Gulf, and opposite the Ormuz of mediæval history, constitute, in combination, an excellent position politically. The British control of this important inland sea had a most honourable origin in the suppression of piracy. The port of Bander Abas near Ormuz is the commercial outlet for the south-eastern extremity of Persia. Bushire itself commands the sea-route to and from Shiraz, the capital of southern Persia. It is also an important station in the line of telegraphic communication between India and Europe. The British Resident there has an escort of Native troops from India. Above Bushire, at a moderate distance opposite the mouth of the Mesopotamian river, is the little island of Karak, which was occupied by British troops during the last Persian war, and was found to be a salubrious station, well situated in a military point of view. The Mesopotamian river above mentioned is the Shat-ul-Arab, or the united stream of the Tigris and the Euphrates, which join near the important city of Bassora, or Basra. Up to Basra the river is navigable for ships of war, of moderate draught, from the Persian Gulf. Under existing political arrangements, these vessels pass to and from Basra, and remain there according to need or convenience. Near Basra, too, is the confluence of the Karûn, and its branches, with the Shat-ul-Arab; and the basin of the Karûn, the ancient Susiana, is one of the most important provinces of Persia. Above Bushire, again, on the Tigris, is Baghdad, where an officer is stationed, who is appointed by the Viceroy of India as Political Resident in Turkish Arabia, and who exercises consular functions directly under the orders of the Government in England. The naval arrangements in the Persian Gulf have been already mentioned in the chapter relating to maritime affairs. Thus the power of England in the Gulf gives moral force to her relations with the countries on its several shores, including eastern Arabia, Mesopotamia and southern Persia. These relations secure to her the control of at least one of the possible routes between Europe and India, strengthen her influence in Persia itself, and render her voice potential in some of those regions which are adjacent to her eastern empire. Her power, too, in this quarter rests upon the sea, which is always for her the best possible base.

The foreign relations of India in the west having been thus mentioned, it is now necessary to turn to her relations in the east.

Although India is not likely to be required to send forces to vindicate British interests in Borneo and Sumatra, yet she may be obliged at any moment to despatch troops to defend the just interests of the Straits Settlements, Singapore, Penang, and Malacca. For example, she supplied troops for the expedition despatched within the last few years to Perak, near Penang. Inasmuch as collisions will occasionally be inevitable between these civilized settlements and the wild aborigines, the necessity for such expeditions may recur.

In Burma, the empire of Alompra, the greatest of Burmese sovereigns, comprised mainly four provinces, Arracan, Tenasserim, Pegu, on the seaboard, and Ava inland. From the issue of wars, provoked by the infatuated arrogance of his successors, the three first have been incorporated in the British dominions and form the fast rising province of British Burma. The fourth, or the inland province of Ava, alone remains to the Burmese dynasty. In this kingdom of Ava, the capital, Amerapura, has been the scene recently of shocking events, when many princes of the blood were slaughtered in order to ensure an undisputed succession after the demise of the late king. A British political mission used to be maintained at Mandalay on the river Irawaddy, near to Amerapura, but was withdrawn last year in consequence of the hostile attitude of the Burmese Court. The relations with the hill tribes east of the Irawaddy, and on the British frontier, at one time rendered war with Ava quite imminent. The king had been long endeavouring to cultivate friendship with powers in continental Europe: he had arranged a commercial treaty with Italy; and on such shadowy foundations he seems to have built some hopes of political support. At the last moment he yielded to the British demands when matters had advanced to the very verge of hostilities. Again, quite recently the aspect of affairs became so threatening that additional troops were rapidly despatched from India to British Burma. Though the outbreak of hostilities was for the moment averted, there is no assurance of peace being rendered permanent. However pacific the people may be in the Irawaddy valley of Ava, the kingdom embraces much hilly territory fraught with elements of trouble: and the Burmese Government is feeble and barbarous in many respects.

The interest of England in Ava chiefly centres in the route which connects it, viâ Bhamo on the upper Irawaddy, with the Chinese province of Yunan. It has long been hoped that in this way the commercial relations between British Burma and south-western China may be improved. The last expedition, which was despatched for this purpose, ended unhappily in the murder of Margary, the officer in charge of it. This deed, perpetrated in defiance of all obligations, was punished in such imperfect manner as the circumstances allowed.

Yunan, however, is not the only province of China adjacent to India; for between Czechuen, on the extreme west of the Chinese empire, and Assam, on the north-east extremity of India, there is a route which is believed by some to be capable of development for purposes of commerce. It was traversed some years ago, by Cooper, starting from the Chinese side, but no marked result is likely to be obtained in the present.

The influence of China is felt in eastern Thibet, of which country the capital is Lhassa, and the spiritual and temporal head is the Grand Lama. The real control, however, rests with the Chinese Government, which maintains a diplomatic official of its own there, supported by a body of Chinese troops. The two Indian, or rather Himalayan, principalities adjoining eastern Thibet are Sikhim and Bhotan. Both these have, in consequence of military and political transactions, become dependent on the British Government, and their trade with Thibet grows, by reason of the exchange of Indian fabrics for Thibetan raw produce, flocks and herds. Thus the political and commercial relations of these States will bring the British into closer communication than formerly with eastern Thibet, and, through Thibet, with China.

China, again, has recently, for a time at least, reconquered and retaken possession of the Muhammadan State of Yarkand and Kashgar combined, with which State the British Government had made a commercial treaty after the despatch of a special mission. Yarkand (the lesser Bucharia of mediæval history), lying between Kokand, a part of the Russian possessions in Central Asia, and Ladakh, a part of the Indian Native State of Cashmir, is a comparatively narrow strip separating the Asiatic empires of England and Russia. Its political condition must, therefore, engage the vigilant observation of England. As the population is Muhammadan, which had apparently shaken off the Chinese yoke, it was hoped that a friendly and independent Muhammadan State might be established under the able Chief with whom the treaty was made. He was killed, however, and the State has again passed under Chinese domination. So long as the Chinese Government shall hold its own there, the British Government may tolerate the situation without absolute dissatisfaction perhaps, though not without some anxiety. But if Russia, advancing from her military position in Kokand, were to occupy Kashgar or Yarkand, then she would come in contact with the outlying dominions of Cashmir and with the British empire. This would arouse apprehension among the English authorities. Such apprehension would, however, refer to the indirect effect which the contact would have on the Himalayan feudatories of England, and through them on the Panjab; and not to the possibility of any direct military movement. For, between the Cashmir dominions and Yarkand there intervene mountain ranges of great altitude, crossed only by passes too difficult for the transit of troops or of military material. But although troops could not march this way, a European power holding Yarkand might, if actuated by hostility, cause embarrassment to England by working mischief in the Himalayan regions which adjoin India.

This review of the foreign relations has now reached the well-known North-west Frontier.

The tribes dwelling on the northern portion of the trans-Indus frontier, Momands, Afridis, Waziris, and others, have for thirty years given trouble to the British Government, that is, ever since the annexation of the Panjab. Therefore it became necessary on many occasions to undertake military expeditions against them; the chastisement, though its necessity must be regretted, was essential for the introduction of civilized order and has been beneficial in its results. Though the tribes still misbehave occasionally, they have yet in many respects yielded to the influence of a system which, sustained by force, is just, merciful, and considerate. In few parts of the empire is improvement more manifest within the last thirty years than the trans-Indus frontier of the Panjab. It has been thought by some that because a less severe system had to be applied on the Sind frontier, the practice adopted by the Panjab Government was too severe. The severity, however, was in proportion to the violent habits of the tribes. The men on the Sind frontier—Beluchis, Bugtis, Marris—though rude and predatory, are less fierce than those on the Peshawur frontier, and therefore did not need such stringent castigation. The principles of the British Government have been the same in both sections of the frontier, though the practice has varied according to circumstances. In all cases the endeavour has been to deter the rude tribes from lawlessness, and to win them over to peacefulness.

The most important of the foreign relations of India are those which relate to Afghanistan, and are involved in the recent or present war, together with the policy whereby it was undertaken. As a commentary on the policy and the war would be beyond the scope of this work, all that can be here attempted is a summary of the phases of opinion in India in respect to the bearing of Afghan politics upon the British empire in the East, with a statement of those considerations which are of permanent importance.

Had foreign powers never threatened that, in event of a general war, some blow should be dealt at India from the north-west quarter, had Russia in particular never moved in the direction of Central Asia, had her movements there not afforded the means of embarrassing England in case of hostilities arising, had the organs of Russian opinion never held forth menaces to this effect, had the history of past invasions not lent some colour to a probability that a similar operation might prove possible in the future,—then no person in India would have ever recommended that the British Government should interfere in Afghanistan. Most persons, indeed, have been anxious to avoid, if possible, such interposition, which they regarded as likely to cause waste of life, loss of treasure, and a host of difficulties. The majority of Anglo-Indian authorities have desired that Afghanistan should remain independent indeed, but in friendly relations with England, and entirely free from the influence of any other power. Such an Afghanistan would have been, as it were, a quickset hedge along the line of British limits, or a chevaux-de-frise in front of the British position. Grave as the objections to interference in Afghanistan undoubtedly are, still graver contingencies may arise. A practical question, therefore, in recent years has been whether such interference, bad as it is, should or should not be accepted as an alternative in preference to something worse. From another point of view, however, the question has been whether, of all conceivable alternatives, interference is not the worst.

Associations hovering round the Indian Caucasus, the classic Oxus, the snow-clad ranges, the rugged hills, the martial mountaineers, used to stir the adventurous spirit which exists in the breasts of so many Englishmen. Still, such impulses have been curbed by prudential considerations. The poverty and bareness of the mountainous regions, the intractable character of the inhabitants, the unsatisfactory nature of any warfare that might be waged there, are likely to deter all save the rash.

For many years past, notably since 1857, when Russia began to operate against Bokhara, and still more since she subjugated Khiva, there have been apprehensions aroused in India. The alarm felt in Afghanistan on account of the Russian operations in Khiva communicated itself to many Indian authorities; and these apprehensions have assumed different shapes. Some persons feared that the proceedings of Russia were tending solely to one purpose, namely, the invasion of India. The plundering of this fertile and populous country was to be offered to the Afghans as a bait for inducing them to join the invaders. These extreme views have been dissipated by the considerations relating to Russia herself. She has too many distractions at home to prevent her from engaging in complications abroad. Her power of aggression is proved by experience to be less than might be supposed from the strength of her army, and her financial resources are restricted. Her position in Central Asia is not, as yet, sufficiently consolidated to serve as a base for operating against a foreign power. If she attempted to establish herself in Afghanistan she would encounter the very difficulties of which England has had such bitter experience.

After the Crimean war, English opinion in the East became favourable to Russia. It was believed that she had acquiesced in the position assigned to Turkey by the Treaty of Paris. She would, it was thought, henceforth devote her energies and resources to the construction of railways in her own territories and to the improvement of her new acquisitions in Circassia and elsewhere. For her railways she would borrow British capital, and thus relations, of the most solid and lasting kind, would be established between her and England. Before the complications began, which led to the last war between Russia and Turkey, the feeling in India towards Russia was becoming quite amicable. There was a hope that the amity would prove enduring between the two European empires in Asia, Russia receiving capital from England, and England drawing interest from Russia. The securities of the Russian Government were highly esteemed in India, and were expected to offer one of the safest and most advantageous fields in the world for the investment of money. The strong belief that the mutual interests of borrower and lender would restrain hostility, induced men for a time to forget their suspicions respecting Central Asia, and to think chiefly of the peaceful course of material improvement upon which Russia had entered. This fair prospect vanished when war was declared against Turkey by Russia in 1877. Then were the apprehensions of Englishmen in India resuscitated in regard to the indirect effect of these events upon the peace of Asia. These apprehensions were aggravated by the diplomatic attitude which Russia was understood to have assumed towards Persia, and especially by the movements of Russian troops from the base of the Caspian towards Merv.

Further, the acquisition by Russia of the three Khanates, as they are termed, Kokand, Bokhara, and Khiva—for Khiva is virtually acquired—was calculated to cause disquietude to Englishmen, if these territories were intended to be used as a basis for operations against India. But respecting the governance of those territories by Russia, Englishmen do not feel any unworthy jealousy. Knowing the barbarism which has disfigured the Native administration, and the cruel incidents of the slavery which used to exist there, they hope that Russia, as a civilized power, will effect humane and beneficent changes in that direction. There never has been any hope of British dominion being established in this region, which may be broadly described as that which lies between the classic rivers Oxus and Jaxartes, and which is too remote from any possible base of English power. Whatever conduces to the good of humanity from European domination in Central Asia, may well be done by Russia, if she be the only power able to effect this. But there is no reason to disguise the fact that Russia has there acquired territories which, with good management, may have a great future before them. It was for some time supposed that Russia was in Central Asia annexing territories which yielded but little and which were sparsely inhabited by untameable tribes. Such is not, however, the case with the three Khanates. They have been in former times reckoned among the very gardens of Asia, possessing one of the best systems of irrigation in the world, sustaining a hardy, industrious, and, on the whole, manageable population. They have more than once afforded the basis on which Asiatic empires have been founded. Though much deteriorated from misgovernment during recent centuries, they are capable of being restored to something like their pristine wealth and power within two or three generations. Fanaticism may drive the inhabitants into rebellion, if an unwise policy be pursued. But if the administration shall be conducted in a judicious and conciliatory manner, the people may become as orderly as many of the subjects of other European powers in Asia.

So far, then, there is no valid ground of rivalry on the part of England with Russia for supremacy in this part of Central Asia. A strip of desert intervenes between the Bokhara territories and the Oxus, not very broad, indeed, but still of sufficient breadth to constitute an obstacle to the passage of a large body of troops at any one time. The Oxus itself constitutes a good boundary in this particular quarter.

It became necessary, however, for England to insist that this boundary should be respected by Russia, though at one time there was doubt whether the Russian Government would acquiesce in this view. Russian officers crossed the Oxus for political exploration up to the northern base of the Indian Caucasus which forms the natural limit of Afghanistan proper, explaining to their countrymen that Russia could never feel at home in Central Asia till she held both banks of the Oxus. Further, they began to interfere in the regions of the Pamir steppes near the sources of the Oxus, and especially in the little province of Wakhan which adjoins the British feudatory State of Cashmir. These difficulties were for a time set at rest in 1873 by the arrangement then concluded between the English and Russian Governments, whereby Wakhan was freed from interference, the Oxus was declared the boundary of the Afghan kingdom down to a certain specified point, whence a line was drawn straight across the desert or thinly inhabited country to a point near Herat, and the Afghan limits both towards Bokhara and Khiva were determined. This provisional delimitation was arranged while Lord Clarendon and Lord Granville successively held the office of Foreign Secretary. It may be called, for the purposes of this narrative, the Clarendon boundary. Afghanistan was then declared by Russia to be beyond the sphere of her interposition. Thus the fears felt by the Afghan sovereign respecting the Russian position at Khiva were apparently quieted, and some progress seemed to have been made in settling the international boundaries between Russia and England, in this part of Asia at least. Here, then, was a hope that at last the grounds of dispute in this quarter between the two empires had been removed. Had Russia adhered to this arrangement, had she never transgressed the boundary thus fixed between her and England, and expressly acknowledged by herself, the recent Afghan war would not have arisen, and all its troublous consequences would have been avoided.

But in 1878, Russia despatched through her representatives at Tashkand, in the Khanates above mentioned, an embassy to Caubul, with the object of negotiating a treaty with the Amir of Afghanistan as against the British Government in India. The particulars of this proposed treaty are not publicly known, but there is no reasonable doubt that they were directly hostile to England. These steps constituted an absolute infringement of the Clarendon arrangement just mentioned, and a positive breach of international engagements. They were, it is true, prepared at a time when hostilities between the two empires, by reason of the Turkish complications, were regarded as imminent, and, so far as the preparation went, England could hardly complain. Still, according to the comity of nations, the embassy ought not to have crossed the Oxus until war was actually declared between the two empires. Nevertheless it did cross, while the international peace, though seemingly likely to be broken, was yet maintained, in fact while the Berlin Congress was in full deliberation. Russia may have claimed, by an extreme stretch of assumption, that she should be excused for committing a deeply hostile act in anticipation of hostilities being declared, expecting that such declaration would soon be promulgated. Even then, however, she was bound to pause the moment that the maintenance of peace was assured by the Treaty of Berlin in July 1878. Nevertheless, the embassy, which started at the time when the Congress began to sit, was not countermanded, notwithstanding the existence of telegraphic communication with St. Petersburg, but proceeded to its destination at Caubul. This occurred, despite the international obligations still subsisting, and the establishment of the general peace by the proceedings at Berlin. Arguments regarding the difficulty of recalling an embassy once on its way and of despatching messengers in time to stop it, and the like, are of no avail whatever in so momentous a matter. The fact remains that the Russian authorities ought to have stopped the embassy, and failed to do so. It may be that the Russian

Government did not intend that the embassy should proceed after the date of the treaty at Berlin; and Englishmen will doubtless desire to give credit to a neighbouring empire for good intentions. But the Government must ultimately be answerable for the proceedings of its lieutenants.

The late Amir of Afghanistan, Shir Ali, did certain acts in connection with this affair, which led to war being declared against him. The question whether he was, or was not, excusable in respect to his conduct, has been much discussed, and need not be re-argued, as it relates to him individually and is no longer of importance regarding the future. It is not necessary to advert to the controversy whether the war was, or was not, the proper means of vindicating British rights respecting Afghanistan. The policy of the war is passing into the domain of history; its results only are the subjects of immediate discussion.

Allusion has been made above to the proceedings of Russia, because they form a subject of abiding interest, and involve principles of permanent importance. She did indeed withdraw the embassy, and it is to be hoped that she acquiesces in the maxim that no such embassy ought to be sent, while the peaceful and friendly relations between herself and England continue what they now are. The Clarendon arrangement continues in full force, whereby Russia engages not to interfere within the Afghanistan of which the boundaries have been defined. These boundaries include Wakhan, near the source of the Oxus, Afghan Turkestan south of the Oxus, mainly represented by the provinces of Badakshan and Balkh, and the territories of Maimena and Herat. Russia has no more right to interfere within these boundaries than England would have to interfere within the boundaries of the Russian empire. England respects absolutely the limits of Russian influence; Russia should do the same regarding English limits. On the other hand, England has throughout these transactions reserved to herself the right to enter into such relations with Afghanistan as she may think fit. It does not necessarily follow that she undertakes to render these relations close, or to control Afghanistan. But she may require that these territories shall be free from foreign interference; and the Russian Government has admitted this claim explicitly.

There are still some territorial points debatable between the two empires, in the region near the sources of the Oxus. But these details, if approached in a good spirit on both sides, ought to be amicably settled without difficulty.

Opinions have been expressed by some authorities to the effect that the mountain range north of Caubul and south of the Oxus, named the Hindu Kush or the Indian Caucasus, might suffice, instead of the Oxus itself, as the boundary of Afghanistan. But apart from the existing arrangement whereby the Afghan boundary is placed beyond, or to the north of, the Indian Caucasus, it would be most impolitic for England to acquiesce in any foreign power establishing itself in the territories on the southern or left bank of that great river. These territories, as already stated, include the well-known positions of Badakshan and Balkh, which are fraught with political importance. They possess capabilities and resources whence a European power could, if so minded, derive the means of warlike operations and the requisite supplies of a military base. It would be impossible to preserve Afghanistan from the influence of a European power established at Balkh. The Indian State of Cashmir could not fail to pay deference to any European authorities who had installed themselves at Badakshan. In other words, the possession of these territories by Russia would be embarrassing to British India.

For some time past, Herat has been ruled by Eyûb Khan, who seems never to have practically tendered submission to his brother, the late Amir Yacûb, and certainly did not make any acknowledgment of the authority of the British Government, when it assumed charge of the general administration after Yacûb resigned his position in 1879. Eyûb's situation was believed to be very precarious, until he recently took the field and advanced towards Candahar, after defeating a British brigade. He has returned to Herat, after his crushing defeat near Candahar, and his condition is more uncertain than ever. In 1879, there were negotiations set on foot for entrusting Herat to Persia, subject to certain arrangements to be made with England. Persia was ambitious of occupying that city and the tract of country immediately adjacent to it, as well as some further portions of Seistan, but a change came over her views in this respect, and the negotiations did not reach any conclusion. Had she been able to place a garrison there, Eyûb would have been reduced to submission, and could not have undertaken the recent expedition against Candahar. The fact of that expedition having advanced so close to Candahar, with a considerable force of artillery and much *matériel* of war, shews how practicable that military route really is. Indeed, topographical information, collected at various times, shews that a good line exists even for a railway from Candahar to a point within forty miles of Herat. These considerations point to the expediency of this route being at least controlled by England.

It is partly on account of Herat that the apprehensions of Englishmen are aroused in reference to the Russian advance towards Merv. These repeated expeditions on the part of Russia are not really needed for the defence or consolidation of her dominions in Central Asia. The harm which Turkomans may occasionally do to the Russian interests on the shore of the Caspian, near Chikishlar, is too insignificant to constitute a reason for important military expeditions to a distant place like Merv. The real aim of these arduous and expensive expeditions can only be the acquisition of influence over Herat and the adjoining province of Persia. If Merv, with its Turkoman tribes, shall fall into the hands of Russia, it can in course of time be made a military base, and it possesses many resources, as its irrigated cultivation, once large but now contracted, can be restored. Among these resources is to be reckoned some of the best material for irregular cavalry, both in men and horses, to be found in all Asia. The hordes of well-mounted Turkomans could, under European guidance, be made to sweep over Afghanistan. From Merv as a base, Herat could be threatened by the route of the Murghab river. It would then require vigilance and skill on the part of England to keep Herat free from Russian influence.

Therefore, it would be conducive to the just interests of England if Russia were again given to understand, as she was in 1875, that any occupation of Merv by her is disliked, and viewed with distrust, as being calculated to cause disquiet among the Afghans, and to disturb the confidence and amity which ought to result from the settlement of the outer boundaries of Afghanistan. The desideratum is that Merv should remain neutral and independent.

It has been already shewn in this chapter that any occupation by Russia of the State of Yarkand-Kashgar would be most injurious to the long-established rights and interests of England in the north-western part of the Himalayas. Such an occupation would also affect the north-eastern boundary of Afghanistan, as already described. The Russians must be well aware of the just jealousy with which England would regard the interposition of a European power in Yarkand-Kashgar; but it is desirable that the weight of the English objections should be impressed upon the Russian Government.

Although the political considerations relating to northern Persia are for the most part beyond the scope of this work, yet it is to be remembered that the north-eastern province of Persia, namely Khorasân, with its capital, Meshed, and its outlying post of Serakhs, adjoins the Herat territory. It is essential to the political independence of Herat, or to its constitution as a part of the Afghan kingdom, that the province of Khorasân should remain free from Russian interposition. As yet Russia has evinced a disposition to interfere, even if she has not actually interfered, in this province of which the northern border adjoins the Turkoman country around Merv. The dominant attitude which she preserves in respect to the northern portions of Persia adjoining the Caspian, and around the Shah's capital, Tehran, affords ground for anxiety lest the progress of relations with the Turkomans should lead to interference on her part within the limits of Khorasân, to which interference England may justly object. Here, again, the force of the English objections should be brought to bear on the Russian Government.

There has been discussion whether it is essential that the control of affairs at Herat should be kept separate from the sphere of Russian interference. As already seen, they were acknowledged by Russia to be thus separate, when the city and its territory were included within Afghan limits by the Clarendon arrangement. The influence of Herat upon the two capitals of Afghanistan proper, Caubul and Candahar, and upon the whole territory of the Afghans, is potential. It would be impossible to preserve Afghanistan from the interference of a European power established at Herat. Therefore it is quite essential to the internal quiet of Afghanistan that Herat should remain free from Russian control. On the other hand, England has, throughout these transactions, reserved to herself the right of controlling the affairs of Herat; though the degree of her control, more or less, may depend on the circumstances of the moment. The position of Herat is of far-reaching importance affecting other countries besides Afghanistan, and involves considerations which cannot well be discussed in this work. It is sufficient here to urge those considerations relating to Herat which concern Afghanistan.

Although England may be desirous of leaving the Afghans to manage their own affairs, and may succeed in avoiding interference with the internal management of Afghanistan, she cannot possibly allow any interposition on the part of Russia, either in the external relations or the domestic administration of that country. It may be said that England, by asserting a right to exercise control on her own behalf, becomes in some degree responsible for acts of aggression committed by Afghans upon neighbouring tribes under the protection of Russia. The responsibility is almost nominal, for the Afghans have neither means nor motives for attempting such aggression, the probability of which thus becomes too remote to be worthy of serious argument. But surely England, as an imperial nation, would never hesitate to accept so limited a responsibility, considering the collateral interests at stake. It is not indeed conceivable that Russia should wish to establish an influence in Afghanistan, except for the purpose either of embarrassing British India, or of acquiring the means for causing such embarrassment at will. A belief is felt that in conquering Central Asia she may have been actuated by a reasonable ambition and by the hope of discharging a beneficent mission. But there can be no such legitimate ambition, and no such fair hope, in respect of Afghanistan. If she really does turn her regards towards Afghanistan—and it is to be hoped that her Government does not, even if individuals among her officers do—then it must be that she expects to find there a vantage-ground from which India may be harassed. It can hardly be that she dreams of attacking India in force, as such an enterprise is of too remote a possibility to fall within the range of practical consideration for the immediate future. The invasion of India cannot at present be compassed, as both English and Russians are well aware. The impossibility of such an invasion is occasionally assigned by some as a reason why England should not be disquieted by a prospect of Russian interference in Afghanistan. This, however, is no reason at all, nor can any satisfaction be derived therefrom. What politicians really dread is, not invasion directly, which is virtually impracticable, but embarrassment indirectly, which is easily practicable. It may be matter for just regret that there should be mistrust between two conterminous empires; but it were vain to ignore the fact that there would be such mistrust if Russian influence were set up in Afghanistan. There is no space here to recount the territorial strides whereby Russia has advanced through Central Asia, nor to illustrate the indisputable fact that her influence immediately fills any space that is left vacant by the English power. This political process has been aptly compared by a very high authority to the natural rushing of air into a vacuum. It follows that if Russia once entered Afghanistan, her influence would not stop till it reached the trans-Indus frontier of the British territories, that is, close up to the right bank of the Indus. In other regions a boundary may be fixed, on either side of which the two European empires in Asia may rest in peace and mutual goodwill. But that boundary must not be on the existing trans-Indus frontier of British India, that is, almost on the Indus itself. It would be impossible then for the two empires to co-exist in mutual trust and amity. Russia might not indeed be able to occupy Afghanistan in force; such occupation might prove as arduous to her as it has proved to the English. But she might maintain diplomatic control or influence there, right up to the mountain passes which are the gates of India facing towards Central Asia. Such events or circumstances would produce a profound impression on the vast population of British subjects of India, especially upon the educated classes, and also upon the Native States. In previous chapters it has been shewn how the spread of superior education is awakening the Natives to an understanding of political affairs, and how important and numerous the Native States really are. The effect not only of the proximity, but actually the contact, of such a power as Russia would be felt throughout the Indian empire. Whether it would sap or undermine the loyalty of so many diverse nationalities need not be discussed, but it would be indefinitely great beyond doubt. The imperial relations of England with India would then be very different from what they now are. One of the momentous consequences must be this, that England would have to maintain a much larger force of European troops in India than at present. If a considerable augmentation of the European garrison were to become necessary, then inevitably a large portion of the English army would be locked up in India. It is not necessary to dwell on the military difficulties that would arise, nor upon the financial embarrassment that would ensue.

The late Amir Yacûb, having executed the treaty of Gandamak with the British Government, was held to have behaved ill, to say the least, during the events connected with the destruction of the British embassy at Caubul in 1879, and is detained virtually as a State prisoner in India. The present Amir Abd-ur-rahman having been recognised as ruler, the British troops have departed from Caubul, leaving him to sustain himself. No treaty has been made with him, but he knows well what England expects in regard to Afghanistan, and what may be the consequences if he deviates therefrom; the fate of Amir Shir Ali is also before his eyes as an example. There is not as yet any assurance in respect to the continuance of his power; rumours are rife from time to time regarding dangers and troubles besetting him at Caubul. Whatever revolutions may occur in that ill-starred capital, some man must ultimately come to the surface, who can be recognised by the British Government as de facto ruler.

Meanwhile, the British Government has territorial rights by the treaty of Gandamak respecting the two military routes leading from India to Caubul, namely that by the Khyber, and that by the Kurram which leads towards the Paiwar and Shutargardan passes, though it does not follow that the Government should undertake to occupy these passes. The Amir of Caubul has ceased to have any claim on the allegiance of the tribes which dwell in this part of the frontier. The British troops, which occupied the passes of Khyber and Kurram, have been withdrawn, but are kept in positions wherefrom they could move for re-occupation at the shortest notice. Arrangements have been made with the frontier tribes for the holding of these several passes, in a manner conformable to the policy of the British Government. During most months, or about two-thirds, of the year, the Kurram route affords comparatively easy and speedy access to Caubul, which is a military and political advantage. The route by the Khyber to Jelalabad, and onwards to Caubul, has been much improved during the recent military operations.

On passing from northern to southern Afghanistan, it is to be noted that the British Government, after occupying Candahar with troops, installed Shir Ali, a relative of the late Amir Shir Ali, as a ruler there, independent of Caubul. He raised some troops for the service of the Candahar province, and with them he marched in June 1880, in company with a British brigade, to oppose the advance of the hostile forces from Herat. His troops, however, mutinied, and he appears to be unable to carry on the administration of his province. If the arrangement made with him is deemed to be terminated in consequence, then Candahar is still at the disposal of the British Government. It seems probable that the British troops will remain there for a time, until the Government can decide either to retain the city, with or without the districts of which it is the capital, or to transfer it to some Afghan chief. Meanwhile there is an advantage in noting the main considerations which affect this question.

By the treaty of Gandamak a long strip of territory adjoining the south-eastern border of Afghanistan was assigned to the British Government for administration. This territory comprises the districts of Thal Chutiali, of Sibi, and of Pishin, the two last of which lie on the route from the Indus to Candahar. The Pishin district also comprises the Khwaja Amran range, which divides the valley of Pishin from the plateau of Candahar. This important range is crossed by the well-known Khojak pass, which is and will be (until the completion of the railway) an obligatory point in the communication between India and southern Afghanistan. The British authorities have taken charge of these extensive districts, and have introduced a civil administration into the best parts of them. The territory is not rich or populous, but it has a considerable extent of cultivation and possesse various resources. A railway has been opened from the Indus to Sibi, and has been begun from Sibi to Pishin, though the operations have been suspended owing to the disturbed state of the frontier, consequent on the events at Candahar during the summer of 1880.

These districts are adjacent to Beluchistan, the territory of the Khan of Khelat. It has been seen, from the previous chapter on Native States, that the internal affairs of Beluchistan have been satisfactorily settled. The Khan of Khelat has made over to the British Government the town and valley of Quetta, adjoining Pishin, and situate on the military route from the Indus to southern Afghanistan by the Bolan pass. Thus Quetta and Pishin together make up a compact territory, commanding effectually the Bolan and Khojak passes and dominating the whole route.

Moreover, the assigned districts, above described, are on the flank of the Marri tribe, which is predatory and in a certain sense formidable, having long been a scourge to its neighbours in Beluchistan, and having often caused trouble on the frontiers of the lower Panjab and of Sind. When British power shall be properly established in the assigned districts, the Marris, and some other tribes heretofore troublesome, will be reduced to order.

Thus the retention of these assigned districts is imperatively necessary for the preservation of order on the frontier near the southern part of the Indus valley, the consolidation of the British position in Beluchistan, the maintenance of control over the great highway from Herat and southern Afghanistan to India, and the fulfilment of the engagements virtually made with the people when the Government assumed charge of this territory.

In support of Pishin lies Quetta, close at hand, an excellent military station, with a bracing climate and with resources for supplying troops. The possession of it enables the British Government to control Beluchistan, and is essential to the safety of the communication with southern Afghanistan in event of need.

The situation of Pishin closely concerns the question whether Candahar should, or should not, continue to be held by a British garrison. On the one hand, it may be said that even if the British troops retire from Candahar to Pishin, a distance of ninety miles and more, the Government will still retain its hold upon southern Afghanistan. Some expense in military transport would be saved. The Khojak pass may still be held, dominating the range of hills which overlook the plains of Candahar, and from the base of which to that city there is good military communication. By the relinquishment of Candahar, there will be averted that enmity and jealousy which some among the Afghans may feel at the sight of a British force at the southern capital of their country. Pishin has a cool climate, and resources which, though moderate, may suffice for a cantonment having supports at Quetta. With the presence of a British garrison, Candahar and its province can hardly form part of an Afghan kingdom. But in the absence of such a garrison, they may be assigned to any chief whom the Government may deem competent to rule over a consolidated Afghanistan.

On the other hand, it may be urged that Pishin, though answering many important purposes, in default of anything better, is yet not at all equal to Candahar as a military and political position. The object is to secure the means of controlling southern Afghanistan and the route to and from Herat. That object is best attained by holding Candahar. The city and its environs are easily occupied, and inexpensively too. Barracks for both European and Native troops already exist, where the men have salubrious accommodation; it is hard to find a station anywhere in which they enjoy such vigorous health as in Candahar during the winter. Whereas, Pishin has not any available accommodation whatever, and barracks would have to be constructed there at a considerable cost. The city of Candahar is rich in supplies of every sort, being an emporium of trade and having in its neighbourhood long lines or strips of irrigated and highly cultivated lands, the productiveness of which will hardly be surpassed anywhere. Good as the position of Pishin may be, that of Candahar is much better. Having on one flank the great desert and on the other flank the mountain ranges dividing it from India, Candahar cannot be turned by any enemy advancing from the Herat direction. The tribes dwelling immediately around it are not fierce, warlike and intractable, like those dwelling, for instance, immediately around Caubul. The British authorities at Candahar never have trouble with the skilful and industrious husbandmen who cultivate the beautiful river-basins all round. The opposition, occasionally met with, comes not at all from the neighbourhood, but from places at some distance, beyond Kelat-i-Ghilzye, or Zemindawar, or the trans-Helmand territory, and the like. As regards the employment of British troops, little would be saved by retirement; most of the troops which held Candahar will be required to hold Pishin. Whereas, if Candahar is occupied in strength, then Pishin is fully covered, and needs no garrison. As British troops must be maintained in this quarter, they should remain, where they now are, in the best possible situation, instead of moving back on Pishin, which, though tolerable, is inferior in every point of view. Respecting the disposal of Candahar and its province, there is no local chief to whom the charge of them could be entrusted. The chief of Herat, Eyûb Khan, though defeated and a fugitive, is still in arms against us. The new Amir of Caubul appears as yet to have a most uncertain tenure even at Caubul itself, and it remains to be seen whether he succeeds in holding his own there, without attempting to found an additional dominion in a distant quarter like Candahar.

Such are, in brief, the considerations on both sides of this question; new conjunctures may at any moment arise; but at present, when all the reasons are weighed, there appears a balance of argument in favour of retaining Candahar.

Besides the general considerations, one particular reason exists at the present time, namely this, that recently in the summer of 1880, a disaster befell a brigade of British troops near the Helmand. The military misfortune has been fully repaired by subsequent achievements, but the moral effect of the defeat has been widely felt. For a time, several of the tribes, occupying various points along the line of communication between Candahar and the Indus, threw off their submissiveness, and rose against British authority. This instance may be added to the many other instances which shew that the spell of invincibility must be maintained in a dominion which partly depends on the force of opinion. It would be injurious to British repute, if the Afghans were to fall into the error of supposing that the Government would be disposed to evacuate a territory because it had been the scene of defeat. It would be well if, on the contrary, they should see that such misfortune hardens the persistency of the Government in pursuing a fixed policy, and stiffens its resolves. On this ground, in addition to other grounds, a display of some tenacity respecting Candahar will tend to the vindication of British interests in that quarter.

The influence of England on Beluchistan and southern Afghanistan will be materially strengthened by the construction of the railway from Sibi, near Bolan, the present terminus of the open line, to the valley of Pishin, with a branch from that valley to Quetta. The line chosen by Nari and Harnai is favourable for the engineers, respecting curves and gradients, and can be permanently maintained at all seasons. It is advantageous politically, as running through the district assigned to the British Government by the treaty of Gandamak, and enabling the authorities to effectively manage that territory. It has been preferred to the alternative route through the Bolan pass to Quetta and thence to Pishin, because a line through that pass, though practicable, offers more engineering difficulties, and fewer political or administrative advantages.

CHAPTER XXVII.

FINANCE.

Publication of budget in India—Statement of income and expenditure—Apprehensions expressed by some authorities regarding Indian finance—Want of elasticity in the revenue—Control of expenditure—The military expenses — Cost of the civil administration — Provincial services — European and Native agency—Cost of material improvements—Guaranteed railways—State railways—Canals and irrigation works—Total outlay on public works—Its results during recent famines—Recurrence of famine—Loss by exchange on remittances by Government of India to England—Former proposals regarding gold standard—The national debt—Equilibrium between ordinary income and expenditure—Audit and account—Government paper currency—Coinage at mints—Savings-banks—Presidency banks—Cash balances.

THE chapter on finance has been reserved for the end, because financial considerations really form the basis of that fabric upon which the Indian empire rests, and afford tests by which other considerations must be finally judged. The circumstances of finance represent an epitome of all other circumstances, economic, administrative and defensive. Good government, military defence, progressive administration, political and diplomatic management, material improvement, moral advancement and spread of civilization would be of no avail to save the empire, if the equilibrum between income and expenditure were permanently lost, and if national insolvency impended. It has been well said that the imperial balance-sheet is the "articulus stantis aut cadentis imperii."

Before 1859, budget estimates of the finances in British India were not regularly prepared for publication. Since that time, however, yearly statements have been promulgated by the Government in India, including the accounts made up for the last preceding year, the revised estimate for the current year, and a budget estimate for the coming year. It is enacted by law that the accounts of the Indian empire shall be annually presented to Parliament. The parliamentary statement, thus rendered necessary, has come to be a commentary on the financial statement already made in India, with such modifications or corrections, and with such additions, as may be deemed fit by Her Majesty's Government. Information is thus afforded to statesmen, economists, capitalists, and to all concerned in the welfare of the Indian empire. The first budget was produced at Calcutta by James Wilson in February 1860.

Although it is by no means intended here to comment on each item of the incomings and the outgoings of the Indian treasury, yet it is well to present, as a foundation for such remarks as may be desirable, a statement of the receipts and expenditure of British India, during the two last completed years, which will be found on pages 444, 445.

In order to convey an idea of the extent to which the finances of the empire have grown, the subjoined statement in abstract shews the total of receipts and of expenditure, as it stood in several previous decades and as it stands at the present time:

Official Years	1839–40	1849–50	1859–60	1869–70	Regular Estimate. 1879–80
	£	£	£	£	£
Receipts .	20,150,000	27,410,000	39,705,822	50,901,081	67,615,205
Expenditure	22,230,000	26,850,000	50,475,683*	50,782,412	67,285,690

The growth is certainly remarkable; but it has been explained in the preceding chapter on the revenues that during the last decade various items have been included which contribute to swell the totals. Still, after allowance has been made for all this, it is patent that there must be much of vital energy and expansive power in an empire of which the finances have thus developed themselves.

* The expenditure was abnormally high after the war of the mutinies.

Some persons, whose position, knowledge and general experience entitle them to high respect, hold that the finances of India are in an unsound state. Some think that the financial situation is even menaced with danger. An answer to a portion of these opinions is presented in a clear and condensed form by the report of the Indian Famine Commission, and by the treatise recently published by Mr. H. S. Cunningham, entitled 'Notes on some disputed Points in Indian Finance and Taxation.' As a judgment can be formed best by studying both sides of a large case like this, a reference ought to be made by the student to the parliamentary speeches of Mr. Fawcett, and to the two articles by Mr. H. M. Hyndman, written for the 'Nineteenth Century' review, and entitled "The Bankruptcy of India."

The objections, which have been propounded at various times, relate to other economic subjects besides finance. Those which relate to finance, so far as they can be gathered from many writings at various times, may be summarized thus. The revenues of the Indian Government are inelastic, and cannot be increased; taxation has been already advanced to the limit of safety. The increase of expenditure is not adequately controlled; the military expenses are overwhelming. The civil and judicial administration is costly and elaborate, beyond the needs and means of the country and people. Expensive European agency is retained, where cheaper Native agency would suffice. Material improvements and public works have been undertaken on a scale too vast, and in a manner which cannot prove remunerative. Even if foreign wars and internal disturbances shall be avoided, still the recurrence of famines must cause a severe drain on the resources of the empire. The necessity of making very large remittances to England, in silver to be measured by a gold standard, renders the finances liable to derangement from loss by exchange. The national debt has grown, and is growing, till its interest amounts to an annual sum which the Indian treasury cannot

ABSTRACT ACCOUNT showing the REVENUE and

REVENUE.	1878-79.	ESTIMATE, 1879-80.
Land Revenue ..	£22,323,869*	£21,679,000
Tributes and Contributions ..	703,660	714,000
Forest ..	605,433	662,091
Excise on Spirits and Drugs ..	2,619,349	2,765,000
Assessed Taxes ..	900,920	797,000
Provincial Rates ..	2,638,835	2,706,000
Customs ..	2,326,561	2,231,000
Salt ..	6,941,120	7,335,000
Opium ..	9,399,401	10,459,000
Stamps ..	3,110,540	3,203,000
Registration ..	266,360*	262,000
Mint ..	172,335	254,038
Post Office ..	911,806	968,000
Telegraph ..	426,694	487,476
Minor Departments ..	84,977	95,266
Law and Justice ..	647,130*	663,000
Police ..	211,108	221,000
Marine ..	250,595	206,017
Education ..	147,425	137,000
Medical ..	44,332	54,751
Stationery and Printing ..	47,096	52,916
Interest ..	628,367	711,325
Receipts in aid of Superannuation, Retired and Compassionate Allowances ..	667,485	531,442
Miscellaneous ..	348,218*	327,246
Railways ..	10,822	—
Irrigation and Navigation ..	168,619	192,000
Other Public Works ..	571,076	479,858
Provincial and Local Deficits ..	973	59,000
Army ..	974,781	947,812
Gain by Exchange on Transactions with London ..	133,313*	324,000
TOTAL	£58,283,200*	59,525,238
Revenue from Productive Public Works:		
Railways ..	6,167,312*	6,701,000
Irrigation and Navigation ..	622,156	678,967
Ditto ditto Portion of Land Revenue due to Irrigation ..	126,934	710,000
TOTAL	£6,916,402*	8,089,967
GRAND TOTAL, REVENUE	£65,199,602	67,615,205

* The reason that these figures do not correspond with those contained in the Finance and Revenue Accounts for 1878-79, is that the new arrangement of these items, which has been adopted in 1879-80, has been applied in the above Account to the year 1878-79, for purposes of comparison.

Expenditure, for 1878–79, and as estimated for 1879–80.

Expenditure.	1878–79.	Estimate, 1879–80.
Refunds and Drawbacks	£406,562	£350,000
Payments in Realisation of Revenue:		
Land Revenue	2,960,010*	2,944,749
Forest	451,934	521,177
Excise on Spirits and Drugs	87,839	110,000
Assessed Taxes	37,617	35,000
Provincial Rates	64,431	50,000
Customs	200,417	201,000
Salt	404,743	356,223
Opium	1,698,730	2,058,856
Stamps	115,452	114,250
Registration	160,801*	162,000
Mint	103,991	91,583
Post Office	1,033,327	1,133,032
Telegraph	470,790	482,038
Allowances and Assignments under Treaties and Engagements	1,826,484	1,899,965
Total of the Direct Claims and Demands upon the Revenues, including Charges of Collection, and Cost of Salt and Opium	£10,026,128*	10,509,873
Interest on Permanent and Floating Debt	4,575,069	4,451,735
Interest on Service Funds and other Obligations ..	378,952	381,027
Administration	1,487,852	1,486 247
Minor Departments	355,347	362,522
Law and Justice	3,297,063*	3,291,049
Police	2,419,119	2,485,000
Marine	548,703	548,363
Education	978,254	971,864
Ecclesiastical	155,200	155,800
Medical	669,059	672,901
Stationery and Printing	471,470	432,757
Political Agencies	448,793	440,440
Civil Furlough and Absentee Allowances	231,561	214,386
Superannuation, Retired and Compassionate Allowances	1,997,327	2,087,279
Miscellaneous	293,094*	314,615
Famine Relief	313,420	99,343
Railways	226,846	360,000
Irrigation and Navigation	630,919	753,551
Other Public Works	4,318,247	4,104,405
Provincial and Local Surpluses	716,878	324,000
Army	17,092,488†	20,974,348†
Loss by Exchange on Transactions with London ..	3,359,144	3,188,000
Total Expenditure, Ordinary	£54,990,433	58,609,505
Expenditure on Productive Public Works (Working Expenses and Interest):		
Railways	6,334,981	6,627,076
Irrigation and Navigation	432,118	462,109
Interest on Debt incurred for Productive Public Works	1,407,824	1,587,000
Total	£8,174,923	8,676,185
Grand Total	£63,165,356	67,285,690
Productive Public Works (Capital Expenditure)	£4,381,898	3,564,140

Revenue	£65,199,602	£67,615,205
Expenditure chargeable thereon	63,165,356	67,285,690
Excess of Revenue over Expenditure	£2,034,246	£329,515

	1878–79.	1879–80.
† Including for Operations in Afghanistan .	676,3~0	3,207,880
" Frontier Railways .	—	1,334,426

properly bear. The Government has failed for many years to preserve an equilibrium between income and expenditure. Therefore some disaster, almost approaching to a collapse, must sooner or later occur.

These apprehensions are chiefly expressed by independent observers, and are entertained by some, but not by the majority, of official men; but they are stoutly controverted by some authorities, and are not admitted by the Government. They are not felt by English capitalists, if the quotations of Indian Government securities in the London money market, and the tenders for the latest Indian loans, may be accepted as indications. Being published in England in the most telling and effective manner, they have elicited much comment in India, but have not been seriously regarded there by the majority of Europeans, official and non-official, though to some they must have caused alarm. They have been noticed by the educated classes of the Natives; a portion of them has been echoed by the organs of Native opinion. In some respects they coincide with the views which influential bodies of Natives have long urged upon the Government. It is impossible to say for certain whether they have affected the Native mind in their extreme conclusion regarding the probability of some national disaster occurring; perhaps they have not. It would hardly be safe, however, to pronounce any positive opinion upon a point which concerns the estimate which the Natives form regarding the ultimate stability of British rule, an estimate which Europeans can hardly divine.

Nevertheless, these apprehensions deserve and doubtless receive the most earnest and constant attention from the Government. For, although they may be rejected in the form whereby they are set forth, they are not destitute of plausible reason, nor wholly devoid of apparent foundation. Indeed, they represent the very dangers to which the Indian empire would be exposed, if it were to be carelessly managed. They point exactly to the pitfalls into which an administration, financially imprudent, or unduly sanguine, or hastily progressive, would lead the country. They give warning of the temptations which beset many of the most benevolent reformers and the most enlightened administrators. They counteract the disposition to overstrain the strength of the country for the sake of immediate effect, and they correct the tendencies of that vaulting ambition which overleaps itself. Therefore, those who declare and expound these apprehensions so lucidly and forcibly, render good service to their country by keeping the public eye fixed on these subjects. Still, if the dangers exist, the country may escape from them; and the question is whether they are being averted or avoided. For the better examination of this all-important question, each of the several apprehensions above mentioned will be briefly noticed.

In respect to the elasticity or otherwise of the revenues, it must be acknowledged that they are inelastic as compared with those of the most advanced European nations, especially with those of Great Britain; as compared also with what many well-wishers might have expected or may still hope to see. There has not been, nor, in all probability, will there be, any bound forward, nor any rebound after temporary depression, of the Indian revenues. This want of fiscal elasticity must have a repressive effect upon the hopes of those who wish to improve the country. Nevertheless, all the branches of the revenue increase slowly, though steadily; in none of them has there been any tendency to decline permanently, notwithstanding the unprecedented calamities from famine and pestilence within the last few years. The land revenue has risen, irrespective of accessions of territory, in consequence of increase of cultivation, notwithstanding that the share in the rent claimable by Government has not been enhanced, and that the rate of incidence per acre has been diminished. It may yet rise considerably further, hereafter, by reason of improvements in agriculture. The revenue from salt, excise and stamps increases by degrees, irrespective of changes in rates of duty. The income from the State forests is likely to increase indefinitely. The customs revenue has decreased, indeed, owing to remission or reduction of duties; irrespective of such causes of diminution, it is likely to increase. Repeated consideration, caused by general warnings in respect to the uncertainty surrounding the opium revenue, has failed to shew any symptom of decline in that branch. The receipts from departments managed by the State, such as the Post-office and the Electric telegraph, are increasing, and promise to increase still further.

In reference to taxation having been already advanced to the limits of safety, it must be admitted that the possible sources of additional taxation are very few. It is a primary object of policy to avoid the imposition of new taxes, although the existing taxation of the country, judged, not by a European, but by an Indian standard, is demonstrably low and light. Still, there is the income-tax which is not new, but is a well-understood impost. However strong may be the objections against this tax, and however great the expediency may be of refraining from its re-imposition after it has been formally remitted, it yet remains as an available resource in the event of absolute necessity, and it will touch some classes who otherwise escape taxation almost entirely. Even those, who do not admit that the general taxation is moderate, will acknowledge that there are some of the wealthier classes who do not at present bear their proper share in the fiscal burdens of the country.

In regard to the national expenses not being adequately controlled, it must be allowed that from official and non-official quarters pressure is incessantly put upon the Government to augment expenditure. All are agreed that in general terms expenditure ought to be kept down. But many, while deprecating existing expenditure on branches in which they have no concern, do not hesitate to recommend expense for beneficent objects in which they feel a just interest. Some, who preach economy as a rule, seem to think that a favourite project is to be the exception; the sense of its particular merits causes the general maxims to be forgotten. Now, the persons of all sorts who have to make proposals for improvements of any kind, may be confidently appealed to for testimony to the fact that the Government in India sets its face against everything that will cause an increase of expenditure. In this respect, too, Her Majesty's Government exercise the strictest supervision; and if under special considerations any augmentation has been allowed in India, it may very possibly be disallowed by orders from England. Thus, whether the control be perfect or not, there is a disposition to exercise it, and therefore it is sure to be exercised in some considerable degree at least.

The military expenses are alleged to be overwhelming; and indeed they constitute by far the largest item of the expenditure. The thought of repressing or reducing them has never been absent from the mind of the Government for many years; the reductions in the forces, European and Native, made during 1859 and 1860 were very considerable; nor has there been any addition to the fighting strength during the subsequent twenty years. Even during the recent Afghan war, when forces, equal to nearly two Army Corps, had to be despatched beyond the Indus, there has not been any actual augmentation of the troops permanently. The slight augmentation ordered for the Native army of Bengal was temporary only, and effect has hardly been given to it. The additional European troops sent from England are employed temporarily, and will be withdrawn on the termination of the war. A high commission has sat in India to consider every practicable means of reducing the military expenditure; though not able to propose any diminution of fighting strength, it has suggested various measures whereby expense may be lessened. Still it must be owned that, despite all precautions, the cost of the army has somewhat, though slightly, increased; but this is owing to the improved armament and equipment rendered necessary by the progress of science in war. The Government could not possibly deny to its Indian armies the fighting advantages which the other armies of the day possess. As to the proportion which the military expenditure bears to the income of the State, it should not, perhaps, be reckoned upon the total receipts, as shewn in the accounts, £66,000,000 sterling, but rather upon the total of the revenue proper as shewn in a previous chapter, namely 43 millions. This expenditure is shewn at 16½ millions in the accounts of recent years; but some critics allege, with a show of reason, that, including cost of barracks and certain other charges, it stands really at more than 17 millions. This sum represents practically the cost which is incurred by India for defence, as her naval charges are insignificant, only £80,000 annually. The proportion will not appear large as compared with the existing defensive expenditure of the United Kingdom, or of any of the Great Powers, excepting the United States.

As to the civil administration becoming too costly and elaborate for the country, there is undoubtedly reason to fear that the demands of civilization may constrain the Government to allow things which, though good in themselves, are more than a poor country like India can afford to pay for. The best intentioned persons commonly press a reform or an improvement upon the Government, thinking only of its merits without counting its cost. If the cost be mentioned as an objection, they will reply that as money was forthcoming for such and such a beneficial measure, it might be, and ought to be, found for this particular proposal. The vehemence of such moral pressure will hardly be understood by any save those who have actually experienced it. Therefore, those do well who emphatically warn the public against expecting too much in the way of a costly and elaborate administration in a poor country. In these respects public opinion is apt to assume different phases; at the present time it would probably support the Government in arresting the course of improvement, as the belief perhaps prevails that enough has been done for the present. But if instead of being, as it is, progressive and civilized, the administration had been backward or halting, because the country could not afford the cost, then a public cry, of a different tone, would have arisen, and the Government would have been reproached as being benighted and as lagging behind the spirit of the age. After all, the administrative improvements which have cost money in India were almost entirely of an obligatory character; they were hardly optional in any degree. The police is corrupt and inefficient; it must be re-organized. Native officials do not receive remuneration enough to keep them in honesty; their emoluments must be raised. The mass of the children throughout the country are growing up in ignorance; something must be done for education. The courts are too few to dispose of the business brought before them, or are too distant from the homes of the suitors; the judicial establishments must be strengthened. A vast territorial area is consolidated under one dominion; it must be fully surveyed. The empire is known to abound in natural resources; something must be effected for physical science. Much mortality is found to arise from preventible diseases; some efforts must be put forth on behalf of sanitation. Prisoners are languishing in badly-ventilated and ill-regulated jails; some outlay for improved prisons must be sanctioned. Instances might be added; but enough is here adduced to convey some idea of the reproaches which would have been justly levelled at the Indian Government by English philanthropists and reformers, if these, and other kindred matters, had been neglected for any reason whatever, even the reason that funds were not available. Had such neglect been brought home to the Indian Government, it is doubtful whether any financial plea would have been accepted by that public opinion in England which, on need arising, always asserts itself and makes its influence dominant. As a case in point, it may be observed that the very critics who condemn the Indian Government for the alleged extravagance of its administration, often reprove it for not having collected and collated a mass of statistical and other information, in addition to all the reports and statistics which are already published. But it seems hardly to be remembered that such information, to be worth anything, is costly to obtain.

Lastly, in the higher salaries, in which Europeans are more concerned than others, there has been no increase but rather a diminution. During the last few years the civil expenditure is shewn to have not increased, but, on the contrary, to have slightly decreased.

An arrangement was commenced in 1872 known by the designation of "Provincial Services," whereby certain sums are allotted by the Government of India to the several Local Governments in the empire for certain services: education, prisons, police, roads, civil buildings and the like. The primary object of the arrangement is this, that the various Local Governments should have resources at their disposal for these purposes, of which resources the most and the best must be made, and which may be supplemented by any legitimate means that can be devised locally, on the understanding that no further demand is to be made upon the general treasury on these accounts. Another object is, that a peremptory limit should be set to expenditure from the imperial finances on these several departments, which are the very departments in which expenditure may be advocated with a moral pressure most hard to resist. The scheme was introduced, under the auspices of Lord Mayo, with an appreciable retrenchment of the average amounts previously allowed for these departments from the general treasury. It has worked well financially, for the limit thus prescribed has been observed and no additional demand has since been made on the imperial finance. It has been found to possess many other advantages, but in this place its financial advantage is dwelt upon, because it distinctly established in several spending departments that very control, which is alleged by some critics to be wanting.

Respecting the retention of expensive European agency, where cheaper Native agency would suffice, it is to be remembered that, despite the expansion of the empire, the European covenanted civil service has not been augmented, but, on the contrary, has been somewhat diminished and is likely to be further reduced in numbers. Natives are being admitted more and more into that service with some saving of expense; for lesser administrative posts the policy of substituting Native for European agency is being carried into effect, in all departments save the police, where European supervision is still indispensable. In the ministerial offices, educated Natives have succeeded in almost entirely supplanting the European or East Indian clerks who used to be employed. For such departments as engineering, telegraphy, forestry, and others, every effort is made to train up Natives for the work. The training, if successful, must have the effect of substituting them ultimately for Europeans to some extent. To this policy, however, manifest necessity has assigned certain limits, which are perhaps overlooked by some critics in the present day, and which, if transgressed, might leave the empire exposed to jeopardy. In most of those places wherein the public safety requires the exercise of what are known as the distinctive British qualities, Europeans must for an indefinite time continue to be employed.

The argument that material improvements have been undertaken on a scale too vast, and in a manner which cannot prove remunerative, would, if substantiated, be serious indeed. It is true that projects of this somewhat extravagant nature are frequently proposed for the sanction of the Government, and that the utmost vigilance is required to prevent their acceptance; but they are usually rejected. Therefore those critics, who insist on a jealous scrutiny being exercised, lend moral support to the Government in performing a duty which often becomes invidious, when the schemes are in their nature excellent and have much to recommend them, barring the prospect of an early financial profit. The question is whether the Government has undertaken any large work which on financial grounds ought to have been postponed, or which from its results can be pronounced to have been wrong in inception and execution. The works in question consist of railways and canals; they are open to inspection by the most independent observers on the spot; the minutest statistical particulars regarding them are accessible to the public. If they were to be taken one by one, it would be difficult to single out any of them which, for financial or any other reasons, ought not to have been undertaken. The only one which, with any semblance of reason, could be indicated as falling within this category, is the canal system of Orissa, as it is not likely to prove remunerative for a long time to come, unless a famine should supervene. Few persons, however, who are acquainted with that which once happened in that province,—and which might happen again if drought occurred in the absence of any means of irrigation,—would assume the responsibility of saying that these works ought not to have been undertaken. For many of the other works, justification could be produced in abundance.

It may be said, however, that although the condemnation of individual works may be difficult when the system is examined piecemeal, yet its results when regarded in the aggregate are financially unfavourable. The works consist of Guaranteed railways, State railways, and canals.

Respecting the Guaranteed railways the excess of guaranteed interest over net traffic receipts, which represents the real charge to the State on their account, for some years stood at 1¾ million sterling annually, and during one year mounted up to more than two millions. It fell, however, to below a million, and in one year dwindled to one quarter of a million; it rose again to three-quarters of a million; in one year it disappeared and was replaced by a considerable profit to the State. It may under these circumstances be expected to disappear permanently ere long.

The State railways have already involved an outlay of 26½ millions sterling, on which the interest would be upwards of one million annually. Though the lines are not all completed, and not in full working order, they are already yielding half a million annually of net earnings for part defrayal of interest charges. It is therefore probable that they will, after completion, soon begin to recoup the State for the interest chargeable on them.

On State railways and Guaranteed railways together, the Famine Commissioners report that the net receipts in 1879–80 amount to 5½ millions sterling on a capital of 114½ millions, and will amount in 1880–1 to 6¼ millions sterling on a capital of 123 millions, the former giving a return a little less, and the latter a return of a little more, than 5 per cent., a result which compares favourably with those obtained in any other country. This success, too, is attained already, notwithstanding that large sums are still locked up in works not yet brought into full operation.

Upon the canals, upwards of 20 millions sterling of capital have been spent. After some trouble and delay the Government has succeeded in making out an exact account of the returns, and that shews a net return of 1¼ million annually, available for defrayal of interest charges, or 6 per cent., as already seen in the chapter on canals, which is satisfactory.

It is satisfactory to note that, notwithstanding the considerable increase in the capital of the debt, the interest will be found to have not appreciably increased when the net income from the productive public works is taken into consideration, as will be seen thus by figures taken from the finance and revenue accounts. On the 31st of March, 1872, the interest-bearing debt stood at £105,581,068 plus £1,378,466, the total being £106,959,534; the charges were—

	1871–2.
Interest on Debt	£5,483,518
On Service Funds	482,781
	5,966,299
Deduct dividend on East India Stock	629,970
TOTAL	£5,336,329

From this, however, £482,781 stated above should be deducted, as the capital of these obligations was not included in the debt; thus the total charge will stand at £4,853,548.

On the 31st of March, 1879, the debt stood at £137,868,043. The charges were—

		1878-9.
Interest, exclusive of productive Public Works ..		£4,575,069
" on Service Funds		378,952
State Railways, working and maintenance		734,377
Irrigation Works, ditto ditto		381,550
Interest on Debt for productive Public Works ..		1,407,824
		7,477,772
Deduct Earnings of State Railways	£966,006	
" ditto Irrigation Works	613,270	
" Land Revenue due to Irrigation	126,934	
		1,706,210
TOTAL		£5,771,562

From this £378,952 for service funds should be deducted, leaving a total of £5,392,610.

Again, it is held by some authorities that the capital outlay on the Guaranteed railways, as forming a part of the State obligations, ought for practical consideration to be added to the national debt. From a technical point of view, however, this position is hardly tenable, or at the best is tenable only to a limited extent. That portion of the national debt, about one-fifth of the whole, which has been borrowed for productive public works, does indeed bear some resemblance to the capital outlay on the Guaranteed railways. In both cases the State has incurred obligations, against which there are to be set valuable properties yielding returns. The remaining, that is much the greater, part of the national debt, incurred for military, political, and administrative necessities, is not at all analogous to the capital outlay on Guaranteed railways, which constitute a productive possession. If, however, the two sorts of State obligations were added together it would be found that the Government is at the present time paying little more than 2 per cent. interest on the whole. As this view will be interesting to some, it may be presented thus by figures taken from the finance and revenue accounts, and from the official statements :—

	1878–9. (Actuals)	1879-80. (Regular Estimate.)	1880-1. (Budget Estimate.)
	£	£	£
Interest on Debt other than that for productive Public Works ..	4,575,069	4,451,735	4,014,000
" on Service Funds	378,952	381,027	400,000
Charges for interest and maintenance on productive Public Works ..	8,174,923	8,676,185	8,615,200
	13,128,944	13,508,947	13,029,200
Deduct Revenue from productive Public Works, including Guaranteed Railways	6,575,230	8,089,967	8,928,000
TOTAL	6,553,714	5,418,980	4,101,200

The amounts for service funds being deducted, the net totals will stand at £6,174,762, £5,037,953 and £3,701,200. For the first of the three years, the charges amount to about $2\frac{5}{8}$ per cent. on the combined national obligations; for the second, to about 2 per cent.; and for the third year, to $1\frac{1}{2}$ per cent. on the total, which may be set down at 138 millions national debt, 98 millions outlay on Guaranteed railways, in all 236 millions in March 1879, and 151 millions plus 98 millions, or 249 millions in March 1880.

The scheme of remunerative public works for the Indian empire was not devised hastily, nor was its execution begun in a desultory manner. The principle of borrowing for such works was sanctioned in 1867 for a scheme of lesser dimensions. Subsequently in 1872–3 the scheme was revised and enlarged, the projects were reviewed, the canals to be undertaken were determined, the number of miles of railways to be made were approximately fixed, a forecast was presented of the time over which the operations were to extend, and a capital outlay of 30 millions sterling was proposed, together with calculations of the returns to be received. These proceedings, initiated by the Government in India, were formally approved by Her Majesty's Government at various times, including both of the English political parties, were officially explained to Parliament when the financial accounts of the empire were submitted, and apparently met with general approbation. Subsequently, again, when embarrassment was caused by the fall in the value of silver, these works were comprehensively reviewed by a parliamentary committee. The leading principles were all maintained ; but further precautions were enjoined respecting the ascertainment of the remunerative prospect before works are sanctioned, and the annual outlay was restricted to the amount which could be advantageously borrowed within India itself.

A retrospect of the recent famines will convince most persons that it was truly fortunate for the Government that the public works, both the former and the latter, had been so far carried out as to place the country in possession of railways and canals when it had to withstand the shock of these calamities. In 1874, when mortality was happily averted, it would have been impossible to prevent some misfortune occurring if there had not been the means of rapidly transporting grain from the port of Calcutta to the banks of the Ganges in Behar. In 1877–8 the famine in southern India, already so widespread, would have extended much further, and the diminished food-supply would have been still further contracted, had it not been for the canals. The importation of food, from long distances to the distressed districts inland, would have been impossible without the railways. Thus the mortality, already lamentable, would have been indefinitely greater, and would have embraced many millions of people in its fatal grasp. Let any one reflect as to what would have been the state of public sentiment in England, so righteously sensitive on these subjects, if such a dire event had come to pass. Many organs of public opinion would have denounced the criminal short-sightedness of those who had failed to store the waters for fertilization, and who, despite the good example before their eyes of all civilized nations, had omitted to apply the ordinary resources of science to providing transport by rail over the long distances which intervene between the different parts of a wide dominion. Then the authorities would have been reproached as being indirectly the authors of at least a part of the great calamity ; and the Government might have had to face the wrath of a justly incensed nation.

One of the objections mentioned may be admitted to the full, namely, that even if political and military causes of financial disturbance be avoided, still the recurrence of famines must cause a drain on the resources of the empire. This prospect must be regarded with resignation to the will of Providence, but with the most resolute spirit of self-help. Material improvements will mitigate, though they cannot avert, the misfortune. The receipts from the public works will in ordinary times reduce the interest on the national debt, so that there may be some margin left for unavoidable increase in time of famine. In view of such misfortunes there must be such a rigid economy, and such a judicious husbanding of resources, that when the trial comes, the Government may be found with its ordinary finance sound and safe, and with its treasury so full that the cash balances can afford a considerable sum for immediate use.

The embarrassment, also, must be fully acknowledged which arises from the loss by exchange on the very large remittances by the Government from India to England in silver, to be measured by a gold standard. The Secretary of State for India in Council draws bills on the Government of India which are sold in London at rates, ranging from a shilling and so many pence to two shillings, for a rupee. It is the fluctuation of the rate thus obtained which causes so much anxiety to financiers. The rate is also of great interest to the general trade, for it is the main indicator of the exchange between England and India. The slightest fall in the value of silver, even by the fraction of a penny, may cause to the State a large additional loss against which no financier can provide. In former days the exchange used not to cause any apprehension: the value of silver was high, approaching the assumed par of two shillings for the rupee, and the amount of the remittances was comparatively small. Of late, while the remittances have largely increased, the value of silver happens to have fallen, and from this double cause much financial trouble has ensued. Within the most recent years, while the finances were strained by famine and by war, the loss by exchange has been superadded. In 1876, the exchange fell below 1*s.* 7*d.* for the rupee, and the alarm in many quarters was great. The chief losers were the State and all the interests depending on it. The European official classes, and some of the non-official classes, suffered severely. Some detriment happened to portions of the foreign trade, but the export trade was not injured, on the contrary, it was affected favourably, and the Natives generally did not feel any ill effect. But on account of the many interests bound up with the State, there were misgivings throughout the empire when the exchange was at its zero, and general satisfaction when it began to rise again. Though risen somewhat after several fluctuations, it is still low (averaging 1*s.* 8*d.* for the rupee) and causes much trouble, though no particular alarm is felt at the present moment.

These serious difficulties arise from the existence of a silver standard and currency. The introduction of a gold standard into India, whereby gold coins would be legal tender to amounts without limit, was strongly recommended by many financial authorities in India, among whom were the finance ministers Mr. S. Laing, Sir Charles Trevelyan and Mr. Massey. The only authority in India of equal rank, who held an opposite view, was James Wilson. But the obstacles were even then found by the Government to be insuperable, when the value of silver relative to gold was high. They have subsequently become aggravated as that value has fallen, and practically there is not any hope of a gold standard being adopted. There is doubt whether the case would be materially altered, even if gold should be discovered in large quantities within India itself, of which some prospect is believed by many to be opening out, on the southern portion of the Malabar coast. It is perhaps unfortunate that originally, at the outset of British rule, a gold standard was not introduced, and some think that at that time circumstances were not unfavourable to the measure. But when once a silver standard has been established in a large empire, and has lasted for many years, a change from silver to gold involves infinite complications; so India must, apparently, continue to bear the burden and the risk entailed upon her by the existing standard. Meanwhile, since the discovery of gold in Australia, there have been anomalies connected with this subject. It was remarked by the late Sir W. Mansfield (afterwards Lord Sandhurst) that the gold of Australia had to go to London to be exchanged for silver, which was then sent out to India after being bought at an artificially high price in Europe. The strange spectacle was exhibited for many years of ships, freighted with gold, traversing half the globe in one direction, crossing ships conveying an equal value of silver in the opposite direction, for the adjustment of balances of trade capable of settlement without either voyage.

Meanwhile the causes of the fall of the value of silver may not prove permanent, and may either abate or disappear, such as the excessive produce of the American mines, the glut of silver in the money market in consequence of the changes made by the German Government, and the altered condition of trade. One of the potent factors in hardening the exchange in favour of India and remedying the losses which have recently occurred, is held to be the briskness of the Indian export trade. Whenever a powerful impulse is given to that trade, then silver is likely to rise in value. The flow of silver to India was enormous when the cotton trade started forward with a bound in consequence of the civil war in America. This subject is well explained in Colonel Nassau Lees' book, entitled 'The Drain of Silver to the East,' and published in 1866.

The next difficulty relates to the national debt, which is said to be growing to an amount that the treasury cannot properly bear. The capital outlay on the Guaranteed railways (97 millions) is held by many to be virtually a part of the national debt; but it is technically excluded and, as already seen, the charge upon the State on account of Guaranteed interest is expected to disappear. The national debt proper, that is the registered interest-bearing debt, may be stated at 151½ millions sterling on the 31st of March, 1880. Of this, 37 millions have been spent on the remunerative public works which are already in part defraying, and are expected ultimately to defray altogether, the interest charges incurred on their account; and 4½ millions on the redemption of the dividend due to the holders of East India stock. Thus, what may be termed the unproductive debt would stand at 110 millions. Of this again something is due to the famines, which are estimated to have cost the Government 16 millions. The national debt incurred for war is considerably less than 100 millions. If 100 millions be taken as the unproductive debt, it amounts to less than two years of the receipts of the Government shewn in the accounts as 65 millions annually. But it has been seen that a part of these receipts cannot be reckoned as revenue proper, which has been shewn to amount to 43½ millions. The revenue proper of two years, then, would amount to 87 millions, a sum not far short of the sum of 100 millions, which sum, therefore, represents a little more than two years' revenue. Judged by the standard of indebtedness in many advanced countries, this amount of national debt in India would not appear excessive. If India, as is understood to be probable, shall receive from England substantial relief in respect to the debt incurred for the recent Afghan war, the only known cause of immediate increase to the Indian debt is the prosecution of the reproductive public works. But it would not thence follow that the interest charges must increase, for, as already seen, they are in part defrayed by the receipts from the works, and do not stand at a materially higher amount now than they stood in 1871, when the debt was much less. These charges amount to upwards of 5½ millions annually; which amount is equal to one-eighth or 12½ per cent of the 43½ millions already shewn as the amount of the revenue proper, or 11 per cent. The normal rate of interest used to be 5 per cent. But of late years the Indian financiers have availed themselves of every opportunity of reducing this rate, till in 1878-9 only 15 millions stood at 4½, £600,000 in India, and £17,200,000 in England at 5, and 1½ millions at 5½ per cent.; all the rest stood at 4 per cent. Even in 1879 the process of reduction went on; 1½ millions at 5½ per cent. were converted into a 4½ per cent., and in July of 1880 the whole of the

English debt, £17,200,000, which bore interest at 5 per cent., was converted into a 4 per cent. stock. In these ways the interest charges are lessened. That the Indian financiers lose no chance which might offer itself of reducing the capital of the debt is shewn by the fact that, between 1861-2 and the end of 1866, it was reduced from 98½ to 90½ millions.

Of the registered debt, 149 millions, 90 millions are held in India and 59 in England. The debt owing in England involves an annual payment there of 2¾ millions, which sum forms an important item of the home charges. There is some reason for satisfaction in the fact that so large a part of the debt is held in India, although, of the whole sum, more belongs to Europeans than to Natives.

Lastly comes the question whether the Government has or has not failed to preserve an equilibrium between income and expenditure depends on the inclusion or exclusion of the expenditure from borrowed money, on the productive public works. In no country are such works largely constructed out of ordinary revenue ; nor is there any reason why India should be made an exception to a rule of such wide application. Most economists and financiers would admit that this expenditure must be excluded from the ordinary account and treated separately. This being excluded, it will be found that during the last 17 years there has been an aggregate surplus of £15,185,000, and an aggregate deficit of £14,026,000, or a net surplus of £1,159,000. This result, too, has been obtained after paying 15 millions for famine relief, and 10 millions on account of loss by exchange. If this very important point be made good, then the ordinary finances of India are clearly seen to have been sound and healthy, to have been capable of sustaining, not only the defence and administration of the country, but also several grave and uncontrollable misfortunes, such as famines and losses by exchange, and to have maintained the desirable equilibrium. In justification of this fundamental proposition the following figures are taken from Mr. Cunningham's pamphlet, which embodies official information :

RETURN of the GROSS REVENUE and EXPENDITURE of INDIA from 1862–63 to 1878–79 (excluding CAPITAL EXPENDITURE on EXTRAORDINARY or PRODUCTIVE PUBLIC WORKS from 1867–68) and the SURPLUS or DEFICIT in each YEAR, including and excluding EXPENDITURE on FAMINE RELIEF and LOSS by EXCHANGE.

YEAR.	REVENUE.	EXPENDITURE.				Comparison of Revenue with Total Expenditure.		Comparison of Revenue with Expenditure, excluding Famine Relief and Loss by Exchange.	
		Excluding Famine Relief and Loss by Exchange.	Famine Relief.	Net Loss by Exchange.	TOTAL.	Surplus.	Deficit.	Surplus.	Deficit.
	£	£	£	£	£	£	£	£	£
1862–63	45,143,752	43,027,689	15,786	272,931	43,316,406	1,827,346	..	2,116,063	..
1863–64	44,613,032	44,319,587	5,230	209,868	44,534,685	78,347	..	293,445	..
1864–65	45,652,897	45,751,136	..	95,282	45,846,418	..	193,521	..	98,239
1865–66	48,935,220	46,128,891	..	40,261	46,169,152	2,766,068	..	2,806,329	..
1866–67 (11 months)	42,122,433	44,078,405	348,575	212,944	44,639,924	..	2,517,491	..	1,955,972
1867–68	48,534,412	49,145,966	230,506	165,635	49,542.107	..	1,007,695	..	611,554
1868–69	49,262,691	51,879,249	4,600	152,872	52,036,721	..	2,774,030	..	2,616,558
1869–70	50,901,081	50,596,844	83,230	102,338	50,782,412	118,669	..	304,237	..
1870–71	51,413,686	49,493,898	448	436,350	49,930,696	1,482,990	..	1,919,788	..
1871–72	50,110,215	46,807,895	5,531	172,612	46,986,038	3,124,177	..	3,302,320	..
1872–73	50,219,489	47,989,381	763	463,673	48,453,817	1,765,672	..	2,230,108	..
1873–74	49,598,253	46,949,852	3,864,707	591,362	51,405,921	..	1,807,668	2,648,401	..
1874–75	50,570,171	47,505,509	2,242,922	502,543	50,250,974	319,197	..	3,064,662	..
1875–76	51,310,063	48,096,261	510,564	1,034,293	49,641,118	1,668,945	..	3,213,802	..
1876–77	55,995,785	54,356,650	2,145,431	1,676,482	58,178,563	..	2,182,778	1,639,135	..
1877–78	58,969,301	56,074,474	5,345,775	1,092,139	62,512,388	..	3,543,087	2,891,827	..
1878–79	65,199,602	59,967,277	313,420	2,884,659	63,165,356	2,034,246	..	5,232,325	..
					TOTAL ..	£15,185,657	£14,026,270	£31,665,442	£5,282,323

The objections urged with so much force and ability against Indian finance have now been briefly reviewed. Of these, some have been fully admitted, others have been controverted, or have been mitigated by counter-considerations. The general effect of the review is, however, decidedly favourable to the position and prospects of Indian finance.

Some few subjects, relating to finance, yet remain to be mentioned.

The system of audit and account is highly organized for the whole empire, sufficiently decentralized to meet the needs of the various provinces, yet so centralized as to admit of control being completely exercised by the central Government in India. There is in each division of the empire an Accountant-General, who works with the local authorities, but who is, as regards audit and account, independent of the Local Government. The several Accountants-General are under a Controller-General, who is the auditor-in-chief immediately under the Government of India, who supervises the keeping of the national accounts, and controls the supply of funds to the various treasuries throughout the empire.

Since 1860 there has been in India a Government paper-currency, which was proposed by James Wilson, when he became finance minister. Previously there was a paper currency pertaining to the three Presidency banks of Calcutta, Madras, and Bombay, which was limited to 5 millions sterling, or 5 crores of rupees, against which one-fourth must be held in specie, while the remaining three-fourths might be issued against securities. This currency was abolished on the introduction of the Government currency, when the right of issue was transferred from the banks to the State by an Act of the legislature.

The principle on which the Government currency was based is thus set forth in a despatch in March 1860 by the Secretary of State for India, Sir Charles Wood, now Lord Halifax:—

"The sound principle for regulating the issue of a paper circulation is that which was enforced on the Bank of England by the Act of 1844, *i.e.* that the amount of notes issued on Government securities should be maintained at a fixed sum, within the limit of the smallest amount which experience has proved to be necessary for the monetary transactions of the country; and that any further amount of notes should be issued on coin or bullion, and should vary with the amount of the reserve of specie in the Bank, according to the wants and demands of the public. The important condition is thus realised that the mixed currency of notes and coin should vary in quantity exactly as if it were wholly in coin."

Upon this principle, then, the Government notes were issued when Mr. S. Laing was finance minister. The circulation amounted to 4½ millions sterling in 1862–63, and rose gradually till it amounts nowadays to 11¾ millions on the average, though it has sometimes exceeded 12, and once mounted to nearly 13 millions.

In the first instance the Government was empowered by law to issue notes on its own securities up to 4 crores of rupees, or 4 millions sterling. In 1870 it was found that the circulation had reached the amount of 11 millions sterling, against which there was a reserve of 4 millions in securities and 7 millions in coin or bullion. This circulation could not, under any possibility that might be reasonably imagined, fall short of 6 millions, or 6 crores of rupees, and power was taken by law to issue notes on Government securities up to that amount. The reserve stands at 5¾ millions sterling worth of Government securities, over 5¾ millions of coin and bullion. The interest saved on the 5¾ millions of Government securities, about £230,000 per annum, less about £30,000 of expenses incurred, represents the profit to the State.

There are ten circles or sub-circles of issue in British India, for each of which notes are issued. The State is bound by law to cash the notes of each circle at the Note office or offices of the circle, but not in other circles. It is not considered safe as yet to undertake the cashing of notes in circles other than that where they are issued. The notes bear the name of the town whence they are issued, and are payable only at the Note office of such town or at the Presidency town of the Presidency within which such town is situate.

The notes range in value from 5 rupees, or 10*s*., to 10,000 rupees, or £1000. About half the total circulation is comprised in notes of £100 and upwards; the notes of the lowest, or 5 rupee denomination, have a total value of ¼ million sterling.

The expansion of the Government paper currency is regarded as satisfactory, though of late years the rate of growth has been but slight. The increase is naturally found at the trade centres where a note currency had previously existed. There is also some circulation, amounting to about 2½ millions sterling, in the interior of the country where notes were formerly unknown. The fluctuations in the circulation have been for the most part inconsiderable, and there never has been any contraction or fall, indicating the slightest degree of public distrust. During times of national danger and disturbance, the currency of notes was maintained. For instance, in 1857, the darkest period which the Indian empire has ever seen, the annual average circulation of the Bank of Bengal notes stood at 1½ million sterling, and between May and August, that is the most critical months of that year, amounted to upwards of 1¾ million; and these amounts were fully equal to any that had been attained before the political troubles broke out.

There were formerly three mints in India, namely those at Calcutta, Madras and Bombay; the Madras mint was closed in 1869. In some seasons, such as the cotton crisis of 1865, the mints have been the scenes of extraordinary bustle and activity; of late years their business has been normal and quiet. During ten years since 1869, £192,263 worth of gold, £54,342,391 of silver, and £611,995 worth of copper, in all £55,146,649, have been coined in the mints of India. Specimen coins from each mint are tested in the London mint; and the coinage is found to be perfectly good.

Government savings-banks have been established at the Presidency towns and at many places in the interior of the country; interest at 4⅙ per cent. is now allowed on deposits up to small amounts not exceeding £50 per annum for a single depositor. The total of deposits, namely 2 millions sterling, has risen to 3 millions; the depositors are tens of thousands in number, chiefly Natives belonging to the professional classes, and certain sections of the mercantile body, but hardly at all to the agricultural community.

It has sometimes been strongly recommended that the Government in India should undertake life insurance to a moderate and limited extent. The measure was designed for the benefit of the Natives, as being calculated to teach them habits of thrifty forethought, and to form ties of the happiest kind between them and the State. Owing to various practical difficulties, also to the objections against interference with private enterprise in this respect, the Government has not yet seen its way to undertaking business of this nature, however desirable that may be on many grounds.

The principle of maintaining some connection on the part of the Government with certain banks has long prevailed in India, though State banks, in the full sense of the term, have never been established. The three Presidency banks of Bengal, Madras and Bombay respectively have existed for many years. The Government used to hold shares in these institutions, and appointed a certain number among the directors who sat on the boards of direction; the paid-up capital of the banks amounted to 4¾ millions sterling, and the Government shares to nearly ½ million in all. During the commercial crisis of 1866 the Bank of Bombay failed, involving serious consequences to the Government and the public, under circumstances which need not now be recounted. The other two banks, especially the Bank of Bengal, have had unbroken careers of successful and prosperous management. The constitution of these banks, and the relations of the Government with them, have been more than once revised by the legislature. The Government no longer holds shares in them, nor takes any part in their direction, but keeps an ordinary deposit account current with them, engaging virtually to maintain at least a certain balance in their hands, and to pay interest if the balance falls below this minimum. On the other hand, the banks are precluded from making advances beyond a certain amount, or any upon securities save those specified in the charter, namely Government securities, guaranteed railway stock and the like. They are styled the Indian or Presidency banks, and are precluded from doing much of the business that is done by the ordinary banks, which are called, in contradistinction, the "exchange banks," namely, the Chartered Bank of India and China, the Chartered Mercantile Bank, the Hongkong and Shanghai Bank, the National Bank, the Agra Bank, and the Oriental Bank. The exchange banks ordinarily keep a large portion of their own balances in the Indian or Presidency banks which have still a special position in the mercantile community, by reason of their connection with the Government, limited though it be. The Government imparts to the Presidency banks some elements of strength, without itself incurring the risk of any real embarrassment. The total capital of these three banks amounts to 3½ millions, the balance which the Government keeps in their hands ranges from ¾ million sterling to 3 millions. While their headquarters are at the Presidency towns, they have branches in the interior of every province in the empire. As now constituted, they are most valuable institutions, adding stability to the trade, and encouraging confidence in the money market. They provide a safe place where money may be deposited, and in times of pressure have the means of affording accommodation, upon securities of the best kind being tendered, serving, in a word, as anchors to the commerce of the country. Their management has during recent years been very successful; they have paid dividends at favourable rates, even during the period of commercial depression from which the empire has hardly yet emerged, and they have produced several bankers eminent in the profession.

Besides the balances in the Presidency banks, the Government in India maintains large sums in cash in its treasuries scattered throughout the empire, which are not less than 250 in number, including only district treasuries, and excluding the lesser treasuries in the interior of the districts. The needs of numerous provinces so widely dispersed cause countless demands to arise at distant points, and it hence becomes necessary to keep large resources of cash in hand. It has been often held by Indian financiers that the Government ought to maintain in India a very high cash balance, so that there should always be a reserve or surplus beyond the ordinary requirements of the public service, which resource would be immediately available in any emergency. The cash balance in India usually rises and falls at certain times in the year, like the flux and reflux of a tide; the lowest point is at the beginning of November, when on the average the amount will be down at 9 millions sterling, and the highest at the end of June, when it may be up at 15 millions; at the end of the official year, that is 31st of March, it ought to be at least 14 millions, even perhaps 15 millions. In March 1870 it stood at 17 millions, in March 1872 at 22 millions, in March 1873 at 18$\frac{3}{4}$ millions. When during 1873 the Bengal famine supervened, then the Government appreciated the national vigour which springs from the possession of a full treasury.

CHAPTER XXVIII.

STATISTICAL SUMMARY.

Area of India—Population—Several religions, castes, professions, and employments of the people—Agriculture—Works of irrigation—Embankments—Tenures—Police—Crime—Prisons—Civil justice—Hospitals and Dispensaries—Education—Universities—Literature—Post-office and electric telegraph—Emigration—Railways—Roads—Foreign sea-borne trade—Coasting trade—Harbours—Shipping—Frontier trade—Tea and coffee—Manufactures of cotton and jute—Exports of wheat and rice—Coal—Forests—Armies—Finance—Revenues and receipts—Expenditure—Coinage and paper currency—Equilibrium of income and ordinary expenditure.

In the previous chapters statistics have been here and there incidentally presented; but no attempt has been made to array or marshal the figures in a connected form; and reference may be had with advantage to the statistical abstract published annually by the India Office in London. Nevertheless the principal statistical facts relating to India, if grouped according to the natural sequence of the subjects, will strike the imagination, and fill it with ideas of the grandeur of the eastern empire. A brief summary will now be given, for the most part in round numbers, of those salient facts which are easily borne in recollection and display the magnitude which the Indian dominions of the British Crown have attained.

The area of the Indian empire amounts to one million and a half of square miles. Of this area, one-third, consisting of upwards of half a million of square miles, belongs to Native States and chiefships great and small, about 450 in number. The remaining two-thirds, or something less than one million of square miles, are British territories. These territories are divided into eight Local Governments or Administrations of various grades, namely two Governorships, three Lieutenant

Governorships and three Chief Commissionerships. The whole are under one central or supreme authority, namely the Government of India, administered by the Governor-General in Council. The executive or administrative unit is termed a district, which is somewhat like a county in England or a department in France. There are 224 such districts in British India, the average area of a district being 4000 square miles. The social unit among the Natives is the township or village, which resembles an English parish. There are 494,000 of such villages in British India; containing 37 millions of inhabited houses.

The population of the Indian empire amounts to 241 millions of souls, of whom 49 millions are in the Native States, and the remainder, or 192 millions, are in the British territories. The population in the British territories shews an average of 211 souls to the square mile. This may appear a low average, but it will be seen presently that nearly half of the whole country is uncultivated. In those provinces which have been surveyed field by field, the population is found to be 446 souls to the square mile of inhabited country, representing a high ratio of density. There is one village to half a square mile, 386 persons on the average to a village, and 5 persons to a house. Of the towns, 44 have 50,000 inhabitants and upwards, and 1358 have from 10,000 to 50,000 inhabitants.

Of the British subjects, there are 141 millions of Hindus, 18 millions of aboriginal races, 41 millions of Muhammadans, 1¼ million of Sikhs, and nearly 3 millions of Jains and Buddhists. The Christians are less than one million in number. There are 6 millions professing religions other than those above stated. Of the 141 millions of Hindus, 10 millions are Brahmins and 5½ millions Rajputs, 105½ millions belong to other or humbler castes, while 8¾ millions are either out-castes or people not recognising caste. The Asiatic non-Indian people, including Arabs, Persians, Armenians, Chinese, Siamese, Malays, Turks, Afghans and Beluches, are 550,000 in number; there are also 3600 Africans. The Europeans, Americans and Australians are

536,000 in all. It may be interesting to those engaged in the work of evangelization to observe that the aborigines and those outside the pale of caste number 26¾ millions, among whom there exist no antecedent obstacles to the reception of a new religion.

In the British territories there are 62 millions of adult males, of whom more than one-half, or 35 millions, are engaged in agriculture. Of the remainder, or 27 millions, the labourers are 8 millions; while nearly 8 millions follow industrial pursuits, and 4½ millions domestic occupation; 3½ millions are employed in commerce, and 2½ millions belong to the various professions, including Government service; 2 millions only being independent. When stress is laid on the excessive dependence of the population on agriculture, it is to be remembered that, still, there are 25 millions of adult males depending on other occupations.

The numbers of adult males employed by Government and municipalities are noteworthy; their total amounts to 1,236,523, of whom 222,594 are military and marine, 442,594 are village watchmen, while no less than 571,335 are employed in general administration. In other words, the Government of British India has more than half a million of civil employés in its service, of whom the vast majority are Natives. Besides these, there are 21,000 employed on railways. Further, there are 33,000 engaged in law, including all from the highest to the humblest, that is, from the barrister to the stamp vendor. Some 61,000 follow the profession of medicine after the oriental fashion. Those who pursue the various Asiatic arts of painting, music, dancing, juggling and the like, are 218,000. The extent to which the trade in money affords employment will be understood from the facts that 118,000 are bankers, 21,000 money-changers, and 110,000 money-lenders. Lastly, the beggars and paupers, not however supported by any poor law, are 1,050,000, or just one million.

Of the 38 millions of adult males engaged in agriculture, 6½ millions are proprietors, of whom ¾ million, or 750,000, do not work, but live as landlords great or small, while the remainder, or 5¾ millions, are engaged in cultivation, more or less, as peasant proprietors. The farm servants and labourers are nearly one million, while the bailiffs and upper servants are 105,000. There are 20,100 cattle dealers, 589,000 herdsmen and graziers, and 260,000 otherwise employed with animals.

The agricultural statistics of the empire are unavoidably imperfect, because the Government has considered itself precluded from insisting on the collection of such information in these provinces which are under the permanent settlement; consequently many interesting particulars which can be rendered for other provinces are not forthcoming for the provinces under the Government of Bengal. With this large reservation, however, many important facts can be stated. Exclusive, then, of Bengal, Behar, and Orissa, there have been 132 millions of acres surveyed and assessed field by field in the manner described in the foregoing chapter on the land-tax. Of this total, 25 millions of acres are irrigated, or less than one-fifth of the whole, the remaining four-fifths being unirrigated. Moreover, there are 10½ millions of cultivated acres not yet surveyed in detail, making up a total cultivated area of 142½ millions of acres. As a remarkable fact in juxtaposition with the above circumstances, it is to be noted that the cultivable area, inclusive of grazing lands, amounts to 102 millions of acres, equal to more than two-thirds of the cultivated area; and there can hardly be any mistake on this point, because out of this cultivable area no less than 88 millions of acres have been surveyed in detail. The grand total of the cultivated and the cultivable area amounts to 244½ millions of acres. Now, the uncultivable area is nearly the same, namely 243½ millions of acres; in other words, only one-half of the entire area is cultivated; a fact which shews how extensive the hill-sides, stony plains and deserts really are. Similar conditions appear to exist also in the provinces under the Government of Bengal, of which the total area (exclusive of rivers and lakes) amounts to 101 millions of acres, of which 54 millions only are estimated as being under cultivation.

In the provinces surveyed as above, 8 millions of ploughs are shewn in the returns, and 31 millions head of cattle (including cows, bullocks and buffaloes). But the information is defective in some provinces, and these figures, high as they are, do not convey an adequate idea of the resources of the empire in such respects.

Out of the 25 millions of acres under irrigation, as shewn above, 6⅓ millions are irrigated from canals, as seen in the previous chapter on canals. The length of these canals has there been stated at nearly 13,000 miles of main channels, besides distributing channels. These works have been constructed by the State at a cost of 21½ millions sterling, already yielding a net return of 1¼ million sterling annually, equal to 6 per cent. interest on the capital outlay. There are, on the other hand, embankments for protecting the lands, near the lower course of the Ganges and the Indus, from injury by floods. The total length of the principal of these embankments amounts to 1370 miles; besides many lesser embankments.

The land is for the most part devoted to the production of edible grains; out of 188 millions of cultivated acres, 161 millions are under food-crops, and only 27 millions under non-food-crops.

The prevalence of the several tenures described in the previous chapter on the land-tax may be illustrated numerically thus. In the provinces under the Government of Bengal there are 130,000 estates, held by landlords great and small; some of whom have large rentals, for instance the Raja of Bardwan with an annual income from land of £400,000, Darbhanga £210,000, Bettia £130,000, Hatwa £90,000, and others. In the Central Provinces there are 28,000 estates, mostly held by small landlords. In the Panjab 91 per cent., North-western Provinces 90 per cent., and Oudh 36 per cent. of the land is held by the village communities described in a previous chapter. In Madras there are 2,392,000 peasant proprietors, holding under the ryotwari tenure, of whom 1,251,750 pay less than £1 of land revenue each year. In Bombay there are 1,367,622 of these peasant proprietors, of whom 737,000 each hold ten acres of land or less.

The selling price of land may be indicated in this wise. In the Panjab the price is 27 years' purchase, of the Government revenue; in Madras it ranges up to £10 per acre unirrigated and £36 per acre irrigated.

Internal order is maintained in this area, and among this population, by a regular police force of 158,000, officers and men. Out of this number, the cost of 27,000 men is defrayed by municipalities and other bodies, while the charges for the remainder, or 131,000 men, falls entirely on the State. That the strength of this police force is moderate, is shewn by the average of one policeman to seven square miles and to 1000 people. Besides these, however, there is the rural police, or village watchmen, of whom the number will be nearly coincident with that of villages, which has been already set down at 442,000.

In so large a population the number of crimes and offences must necessarily be large; it stands at nearly 880,000 in the year. Then, the number of persons brought to trial in the year amounts to 970,000, or nearly one million, of whom 350,000, on the average, are discharged, and 550,000 convicted or committed, the rest being under trial. These facts will give some idea of the business devolving on the police and the magistracy.

There are 211 prisons in the whole country, exclusive of 386 lock-ups, and the daily average of prisoners amounts to 118,500, of whom only 5500 are females.

The civil litigation is considerable, as will be seen from the number of suits instituted in the year, namely 1,500,000. Of this number two-thirds are for money and the remainder for rent and other things. The estimated value of the suits, that is, the amount claimed and disputed, stands at the large sum of upwards of 14 millions sterling annually. Out of this number the suits for small amounts up to £10 are upwards of 1,100,000, valued at 3¾ millions sterling. These facts throw some light on the question so often debated as to whether there is much wealth in the country.

The main result of the organization of public charity by the State will be comprehended in the facts that there are 1150 charitable dispensaries and hospitals, which receive 270,000 indoor patients during the year, and afford outdoor relief in 6½ millions of cases. The total of indoor and outdoor patients exceeds 6,900,000 in the year, exhibiting a daily average of 19,000 persons. There are also 22 lunatic asylums, having 3470 inmates. The returns shew that 3½ millions of persons are successfully vaccinated annually.

In a year 20,000 persons and 50,000 head of cattle are destroyed by wild beasts and snakes. Reference may be had to Sir Joseph Fayrer's illustrated work on the venomous snakes of India.

The three Presidency towns, Calcutta, Madras, and Bombay, have a population within municipal limits of 1,471,492 souls; the members of the three corporations are 176 in number, of whom 122 are Natives and the remainder Europeans; the income administered by them amounts to £668,400 annually. The district municipalities in the interior of the country are 894 in number, and the members of the municipal committees are 7519, of whom 5725 are Natives and the remainder Europeans; the income administered by them amounts to £1,284,312 annually; the population within their municipal limits stands at 12,380,000 souls. The average incidence of municipal duties and taxes is 9*s.* per head per annum in the Presidency towns, and only 2*s.* in the district municipalities.

The national education is promoted by about 65,500 institutions including schools and colleges of all sorts supported in some degree, or inspected, by the State. The number of students is returned as 1,900,000, or nearly two millions. Out of this number there are 72,200 girls at schools maintained for them specially, besides a considerable number at mixed schools of boys and girls. The colleges are 82 in number, with 8900 students, the normal and technical schools are 155, with 6900 students. In the returns are included 104 schools for Europeans, with 9100 students of both sexes. The total of these numbers, in themselves great, is relatively not large, for in all they shew only nine scholars to 1000 of the population. It appears to be thought by some that the State undertakes too much in the way of public instruction through its own direct agency. But the purely Government institutions are only 14,500 in number, with 550,000 students, equal to less than one-fourth of the whole. Again, it seems to be supposed that the State maintains inadequately the grant-in-aid system; but the aided schools are 28,500 in number, with 650,000 students; while the remaining institutions are under State inspection.

Some light is thrown upon the effect of the high education by the result of the examinations at the Universities. During the ten years preceding 1879, 49,000 candidates, Natives with but few exceptions, presented themselves for entrance; of whom 18,500 only passed, a fact which is creditable to the strictness of the examiners. During the same period, in round numbers, 4200 passed the first arts examination, which, as explained in the chapter on education, is only an intermediate one; 1610 became Bachelors of Arts, and 305 Masters of Arts; 890 took a degree in law, 950 in medicine, and 255 in civil engineering. As passing the first arts examination is not equivalent to taking a degree, it follows that during ten years, out of 18,500 young men who entered the Universities, only 4040, or less than one-fourth, took degrees.

Some literary activity prevails in British India, as seen from the registration of publications under the law. In the course of a year 4900 works are published, of which 550 are in English, 3050 in the vernacular, 730 in the classical languages of India, and 570 in more than one language.

In Bengal there are 38 vernacular newspapers, in Madras 22, in Bombay 78, in upper and Central India 65. In Bengal the circulation is represented by 19,360 copies, in Madras 5,750, in Bombay 15,587, in upper and Central India 15,608.

The State expenditure on education shews variations according as certain items are excluded or included, and the total ranges from £750,000 to £970,000 annually; in the previous chapter on education the sum of £800,000 has been taken as an average.

The progress of the country in general intelligence may be illustrated by the principal facts of the postal and telegraphic departments. There are 5500 post-offices in the whole country, 58,000 miles of postal lines, £660,000 of cash receipts annually from the public, exclusive of official postage, and 131 millions of letters and covers despatched in the year. There are 240 signal offices open for telegraphic communication, and 1¼ million of private messages are despatched annually, exclusive of State and service messages. The telegraphic lines extend over 19,100 miles, have involved an outlay of 3½ millions sterling, and despatch 1¾ million of messages a year either for the State or the public, including the private messages stated above.

The total number of persons, Natives, who have emigrated from India to the colonies during the ten years between 1869 and 1879, is 173,420, of whom 29,600 went to French, and 4200 to Dutch colonies, while the remainder proceeded to the British possessions.

It has been seen in the chapter on railways that the lines opened for traffic comprise 8600 miles, of which 6073 miles belong to guaranteed companies, 2363 miles to the Government, and 175 to Native States. Besides these, there are 1850 miles of lines proposed to be executed soon. The passenger traffic is represented by 43 millions of passengers in the year, and the goods traffic amounts to 8 millions of tons annually. The rolling stock employed in working the railways consists of 1850 locomotives, 4294 passenger carriages, and 34,856 trucks. The capital outlay by the guaranteed companies amounts to 97¼ millions sterling, that by the Government to 24½ millions, that by Native States to 1½ million, or 123¼ millions in all. The gross receipts on the guaranteed lines amount to 9¾ millions sterling in the year, and the expenses to 4¾ millions; and on the State lines (incomplete) the gross receipts amount annually to 1½ million, the expenses to something over 1 million. The extent to which the moneyed classes in England are interested in the guaranteed railways may be understood from the fact that the stock and debentures of these companies are held by 63,290 persons, of whom only 301 are registered in India.

Out of the 58,000 miles of postal roads, at least 20,000 miles are metalled or macadamized, and partially bridged.

The external sea-borne trade is valued at 110 millions sterling annually; for one recent year it stood at 120 millions. Out of the 110 millions, 60 millions represent exports of merchandise and 36 millions imports; the remainder is made up by treasure. Out of this foreign trade 60 per cent. is with the United Kingdom, and 40 per cent. with other nations. India sends to England 28 millions sterling worth of produce, and receives 30 millions worth of merchandise; in other words, regarding this part of the trade the imports are fully equal in value to the exports. But in the trade with other countries, India has during recent years sold more of her produce to them than she has taken of their products in return. On the whole trade the value of the exports has for recent years exceeded that of the imports by 16 millions sterling per annum on the average. The value of the stores imported by the Government now stands at 2¼ millions sterling annually, and during the ten years between 1869 and 1879 has amounted to 13½ millions sterling.

The coasting trade between the various ports is now considerable, and has risen in value from 44 millions sterling in 1873 to 67¾ millions in 1877–8. There are 9185 miles of coast, and 300 places which are recognised as ports, most of which are very small.

This foreign trade is entirely sea-borne; the shipping engaged in it may be stated at 12,500 vessels, with a total tonnage of 5½ millions of tons, of which 2000 vessels, with a tonnage of 2¼ millions of tons, are steamers; of the steamers about two-thirds come and go by the Suez Canal. Of the total shipping, 88 per cent. is British, and the remainder, or 12 per cent., is foreign.

The Suez Canal was opened on November 17, 1869; the

figures of the shipping are not recorded until the year 1871–2. During the nine years which have since elapsed, nearly 8000 steamers, with a tonnage of 10 millions of tons, have passed through the Canal. On the average, 1200 steamers, with a tonnage of 1¾ million of tons, use the Canal annually.

The external trade by land with Afghanistan, Beluchistan and the Himalayan regions, though small as compared with the sea-borne trade, is yet considerable, and amounts, exports and imports together, to 4¼ millions.

Some interesting particulars may here be summarized regarding the products and manufactures.

Of tea, 34 millions of pounds, valued at 3 millions sterling, are produced annually; and of coffee, 350,000 cwts., valued at 1⅓ million sterling. The exports of wheat fluctuate in amount, in 1877 they amounted to 5½ millions of cwts., and in 1878 to 6½ millions. The quantity of rice exported amounts to nearly 21 millions of cwts.

There are 53 spinning and weaving mills in India, which employ 10,500 looms and 1½ million of spindles. On the average 4 millions of cwts. of raw cotton are exported annually. Of jute 5 millions of cwts. are exported annually, valued at 3 millions sterling; the jute manufactures in India itself are valued at ¾ of a million yearly.

The total out-put of the collieries is reckoned at 1 million of tons annually; the local consumption amounts to ½ million of tons; and upwards of ½ million of tons of English coal and coke are imported. The coal industry affords employment to 60,000 men.

The forests more or less under protection or conservation cover an area of 68,100 square miles, of which less than one-half is fully preserved. Indeed the Famine Commission reckon that hardly more than one-third, or 24,000 square miles, are thus preserved.

In the previous chapter on the material progress of the Natives allusion has been made to the doubts expressed by some as to whether British India raises enough of food-crops for the sustenance of the people, and whether the value of the total produce, agricultural and non-agricultural, indicates an income sufficient for meeting their wants and for enabling them to pay the revenue without impoverishment. The Famine Commission have been at some pains to present calculations bearing on this point. Exclusive of British Burma, there are 166¼ millions of acres under food-crops and 27 millions of acres under non-food-crops. The gross annual value is set down at 331 millions sterling per annum, at £5 per ton for food and £3 per acre for non-food-crops. If British Burma were included, the grand total would not be less than 345 millions; which is considerably in excess of calculations recently made by some able writers, which shewed a total value of under 280 millions, exclusive of British Burma. Upon this area the average out-turn of food is estimated at 51½ millions of tons; of which amount 38 millions are required for consumption by the people, 3½ millions for seed, 3 millions for cattle-fodder, while 2½ millions are allowed for wastage; leaving 4½ millions of tons surplus, available for storage at home or exportation abroad. To which must be added ¾ million, the exportable surplus of British Burma; making up the total to 5¼ millions of tons. This calculation is offered by the Commission as approximate only; the known movements of grain during the famines of 1874 and 1877–8 prove it to be moderate; it is indeed probably below the reality. During the famine of 1877–8, 2 millions of tons of food were imported by sea into the distressed districts and 4 millions of tons were moved by rail in different parts of the country.

The established strength of the European army stands in round numbers at 4570 officers and 60,156 non-commissioned officers and privates, in all 64,726 officers and men; that of the Native army stands at 1617 European officers and 123,254 Native officers and men, in all 189,597 officers and men. Out of the last-named total, 104,216 officers and men belong to the army of Bengal, 47,026 to that of Madras, and 38,355 to that of Bombay.

The principal financial facts may be thus epitomized. The ordinary revenue and receipts amount to 58¼ millions sterling annually, to which are added 7 millions sterling receipts from productive public works, making up a grand total of 65¼ millions. It is expected that during the current year 1880 this total will exceed 67 millions. Of the 7 millions above stated, ¾ million pertain to canals and works of irrigation, and the remainder to railways belonging to Guaranteed companies and to the State. From the chapter on the revenues it has been seen that, out of the grand total, the revenues proper amount to 43½ millions sterling annually.

The ordinary expenditure amounts to 55 millions sterling annually, including 5 millions of expenditure on ordinary public works, civil and military buildings and the like. To this are added 8¼ millions of expenditure on productive public works, working expenses and interest, making up a grand total of 63¼ millions annually. The capital expenditure on productive public works amounts annually to 4⅓ millions, which may perhaps be diminished in future years.

The 65¼ millions sterling above mentioned have risen to 67½ and 66¾ during the years 1879–80 and 1880–1, gross; but the charges of collection and the like are considerable, and these being deducted, the net revenue stands at 44½ millions.

In the total of 55 millions sterling of ordinary expenditure there are comprised 10 millions of direct claims and demands upon the revenues, including charges of collection; 4½ millions of interest on permanent and floating debt, 3¼ millions of expenditure on law and justice; 2½ millions on police; 17 millions on the army, and 3½ millions of loss by exchange on transactions with London.

The incidence of the existing taxation has been mentioned in the previous chapter on revenue. It is further described in the following extract from the report by the Famine Commission:

"The general incidence of all taxation, including the land revenue in this term, on the whole population is 4*s.* a head. The landed classes pay about 5*s.* 6*d.* (44 annas) per head; but, excluding the revenue they pay for their land to the State, their share of taxation is 1*s.* 9*d.* (14 annas) per head. The agricultural labourers pay taxes on their liquor and salt, amounting to 1*s.* 8*d.* (or 13½ annas) per head, or each family pays about a fortnight's wages in the year. The artisans pay about 2*s.* (16 annas) each, or about the average earnings of five working days. Traders pay 3*s.* 3*d.* (26 annas) each. But any native of India who does not trade or own land, and who chooses to drink no spirituous liquor or to use no English cloth or iron, need pay in taxation only about 7*d.* a year on account of the salt he consumes personally; and on a family of three persons the charge amounts to 1*s.* 9*d.*, or about four days' wages of a labouring man and his wife."

The public debt proper, that is, the registered interest-bearing debt, amounts to 149 millions sterling, of which 33½ millions have been spent on productive public works. The portion of the public debt incurred for war is less than 100 millions, or little more than two years of the annual revenue proper of 43½ millions, or 87 millions, and much less than two years of the total revenues and receipts, which amount to 65 millions annually. With the exception of 17 millions, this debt bears a 4 per cent. rate of interest.

The credit of the Government of India has stood, and still stands high, as is proved by the prices of the Indian securities in India and in England. Of the rupee debt (in silver) the 4 per cent. Government securities some years ago used to be sold in India at 91 for 100 rupees; then gradually rose to par and reached 105, or 5 per cent. premium in 1873. They have since receded, owing partly to the fall in the value of silver, and now stand at 97. For several years before 1878 the Government obtained its loans at 4 per cent., whereas the rate used formerly to be 5 per cent. Since 1878 the rate has been

4½ per cent., and the securities under this category were sold in India at 99½ and 100½; they now stand at 105.

Of the sterling debt (in gold) the 4 per cent. securities have ranged from 92 to 106. They now stand at 105, a rate which is one of the most favourable rates in the world, and may be regarded as second only to the rate at which the Government of England itself would be able to borrow.

In a previous chapter on the material progress of the Natives, the proportion held by them out of the total public debt in India and in England was set down at 18 millions sterling, or one-eighth. The latest returns, however, raise this amount to 20 millions. Now, the debt held in India amounts to 80 millions sterling in assumed value, of which 20 millions are enfaced for payment of interest in England and are presumably held by Europeans; leaving 60 millions, of which the interest is paid in India. Out of the latter sum, 20 millions, equal to one-third, belong to Natives.

It is noteworthy that in June 1880, when three crores of rupees, or three millions sterling, were borrowed by the Government in India at 4½ per cent., the large sum of 26½ crores was tendered, of which no less than 9¼ crores or millions were offered by Natives.

The total coinage at the two mints during the decade ending with 1878 amounted to 52½ millions sterling, of which 51⅓ millions' worth were in silver. The circulation of the Government currency notes on the average amounts to 11½ millions sterling. The deposits in the Government savings-banks amount to more than 2 millions sterling. The total capital of the three Presidency banks amounts to 3½ millions sterling.

Some light is thrown on the wealth of India by the facts that, during the ten years ending with 1879, 25 millions' sterling worth of gold and 66 of silver, in all 91 millions of specie and bullion—while 6 millions' worth of gold and 16 millions of silver were exported, in all 22 millions, leaving a net amount of 69 millions in the hands of the Indian people, being an average of about 7 millions a year.

In the previous chapters on canals, on railways and on finance, it has been seen that the public works are now proving remunerative to the State, and that, owing partly to this cause and partly to reduction of the rates of interest, the interest charges on the public debt have not materially increased, notwithstanding the considerable augmentation of the capital of the debt. On this subject the Famine Commission report that "in the present year for the first time the public accounts contain a correct statement of the financial results of the class of works now known as "productive," that is, all those carried out with the help of borrowed capital, or under a guarantee of interest. It appears from the estimates of 1880–1 that a surplus of income is expected from these works over all charges, including the whole of the interest on all the capital laid out, whether that capital was specially borrowed or provided from the revenues of last years, or raised under guarantee, and whether the works on which it has been expended are in operation or not."

In further illustration of this subject, the Commission present the following table. They say:—

Year.	Net Interest on Ordinary Debt. (1.)	Net Charge for Productive Works. (2.)	Total of (1) and (2).	Net Charge Ordinary Public Works. (3.)	Grand Total.
	£	£	£	£	£
1868–69 .	5,383,000	2,011,000	7,394,000	5,751,000	13,145,000
1869–70 .	5,155,000	1,737,000	6,892,000	4,349,000	11,241,000
1870–71 .	5,338,000	2,084,000	7,422,000	3,409,000	10,831,000
1871–72 .	5,386.000	2,012,000	7,398,000	3,399,000	10,797,000
1872–73 .	5,058,000	2,687.000	7,745,000	3,532,000	11,277,000
1873–74 .	4,930,000	2,124,000	7.054,000	3,072,000	10,126,000
1874–75 .	4,305,000	1,913,000	6,218,000	3,392,000	9,610,000
1875–76 .	4,268,000	1,697.000	5,965,000	3,550,000	9,515.000
1876–77 .	4,371,000	1,161,000	5,532,000	3,311,000	8,843,000
1877–78 .	4,500,000	35,000	4,535,000	3,305,000	7,840,000
1878–79 .	4,326,000	1,600.000	5,926,000	4,425,000	10,351,000
1879–80 .	4,121,000	586,000	4,707,000	4,546,000	9,253,000

"N.B.—The charge for ordinary public works has been increased in the last two years by including expenditure of local funds not entered before, and from a proper comparison with the earlier years about 1,200,000*l.* should be deducted from the charge for the two last years.

"The sudden reduction of charge for productive works in 1877–78 is due to the greatly increased railway receipts from the grain traffic during the famine."

"The financial effect of the public works policy of the Government during the last 12 years is further, and more completely, exhibited in the following figures" [in the table on p. 486], "which shew (1) the net charge for interest on the public debt, excluding the amount borrowed for productive works as defined in par. 12; (2) the net charge for interest on capital and working expenses of all productive public works after setting off the income received from them—under this head are included guaranteed railways, State railways, and irrigation works; (3) the whole ordinary outlay on all other public works."

Lastly, it has been seen that an equilibrium is maintained between income and ordinary expenditure. Some of the deficits, which used during several years to be exhibited in the national accounts, were attributable to the inclusion of the capital outlay on productive public works. When this outlay is excluded, and shewn separately, as it ought to be, then upon the latest series of years there will be found to exist a net surplus of 1½ million sterling of income over ordinary expenditure during the period.

CHAPTER XXIX.

CONCLUSION.

Recent war in Afghanistan—Its results and lessons—Prosperity of the Indian empire, despite some inevitable drawbacks—Adverse calculations contradicted by existing facts—Satisfactory answer to question as to why England should retain possession of India—Virtues and merits in the character of the Natives—Their general contentment under British rule—Happy prospect rising before them.

THE beginning of the end of this exposition may well comprise a brief notice of the second Afghan war.

Hostilities carried on, from the autumn of 1878 to the present time, in Afghanistan, have been brought near to a conclusion, though no man can yet say whether they are actually concluded. Their political effect is connected with the considerations set forth in the previous chapter on foreign relations The Indian Government, when Lord Lytton was its head, propounded a definite policy, which was calculated to have such permanency as is possible in a troublous region. The broad results of that policy were embodied in the treaty of Gandamak. Of these results a small portion has been lost, owing to events beyond the control of the Government; whether the remainder, or greater portion, shall be preserved, depends on the action of the Government itself, of which action the future course is not as yet publicly known. Be this course as it may, however, some results have actually been obtained. The might as well as the right of England to control the foreign relations of Afghanistan, irrespective of its internal administration, has been vindicated before the world. The resolution of the British Government to take up arms, if necessary, in defence of claims which have once been deliberately asserted, has been proved in the face of all Asia. The hostile power of the late Amir Shir-Ali has been overturned. The military means possessed by the Indian Government for overrunning Afghanistan, after one month's preparation, have been demonstrated. This display will serve as a serious warning to the future rulers of that country. The moral effect upon neighbouring nations has been salutary, and the impression upon Persia decisive. The military power of the Indian Government was already respected by Asiatic nations. Still, inasmuch as deterioration during a long peace of twenty years is, according to common experience, but too common, it is well that all men should know by these events that this power is at least kept up to its historic standard, and is probably greater than ever. Since the completion of the present railway system, this was the first occasion when war on a considerable scale had been carried on. On the commencement of hostilities in 1878, the advantages of railway communication were remarkable, as the troops were brought up to the frontier by rail from great distances. The enemy must have been struck with surprise on perceiving that an invasion, which in the first war of 1839 occupied several months of preparation, took only as many weeks in the second war of 1878, and at some points only as many days. There had of late years been debates as to what force the Government of India could send to the field. It is now seen that a force equal to two army corps of 33,000 men each, or 66,000 men, was sent to the frontier or across it. During the time of this war, the conduct of the vast Indian population was loyal and exemplary, with one unimportant exception on the east coast, and one notable exception in the Deccan, as explained in the previous chapter on crime. The Native troops behaved well, even better on the whole than during the war of 1839; the Gorkha and Panjabi soldiers being specially distinguished. One regiment only, that of Jacob's Rifles, formed an exception to the general standard of merit. But the experience of this war is held to have proved the correctness of what had been urged by many authorities regarding the paucity of European officers, and the need of properly maintaining the complement of these officers. It is also found that, although the Native soldiery proceeded with the utmost alacrity to Afghanistan for a campaign, yet protracted service in that country proves to be unpopular with some of the Indian races which have heretofore furnished recruits for the Native army. Among the European forces, the cavalry and artillery proved quite worthy of their ancient renown. Of the infantry, those regiments which consisted of comparatively old soldiers displayed all the best fighting qualities for which the British army has been famous. Some corps, however, in which the new short service regulations had produced a considerable effect, exemplified the very defects attributed to that system by so many military authorities, and the inconvenient consequences which had been predicted as likely to result. It is to be hoped the serious teachings of this experience will be duly noted. The difficulties of the transport in the field have been already described in the chapter on the army. It should never be forgotten that, if military operations are undertaken in the winter, the animals have to traverse frost-bound regions without a blade of fodder, and must soon succumb to inanition unless the difficult task of conveying and storing food for them shall be accomplished. These difficulties were overcome by the strenuous exertions of the officers of all grades from the highest to the lowest, and thus the resources of India were brought into full play. It is very desirable that a permanent organization of this important branch of the service should be undertaken for the future.

The Afghans, as a fighting race, recently displayed all the characteristics which have so often proved embarrassing to British commanders. They are in the first instance beaten without difficulty, upon being regularly attacked, and then seem ready to tender a virtual submission. But they soon rally again for resistance, and await a favourable moment for assailing their conquerors. If they find their enemy placed at any disadvantage, they are wonderfully prompt and skilful in seizing their opportunity. Their clans muster rapidly in thickly gathering numbers, and every husbandman is a ready-made soldier after his kind. The word passes round, and all the men of the fighting age turn out under arms instantly. This is the reason why it so often becomes impossible for British commanders to learn the strength of the Afghan forces in the field. It would not be just to blame British officers for failing to ascertain that which is not ascertainable. The Afghans are in their homes one day, apparently non-combatant, the next day they are in the field arrayed for battle, a few days afterwards they are in their villages again, assuming the appearance of peaceable inhabitants. It is possible that they might submit to foreign domination so long as they saw that their rulers were in too great strength to be displaced and that resistance was hopeless. But they would be ever on the watch for a chance of striking for their independence; and if among the many accidents which are but too possible in such a country as theirs, an occasion were to present itself, they would break out into insurrection with unsubdued energy. This description is applicable fully to the country around Caubul and to northern Afghanistan, but in a much less degree to the country around Candahar and to southern Afghanistan; indeed many believe that the city and district of Candahar could, if necessary, be permanently held. There is a considerable difference between the character of the northern tribes and that of the southern.

The fight at the Paiwar pass in the autumn of 1878, the rapid advance upon Candahar somewhat later in the same year, the march from Kurrum upon Caubul in 1879, and the battle on the heights before that city, the fight near Ghazni, in 1880, and the fine movement from Caubul for the relief of Candahar, followed by the decisive battle near that city, make up a sum of success fit to be included in the military annals of England, and chequered by only one defeat, namely, that at Maiwand. The memory of Sir Frederick Roberts and Sir Donald Stewart will be handed down to posterity as belonging to that long and illustrious roll of commanders whom the Indian service has produced, and with them will be associated the names of their able coadjutors Generals Baker, Macgregor, Macpherson, and Gough.

Signal as the successes of the Indian Government have been in war, its achievements in peace have been equally great. Sir James Stephen wrote, in 1877, regarding the administration of British India, that he had enjoyed the privilege of being a close spectator of one of the greatest sights in the world. Of the East India Company he truly said that it ceased to exist in the full pride of its strength, in the moment of its crowning triumph, at the hands, not of the mutineers who tried to throw it down, but of men who raised the imperial Company to its proper place when they made it a permanent member of the Government of England. Though the corporation had gone, yet, he declared, the corporators remain, and men of the same stamp do the same work, as of old. The Company's colours, which had been displayed on many seas and many battle-fields, were struck twenty years ago, and the flag of England was hoisted in their place.

The various phases and conditions presented by the Indian empire have now been described. The motto of the imperial administration should be "festina lente." By "festina" is meant that confident energy which must ever be the main-spring of progress. By "lente" is meant that circumspect caution which is essential to success.

If the views of the existing facts and circumstances which have been set forth in the foregoing chapters shall find acceptance, the effect must be to mitigate the apprehensions of those whose gaze has dwelt on the darker side of current affairs, and to confirm the hopefulness of those whose regards are attracted towards the brighter. Though endeavour has been made to paint broadly the veritable shadows in the picture, still the lights of various degrees have forced themselves into prominence. With some few manifest exceptions, the state of the empire is such as to cause pride on the retrospect of a glorious past, satisfaction on the survey of an animated present, and hope on the contemplation of a pregnant future.

Three grave and abiding dangers must indeed be borne in remembrance, namely, the reappearance of famine to lay its fatal hand on the lives of millions, the financial disturbance from the fluctuating value of silver in the foreign exchanges, and the war-cloud hanging heavily over the regions which divide Afghanistan from Central Asia. But while these elements of evil are borne in mind, the many grounds of safety must be observed. During seasons, ordinarily propitious in respect of rain and sunshine, the population increases, cultivation expands, wealth is stored, capital is accumulated, trade grows, and the revenue rises. While the material condition of the people, from one generation to another, is gradually being raised, the Government adopts all practicable measures for the protection of their rights, the encouragement of their industry, the elevation of their social status and the advancement of their education. The moral development of the classes who most immediately come under these influences is remarkable. The temper of the masses is peaceful, their mind contented, their disposition law abiding. The vast majority of the people, including British subjects and feudatory States, is actuated by loyalty towards the Sovereign, and by good-will towards the British nation. In times of prosperity the Government, though claiming so much of success, searches vigilantly for the evils yet to be cured, the shortcomings to be retrieved, the defects to be remedied. In times of adversity, improvements are devised which not only relieve the pressure of the emergency, but also produce permanent benefit when the storm shall have passed away.

Elaborate calculations are sometimes made to shew that the population is outgrowing the limits of agriculture, that the people do not raise enough income to enable them to live in reasonable comfort, that even sometimes the land is being cultivated at a loss, and does not yield enough to enable the landowners to pay their land revenue. Such calculations are instructive, and evince an enquiring spirit, which conduces to administrative improvement. But they often rest on assumed data which do not admit of exact verification. Their extreme conclusions cannot be accepted in opposition to large facts which are patent to all who take a comprehensive survey of the country. That they must have some flaw destructive to their validity is proved by the known circumstances of the empire. It were vain to estimate that the people must ere long be famished for lack of agriculture, when vast cultivable areas within India itself are seen to be inviting the approach of the plough. It were futile to offer statistical proof that the food-supply must be insufficient, when large quantities of edible grain are being stored at home and exported abroad. The Government is not likely to credit calculations shewing that the cultivation, being burdened with the existing land-tax, cannot prove remunerative, when the revenue is collected with ease and punctuality; when it actually increases from time to time notwithstanding the reduction in its rates, because new lands are brought under cultivation; when landed property is treated by the people as a valuable security; when land commands a selling price unknown in any previous era; when the fiscal demand is demonstrably much below that which prevailed under the preceding Native dynasties and which prevails among the Native States at the present time. Let the revenues of the Queen-Empress of India to-day be compared with the most authentic account of those of Akber the Great or the Emperor Shah Jehan, and it will be observed that upon at least an equal population, a probably wider area of cultivation, and a greater trade, a lower fiscal demand is made now than formerly. If any one of the Native States, in which the administration is wisest and the taxation mildest, be now contrasted with the adjacent British territories, it will be found to exact much more proportionably from its subjects than is levied under Her Majesty's Government.

Nor will reliance be placed on vague estimates, accompanied with broad assertions that the people are becoming poorer, in the face of the improvement of their dwellings, the rise of their wages, the expansion of their trade, foreign and domestic, and the growth of new industries. The fact that many persons will die during famine, unless relieved by the State, is not to be admitted as a proof of deepening poverty, because no labouring class in any country can withstand without mortal injury the cessation of employment and of wages for several consecutive months. But the experience of the recent famines has proved, what was quite believed before, that large classes habitually hoard, in times of plenty, some stores of grain for their sustenance in the day of dearth. Indeed, these calamities, while exposing some chinks in the armour of the body politic, have yet afforded substantial encouragement, in that so many sections of the population were found to possess resources for self-support as well as a resolute spirit of self-help.

These fears and apprehensions tend avowedly to certain practical conclusions, and will in some degree be judged by those conclusions, as a tree is esteemed according to its fruits. These conclusions are set forth somewhat in this wise. The agencies of steam and electricity, which have revolutionized so beneficently the condition of Europe, cannot be afforded for the Indian empire. The attempts to protect the country, by works of material improvement against famine, result from a mistaken policy. The introduction of a civilized administration, calculated to humanize and elevate Native society, is beyond the present needs of the people. Laws, derived from the best traditions of bygone times and from the practice of the most advanced nations, are not conducive to the welfare of Indians. The virtue, energy, and resolution of British administrators, whereby an imperial dominion has been established, may be dispensed with. Even the military strength of the empire may be reduced, till India shall be left with her breast bare to every foe. The mere statement of such conclusions shews that there must be a radical defect in the reasoning which gives birth to them.

The train of argument is even carried further by some persons, till at length the electors of the United Kingdom are asked to consider why they should vote for keeping India at all. Stress seems to be laid but slightly upon the sense of national responsibility, and the spirit of patriotic duty, which stir Englishmen to a degree never surpassed by any race at any era; these sentiments are apparently set aside, as pertaining to the pride of empire. But attention is drawn to the risks which are supposed to be inseparable from the possession of foreign dominion, and to far outweigh the advantages of commerce being extended, or fresh fields being opened abroad for British energy and capital. It almost seems to be thought that India is a source of expense to England, a clog upon the resources, and a drain upon the population of the United Kingdom. The cutting adrift of the encumbrance is pronounced to be the true remedy for the alleged embarrassment. Englishmen are actually advised to relinquish the heritage of their fathers, and other nations are invited to don, if they have the courage, the imperial mantle when England shall have cast it off. Still, it is well that, as a prudent nation, England should address searching enquiries to herself, and among such investigations may be the question why she should keep India, together with the answer thereto.

England, then, must keep India

—because during more than a century she has assumed the government of a vast population, rescued by her from anarchy, revolution, and internecine strife, and now living in loyalty contentment and prosperity under her sway;

—because, in the faith of British power being permanent, immense interests have arisen, which depend on the security of rights under fixed laws with a competent executive, and would be imperilled by the withdrawal of the paramount authority, letting loose the destructive elements that the British Government now restrains, as Æolus imprisons in his cave

"Luctantes ventos, tempestatesque sonoras;"

—because the abnegation by England of responsibilities, persistently taken up by her, would leave her friends, allies, and supporters in India, and all, who have there prospered under her ægis, to become the prey and sport of disruptive forces;
—because the influences of Western civilization, especially education, have called into being new schools of thought and belief, comprising men who have sacrificed social status and broken ancestral ties, in order to follow the light of European guidance, and who ought not now to be deserted by England;
—because a vast amount of British capital has been sunk in the country, on the assurance of British rule being, humanly speaking, perpetual, the said capital being invested in railways and canals, or in industrial and commercial enterprises;
—because the British Government has incurred a considerable debt by issuing securities, of which a large portion is held by Europeans and a considerable part by Natives;
—because under the British flag a great trade has sprung up, which, though sea-borne, does yet wholly depend on the maintenance of order in the interior of the country, and would languish if British power were to cease;
—because extensive markets have been, and are being, opened for British manufactures, all which must be, more or less, closed if the country should revert to disorder on the retirement of the British authorities;
—because the Indian empire is self-supporting financially, has borne the cost of all its wars, without imposing any charge or burden upon the United Kingdom, and has on the other hand rendered assistance in British wars waged beyond its own limits in Persia, Abyssinia and China;
—because England does not incur any expense for maintaining

the communications to the east of Egypt and in the Red Sea, and because the intermediate stations of Gibraltar and Malta are held in force for guarding British interests on the shores of the Mediterranean, besides protecting the overland route to India;

—because the Indian empire does not cause any real drain upon the English people, inasmuch as all Englishmen who go there, proceed upon service which they have voluntarily undertaken for their own benefit; and because, on the contrary, such service affords employment to the surplus of a fast-growing population;

—because India offers to England an unequalled scope for giving effect to the purest philanthropy, the noblest ideas, the loftiest aspirations by which the English nation can be moved and actuated; and

—because England herself is elevated morally by the obligation of caring humanely and unselfishly for the good of a vast population which Providence has committed to her charge.

Nor has England, in assuming the governance of so vast a people, undertaken an ungrateful task. A happy experience has shewn that the Natives are morally improvable by education, and it has been explained in previous chapters how a good standard of probity and rectitude has been established among the educated classes. The complex mass of Native society does indeed present numerous difficulties to its foreign rulers, and many of the phases of the Indian mind seem obscure to European eyes. Still there is, in the Native character, much to engage the sympathetic regards of Englishmen, over and above their sentiment of duty towards those whose destiny has been linked with that of England. The Native character, as a whole, may be disparaged by some whose experience is short and whose knowledge is not profound. But with an Englishman who lives and labours in the country, the wider his acquaintance with the Natives and the deeper his insight, the greater is his liking for them. He who has the best and longest acquaintance with the Natives, esteems them the most. Probably every Englishman, without exception, who has, during a lengthened residence, been brought much into contact with the Natives, parts from them with sincere regret, remembers them with the most kindly regards and breathes heartfelt aspirations for their welfare and happiness. He who has the best data for an opinion regarding them and the firmest ground on which to found his belief, will have the most hopeful faith in their mental and moral progress. He who has to deal with many millions of them, who has been more or less intimately acquainted with some thousands of them, will have formed friendships that will survive so long as life endures. Many of their virtues are of a type or mould different from the Anglo-Saxon, but their domestic qualities shine with a quiet unobtrusive light which deserves the admiring gaze of even the most civilized nations. While bowing down before graven images, they still reflect inwardly on an all-pervading power, believing that,

> "Its threads are love and life, and death and pain
> The shuttles of its loom."

There is, in their disposition, a cheerful and courageous patience nurtured in the midst of national tribulations, a willingness to submit the unruly will to the dictates of a venerated law, and a reliance on an almighty power as the refuge of the weak, and the helper of the helpless, which are akin to the best forms of religion. Those primeval characteristics which denote the refinement and elevation of human nature in all climes, and which are mirrored in the oldest epic poetry of the East and West, have ever been, and are to this hour, exemplified in the Natives of India. Though there is with them a calm resignation to the decrees of ill, yet the remembrance is never lost of the eternal benevolence, in the thought, that

> "Unseen, it helpeth ye with faithful hands,
> Unheard, it speaketh stronger than the storm."

The social and political life of India is like an ocean that has long been swept and lashed by storms following each other in too rapid succession. The heaving and the long swell, which ensue after such events, may cause some to think that the national agitation has not wholly subsided. There will always be those whose pulse throbs at the anticipation of coming tempest, and who wait expectantly for disturbance, like as the stormy petrel in its flight hangs low over the rising waves. But the mass of the teeming Indian population desire nothing so much as that sort of repose which they enjoy under the strong, mild and just rule of England, when every man gathers in quiet the fruits of his toil, is not forced to render up his goods against his will, sleeps without fear of violence, has redress for wrong done to him by his neighbour, performs his religious rites, and follows his caste observances, undisturbed, and lifts his eyes towards the State as to a father. They love to dwell under a Government as they repose under the banyan-tree, of which Milton sings, as

> "... a pillar'd shade
> High o'erarched ...
> There oft the Indian herdsman, shunning heat,
> Shelters in cool ..."

They desire of their Government that its policy shall be truly benevolent, and that it shall have the power of giving real effect to its good intentions. Whatever be the exceptional view of some classes among the people, the overwhelming majority think that, in this iron age, the marks of imperial qualification are found in the British Government more than in any government that has been seen since the golden age of an ideal antiquity. They picture to themselves the Queen-Empress seated on the throne of justice under the canopy of mercy. They were rejoiced at the presence of the Heir-Apparent, and founded charitable and educational institutions in memory of the royal visitor. Some Natives, who are beginning to be imbued with the Western education, occupy a comparatively high range of thought, and these feel grateful to the State for placing intellectual resources at their disposal. Others soar higher still, enjoying that mental independence and moral freedom into which they have been initiated by studious preparation, and they derive encouragement from the example of their foreign rulers. Among them, many consider that the Government must ere long offer higher careers than heretofore to Native talent in the public service, and concede to qualified Natives a larger share in the management of the country. Undoubtedly such opportunities will be afforded gradually, and the advancement of the Natives will proceed so far as may be consistent with the maintenance of a due proportion of European administrative strength in all those situations where the absolute safety of the imperial interests is concerned. Here also the Natives, though regretting what seems to them the slow rate of such advancement, yet note the onward movement which is already effected, and feel assured that their claims will meet with consideration from English justice.

Although the loyalty and fidelity of the Natives will remain unchanged, if the British administration shall continue to be wisely conducted as heretofore, their minds will in many respects be powerfully affected by the mental and material progress which is being wrought. The morning of a new day is about to break for them. Those who look for this light are like travellers in the Himalayas, who during the last hour of the night arise from their beds, and sit outside their tents on the mountain summits, watching for the dawn to appear behind the distant range of everlasting snow. At first a faint glimmer steals over the eastern horizon, and the peerless peaks are reared up black as Erebus, with no promise as yet of the shining robes in which they are shortly to be arrayed. As the sky becomes illuminated with amber hues, the outline of the peaks, with their needles, spires and pinnacles, is defined with an amazing sharpness, till the whole range presents for a moment the jagged teeth of a gigantic saw. Then, as the orb of day surmounts the horizon, the darkness of the snowy range yields gradually; parts of the range become suffused with a purple mist, some points are obscured by a veil of golden gauze, while others, fronting the sun, are smitten with splendour and seem to catch fire. At length, the whole mass of mountains subsides into a state of radiant whiteness.

So it is with those who wait for the good time coming to India. Formerly

> "midnight hushed the world
> Save where the beasts of darkness in the brake
> Crept and cried out, as fear and hatred cry.
> As vice and avarice and anger creep
> In the black jungle of man's ignorance."

As the daylight for the nation approaches, many points, which as yet stand out gloomily, will be irradiated, many mists of superstition, prejudice and error will be cleared away by a sounder knowledge, a higher morality, a purer faith. Then there will be a bright epoch for these Eastern races under the guidance of Western civilization. This era will arise as the sunrise manifests itself to the earth;

> ". . . high as the herald star which fades in floods
> Of silver, warming into pale gold, caught
> By topmost clouds, and flaming on their rims
> To fervent glow, flushed from the brink
> With saffron, scarlet, crimson, amethyst;
> Whereat the sky burns splendid to the blue,
> And, robed in raiment of glad light, the King
> Of life and glory cometh!" *

INDEX.

EMIGRATION.

FINANCE.

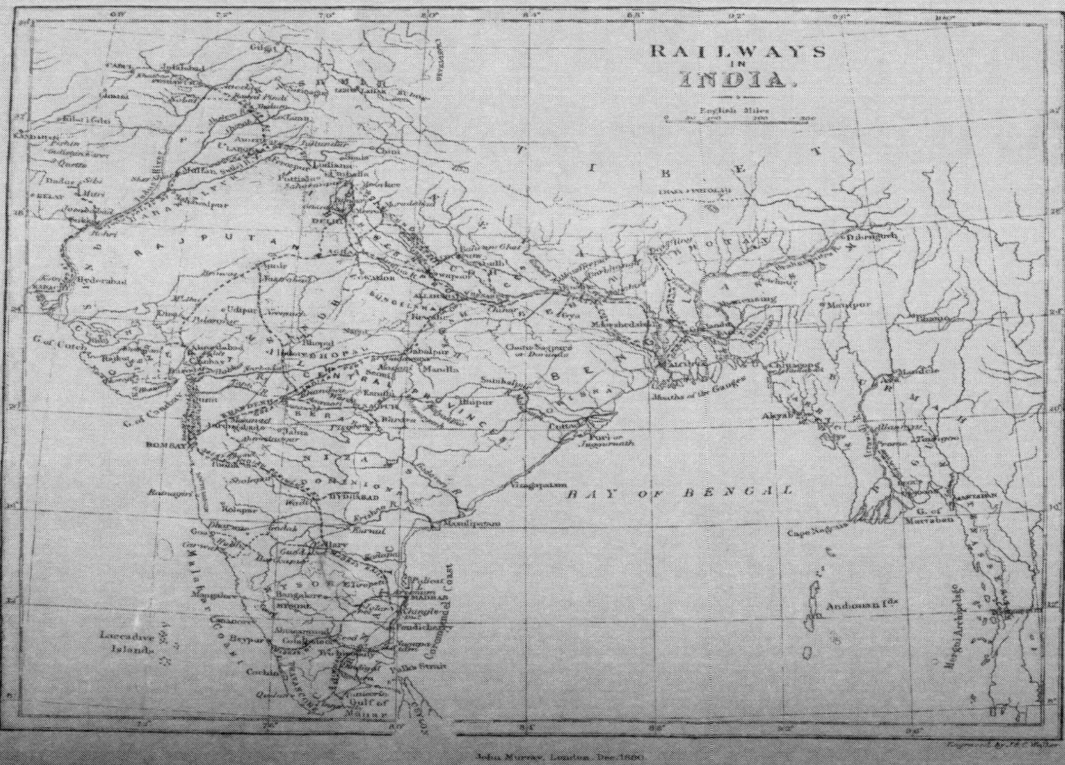
RAILWAYS IN INDIA.
English Miles
TIBET
BAY OF BENGAL
RAJPUTANA
CENTRAL PROVINCES
BENGAL
BOMBAY
HYDERABAD
MADRAS
DELHI
Hyderabad
G. of Cutch
Jabalpur
Chota Nagpur or Doranda
Mouths of the Ganges
Puri or Juggernath
Vizagapatam
Masulipatam
Bangalore
Mangalore
Cochin
Beypur
Laccadive Islands
Malabar Coast
Coromandel Coast
Palk's Strait
Gulf of Manaar
Akyab
Cape Negrais
G. of Martaban
Andaman Ids
Mergui Archipelago
Bhamo
Manipur
John Murray, London. Dec. 1880
Engraved by J & C Walker

ALBEMARLE STREET,
April, 1888.

MR. MURRAY'S
New and Recent Publications.

[*UNIFORM WITH THE "SPEAKER'S COMMENTARY."*]

The Apocrypha,

WITH A COMMENTARY, EXPLANATORY AND CRITICAL,

AND A REVISION OF THE TRANSLATION.

BY THE FOLLOWING CLERGY OF THE ANGLICAN CHURCH.

Introduction	GEORGE SALMON, D.D., Provost of Trin. Coll., Dublin.
Esdras	J. H. LUPTON, M.A., Sur-master of St. Paul's School.
Tobit & Esther . . .	J. M. FULLER, M.A., Professor of Ecclesiastical History, King's Coll., London.
Judith	C. J. BALL, M.A., Chaplain of Lincoln's Inn.
Song of Three Children .	
Susanna	
Bel and Dragon . .	
Manasses	
Wisdom	Archdeacon FARRAR, D.D.
Ecclesiasticus	ALFRED EDERSHEIM, D.D.
Baruch & Jeremy . . .	Archdeacon GIFFORD, D.D.
Maccabees	Canon RAWLINSON, M.A.

Edited by HENRY WACE, D.D.,

Preacher of Lincoln's Inn, Prebendary of St. Paul's, and Principal of King's College, London.

2 *Vols. Medium 8vo.* 50*s.*

Handbook—Spain and Andalusia.

MADRID, THE CASTILES, THE BASQUE PROVINCES, LEON, THE ASTURIAS, GALICIA, ESTREMADURA, RONDA, GRANADA, MURCIA, VALENCIA, CATALONIA, ARAGON, NAVARRE, THE BALEARIC ISLANDS, &c., &c.

Seventh Edition Revised. Maps. Post 8vo. 20*s.*

Handbook—Egypt and the Nile.

THE COURSE OF THE NILE, THROUGH EGYPT AND NUBIA, ALEXANDRIA, CAIRO, THE PYRAMIDS AND THEBES, THE SUEZ CANAL, THE PENINSULA OF SINAI, THE OASES, THE FYOOM, &c.

Seventh Edition, Revised. Map. Post 8vo. 15*s.*

Handbook—Rome and its Environs.

Fourteenth Edition, Revised. Maps and Plans. Post 8vo. 10*s.*

Handbook—Russia, Poland and Finland.

THE CRIMEA, CAUCASUS, SIBERIA, AND CENTRAL ASIA.

Fourth Edition, Revised. Maps and Plans. Post 8vo. 18*s.*

The Country Banker:

HIS CLIENTS, CARES, AND WORK.

FROM THE EXPERIENCE OF FORTY YEARS.

By GEORGE RAE,

Author of "Bullion's Letters to a Bank Manager."

New Edition, Revised. Crown 8vo. 7s. 6d.

"Mr. Rae may be congratulated on having produced a book which can be recommended to the student who wishes to gain an insight into the subject."—*Times.*

"We have seldom taken up a book on the business of banking which is at once so interesting and so full of shrewd common sense as this of Mr. Rae's."—*Economist.*

MR. DARWIN'S LIFE AND WORKS.

Life of Charles Darwin, F.R.S.

WITH AN AUTOBIOGRAPHICAL CHAPTER.

By his Son, FRANCIS DARWIN, F.R.S.

Seventh Thousand. With Portrait and Woodcuts. 3 *Vols. 8vo.* 36*s.*

NEW EDITIONS OF MR. DARWIN'S CHIEF WORKS.

Library Editions.

Descent of Man, and Selection in Relation to Sex.

2 *Vols. Crown 8vo.* 15*s.*

The Origin of Species by means of Natural Selection.

2 *Vols. Crown 8vo.* 12*s.*

Cheaper and Uniform Editions.

A Naturalist's Voyage round the World. 7*s.* 6*d.*

The Origin of Species by means of Natural Selection. 6*s.*

The Various Contrivances by which Orchids are fertilised by Insects. 7*s.* 6*d.*

Variation of Animals and Plants under Domestication. 2 Vols. 15*s.*

The Descent of Man, and Selection in relation to Sex. 7*s.* 6*d.*

Movements and Habits of Climbing Plants. 6*s.*

Effects of Cross and Self-fertilization in the Vegetable Kingdom. 9*s.*

Different Forms of Flowers on Plants of the same Species. 7*s.* 6*d.*

Formation of Vegetable Mould through the action of Worms. 6*s.*

Life of Erasmus Darwin. New Edition. Portrait. 7*s.* 6*d.*

Geographical Etymology.

A DICTIONARY OF PLACE NAMES,

GIVING THEIR DERIVATIONS.

By **C. BLACKIE.**

Third Edition, Revised and Enlarged. Crown 8vo. 7s.

"Of speculating on place names there is no end. The tourist who has ever had his curiosity awakened—what intelligent tourist has not?—by the names of the places he passes through, will find this volume a delightful companion, opening up to him novel sources of interest, and conveying no small amount of information and suggestion of a curious kind."—*Daily News.*

An Introduction to the Study of the New Testament;

AND AN INVESTIGATION INTO MODERN BIBLICAL CRITICISM,

BASED ON THE MOST RECENT SOURCES OF INFORMATION.

WITH A CHAPTER ON THE NON-CANONICAL BOOKS.

By **GEORGE SALMON, D.D., D.C.L., &c.**

Provost of Trinity College, Dublin.

Third Edition, Revised. 8vo. 16s.

"If Professor Salmon had done no other service, he would deserve the sincere gratitude of serious theological students, to whatever school they may belong, for having in this volume put down his foot upon a very large amount of nonsense given forth in the name of criticism. It is perhaps too much to hope that in the future we may be spared at least some of it; but the general public has now the means of appraising the real value of what so many have taken on trust as the outcome of the best scholarship."—*Saturday Review.*

Murray's Magazine.

HALF-YEARLY VOLUMES, bound in Cloth, Medium 8vo. 7s. 6d. *each.*

VOLUME I., JANUARY—JUNE, 1887.

VOLUME II., JULY—DECEMBER, 1887.

"*Murray's Magazine* seems to stand out head and shoulders above its competitors."—*Glasgow Herald.*

"Though only a year old, *Murray's* has fairly won its way to the very front rank among magazines."—*Nonconformist.*

"*Murray's Magazine* improves with every new month. More convenient in form and eighteenpence cheaper, it seems to contain all that we expect to get in the big monthlies."—*Land and Water.*

COMPLETION OF THE

Dictionary of Christian Biography.

Edited by WM. SMITH, D.C.L., and HENRY WACE, D.D.,
Principal of King's College, London.

THIS WORK CONTAINS A COMPREHENSIVE ACCOUNT OF THE PERSONAL, THE LITERARY, THE DOGMATIC, AND THE ECCLESIASTICAL LIFE OF THE CHURCH DURING THE FIRST EIGHT CENTURIES OF CHRISTIANITY.

Vol. IV. (N to Z), completing the work (1240 *pp.*). *Medium* 8*vo.* £2 2*s.*

The unique position of this work, and its very great value to all theological students, have been recognised by the principal scholars of England and Germany. The *Times* reviewer wrote—

"The value of the work arises, in the first place, from the fact that the contributors to these volumes have diligently eschewed mere compilation; and, in fact, the articles include many really important monographs by highly competent scholars, frequently adding to a summary of what had been already known the results of new and original investigations. Essays of this class deserve the better welcome on account of their comparative infrequency in this country. . . . *In these volumes we welcome the most important addition that has been made for a century to the historical library of the English theological student.*"

And in *Hilgenfeld's Zeitschrift* we read:—"Bei dieser Gelegenheit aufmerksam auf das vorzügliche Dictionary of Christian Biography, &c., wo man über alles Betreffende in den ersten 8 Jahrhunderten der Christlichen Kirche, kurz und gut Nachricht findet. Ein solches Werk gereicht der Englischen Theologie zur hohen Ehre."

"At last this work is finished, after the lapse of ten years from the publication of the first volume. The time spent upon its production is certainly not out of proportion to its value; for the amount of information, research, scholarship, and ability devoted to this cyclopædia is enormous, and there is ample reason to congratulate the editors, contributors, and public alike on the successful completion of a work which is not only without equals, but even without a rival. It is the best vindication of English scholarship in its best and most practical form. The quality which renders the Dictionary unique is the comprehensiveness with which it has treated the whole sphere of Christian or ecclesiastical life and order during eight centuries."—*Scotsman.*

Volumes I., II., III., 31*s.* 6*d. each.*

*** *Subscribers are recommended to complete their Sets.*

Life and Labour.

OR CHARACTERISTICS OF MEN OF CULTURE AND GENIUS.

By SAMUEL SMILES, LL.D.
Author of "Self-Help," "Character," "Thrift," "Duty," etc.

Post 8*vo.* 6*s.*

"As years roll on, the author's store of apt illustrations becomes ampler, while in the case of Dr. Smiles, his skill in dealing with them shows no failure. *Life and Labour* is a companion volume to *Self Help* and *Character*, and its publication at this season will be regarded as opportune. . . . No more suitable volume could be found (for a prize book) to bear the inscription *Laboris præmium.*"—*Academy.*

Letters from a Mourning City.

NAPLES DURING THE AUTUMN OF 1884.

From the Swedish of AXEL MUNTHE.

Translated by MAUDE VALÉRIE WHITE.

With Frontispiece. Post 8vo. 6s.

"There are few books of the season we could have spared so little as this fantastic pilgrimage across the terrible stage of the South as it exists."—*Athenæum.*

"We almost feel as if we were hearing the story of some other world, so different is it to all we are most familiar with."—*Guardian.*

"There is excellent work in the 'Letters from a Mourning City.' Much has been written about Horrible London; here is something to the full as moving and instructive about Horrible Naples, and there is scarce a line of it but should be read and pondered."—*Saturday Review.*

The Bible in the Holy Land.

EXTRACTED FROM

DEAN STANLEY'S "SINAI AND PALESTINE."

FOR THE USE OF VILLAGE SCHOOLS AND YOUNG PERSONS.

4th Edition. Illustrations. Post 8vo. 3s. 6d.

Wealth and Welfare:

AN EXAMINATION OF OUR NATIONAL TRADE POLICY AND ITS EFFECTS ON THE GENERAL WELFARE OF THE NATION.

By HASTINGS BERKELEY, Commander R.N.

Crown 8vo. 6s.

"The author's deductions are sound, and bear the stamp of common sense, and it is to be hoped will be largely read."—*Bullionist.*

"There is also a well-written chapter on the relation between labour and capital. Commander Berkeley has evidently thought the matter carefully out, and his book is throughout marked by a lucidity and moderation which render it deserving of careful study by those who are interested—as all of us ought to be—in the 'wealth and welfare' of our native land."—*Morning Post.*

Sermons and Addresses to Children.

INCLUDING THE BEATITUDES—AND THE FAITHFUL SERVANT.

By **ARTHUR PENRHYN STANLEY, D.D.,**
Late Dean of Westminster.

Post 8vo. 3*s.* 6*d.*

Kugler's Handbook of Painting.

THE ITALIAN SCHOOLS.

Fifth Edition, Revised, incorporating the most recent discoveries.

By Sir A. HENRY LAYARD, G.C.B., D.C.L.,
Corresponding Member of the Institut de France, Académie des Inscriptions et Belles Lettres; Trustee of the National Gallery, &c.; Author of "Nineveh and its Remains."

With 200 *Illustrations. Two Vols. Crown 8vo.* 30*s.*

England's Case Against Home Rule.

By A. V. DICEY, B.C.L., of the Inner Temple,
Fellow of All Souls, and Vinerian Professor of English Law at Oxford.

Third Edition. Crown 8vo. 7*s.* 6*d.*

"This is a book which will richly repay the most careful study by Home Rulers as well as by Anti-Home Rulers."—*Scotsman.*

"It is in our judgment absolutely conclusive."—*Saturday Review.*

"A deep feeling of political duty pervades the whole argument, which adds a weight and dignity to the reasoning, and increases the impressive effect of a work that is already noteworthy for its vigour, its acuteness, and its learning."—*Guardian.*

Why England Maintains the Union.

A POPULAR RENDERING OF THE ABOVE WORK. **By C. E. S.**

Post 8vo. 1*s.*

Dean Hook's Church Dictionary:

A PRACTICAL MANUAL OF REFERENCE FOR CLERGYMEN AND LAYMEN.

Edited by **WALTER HOOK, M.A.**, and **W. R. W. STEPHENS, M.A.**
Rector of Porlock. Prebendary of Chichester.

14th Edition, thoroughly Revised. One Volume. (790 *pp.*) *8vo.* 21*s.*

"No book could have gone through so many editions, and have become so widely appreciated, without having well deserved its reputation . . . the revision has been conducted with the utmost care, while the judicious impartiality with which editors have treated matters on which opinion is still divided, deserves our warmest acknowledgment."—*Saturday Review.*

MOUNTSTUART ELPHINSTONE'S HISTORY OF INDIA.

PART I.—*Hindu and Mahommedan Periods.*

Edited by **E. B. COWELL.**

5th Edition, with Map. 8vo. 18*s.*

PART II.—*Rise of the British Power in the East.*

Edited by Sir **EDWARD COLEBROOKE**, Bart.

With Maps. 8vo. 16*s.*

The Great Silver River.

NOTES OF A RESIDENCE IN BUENOS AYRES.

By Sir **HORACE RUMBOLD**, Bart., K.C.M.G.
H. B. M. Minister at Athens.

With Illustrations. Crown 8vo. 12*s.*

"We cannot help being surprised at the amount and accuracy of the information gathered in so short a time. The important subject of emigration is admirably treated."—*Athenæum.*

"The title conveys a most inadequate idea of the varied contents and comprehensive scope of this graphic picture of S. American life and scenery."—*Academy.*

The Twining Family.

I.—RECREATIONS OF A COUNTRY CLERGYMAN OF THE 18TH CENTURY.

II.—SELECTIONS FROM THE PAPERS OF THE TWINING FAMILY.

Edited by **RICHARD TWINING.**

2 Vols. Crown 8vo. 9s. each.

A Glossary of Anglo-Indian Colloquial Words and Phrases,

ETYMOLOGICAL, HISTORICAL, GEOGRAPHICAL, AND DISCURSIVE.

By Col. **YULE, C.B., & ARTHUR BURNELL, C.I.E.**

Medium 8vo. 36s. Half bound.

THE NEW SERIES OF ETON COLLEGE SCHOOL BOOKS.

The Elementary Eton Latin Grammar.

FOR USE IN THE LOWER FORMS.

Crown 8vo. 3s. 6d.

A First Latin Exercise Book.

Adapted to the Eton Latin Grammar.

Crown 8vo. 2s. 6d.

COMPILED WITH THE SANCTION OF THE HEADMASTER,

By A. C. AINGER, M.A., Trin. Coll., Cambridge; and H. G. WINTLE, M.A., Ch. Ch., Oxford;

Assistant Masters at Eton College.

The Preparatory Eton Latin Grammar.

CONTAINING THE ACCIDENCE AND THE SYNTAX RULES.

ABRIDGED FROM THE LARGER WORK.

By **A. C. AINGER, M.A., and H. G. WINTLE, M.A.**

Crown 8vo. 2s.

The Eton Horace.

PART I. THE ODES, EPODES, AND CARMEN SÆCULARE.

WITH NOTES.

By F. W. CORNISH, M.A.,

Assistant Master at Eton College.

In Two Parts. With Maps. Crown 8vo.

*** *As it is considered desirable that the Notes should be used only in the preparation of the Lesson, and not in the Class, they are bound up separate from the Text.*

"The idea of publishing the notes separately seems to us a good one in the case of a text-book for schools. The notes can then be employed in preparing the lesson, while the text alone is brought into class. The Eton Horace is a thoroughly sensible and useful book. The notes are sufficiently full without sacrificing brevity, and, as far as we can see, they do not shirk difficult passages."—*Literary World.*

THE ETON MATHEMATICAL SERIES.

I.—* Exercises in Algebra.

By EDWARD PEAKE ROUSE, M.A., and ARTHUR COCKSHOTT, M.A.,

Assistant Masters at Eton College.

Crown 8vo. 3*s.*

II.—* Exercises in Arithmetic.

By Rev. T. DALTON, M.A.,

Assistant Master at Eton College.

Crown 8vo. 3*s.*

"These handbooks of 'Exercises' should be widely used, as they embrace almost every conceivable kind of question that the ingenuity of an examiner could devise. To teachers who 'coach' students for the various public examinations they will be indispensable. The volumes have therefore our warmest commendation."—*Practical Teacher.*

* Keys to these works supplied to authenticated teachers on application to the publisher.

The Consulting Architect.

PRACTICAL NOTES ON DIFFICULTIES CALLING FOR ARBITRATION.

By ROBERT KERR,

Author of "The English Gentleman's House," "A Small Country House," &c.

Crown 8vo. 9*s.*

Bolingbroke:

AN HISTORICAL STUDY.

Contents.—The Political Life of Bolingbroke: Bolingbroke in Exile: Literary Life of Bolingbroke.

Reprinted from the "Quarterly Review," to which is added an Essay on "*Voltaire in England.*"

By J. CHURTON COLLINS.

Crown 8vo. 7s. 6d.

The Land of the Midnight Sun;

SUMMER AND WINTER JOURNEYS THROUGH SWEDEN, NORWAY, LAPLAND, AND NORTHERN FINLAND,

With Descriptions of the Inner Life of the People, their Manners and Customs, the Primitive Antiquities, &c., &c.

By PAUL B. DU CHAILLU,
Author of "Explorations in Equatorial Africa," &c.

4th Edition. With Map and 235 Illustrations. 2 Vols. 8vo. 36s.

"Mr. Du Chaillu's work is likely to become one of the most popular books of the season."—*Times.*
"Full of interest from beginning to end."—*Pall Mall Gazette.*
"One of the most interesting and valuable works of the season."—*Nonconformist.*
"No writer has made travel in desolate regions more attractive."—*Spectator.*

The Western Pacific, and New Guinea.

WITH NOTICES OF THE NATIVES, CHRISTIAN AND CANNIBAL, AND SOME ACCOUNT OF THE OLD LABOUR TRADE.

By HUGH HASTINGS ROMILLY,
Deputy Commissioner for the Western Pacific, and Acting Special Commandant for New Guinea.

Second Edition, with Map. Crown 8vo. 7s. 6d.

"One of the most amusing books of travel that have been published for some time."—*Times.*

Some Verdicts of History Reviewed.

By WILLIAM STEBBING.

Late Fellow of Worcester College, Oxford.

8vo. 12*s.*

"Mr. Stebbing's primary object is to search out the truth, and he seems to us to have been singularly successful in his various researches. . . . The most interesting and important of the biographical essays is that which takes St. John for its theme. . . . The volume closes with delightful companion pictures of New England and Virginia."—*Times.*

Lord Beaconsfield's Letters to His Sister. 1830–1852.

WITH ADDITIONAL LETTERS AND NOTES.

Edited by HIS BROTHER.

A popular Edition. Portrait. Post 8vo. 2*s.*

The Croker Correspondence and Diaries, 1809–1830.

Relating to the Chief Political Events of the present Century.

By LOUIS J. JENNINGS, M.P.

Second Edition. Portrait. 3 *Vols. 8vo.* 45*s.*

BULGARIA.

Struggle of the Bulgarians for National Independence.

A History of the War between Bulgaria and Servia in 1885.

By Major A. VON HUHN.
Map. Crown 8vo. 9*s.*

The Growth of Freedom the Balkan Peninsula.

Notes of a Traveller in Montenegro, Servia, Bulgaria, & Greece.

By J. G. COTTON MINCHIN.
Crown 8vo. 10*s.* 6*d.*

A Child's First Latin Book.

COMPRISING A FULL PRACTICE OF NOUNS, PRONOUNS, AND ADJECTIVES, WITH THE VERBS.

By Professor T. D. HALL, M.A.

A new and Enlarged Edition, including the passive verb.

16mo. 2*s.*

COMPLETION OF THE

Student's History of the English Church.

FROM THE EARLIEST TIMES TO THE PRESENT DAY.

By G. G. PERRY, M.A.,
Canon of Lincoln, and Rector of Waddington.

THIRD PERIOD. FROM THE ACCESSION OF THE HOUSE OF HANOVER TO THE PRESENT TIME. 1717—1884.

Post 8vo. 7s. 6d.

Amongst other matters dealt with in this volume are the Great Revival Movement of the latter half of the last century—the foundation of the Colonial Church—the Oxford Movement—the Papal Aggression—the Rise of Ritualism—the Disestablishment of the Irish Church—the Pan-Anglican Conferences—the Gorham Case—Essays and Reviews—Bishop Colenso's Works—the Ridsdale Case, &c., &c.,

Already published.

FIRST PERIOD, 596—1509; SECOND PERIOD, 1509—1717.

Post 8vo. 7s. 6d. *each.*

"A most valuable history, full of information well digested and arranged, and enriched by well-chosen quotations from documents which are buried in blue books and law reports, or 'live dispersedly' in numerous biographies and memoirs."—*Journal of Education.*

"We have repeatedly commended this careful and excellent abridgment of the *Speaker's Commentary.* It is beyond all doubt superior to any other commentary of the same size. With respect to this last volume we may venture to say that it attains to a higher level of general excellence than any of its predecessors. . . . As good a book as we are likely to meet with for many a day."—*Church Bells.*

Sketches of the History of Christian Art.

By the late **LORD LINDSAY.**

Second Edition. 2 *Vols.* 8*vo.* 24*s.*

Symbols & Emblems of Early Christian Art.

By LOUISA TWINING.

Illustrations. Crown 8*vo.* 12*s.*

Persia and the Persians.

By S. G. W. BENJAMIN,

Late United States Minister to the Court of Persia.

With 60 *Illustrations.* 8*vo.* 24*s.*

England's Chronicle in Stone.

By J. F. HUNNEWELL.

Derived from her Cathedrals, Churches, Abbeys, &c.

With 60 *Illustrations.* 8*vo.* 24*s.*

DR. SCHLIEMAN'S WORKS.

Tiryns.

A Prehistoric Palace of the Kings of Tiryns. Disclosed by Excavations in 1884-85.

Illustrations. 42*s.*

Ancient Mycenæ.

Discoveries and Researches on the Sites of Mycenæ and Tiryns.

Illustrations. 50*s.*

Troja.

Researches and Discoveries on the Site of Homer's Troy, and other Sites.

Illustrations. 42*s.*

Ilios.

History of the City and Country of the Trojans.

Illustrations. 50*s.*

Sir Hector's Watch.

A STORY.

By CHARLES GRANVILLE.

Post 8vo. 2*s.* 6*d.*

COMPLETION OF THE

Student's Commentary on the Holy Bible.

ABRIDGED FROM THE "SPEAKER'S COMMENTARY."

Edited by JOHN M. FULLER, M.A.,

Vicar of Bexley, and Professor of Ecclesiastical History, King's College, London.

6 vols. Crown 8vo. 7s. 6d. each vol.

OLD TESTAMENT.

Vol. I.—GENESIS TO DEUTERONOMY.
,, II.—JOSHUA TO ESTHER.
Vol. III.—JOB TO ECCLESIASTES.
,, IV.—ISAIAH TO MALACHI.

NEW TESTAMENT.

Vol. I.—GOSPELS AND ACTS. Vol. II.—EPISTLES AND REVELATION. [*Just out.*

"The result of a careful examination of this new Commentary is in all respects satisfactory. The execution is as good as the idea—which is saying a great deal."—*Church Bells.*

"There can be no question that the Speaker's Commentary has marked an era in Biblical literature, as the most successful of all scientific expositions of the Bible yet given to the public . . . . in this abridgment we are glad to see the essential portion of the great original is faithfully preserved."—*English Churchman.*

NEW AND CHEAPER EDITIONS OF DR. WM. SMITH'S LATIN DICTIONARIES.

I.—*A Complete Latin-English Dictionary.*

WITH TABLES OF THE ROMAN CALENDAR, MEASURES, WEIGHTS, AND MONEY.

AND

A DICTIONARY OF PROPER NAMES.

By WM. SMITH, LL.D., D.C.L.

19th and Cheaper Edition. (1250 *pp.*) *Medium 8vo.* 16*s.*

This work holds an intermediate place between the Thesaurus of Forcellini and the ordinary School Dictionaries, performing the same service for the Latin language as Liddell and Scott's Lexicon has done for the Greek. It therefore avoids those minute subdivisions and numerous quotations which, however useful in a Thesaurus, render a Dictionary less practically useful to students.

"A *most useful book*, and fills for Latin Literature the place now occupied by Liddell's and Scott's Lexicon for Greek."—Sir G. CORNEWALL LEWIS.

"Dr. Wm. Smith's 'Latin Dictionary' is a great convenience to me. *I think that he has been very judicious in what he has omitted*, as well as in what he has inserted."—Dean SCOTT, D.D., *Author of the "Greek Lexicon."*

II.—*A Copious English-Latin Dictionary.*

COMPILED FROM ORIGINAL SOURCES.

By WM. SMITH, LL.D., and Prof. T. D. HALL, M.A.

5th and Cheaper Edition. (970 *pp.*) *Medium 8vo.* 16*s.*

It has been the object of the Authors of this work to produce a more complete and more perfect ENGLISH-LATIN DICTIONARY than yet exists, and every article has been the result of original and independent research.

Great pains have been taken in classifying the different senses of the *English words*, so as to enable the student readily to find what he wants.

Each meaning is illustrated by examples from the classical writers; and those phrases are as a general rule given in both English and Latin.

"This work is the result of a clear insight into the faults of its predecessors as to plan, classification, and examples. In previous dictionaries the various senses of English words are commonly set down hap-hazard. This has been avoided in the present instance by the classification of the senses of the English words according to the order of the student's need. Not less noteworthy is the copiousness of the examples from the Latin, with which every English word is illustrated; and, last not least, the exceptional accuracy of the references by which these examples are to be verified."—*Saturday Review.*

ALBEMARLE STREET,
April, 1888.

MR. MURRAY'S FORTHCOMING WORKS.

The Correspondence of Daniel O'Connell,

THE LIBERATOR.

NOW FIRST PUBLISHED, WITH A MEMOIR AND NOTES.

By WM. J. FITZPATRICK.

With Portrait. 2 Vols. 8vo.

Lives of Twelve Good Men.

By JOHN W. BURGON, B.D., Dean of Chichester.

I.—*The Learned Divine.* MARTIN JOSEPH ROUTH.
II.—*The Restorer of the Old Paths.* HUGH JAMES ROSE.
III.—*The Saintly Liver.* CHARLES MARRIOTT.
IV.—*The Great Provost.* EDWARD HAWKINS.
V.—*The Remodeller of the Episcopate.* SAMUEL WILBERFORCE.
VI.—*The Humble Christian.* RICHARD LYNCH COTTON.
VII.—*The Faithful Steward.* RICHARD GRESWELL.
VIII.—*The Pious Librarian.* HENRY OCTAVIUS COXE.
IX.—*The Christian Philosopher.* HENRY LONGUEVILLE MANSEL.
X.—*The Singleminded Bishop.* WILLIAM JACOBSON.
XI.—*The Earnest Parish Priest.* CHARLES PAGE EDEN.
XII.—*The Good Layman.* CHARLES LONGUET HIGGINS.

Two Vols. Crown 8vo.

Three Generations of English Women.

OR THE MEMOIRS AND CORRESPONDENCE OF MRS. JOHN TAYLOR, MRS. SARAH AUSTIN, AND LADY DUFF GORDON.

By JANET ROSS (née DUFF GORDON).

With Portraits. 2 Vols. Crown 8vo.

Among Cannibals.

TRAVELS IN AUSTRALIA, INCLUDING A YEAR'S RESIDENCE AMONG THE LITTLE KNOWN SAVAGE TRIBES IN THE N.E. PART OF THE CONTINENT.

By CARL LUMHOLTZ, M.A.,
Member of the Scientific Academy of Christiania.

With Maps and 100 *Illustrations. Medium 8vo.*

Principal Shairp and his Friends.

By WM. KNIGHT,
Professor of Moral Philosophy in the University of St. Andrews.

With Portrait. 8vo.

The Whewell Lectures on International Law.

By SIR HENRY SUMNER MAINE, K.C.S.I.,

Late Master of Trinity Hall, Cambridge, and Member of the Indian Council, formerly Corpus Professor of Jurisprudence in the University of Oxford, Foreign Associate Member of the Institute of France.

8vo.

Finance and Politics; an Historical Study.

By SYDNEY BUXTON, M.P.,

Author of "A Handbook of Political Questions," &c.

2 *Vols.* *8vo.*

Stephen Hislop.

PIONEER, MISSIONARY AND NATURALIST IN CENTRAL INDIA. 1844–1863.

By GEORGE SMITH, LL.D., C.I.E.,

Author of "The Life of William Carey," &c.

With Portrait and Illustrations. *8vo.*

MEMOIR OF

George Edmund Street, R.A.,

ARCHITECT.

By his Son, ARTHUR EDMUND STREET.

With Portrait. *8vo.*

The Viking Age.

THE EARLY HISTORY, MANNERS, AND CUSTOMS OF THE ANCESTORS OF THE ENGLISH-SPEAKING NATIONS.

ILLUSTRATED FROM

THE ANTIQUITIES DISCOVERED IN MOUNDS, CAIRNS, AND BOGS, AS WELL AS FROM THE ANCIENT SAGAS AND EDDAS.

By PAUL B. DU CHAILLU,

Author of "The Land of the Midnight Sun," &c.

With 1200 *Illustrations.* 2 *Vols. Medium* 8*vo.*

Very crude and mistaken ideas have long prevailed concerning the races of Northmen, who at the decadence of the Roman Empire overran and settled in Britain and the Northern Coasts of Germany and France, and became the progenitors of the great English-speaking community throughout the world. These ideas were derived from hostile or prejudiced sources, and have been adopted by one historian after another. More recent research has, however, established the fact that these Northern ancestors of ours were no barbarians, but a most highly civilized and accomplished people, pre-eminent not only in the science of war, but in all the arts of peace. Vast quantities of objects, including arms and armour, gold and silver ornaments of the most skilful workmanship and refined beauty; wood carving, filigree work, agricultural and domestic implements, magnificent carriages, &c., have been unearthed and are now deposited in the Museums of Scandinavia. But besides these material testimonies to the greatness of these Northmen, we have the literary and historic records of the Sagas and Eddas, and by testing the evidence of one with the other we can obtain a wonderfully vivid idea of the manners, customs, laws, traditions, and domestic life of a bygone age.

Mr. Du Chaillu has devoted seven years of incessant labour to the collection of materials from every available source, and has written a book which bids fair to do for our ancestors what Sir Gardiner Wilkinson did for the ancient Egyptians. The work will be embellished by over 1,200 illustrations.

THE LIFE OF

Sir William Siemens, F.R.S.,

CIVIL ENGINEER.

By Dr. WILLIAM POLE, F.R.S.

HON. SECRETARY OF THE INSTITUTE OF CIVIL ENGINEERS.

With Portrait and Illustrations. 8*vo.*

A SELECTION FROM

The Scientific Papers of the late Sir Wm. Siemens, F.R.S.

2 *Vols.* 8*vo.*

RECORD OF THE SERVICES IN

Afghanistan and the Punjab

OF

Major George Broadfoot, C.B.

GOVERNOR GENERAL'S AGENT ON THE N.W. FRONTIER OF INDIA.

COMPILED FROM HIS PAPERS AND THOSE OF

LORDS ELLENBOROUGH AND HARDINGE.

By **MAJOR WM. BROADFOOT, R.E.**

8vo.

THE NEW SERIES OF ETON COLLEGE SCHOOL BOOKS.

The Eton Latin Grammar.

FOR USE IN THE HIGHER FORM.

By **FRANCIS HAY RAWLINS, M.A.,** AND

WILLIAM RALPH INGE, M.A.,

Fellows of King's College, Cambridge, and Assistant Masters at Eton College.

Crown 8vo.

Lectures on the Infallibility of the Church.

By **GEORGE SALMON, D.D., D.C.L., &c.,**

Provost of Trinity College, Dublin, Author of "An Introduction to the Study of the New Testament."

8vo.

THE DUKE OF ARGYLL'S WORKS.

New Editions.

The Unity of Nature.

By the DUKE OF ARGYLL, K.G.

Third and Cheaper Edition. 8vo. 12s.

The Reign of Law.

By the DUKE OF ARGYLL, K.G.

19th Edition. With Illustrations. Crown 8vo.

THE

Works of George Borrow.

A Re-issue in Monthly Volumes, Post 8vo, 2s. 6d. each.

"The career and works of George Borrow are well worthy of study; he may have been 'a vagabond' by taste and habit, but he was eminently a Christian and a gentleman, and many men have earned greater name and fame without half his claims to the gratitude of society."—*Saturday Review.*

I. The Bible in Spain; or, the Journeys and Imprisonments of an Englishman in an attempt to circulate the Scriptures in the Peninsula. With Portrait. [*Ready.*

II. The Zincali: an Account of the Gypsies of Spain; their Manners, Customs, Religion, and Language. [*Ready.*

III. Lavengro; The Scholar—the Gipsy—and the Priest. [*May.*

IV. The Romany Rye: a Sequel to Lavengro. [*June.*

V. Wild Wales: its People, Language, and Scenery. [*July.*

Also, uniform with the above, Post 8vo, 5s.

VI. Romano Lavo-Lil; With Illustrations of English Gypsies, their Poetry and Habitations.

The Holy Places of Jerusalem.

By J. HAYTER LEWIS, F.S.A.

With Illustrations. *4to.*

A

Readable English Dictionary.

GIVING THE GREEK AND LATIN ROOTS WITH THEIR DERIVATIVES IN THE ORDER OF CLASSICAL GRAMMARS,

WITH A COMPLETE ALPHABETICAL INDEX, INCLUDING WORDS OF TEUTONIC ORIGIN.

By DAVID MILNE, M.A.

Crown 8vo.

The English language is composed of two elements, the Saxon and the Classical. Words of Saxon origin, such as *hand, shoe, cat, cow, hard, high, go, get,* &c., are familiar to us from infancy and need no explanation. Nearly all our harder words come to us directly or indirectly from Latin and Greek roots. The main purpose of this work is to provide for those who either do not get a classical education, or who are mere beginners in the study of Greek and Latin, an easy, interesting and instructive method of acquiring a thorough knowledge of the derivatives from these languages common in English.

A Dictionary of Hymnology.

SETTING FORTH THE

ORIGIN AND HISTORY OF THE CHRISTIAN HYMNS OF ALL AGES AND NATIONS,

WITH SPECIAL REFERENCE TO THOSE CONTAINED IN THE HYMN BOOKS OF ENGLISH-SPEAKING COUNTRIES, AND NOW IN COMMON USE;

TOGETHER WITH BIOGRAPHICAL AND CRITICAL NOTICES OF THEIR AUTHORS AND TRANSLATORS, AND HISTORICAL ARTICLES ON NATIONAL AND DENOMINATIONAL HYMNODY, BREVIARIES, MISSALS, PRIMERS, PSALTERS, SEQUENCES, &C., &C.

BY VARIOUS WRITERS.

Edited by JOHN JULIAN, M.A.,
Vicar of Wincobank, Sheffield.

One Volume. Medium 8vo.

NEW EDITION OF GROTE'S GREECE.

A History of Greece

FROM THE EARLIEST PERIOD TO THE TIME OF ALEXANDER THE GREAT.

By GEORGE GROTE.

With Portrait, Map, and Plans, 10 *Vols., Post 8vo,* 5*s. each.*

*** *The Volumes may be had separately.*

CONTENTS:

I. LEGENDARY GREECE.

II. EARLY SOCIETY; HOMERIC POEMS; GEOGRAPHY; RACES; MIGRATIONS; LYKURGUS; MESSINIAN WARS; CONQUEST OF SPARTA; AGE OF DESPOTS; SOLÔN.

III. GREEKS OF ASIA; PHŒNICIANS; ASSYRIANS; EGYPTIANS; CARTHAGE; GREEK COLONIES; PAN-HELLENIC FESTIVALS; LYRIC POETRY; PEISISTRATIDÆ AT ATHENS; PERSIAN EMPIRE; IONIC REVOLT.

IV. MARATHON; IONIC PHILOSOPHERS; THERMOPYLÆ; SALAMIS; PLATÆA AND MYKALE; SICILY AND THE GELONIAN DYNASTY; THEMISTOKLES AND ARISTEIDES; GROWTH OF ATHENIAN EMPIRE; PERIKLÊS; BLOCKADE OF POTIDÆA.

V. PELOPONNESIAN WAR; PEACE OF NIKIAS; BATTLE OF MANTINEIA; SICILIAN EXPEDITION PLANNED; ALKIBIADÊS.

VI. OPERATIONS IN SYRACUSE AND DESTRUCTION OF THE ATHENIAN ARMAMENT; OLIGARCHY OF THE FOUR HUNDRED; RESTORED DEMOCRACY; CYRUS THE YOUNGER IN ASIA MINOR; BATTLE OF ARGINUSÆ; THE THIRTY TYRANTS AND THEIR EXPULSION.

VII. DRAMA; RHETORIC AND DIALECTICS; SOPHISTS; SOKRATÊS; TEN THOUSAND GREEKS; LACEDÆMONIAN EMPIRE; CORINTHIAN WAR; AGESILAUS; BATTLE OF KNIDUS; PEACE OF ANTALKIDAS.

VIII. SUBJUGATION OF OLYNTHUS BY SPARTA; BATTLE OF LEUKTRA; EPAMEINONDAS; HEADSHIP OF THÊBES; PELOPIDAS; MANTINEIA; SICILIAN AFFAIRS; ELDER DIONYSIUS.

IX. CARTHAGINIAN ARMY AT SYRACUSE; DIONYSIUS THE YOUNGER; DION; TIMOLEON; ACCESSION OF PHILIP OF MACEDON; SACRED WAR; EUBOIC AND OLYNTHIAN WARS; DEMOSTHENÊS; CHÆRONEIA; ALEXANDER THE GREAT; CAPTURE OF THÊBES.

X. ASIATIC CAMPAIGNS OF ALEXANDER; BATTLE OF ISSUS; SIEGE OF TYRE; DEATH OF ALEXANDER; SAMIAN WAR; EXTINCTION OF GRECIAN FREEDOM; SICILIAN AND ITALIAN GREEKS; AGATHOKLÊS; OUTLYING HELLENIC CITIES; GENERAL INDEX.

*** *THIS IS NOW THE ONLY EDITION IN CIRCULATION.*

UNIFORM WITH THE ABOVE WORK.

Grote's Plato.

Edited by Professor BAIN.

New and Cheaper Edition. 4 *Vols. Crown 8vo.* 6*s. each.*

BY A NEW ARRANGEMENT OF THE CONTENTS, EACH VOLUME IS COMPOSED OF NEARLY RELATED SUBJECTS.

*** *The Volumes may be had separately.*

CONTENTS.

I. Speculative Philosophy in Greece before Sokrates; Growth of Dialectic; other Companions of Sokrates: Xenophon; Life of Plato; Platonic Canon; Platonic Compositions generally; Apology of Sokrates; Kriton; Euthyphron.

II. Alkibiades I. and II.; Hippias Major, Hippias Minor; Hipparchus—Minos; Theages; Erastæ or Anterastæ—Rivales; Ion; Laches; Charmides; Lysis; Euthydemus; Menon; Protagoras; Gorgias; Phædon.

III. Phædrus—Symposion; Parmenides Theætetus; Sophistes; Politikus; Kratylus; Philebus; Menexenus Kleitophon.

IV. Republic; Timæus and Kritias; Leges and Epinomis. General Index.

Kamschatka and New Guinea.

WITH NOTICES OF FORMOSA, LIU-KIU, AND THE ISLANDS OF THE MALAY ARCHIPELAGO.

By **F. H. H. GUILLEMARD, F.L.S.**

New Edition. Maps and Illustrations. Medium 8vo.

Buddhism.

WITH A CHAPTER ON JAINISM.

By **SIR MONIER WILLIAMS, K.C.I.E., D.C.L.**

8vo.

London;

Its Historical Associations, Antiquarian and Modern.

ORIGINALLY COMPILED BY THE LATE PETER CUNNINGHAM, F.S.A.

A Library Edition, Revised, Re-written and Re-arranged.

By **JAMES THORNE** and **H. B. WHEATLEY.**

3 *Vols. Medium 8vo.*

Life of Alexander Pope.

By **W. J. COURTHOPE, M.A.**

FORMING THE COMPLETING VOLUME OF THE

LIFE AND WORKS OF POPE.

With Copious INDEX *to the Whole Work. 8vo.*

The Student's History of the Roman Empire.

FROM THE ESTABLISHMENT OF THE EMPIRE TO THE ACCESSION OF COMMODUS, A.D. 180.

Post 8vo.

*** This work will take up the History at the point at which Dean Liddell leaves off, and carry it down to the period at which Gibbon begins.

A Portable Handbook to the English Cathedrals.

WITH A CONCISE DESCRIPTION OF EACH.

With Plans and Illustrations. One Volume. Crown 8vo.

The Expression of the Emotions in Men and Animals.

By CHARLES DARWIN.

New Edition, revised, with Illustrations. Crown 8vo.

THE

Power of Movement in Plants.

By CHARLES DARWIN.

New and Cheaper Edition. Crown 8vo.

Insectivorous Plants.

By CHARLES DARWIN.

New and Cheaper Edition. Crown 8vo.

Handbook—England & Wales.

ALPHABETICALLY ARRANGED.

New and Revised Edition. One Volume. Map. Post 8vo.

Handbook—Surrey, Hants, and Isle of Wight.

New and Revised Edition. Map. Post 8vo.

Handbook—Durham and Northumberland.

New and Revised Edition. Map. Post 8vo.

Handbook—Huntingdon and Bedfordshire.

Map. Post 8vo.

Handbook—Lincolnshire.

Map. Post 8vo.